W9-DDD-494

PETER WARLOCK

PETER WARLOCK

The Life of
Philip Heseltine

BARRY SMITH

Oxford   New York

OXFORD UNIVERSITY PRESS

1994

Oxford University Press, Walton Street, Oxford OX2 6DP

Oxford New York Toronto
Delhi Bombay Calcutta Madras Karachi
Kuala Lumpur Singapore Hong Kong Tokyo
Nairobi Dar es Salaam Cape Town
Melbourne Auckland Madrid
and associated companies in
Berlin Ibadan

Oxford is a trade mark of Oxford University Press

Published in the United States
by Oxford University Press Inc., New York

British Library Cataloguing in Publication Data
Data available
ISBN 0-19-816310-X

Library of Congress Cataloging in Publication Data
Smith, Barry, 1939-
Peter Warlock: the life of Philip Heseltine / Barry Smith.
Includes bibliographical references (p.) and index.
1. Warlock, Peter, 1894-1930. 2. Composers—England—Biography.
I. Title.
ML410.W2953S6 1994 782.2'092—dc20 [B] 93-44931
ISBN 0-19-816310-X

Set by Hope Services (Abingdon) Ltd
Printed in Great Britain
on acid-free paper by
Biddles Ltd
Guildford & King's Lynn

To FRED TOMLINSON
*in acknowledgement of his unequalled
contribution to Warlock scholarship*

> The darke is my delight,
> So t'is the Nightingalls.
> My Musick's in the night,
> Soe is the Nightingalls.
> My bodie is but little,
> Soe is the Nightingalls.
> I love to sleepe against ye prickle,
> Soe doth the Nightingale.

Anonymous poem quoted by Philip Heseltine in a letter to Robert Nichols, 3 March 1929.

For myself I'd like to see Phil—sooner or later—but drawn absolutely plain, as he was . . . Whatever happens, his memory must not be betrayed by hypocrisy. He mustn't be made feeble.

Robert Nichols to Cecil Gray, 13 February 1933

A book is never finished, especially if it is about real rather than fictional people. There are always mistakes, reassessments, unanswered questions. . . . a book is the product of a particular person at a particular time and cannot even aim at completeness.

Carole Angier, *Jean Rhys: Life and Work*

PREFACE

My FIRST unwitting meeting with one of the characters in the Peter Warlock story took place when I was a small boy and had been entered for a class (scales and arpeggios 8 years and under) in the local Eisteddfod in Port Elizabeth, South Africa. The examiner was one Colin Taylor, then a spry 67 years of age who I remember vividly as a tall man with a bow-tie, who sat next to me at the piano whilst putting me through my paces. As I rose to leave he said a few words of encouragement and then attempted to shake my hand, whereupon, in my childish confusion, I somehow proffered my left hand by mistake. I can still remember as if it were yesterday my acute embarrassment and how that kind and elegant gentleman showed me the correct way to shake hands. Forty years earlier Taylor had shaken the hand of the young Peter Warlock when he met him for the first time as a new piano pupil at Eton.

It was to be another eight or nine years before I was to discover the music of Peter Warlock. The particular work in question was the *Capriol Suite*. As I heard those dreamy chords at the end of 'Pieds en l'air' I suddenly knew that this composer was saying something that spoke to me very directly. I was just 17 and at University and, when I told an older student about the piece, he amazed me by knowing all about Warlock, directing me to Cecil Gray's memoir. From then on I was hooked and desperately tried to find every piece of music that Warlock had written—not an easy task in a provincial South African town in the late 1950s when, even in England, many of his songs and choral works were out of print.

A few years later, in 1960, I found myself in England as a post-graduate student. There I met by chance a fellow Warlock enthusiast who suggested that I take a trip down to Eynsford to speak to some of the people there who still remembered Philip. On arriving at the station I thought the best person to ask for advice and directions would be the station-master. I could hardly believe it when he nonchalantly announced that it was he who had to watch out for the train containing the sleeping and sometimes inebriated Philip returning from his London binges! I have in my diary for that year an enigmatic entry about Philip anecdotes that he told me: 'Barbara [Peache] and the spittoon' and 'the villagers and barley-wine' but I fear I cannot remember any details. On another occasion I also had the privilege of meeting the legendary Charles Kennedy Scott, who had given a number of first performances of Warlock choral works and who told me of Philip's attempts to get him to sign various petitions against certain London music critics.

On my return to South Africa I met up with Colin Taylor again. He was now 83 and I had just been appointed Organist of St George's Cathedral in Cape Town. Yet I still did not associate him with the Colin Taylor of the Gray memoir which I had read so many years earlier. It was only when he invited me to visit him in Stellenbosch that everything suddenly fell into place. As I entered his tiny flat, the first thing I saw was a photograph of Philip with its inscription, 'To Colin with love from his old friend Peter Warlock, January 1926', which hung in pride of place over his piano. We soon struck up a real friendship and it was one of my great privileges to have spent many happy hours with him during the last nine years of his life, listening to his anecdotes about so many musicians, absorbing his philosophy of life, and falling completely under his spell. He was a truly remarkable man: the quintessence of an English, Edwardian gentleman. His old-world courtesy was coupled with a razor-sharp mind and a personality as gentle and sensitive as it was full of empathy and charisma. Among his most precious possessions were the many letters which Philip had written to him between 1911 and 1929 and which he presented to the British Library in 1967. These he let me read and I was able to learn more about Philip, his personality, his musical and personal likes and dislikes, and, not least, his humour.

But the South African connections with Philip did not end here. I discovered to my amazement that two of Philip's first cousins lived in South Africa: Irene ('Freddie') Heseltine (who he once described as his favourite cousin) in Harrismith, and her brother, 'Sonny' Heseltine in Wynberg, a suburb of Cape Town. Unfortunately I only had the pleasure of meeting Sonny once, for he died a short while later and I had foolishly delayed accepting his invitation to come and hear his reminiscences about his cousin. I also have the privilege of knowing Sonny's wife, Vicky, and one of Philip's grandsons, Dr Peter Heseltine. Their friendship and support has been a source of great encouragement over the past years.

This book has its origins in a thesis which I submitted for a doctoral degree some years ago. When I wrote in that work that 'the definitive biography has yet to be written' I little thought at the time that I would undertake that rather daunting task. It seemed to me, however, that the centenary of Philip's birth should not go unmarked and this contribution is submitted with affection and appreciation to mark the life and work of a great English songwriter whose contribution to music and musical scholarship is, in many ways, still grossly underrated.

My thanks are due to many people, but most especially to Fred Tomlinson—most sensitive and perceptive of all Warlock scholars. Anyone writing about Peter Warlock is eternally in his debt. Without his enthusiasm and the enormous amount of research he has undertaken over many years my task would have been well-nigh impossible. He answered endless questions and made his unrivalled knowledge of Warlock and his music unselfishly available to me.

I would also like to thank Dr Denis ApIvor for his friendship, unceasing encouragement, interest, and support in this project. He too answered many appeals for assistance and I was able to draw on his wide experience and knowledge on many occasions. One of the added bonuses of writing this book has been the gaining of his much-valued friendship. There are many others who gave of their time and expertise and I would like to record my indebtedness for their valuable assistance: Dr John Allison, who helped me in innumerable ways, from taking a number of splendid photographs to researching vital information; Professor Peter Alexander, Associate Professor of English, Sydney University; Mr Richard Andrewes, Head of Music, Cambridge University Library; Miss Carole Angier; Mr Felix Aprahamian; Mr Robert Beckhard; Mrs Mary Bernard; Mr John Bishop; Dr Lionel Carley, archivist of the Delius Trust; Mr Peter Carr, Mrs Barbara Churms, and Mr Mark Buckle for proof-reading; Professor Kathy Coleman, Professor of Classics, Trinity College, Dublin, for Latin and Greek translations; Mrs Helene Cooke and Mr Rainer Strauss for German translations; Mr David Cox, former editor of the *Peter Warlock Society Newsletter*; Mr Mark Curthoys, archivist of Christ Church, Oxford; Miss Eiluned Davies; Miss Etaine Eberhard, formerly of the staff of the Manuscripts and Archives Department of the University of Cape Town Library; Mrs Tony Edwards for her research in Somerset

House; Mrs Paula Findlay; Dr Philip Hazel; Dr Michael Herbert, Lecturer in English, St Andrew's University, for help and advice on D. H. Lawrence; Ms Elisabeth Heseltine; Mrs Natalia Heseltine; Dr Peter Heseltine; Mrs Vicky Heseltine; Dr Donald Hunt, organist of Worcester Cathedral; Mr Robert Johnson; Mr David Jordan; Mr Ewald Junge; Miss Jenny Keen of the EMI Music Archives; Professor Mark Kinkead-Weekes, formerly Professor of English at the University of Kent, for sharing his tremendous knowledge of D. H. Lawrence; Dr Jean Le Brocquy; Miss Valerie Lewis for French translations; Mr and Mrs Robert Loades of Newbold Pacey Vicarage; Miss Veronica Manoukian; Mr Robert McQuillan; Mme Anna Merle D'Aubigné for her hospitality at Grez-sur-Loing; Mrs Kate Nelson of Cefn Bryntalch; T. Otake, Reference Librarian, University of Tokyo Library System; Professor-Emeritus Ian Parrott; Mr and Mrs Geoffrey Peel of Didbrook Vicarage; Mr Richard Pooler; Mr James Poston; Professor Brian Priestman, formerly Professor of Music at the University of Cape Town; Mr Paul Quarrie, College Librarian, Eton College; Dr Tim Radloff, Senior Lecturer in Music, Rhodes University, Grahamstown; Sir Anthony Reeve, British Ambassador to South Africa; Mr Christopher Robinson, organist of St John's College, Cambridge; Mr Malcolm Rudland, secretary of the Peter Warlock Society; Ms Miranda Seymour; the late Mr Colin Taylor; Mr Hugh Taylor; Miss Elizabeth Wells of the National Sound Archive; Mr Pierre van Wyngaard for help with computing; Dr Percy Young; the director of the Universitäts- und Stadtbibliothek, Cologne; Mr Gerard Hayes of the State Library of Victoria, Melbourne; Miss Ann-Marie Baker and Mrs Rosemary Florrimell of the Grainger Museum, University of Melbourne; the staff of the Humanities Research Center of the University of Texas at Austin; Mr Hugh Cobbe, Mr Arthur Searle, and the staff of the Manuscripts Students' Room of the British Library; Ms Maria Calderisi and the National Library of Canada; the Library of Trinity College, Dublin; Ms Lori Curtis of the special collections of the Library of Tulsa; the National Library of Wales; the staff of the South African Library, Cape Town; Miss Eugénie Söhnge and Mrs Lesley Hart of the University of Cape Town Medical Library, Miss Leonie Twentyman-Jones and the staff of the Manuscripts and Archives Department and of the South African College of Music Library of the University of Cape Town.

Thanks are also due to the following copyright holders for allowing me to reprint from their material: Fransisco Campbell Custodio and Ad. Donker (Pty) Ltd., and Faber & Faber Ltd., for permission to quote Roy Campbell's poem 'Dedication of a Tree'; John Murray (Publishers) Ltd. for permission to quote from *Another Part of the Wood* by Kenneth Clark; Laurence Pollinger Limited; the Estate of Frieda Lawrence Ravagli and Viking Penguin, a division of Penguin Books USA Inc., for permission to quote from D. H. Lawrence's *Women in Love*; Laurence Pollinger Limited, the Estate of Frieda Lawrence Ravagli and Cambridge University Press for permission to reprint extracts from D. H. Lawrence's correspondence, vols. ii, iii, and iv; Scolar Press for permission to quote from Lewis Foreman's *Bax: A Composer and his Times*; Severn House Publishers Limited for permission to quote from Sir Thomas Beecham's *Frederick Delius*; Thames Publishing for permission to quote from Christopher Palmer's *Herbert Howells: A Centenary Celebration*; A. P. Watt Ltd. on behalf of The Executors of the Estate of Cecil Gray for permission to quote from Gray's *Peter Warlock: A Memoir of Philip Heseltine*.

Whilst I have made every effort to obtain the necessary permission to quote copyright material, in a few instances it has proved impossible to trace the copyright holders. I apologize therefore if I have inadvertently infringed any laws of copyright.

B.S.

Cape Town
13 May 1993

CONTENTS

LIST OF PLATES

(between pp. 174–175)

THE EARLY YEARS
(1894–1911)

IN OCTOBER 1894 the 75-year-old Queen Victoria had been on
the throne for fifty-seven years and was no doubt still delighting in
the fact that her *bête noire* Gladstone had been forced to resign as
Prime Minister in March. She had once summed up her feelings
about him in the famous remark: 'He speaks to me as if I was a
public meeting.' Unadvised, the Queen and Empress had recently
appointed Lord Rosebery as his successor and would, doubtless, not
be amused to see his government collapse after only sixteen months.
However, on the last Tuesday of October, the 30th, Her Majesty
was temporarily unconcerned with matters of State. She had lunched
with the Duke and Duchess of Fife during a late autumn visit to
Balmoral and her thoughts were, no doubt, very much occupied
with the condition of the dying Tsar of Russia, Alexander II.

That same year, highly displeased by a development called Queen
Anne's Mansions which disturbed her view, she had imperiously
pressurized Parliament into limiting the height of London buildings
to 150 feet: an act which meant that no skyscrapers would be
erected in London for the next sixty years. Despite this ban there
was, however, considerable activity on a grand scale in London.
Tower Bridge, costing £1 million, had just been opened, as had
Queen's Hall, destined to become one of London's most important
music venues until its destruction in 1941 during the Second World
War. The first white-fronted and gold-lettered Lyons tea-shop had
opened in Piccadilly, and Harrod's, which had recently instituted a 7
o-clock closing time, had begun acquiring land for a large new store
which would eventually swallow up the Heseltine residence in
Knightsbridge. It was the year that saw the appearance not only of
the first of Kipling's popular *Jungle Books*, but also the notorious
Yellow Book containing Aubrey Beardsley's illustrations, and
Debussy's impressionistic *Prélude à l'Après-midi d'un faune*. The 20-
year-old Schoenberg had just begun counterpoint lessons, Bartók

was only 13, Stravinsky 12, whilst the 37-year-old Elgar still had five years to wait before his reputation as a composer would be firmly established.

The popular Victorian farce, *Charley's Aunt*, was playing at the Globe, while at the Savoy Theatre Rupert D'Oyly Carte, no longer able to extract an annual new work from the money-spinning duo Gilbert and Sullivan, was offering the London public André Messager's operetta *Mirette*. It was also the year in which, at the adjacent five-year-old Savoy Hotel, Auguste Escoffier created his immortal dessert, *Pêche Melba*, to honour the great Australian diva, Dame Nellie Melba. On a typically dull, wet London day, while the busy Savoy chefs were placing scoops of vanilla ice-cream on cooked peach halves and topping them with a purée of raspberries and almond slivers, in another room in the same hotel another event was taking place: an event that would prove of great musical significance in the years that lay ahead.

Philip Heseltine (alias Peter Warlock) described the occasion in rather jocular terms when being interviewed some twenty-nine years later. 'I was born in 1894 on the Embankment . . . It was in the Savoy; but the Embankment sounds better.' Somehow it is in keeping with his subsequent unpredictable life-style that on 30 October 1894 he should have been born in as unusual a place as London's most fashionable hotel. Typical too that he should have made such a facetious remark to the interviewer Rodney Bennett, father of the composer Richard Rodney Bennett.[1] One immediately has mental pictures of the young Philip Heseltine making his entrance into the world, prematurely and dramatically, in the middle of a lavish dinner-party! Mysterious as the reference might at first sound, the explanation is, in fact, quite simple. Writing to Delius in 1916 Philip remarks how his parents 'lived lavishly for years in the Savoy Hotel',[2] while, in a letter written to his mother from the Grand-Hôtel in Rome in 1921, he makes the significant remark: 'In this excellent place I begin to understand how you must have loved your years at the Savoy!'[3]

In the same interview Philip continued by saying that he had a horoscope which had been cast for him sometime about 1917 and that he was born under Gemini which signified duplicity. This, too, was a tongue-in-cheek remark. He was, in fact, born under the sign of Scorpio, but the idea of being a Gemini fitted in better with the Heseltine/Warlock image he was by then assiduously creating. It is quite uncanny how many accurate assessments and predictions about Warlock's life and personality appear in this very horoscope which he mentioned:

You have Aries rising, and this is the sign of the Pioneer. You like a good fight, particularly a battle of brains, and you don't care how many difficulties you find in your path, you charge straight at them and rather enjoy it all. You are neither shy nor pessimistic; you have a happy knack of forgetting any failures you may experience, and you carry through your undertakings with a confidence, dash and brilliancy that disarm criticism. You are enthusiastic and warmhearted in your friendships almost to a point of rashness. You like a change of surroundings and acquaintances; in fact you like to dash about over the face of the world, here to-day, and goodness knows where to-morrow. . . . much of your present life will revolve about the question of partnerships and associations with others. You will be a determined lover, difficult to turn aside in your affections and desires. A mental awakening in 1911 was the result of Mercury (the planet of intellect) measuring by primary directions to the ascendant at about that date. You naturally have an active mind and a good memory. You can be sarcastic when roused by any injustice, and you have a ready wit. Your Sun (representing the individuality) is also in Scorpio. This makes you very determined, gives you great magnetic power, and critical perception. Scorpio is a sign of extremes; its sons are either saints or sinners—they never do anything by halves. The conjunction of the Sun and Venus gives you a love of art and refinement. The trine with Jupiter gives you abundant vitality . . . The nerves are inclined to be very tensely constituted. You are liable to meet with some danger in connection with electricity, so keep this in mind. You are at times pessimistic but this does not last for long . . . Your Moon (or personality) is in the sign of Sagittarius. This makes you often at loggerheads with convention. It also gives you a gift for prophecy and a fondness for dual experiences. Neptune is in Gemini, and this is a good position for developing occult or inspirational faculties. It is the signature of genius in many directions, but it makes you restless, and makes it difficult for you to concentrate on one thing for a great length of time. You will . . . succeed in any field of endeavour where mental ingenuity is essential. . . . You will have an irresistible impulse to do at least two things at the same time and, what is more extraordinary still, you will succeed in doing them.[4]

Christened Philip Arnold, his father Arnold Heseltine (1852–97), a younger son in a family of eleven children, was a partner in a firm of solicitors. Writing about his father in 1913, Philip told Delius that he understood he was 'excessively pious', adding, with a certain degree of cynicism, 'fervent in his devotion to the "grand traditions" of Christianity and the British nation and empire, no doubt!'[5] The Heseltines were a well-to-do upper middle-class London family, many of whom had had distinguished careers. Philip's paternal grandfather had been a successful stockbroker and two of his uncles had entered the same profession, amassing considerable fortunes. His grandmother had been a brilliant classical scholar, an unusual achievement for a woman in those days, and a cousin, Michael Heseltine (1886–1952), followed in her footsteps, producing in 1913 one of the early, standard English editions of the works of the Roman poet, Petronius. Philip was, however, not overimpressed with his cousin's editorial achievement—mainly on account of the fact that he had severely expurgated the original Latin text, leaving, in his own words, 'whole pages in the decent obscurity of Latin'.[6] Philip also wrote a short, sarcastic review of his cousin's poetry in the October 1913 edition of the *Oxford Magazine*, describing it in a letter as 'frightful hogwash . . . *damned* nonsense'.[7]

There were also artistic connections in the family: one of the uncles, John Postle Heseltine (1843–1929), a well-known connoisseur and art-collector, was a trustee of the National Gallery for more than forty years and numbered drawings by Dürer, Rembrandt, and Watteau in his own collection. Another uncle, the wealthy Evelyn Heseltine (1850–1930), contributed £5,000 towards the erection of a remarkable art nouveau church near his family home at Great Warley, Essex in 1902, in memory of Philip's father. Yet another uncle, Arthur Joseph ('Joe') Heseltine (1855–1930), was a rather eccentric, though not particularly good, painter and engraver who had left the Victorian respectability of the London family to settle in Marlotte, a village some 80 kilometres south of Paris where a number of distinguished painters of the day had studios. Three of his works (two etchings and an oil-painting entitled 'Chalands') may be seen hanging in the Marie de Bourron-Marlotte. He had studied in England with Sir Edward Poynter (1836–1919), and with the French painter and sculptor Carolus Duran (1838–1917), and had married Céline Guillet, the daughter of an artist. Theirs was a curious relationship. Uncle Joe lived in a house called Villa Heseltine where he had his studio (in a side street in Marlotte which now bears the name Passage Heseltine) whilst she lived in another house nearby. They did, however, meet at mealtimes, though Uncle Joe obviously found being married to her a bit of a trial, telling Philip that his aunt was 'neurasthenic & hypochondriac, which is not at all amusing to live with in hot weather or in cold either'.[8] In fact Joseph Heseltine seems to have been something of an oddity and no doubt Philip, who was rather fond of him, could identify with him when he later wrote: 'He has, of course, a certain very decided *kink* somewhere, but his ideas on everything are absolutely free, and he dislikes most of his relatives as much as I do: we criticize them freely—mostly "damned fools"!'[9] There appears to have been a good rapport between the two of them and in the early years they exchanged numerous letters and Philip visited him twice while still in his teens.

Arnold Heseltine died suddenly in March 1897, at the early age of 45, when Philip was only 2 years old. He had been previously married to the sister-in-law of his brother Evelyn, Florence Marion Hull, who died in 1880. Arnold's second wife, Philip's mother, Bessie Mary Edith Covernton (nicknamed 'Covey') (1861–1943), who he married in 1889, was of Welsh stock and came from Knighton in Radnorshire,[10] a part of Britain with which Philip was to have strong ties throughout his life. The 'admirable and tranquil'[11] Welsh countryside, as he described it, was of particular importance to him and he often wrote of its beauty and 'enchantment . . . stronger than wine or woman and intimately associated with music'.[12]

Edith Covernton's mother had died when she was 10 and Edith had the task not only of helping bring up her brothers and sisters, but also of keeping house for her father, Charles, who had qualified as a doctor in Edinburgh. On his death Edith, then in her early twenties, moved to Canada where she had relatives, returning to England some seven years later when the man she had hoped to marry in Canada died of tuberculosis. From all accounts she appears to have had a dominant and powerful personality: in fact Philip's composer-friend, E. J. Moeran (1894–1950), described her as 'the most dominating woman he had ever met'.[13] Her daughter-in-law, Natalia Heseltine, found her 'essentially Edwardian in her attitude and very attached to traditions', describing her as 'pretty authoritarian with a strong personality', though admitted that she had a wonderful sense of humour.[14] The art historian Sir Kenneth Clark (1903–83) adds a little to what information we have about her. In some ways it contradicts the impression that will be gained of her in subsequent chapters:

[My mother's] greatest friend, called Mrs Buckley-Jones, had a son by an earlier husband named Heseltine . . . She was my favourite playmate and a great uninhibitor, who could make even my mother laugh. Her son, Philip, was a musician of considerable talent . . . As a boy he had been gentle and withdrawn; I always remember him on our yacht suffering tortures of sea-sickness, but soldiering on through a score of Purcell. It seemed admirable to me though ridiculous to the rest of the party. But when he broke loose on the world he developed a strain of combative amorality which made him legendary in the life of the early 'twenties . . . His mother was not at all straitlaced, but Phil went too far for anyone brought up in nineteenth-century England, and she used to send my mother long, despairing letters relating all her son's misdoings. My mother would read them at breakfast with ill-disguised relish and when I came in to see her would roll her eyes to heaven and say in a tragic voice: 'Phil's broken out in a new place' . . . From about 1915 onwards Phil was held up as an awful example of what could happen to me if I became an artist, and I was never allowed to see him; but we kept in touch.[15]

After Arnold's death Edith Heseltine continued to live in their Knightsbridge house, 27 Hans Road, Hans Place, and some of Philip's earliest letters date from this period. Over 300 letters from Philip to his mother have survived, the earliest written in 1899 when he was only 4 years old, the last written in late 1930, very shortly before his death. In the early letters he often addressed his mother as 'Dear darling Wooley Sheepkin' and signed himself 'dear darling Lambkin',[16] which not only hints at the dependence each had on the other but indicates how strongly the two had been bonded in the boy's formative years. She was no doubt one of the major problems in his life, attempting as she did to control and influence him whenever she could. Although aware of her obvious machinations and manipulations, Philip was never quite able to break the filial ties. This was partly due to the fact that Arnold Heseltine had made no special financial provision for his young son. Any allowance Philip was to receive in future years depended entirely on his mother's goodwill. This fact, coupled with his singular lack of business sense, meant that he was constantly having to ask her for money. Time and time again, usually after some disastrous scheme or undertaking, he was fortunate in being able to return to his home in Wales. Although in 1913 he wrote that when he was 21 he would have an income of his own of £80 a year, there is no reference to anything of the kind in the will which Arnold Heseltine signed a month before his death. He left his entire estate to his wife, Edith, naming her and his brother, Evelyn, as trustees, stipulating that they 'shall stand possessed of my said residuary moneys and the investments . . . in trust to pay the income thereof to my said wife during her life for her sole and separate use'. Whatever kind of person Philip's mother may have been, it is to her credit that throughout his life she was prepared to provide a place where her son could retire to in comparative security and tranquillity. As we shall see, much of his creative work was produced during these periods in Wales.

At the age of 5 Philip Heseltine started school at an establishment run by a Miss Quirinie, 35 Cliveden Place, just off Sloane Square and very near his home in Hans Road. This was 1899, the year in which the Boer War began, Elgar's *Enigma Variations* received its first performance, and the appearance of Scott Joplin's *Maple Leaf Rag* heralded a musical genre that would change the whole course of popular music in the years ahead.

As a small boy Philip was noted as having 'an entirely individual character, and . . . a highly original mind . . . fond of improving on, and usually dramatizing, any game [he] happened to be playing'.[17] In the British Library there is a letter to Philip's mother from a Florence Peck describing the 7-year-old boy as being perfectly charming, with very delightful manners: 'He was slim, had a pale oval face, wonderful blue-grey eyes and soft fair hair, and had a quite unusual bearing for a child of his years . . . He was intensely interested in all matters appertaining to music, and would discuss with me the way the orchestra would sit, how many violinists there would be at such a concert, etc.'[18] Though he later professed to have hated them, Philip began piano lessons at the age of 6 and he was said to become 'very emotional when moved by any tune'.[19] In November 1902 he was first in a class of five and his report noted that he had 'been more attentive of late . . . Conduct good.'[20]

In 1903 his mother married Walter Buckley Jones (1864–1938), a wealthy bachelor four years her junior, who was descended from a Welsh family who had made their money in the flannel trade in the early part of the nineteenth century. After studying law at Cambridge, Walter had been called to the bar but chose not to practise, living instead a life of leisure in London for over fifteen years. Like the young Philip he had a passion for railways and it would appear that he and his stepson had a good relationship and 'were always the best of friends and companions'.[21] The Jones family also owned a fine house, Cefn Bryntalch, set in spacious grounds not far from Abermule in Montgomeryshire, in the middle of the Severn valley. *Talch* in Welsh means fragment, *bryn* means hill, and *cefn* means ridge, the house is therefore on the 'ridge of part of a hill'. Philip once wrote helpfully to a friend that it was pronounced 'Keffen Brŭntach, the *ch* being aspirate'.[22] Built by G. F. Bodley and Philip Webb in 1869, it is regarded as marking the beginning of the Georgian revival of the 1870s. It is a large and imposing building with an exterior of cleanly detailed red brick and three big gables on the south-east front. The interior is largely in the neo-Georgian style—one of the most impressive features being the imposing, broad staircase leading towards a Venetian window and then dividing into two flights which double back to a gallery.

After living in London for a while, Walter Buckley Jones and his wife moved to Cefn Bryntalch in 1908, regarding it as their home, although the house in Hans Road was kept on until October 1910, when it was bought by Harrod's Department Store for extensions to their new premises. Once installed in Cefn Bryntalch, Edith Buckley Jones soon assumed the role of lady of the manor and it would seem that Walter became very much under his wife's control, content to take a back seat while she ran their affairs and controlled the purse-strings. Philip was delighted with the move, immediately identifying with the magnificent surrounding countryside, and soon developing a deep love for Wales and the Welsh people.

Philip undoubtedly showed remarkable precocity in his early years, constantly writing funny little poems and plays, as well as inventing stories and people with strange names. One such was 'The History of Golly Land' which included characters with weird names such as P. A. Phatboy (Philip Arnold himself?), a King and Queen called Ehtgnikfoehtstac and Ehtneeuqfoehtstac (the king (and queen) of the cats, spelt backwards!) and Sir C. F. Tatters and General Sir J. L. Rags. It is also interesting to note amongst this juvenilia of 1904 the mention of one Bulgy Gogo, 'the Prize fool of Chiswick', a name which Philip would use again in later writings. In view of his considerable interest in limericks in adult life, it is perhaps worth noting that his first recorded attempts in this form were written in 1905: a series of eight entitled 'Ye Jones Familie Rhymes', including one about his stepfather very much in the Edward Lear style:

> There once was a small boy called Walter
> Who chanted sweet chants from a psalter
>   When told he must stop
>   Away he did hop,
> With his song-book, his hymn-book & psalter.[23]

The limericks we shall encounter in later years will not be quite so innocent.

On 28 April 1904, at the age of 9½, Philip was sent to Stone House, a private boarding-school for some sixty boys, which had been founded in 1883 in Broadstairs, Kent, and where he was to spend the next four years. Surrounded by a belt of trees and a towering flint wall, Stone House stands on the high ground of the North Foreland, overlooking the sea where, on a clear day, the coast of France is visible on the far horizon. After the school's closure in 1969 the building was converted into fashionable apartments, and it remains a dignified and distinctive Georgian building, with bow-fronted windows and wide-spreading balcony. The headmaster, a Cambridge man, the Reverend William Henry Churchill, had bought the school in 1895 and seems to have been a good teacher, particularly of history, inspiring awe and affection in his pupils, though to some he came across as a bit of a snob. A strict disciplinarian, he was insistent on good behaviour and good manners at all times and boys were expected to sit absolutely still, both in class and chapel. On Saturday afternoons they would be taken for walks. One can picture them dressed in their little Eton jackets and top hats making their way in crocodile formation across the Foreland and down the chalk tracks to the sea. There was also a fair amount of music performed in the school. The music-master and organist, Mr W. E. Brockway, produced a full, albeit largely Victorian, programme of chapel and organ music, and Saturday night concerts in winter included vocal music by Handel, Schubert, and excerpts from Gilbert and Sullivan. A contemporary of Philip's noted Brockway's 'aggressive manner' while Philip himself subsequently declared that he 'had probably destroyed more musical talent than any man in England'.[24]

A large number of Philip's prep-school letters to his mother give an interesting account of his early progress and development. It was also a period of his life when a number of the problems which were later to beset him were beginning to form within his sensitive temperament. Parted from his possessive mother for the first time, we find him writing significant sentences such as: 'I think your love is coming down on me every night', whilst in the same letter the guilt that had already been ingrained by the powerful Mrs Buckley Jones surfaces in the small boy's almost pathetic request and confession: 'Please kiss all your letters . . . We have been told not to go on to other boys mats in the dormitary [sic] and I went on one by mistake but when I said my prayers I asked to be forgiven.'[25] His mother was determined not to neglect her son's religious life. Prayer-books, hymn-books, and church services were promptly dispatched to him in the first few weeks of his first term. She exhorted him not to read in bed unless it was his work or the Bible, whereupon Philip immediately tried to put her mind at rest by saying he had just that night read St Luke 89: 26, the account of Jesus casting out devils. In these early letters there is, in fact, a strong religious element, and we find him requesting books such as *Three Martyrs of the Nineteenth Century*, *Helps to Study the Bible*, and the *Cathedral Psalter*, though, to be fair, he was also asking for a cricket ball and copies of the *Railway and Locomotive Magazine*, trains and photography being two of his earliest enthusiasms. But his mother's over-effusive and affectionate postcards soon proved an embarrassment, particularly when read by teasing or bullying schoolmates, and after three months we find him writing tactfully: 'If you do not mind dont send any more postcards here (much as I like them).'[26]

Despite these accumulating pressures, he was proving an outstanding pupil and after only two weeks was top of his form by 60 marks, a pattern of excellence which he steadily maintained. By 1905, even though he was the youngest boy in the class, he came top in the Lower Sixth, the following year he was made captain of his dormitory, and at the age of 12 was appointed head of school. Although he played cricket, football, and hockey, he confessed in his letters home that he was not much of a success at games. Yet, despite his academic achievements and positions of responsibility, he was never really happy at Stone House and his letters to his mother betray signs of intense homesickness. He was often physically sick on the train when returning to school, a sign of apprehension and anxiety, and his early letters constantly refer to the number of days remaining before he and his mother would be reunited. Even after two years away from home he could still write: 'I *shall* try to do my level best . . . but I would MUCH prefer to be sitting with you and the Jones family as you know well.'[27] It is also slightly disturbing that at the age of nearly 12 he could be writing to his mother words such as these: 'I am still you [sic] own VERY *extra* loving lambkin *Phil*. I hope you don't show this letter or any of my letters to anyone . . . Of course I know you wouldn't but I like to make certain that our little loving talks are quite private.'[28]

Even as early as 1906, one can sense the demanding Edith Buckley Jones putting some kind of religious pressure on the young Philip. He wrote to her in March 1906 saying that he had composed a five-verse hymn about what she had been telling him:

> Thou knowest, Lord, that we are weak;
> O give us strength to conquer sin
> That we may crush all evil down
> And finally prevail and win.[29]

More disturbing, however, was the fact that she was now beginning to use subtle methods of emotional blackmail on her as-yet-unsuspecting son—methods which would intensify as the years pro-

gressed. We see in this reply written in December 1906 his first confused and apologetic reaction to her unexpected allegations:

I was sorry to get your letter today, at least to read what you said. I didn't
think my last letters were so very much shorter than those before. But I hope
those of this term up till now have been alright . . . only please whatever you
do DONT think that I dont care whether I get your letters or not as I *really* do:
you cannot really think that I know. But above all *dont* think I forget you
here as I know also that you couldn't think that.[30]

It was during his years at Stone House that his interest in music
seems suddenly to have been awakened. Almost as soon as he
arrived he wrote to tell his mother of Brockway's comments on his
musical ability: 'He says I can play but that I dont know how to
read and that I dont know how to make brieves & sembrives [*sic*].'[31]
In the years that followed he often reported home on his progress at
the piano, commenting on the works (by composers such as
Mendelssohn, Heller, and Moszkowski) that he was learning. There
was also a pianola which belonged to one of the masters at the
school and it was through performances on this instrument that he
was first introduced to some of the music of Beethoven, Schubert,
Mendelssohn, Chopin, and Liszt.[32] There were also school concerts
in which the young Philip took part, playing piano solos or duets
with Brockway, as well as singing solos and duets from several of
the Gilbert and Sullivan operettas. There is even a brief reference in
a letter of 1906 to what must surely be some of his first attempts at
musical composition: 'I shall copy out the music I have composed
for Miss Oakley to see, but that's extremely dull and boring when
you have been doing it for some time.'[33] He also told his mother
about a lecture on Shakespeare's songs which one of the masters
had given and in which 'It was a lover and his lass' by Thomas
Morley and 'The poor soul sat sighing' made an obvious impression
on him, even to his noting that the manuscript of the latter song
was in the British Museum. Were the seeds of important future
scholarship perhaps sown that October evening in 1907?

Even at this early age, during his school holidays in London or
Wales, he seems to have shown a flair for organizing concerts.
Family and friends were often pressed into taking part in these
entertainments, for which he wrote more plays and poems, recited,
sang, and played the piano, zither-harp, and flageolet. His mind was
already highly creative and at the age of 11 he was able to produce
original and amusing poems such as this one written rather in the
style of Hilaire Belloc's *Cautionary Verses*:

> In castles and old mansions too
> There oft are haunted rooms a few.
> Where hands appear and strangle men
> All bloody & with fingers ten
> For instance once a man was told
> In order that he might be bold
> That ghastly fingers would appear,
> Which in the dark would seem quite clear,
> That they would rise above his bed
> Until their nails should pierce his head
> So then he two revolvers got
> So that these fingers might be shot.
>
>   *   *   *   *   *   *
>
> The night approached: he went to bed
> And stayed up in his nightshirt red.
> All was quite silent in the dark
> He heard not e'en a dog to bark—
> When suddenly!—O gracious my
> Two hands appeared—so with a cry
> He snatched up the revolvers two
> A ghastly screm [*sic*]—what did he do
> Alas! it was no ghostly foe
> For he'd shot off his own big toe.
>
> MORAL So if with Lux you wash your sheet
>   You'll never these disasters meet.[34]

At the same time he was gradually expanding his musical horizons and by January 1907 was beginning to sample the varied opportunities of the London musical scene, attending, for example, a performance of Handel's *Messiah* in the Albert Hall on New Year's Day. During the last months of his time at Stone House his letters were increasingly full of references to music, either with details of what he was playing on the piano at school, his determination to learn the clarinet (despite his mother's lack of enthusiasm for the idea), requests for a complete gramophone catalogue from Harrod's, or references to concerts and operas in London. She again berated her 13-year-old son for not writing regularly enough and his reply has a pathetic, almost desperate quality:

I *really am sorry* I did not write, I can't think how I could have been so unkind as I realize now how it *must* have hurt you . . . *Please* forgive me, my own darling mother: I am sure you will when you know that I didn't really mean to be unkind, and I *really* do love you just as much as ever so dont please think that I dont.[35]

By June 1908 he could proudly announce to his mother that he was five foot three and a quarter inches tall (in his boots) and the next month (7–9 July) he sat the prestigious Eton scholarship examination. Although he came fourth and was thus eligible for a scholarship, the Reverend Mr Churchill advised his mother not to send him into College, saying that he believed it would do his character far more good to be an Oppidan, a fee-paying pupil who was a member of one of the twenty-four houses presided over by a housemaster. At that time it was not considered the 'done thing' for wealthy parents to accept such scholarships and so the family duly declined it.

Appropriately equipped with two Eton jackets, three pairs of trousers, fourteen shirts, three night-shirts, one pair of pumps, twelve pairs of socks, fourteen collars, four pairs of drawers and numerous other articles of clothing (as laid down in the school handbook), Philip started Eton on 17 September 1908. He was placed in Warre House, a late Victorian building a few minutes' walk from the main school, together with some other fifty boys under the care of the housemaster Hubert Brinton (1862–1940), who was also one of the classics masters. From all accounts his years at Eton were not particularly happy ones. In his interview with Rodney Bennett, Philip had harsh words to say about his schooling there: 'I shall always hate that housemaster . . . I became a moody, vindictive youth and absolutely lost a rather real concentration that I had.'[36] In his later letters the few references to the Eton days are not particularly complimentary. Writing in 1914, for example, he gave vent to his feelings about the inadequacies of his education: 'this accursed public school and university "education" (!!) fits one for nothing: at the age of 19, the product of Eton and Oxford is worth a thousand times less than the product of the national board-schools'.[37] Writing about a schoolboy contemporary the year before, he had observed that he seemed 'tremendously Anti-Eton: and anyone of this opinion is immediately beloved of me, ex-officio, as it were!'[38] Gray gathered that Philip had been bullied at Eton and suggested that 'the explanation of many aspects of his life and character that are difficult to understand is to be sought in the miseries and humiliations endured in those early years at Eton'.[39] He had once confided to Gray that a recurring nightmare was one in which he found himself back at school. On the other hand, his poet friend Robert Nichols (1893–1944) had the impression that he had not really detested life at Eton all that much.

The Precentor (Director of Music) at the time was Dr Charles Harford Lloyd (1849–1919), known by the nickname 'Pussy'. He had been organist at Gloucester Cathedral and Christ Church,

Oxford, and had been appointed to Eton in 1892 where he remained for twenty-two years until his retirement in 1914. He was regarded as a fine improviser on the organ and also composed a modest amount of not very distinguished church and choral music. After an interview with Lloyd, Philip joined the College Musical Society (costing an extra £1. 11s. 6d. a term) which meant that, despite his 'cracking voice',[40] as he described it, he was able to experience at first hand the works of such composers as Palestrina, Bach, Handel, Schubert, and Brahms. There was even the opportunity to take part in a performance of the *Eton Memorial Ode*, especially written by two old Etonians, Sir C. Hubert H. Parry and Robert Bridges, for the celebrations when Edward VII came to open the Memorial Hall in November 1908. Dr Lloyd had engaged a professional orchestra for the occasion and the impressive choir, the Eton College Musical Society, consisted of some 229 voices.

Philip also became involved in a number of other musical activities and for a while he studied the clarinet with the school bandmaster and played the percussion in the college orchestra, which was conducted by the composer Thomas Dunhill (1877–1946), one of the assistant music-masters (from 1899 to 1908). He noted two occasions on which he took part in performances as a percussionist: in December 1909 he played cymbals and bass drum in Grieg's *Peer Gynt Suite*, while in February 1911 he wrote wittily that he had been 'admitted free of charge [to a concert of the Windsor and Eton Amateur Musical Society] for striking the cymbals a dozen times in one piece'.[41] In the same letter he added critically that he thought 'the orchestra were bad . . . worse than before'. It is interesting to note that in that particular concert the Reverend E. H. Fellowes (1870–1951), the pioneer musicologist and editor, and minor canon of St George's Chapel, Windsor, was playing in the back desk of the first violins. In less than a decade he would be crossing swords with the young lad then clashing the cymbals.

Philip's interest in music continued to grow rapidly and in December 1908 we find him writing to his mother asking her to book seats for performances of the complete *Ring* cycle at Covent Garden which the great Hans Richter (1843–1916) was to conduct. But by far the most important and lasting influence at Eton was his remarkable piano-teacher, Colin Taylor (1881–1973). To quote the words of Cecil Gray: 'He was fortunate in finding a sympathetic and stimulating influence in the person of the assistant music-master, Mr Colin Taylor, from whom he received piano lessons which he now actually enjoyed, though he was never to attain to any great proficiency on the instrument.'[42] Taylor, the son of Dr James Taylor (1833–1900), a former organist of New College, Oxford, was a kind and sympathetic man, as well as an enlightened teacher who was later to become a close friend and confidant. He had been educated in Germany and at the Royal College of Music and in those early days was already playing and teaching advanced modern piano works. It was he who encouraged the young boy in his music studies, imparting to him an especial interest in modern music. As Philip was to tell Delius: 'Colin Taylor is a splendid man: I owe most of my love for music to him.'[43] Some fifty-six years later Colin Taylor's memories of the young schoolboy were still vivid:

When Heseltine came to Eton in 1908 at the age of fourteen I was twenty-seven, and had already been an assistant music master at the College for four years. Dr Charles Harford Lloyd was Precentor . . . a kindly, gifted and excitable little man who lived in a perpetual state of imagined haste.

From the very outset of Heseltine's advent it was apparent that in this well knit and rather pale little boy there was something arresting, something apart, something strikingly different from the ordinary run of our music students. Not that he showed musical or pianistic precocity, but it was his approach, his attitude that differed. This posed a problem.

Sensing, and I hope rightly, that had I insisted on the stereotyped drill commonly meted out to those in my charge, the boy as likely as not would give up music altogether. The upshot was that I devoted the greater part of lesson time to an attempt to enlarge his musical horizon. This was done by playing the accepted classics, romantics and moderns to him, and by discussing and exploring music. By these means his keenness grew and his interest consolidated. In those days I probably considered myself the deuce of a go-ahead modern, for I was playing and teaching Debussy, Ravel, Schoenberg, Scriabin and the then available Bartók hot from the press, so to speak . . .

Of course pianistic drill was not altogether neglected. My bait in his case as in many another, was to extol sightreading as a means towards exploration. The boy was sensible enough to see that lacking at least a workaday technique the bulk of our musical heritage would be literally a closed book to him. We must remember that mechanical reproduction barring the pianola was then virtually non-existent.[44]

Here at last was someone who Philip felt really understood him and could show him how to unlock the doors to the world of music. It was from those teenage days that a real friendship was to develop and blossom and he remained grateful to Taylor throughout his life, keeping in touch with him until the year before his death.

In the meantime he had been producing excellent results, not only in musical activities (winning prizes for Musical Holiday Tasks), but also in the academic sphere, where he won prizes for coming second in his form in 1909 and for Latin verse in 1910. Life at Eton was perhaps gradually beginning to show its unhappy effect on his personality, for his classics report for Michaelmas School-Time 1909 referred to him as 'a precise and steady worker—rather too precise, I have sometimes thought—with perhaps a faint suspicion of priggishness'.[45] His experience of life in the school army corps was also not to his taste and he predictably described the month spent on an officers' training course on Farnborough Common in August 1910 as 'most unpleasant'. He would, no doubt, have also been highly cynical of instructions issued by the headmaster late that same year, which suggested to pupils 'that the correct position to stand in Chapel is either with the arms folded, or to clasp the front of the coat about the height of the top waistcoat button'[46] but *not* with their hands in their pockets! In short, for Philip Heseltine life at Eton was endlessly dull and monotonous. In an interview with the composer Alec Rowley (1892–1958) in 1927, he dismissed it as 'a scholastic sausage machine' where individualism was discouraged: 'I was put back into a class in which my mental juniors by years dominated, and I have never really recovered. Indeed, the iron entered into my soul, and *that* at fifteen years of age. The harm was that it broke the continuity of my development.'[47] He was duly confirmed in December 1909 by the Bishop of Oxford, the Right Reverend Francis Paget (1851–1911), his godfather, Uncle Evelyn, attending the service. From time to time he appeared in concerts in the School Hall. The pieces he played were certainly not show-pieces: the 'Sarabande' from Grieg's *Holberg Suite*, 'Seguidilla' by Charles Vincent, 'Two Tone-Stanzas' by Ernest Austin and a piano duet by Schubert ('Marche caractéristique', Op. 121 No. 1). At the end of his Eton career, in his final appearance at a concert given by the school-leavers in July 1911, besides accompanying a number of items, he and another pupil played a duet, 'Paraphrases on "Chop-sticks"' by various Russian composers (Borodin, Cui, Lyadov, and Rimsky-Korsakov), which went down well with the audience and was 'roundly applauded'.[48]

His many letters home tell us much of his developing musical interests and activities during these years. They also often show how his mother was still keeping a firm emotional grip on him. The following was written after a bad report from his housemaster:

I really mean to turn over a new leaf altogether to-day for the New Year and show you that I really am your loving son and do more to reward you for all you have done for me, as I know I have been *very* unkind and selfish this term

so far . . . I know how this must have grieved you . . . as I really *do* love you
so and I really am more sorry than I can say. But please forgive me, although
I know it must seem as if I did not love you, but I *do* really love you.[49]

On reading through these early letters certain aspects of the
mother–son relationship appear, certainly to the modern-day reader,
as very unhealthy. For example, on his sixteenth birthday she sent him
a bunch of violets—a strange gift for a teenage boy at an English public school! His thank-you letter has disturbingly Oedipal overtones:

How can I thank you enough for your *more* than generous present and kind
letter; it is very kind of you and thank you a thousand times. I think I was
more touched by the lovely violets you sent than by almost anything you have
ever sent me; they smell most beautiful and so indeed remind me of your
love.[50]

As if this was not enough, Philip then goes on to quote Shelley's
poem 'Music, when soft voices die' which contains the significant
lines:

> Odours, when sweet violets sicken,
> Live within the sense they quicken
>
> .   .   .   .
>
> And so thy thoughts, when thou art gone,
> Love itself shall slumber on.

In 1910, rather as schoolboys today develop a craze for a certain
pop-star or group, Philip's gradual interest and eventual obsession
with the music of Delius began to manifest itself. As early as 1908
he had written to his mother announcing his intention of obtaining
Delius's autograph for Mr Brockway's collection, through the
agency of his Uncle Joe, who lived not far from Delius, who had
been living at Grez-sur-Loing since 1897. Perhaps it was Brockway's
interest in Delius's autograph that first attracted Philip's attention to
his music. Apart from this early recorded comment, there is no
other obvious reason as to why Philip should suddenly have developed this all-consuming interest; there are simply increasing references to Delius's music in his letters home. No doubt the immense,
emotive power of Delius's chromatic, impressionistic style appealed
in some way to Philip, a relatively naïve listener with an obviously
sympathetic temperament. Again in February the next year he wrote
to his mother expressing the hope that Delius's opera *A Village
Romeo and Juliet* would 'be a big success' under Beecham, 'the eminent pillmaker's son [who has] done and is doing a great deal for
music in England'.[51]

Besides Taylor, the young Philip had also been befriended by Edward Mason (1878-1915), a cellist who visited the school as a part-time music teacher, and who he described to his mother as someone who 'used to be a kind of sub-conductor at Thomas Beecham's orchestral concerts . . . now in the New Symphony Orchestra and several quartets, and runs a choir of his own'.[52] Mason was also a great devotee of Delius's music and no doubt communicated his enthusiastic first-hand knowledge to the youthful fellow-admirer. So much so that Philip wrote to his mother in the following excited terms:

[Mason] is an enthusiast in the cause of that really great and (here in his native land only) much neglected composer Frederick Delius, whose works I positively adore; I am studying his operas and songs now with very great plea-sure . . . And although I have heard nothing of his music, yet from what I can discover at the piano, I may say that so far as I have yet found, Delius comes the nearest to my own imperfect ideal of music, though when I say nearest I mean 'one of the nearest', as I could not say I like him better than Elgar or Wagner, but I still think he is wonderful. There is one little work of his: a part-song for voices unaccompanied, to words by Arthur Symons, On Craig Ddu: I think that song appeals to me as much as almost anything I have ever heard, by the way it absolutely catches the spirit of the Welsh hills and trans-fers it to music. I would give anything to hear it sung, as it seems to me noth-ing short of wonderful.[53]

When reading this letter it is important to remember that Philip was only 16 at the time and that he had managed, without assis-tance and without the aid of recordings (taken so much for granted these days), the remarkable feat of studying complicated scores of difficult contemporary music. In October 1910 he wrote to his mother saying that he intended making an arrangement for two pianos of parts of A Village Romeo and Juliet from the vocal score and, when it was time for Christmas presents that year, his request was for 'cash' as he was determined to buy 'one or other of those Delius Scores, probably the Dance Rhapsody'.[54] Understandably he now longed for an opportunity to hear some of Delius's music. Mason had lent him a copy of Delius's Sea Drift and the beauty of the music had sent him into further raptures. He wrote to his mother saying: 'It is absolutely heavenly, and, to my mind, as near perfect almost as any music I have ever seen. What it must be with the proper orchestral colour! O that I could hear some Delius!'[55] At last it looked as if this seemingly impossible wish was to be granted. On Friday 16 June 1911, Beecham was due to conduct a concert devoted entirely to the works of Delius, including *Appalachia*, *Paris*, and the *Dance Rhapsody*:

Is it not too absolutely tantalizing, after having made all my plans for going to the Beecham concert with Mr Leigh Spencer[56] on May 3rd, in the hopes that *some* work of Delius *might* be performed, that concert is cancelled, and in yesterday's paper I see the announcement that the Beecham Symphony Concert on Friday June 16th will be *entirely devoted* to the works of Frederick Delius. It is too exasperating for words: my enthusiasm for his most magnificent and all too neglected and rarely performed works grows more and more every time I play or study or even think about those I have copies of, yet I never get a chance of hearing one; if you remember, the Sunday of my long leave last winter was sandwiched in between two Sundays, on both of which Delius works were played at Covent Garden: his opera was performed in London a fortnight after the beginning of one term . . . and I was done out of Mr Mason's concert, at which his lovely 'Sea Drift' poem was sung. Though he is not strictly speaking English, yet he is called a British composer and is a naturalized Englishman, and yet, in the triennial *International* Musical Congress, which is being held this year in London & only British works are being performed, no work of his appears in the scheme. It is a positive disgrace. But I am sure he will come to his own some day, and perhaps his greatness will be all the more widely recognized for it, but people are not given a chance nowadays.[57]

In the meantime his mother wrote telling him that she herself would be meeting Delius during his visit to London. The reasons for and circumstances surrounding the event are somewhat mysterious. Whilst in London Delius stayed at 9 Hans Road (not far from where the Heseltine residence had once been) and it is just possible that the meeting was arranged through mutual friends or perhaps through the agency of Uncle Joe. Perhaps the meeting was occasioned by her wish to know more about the composer of whom Philip had written so enthusiastically or was merely a coincidence— a chance to do a little social climbing? Whatever the reasons, the young boy found the very thought unbelievably exciting:

The second sheet of your letter at once tantalized, mystified and also pleased me more than I can possibly express. I cannot possibly describe how great, how passionate a love I have for Delius and his music, and, as you may well imagine, it would be one of the very greatest pleasures and highest honours of my life to meet him. I would a thousand times rather know him than King George himself! You do not tell me what Uncle Joe said besides in his letter and whether it was his own idea or Delius' that you should call upon him . . .

. . . it is to me very surprising and of the highest interest to know if you have been honoured with special permission to call on this truly great man, or whether it is Uncle Joe's idea . . . as you may readily understand, I am simply *longing* to know all about it and what Uncle Joe said, as if you knew Delius, I should feel that I did also through you . . .

I would give *anything* to come myself, but it is unfortunately an evening concert. If you knew Delius, I might perhaps get permission to come, but I don't know.

Please forgive this long wrigmerole [*sic*], but I am *so* excited about this I hardly know what to do![58]

His mother even went so far as to suggest that Delius could perhaps be persuaded to visit Eton. Philip's ecstatic reply is particularly interesting as in it he mentions the earliest surviving transcription that he had made of one of Delius's orchestral pieces:

It is too perfectly glorious about Delius, and to know him would be the greatest joy of my life . . . It would be the greatest possible honour for me to receive him here, though I am afraid my room offers very limited space for so great a man. It is quite unworthy of him—I am working with redoubled enthusiasm at my transcription of *Brigg Fair*, so that I may have it finished in case you persuade him to come down: it will at least afford a proof (though a humble and unworthy production on my part through lack of skill) of my enthusiasm for him.[59]

Philip had, of course, heard all about the forthcoming concert from Mason. The *Songs of Sunset* were to be given their first London performance by the Thomas Beecham Orchestra and Edward Mason Choir. This choir, which had been formed by Mason in 1907, consisted of some 100 voices, its aim being to produce new works by young British composers. Philip waxed lyrical to his mother about his new discovery, saying that Mason had shown him a copy of the *Songs of Sunset* 'and though I only had half an hour's strum at it, I am absolutely raving over it: I consider it is one of if not the finest and most lovely pieces of music I have ever come across: it is very sad in character, but will be glorious when performed. I do envy you going to the concert.'[60] As the day of the concert drew nearer, his frustrations grew at the thought of not being able to attend. Mason had described one of the final rehearsals at which Delius had been present: 'I cannot tell you how *absolutely* tantalizing it is for me to hear them all talking about it—I who would give anything to hear one work of the composer whom I adore above all others.'[61] It is here that Taylor made his appearance as the *deus ex machina* for, to use his own words, he 'wangled permission'[62] from the school authorities to take the boy to the concert, an event which was to have a profound effect on his impressionable pupil. An elated young Philip wrote to his mother the day before this great event:

I am so excited I hardly know what I am doing. I have permission to come to the Delius concert tomorrow night, under the supervision of Colin Taylor. Mr

Brinton has been extremely nice about it. I am to report myself to him at 6 o'clock tomorrow, come up by the 6.28 from Slough and report to Colin Taylor at Paddington: he is coming straight up from Oxford where he teaches on Fridays, and his train arrives at Paddington five minutes before mine. I shall come up with him to Queen's Hall where I will meet you (main entrance) shortly after 8. I shall go back with him, as he returns here.[63]

One can but imagine the incredible emotional intensity of that evening for the young, adolescent Philip. Not only was he at last hearing a whole programme of Delius's music but he actually managed to meet the great man himself during the interval—'when he was beset by so many friends . . . he spoke so very nicely and kindly to me'.[64] By the same token he was annoyed when, travelling back to Eton after the concert, Thomas Dunhill, who was in the same train, announced 'that he almost went to the concert but didn't think he could stand a whole evening of Delius, so went to the White City instead!!'[65]

The next day, still intoxicated by the heady music, the boy began what was to be a life-long correspondence with Delius:

I feel I must write and tell you how much I enjoyed your concert last night, though I cannot adequately express in words what intense pleasure it was to me to hear such perfect performances of such perfect music. I hope you will not mind my writing to you like this, but I write in all sincerity, and your works appeal to me so strongly—so much more than any other music I have ever heard—that I feel I cannot but tell you what joy they afford me, not only in the hearing of them, and in studying vocal scores at the piano, (which, until last night, was my only means of getting to know your music) but also in the impression they leave, for I am sure that to hear and be moved by beautiful music is to be influenced for good—far more than any number of sermons and discourses can influence.

It was extremely kind of you to see me in the interval, especially as you had so many friends to talk to. I am most grateful to you for allowing me to make your acquaintance, and I shall value it very highly . . .

I cannot thank you enough for allowing me to meet you and for the most glorious evening I have ever spent.[66]

Two days after the concert he wrote an equally ecstatic letter to his mother:

I have not yet got over Friday night—the recollections of that music and the impressions they made haunt me, and the more I study the score of 'Songs of Sunset' the more wonderfully beautiful they seem to me—standing absolutely apart from any other music in their loveliness. . . . I have never heard any music to touch it, and truly, words fail me to describe it at all—it is too divine. Colin Taylor enjoyed it immensely: he said he had not for a long time been so moved and described parts of the music by a singularly happy phrase, saying 'it was so beautiful that it almost hurt', which I think is an excellent description . . . Yes, Friday evening was the most perfectly happy evening I have ever spent, and I shall never forget it.[67]

In this same letter he included one very telling sentence which was to prove uncannily prophetic: 'I am sure music like that must have a very powerful influence on one's life.' From that first meeting at Queen's Hall began a quite remarkable friendship. Delius was obviously impressed by the young boy, telling Taylor later that year: 'Heseltine seems to me to have remarkable musical intelligence and also to be very gifted—I like him very much and find his enthusiasm very refreshing.'[68] In the following years Delius would become his mentor and friend, one of his principal correspondents, and an influence that was to have a profound and lasting effect on his life.

Although Philip was not yet 17 and should have spent another year at Eton, he had by now become restless and exceedingly dissatisfied with school life. In October 1909 he had already expressed a wish to join his father's old office rather than become a stockbroker like some of his uncles. Now, in early March 1911, he begged his mother to let him leave school that year and spend some time abroad:

. . . . I want to go into the office at 18 and begin work: also to have some time abroad—a year is the very least I could do with abroad . . . Please understand that if I go abroad, I shall go there with a fixed intention of learning the language, and not for the fun of being there, though in any case it would be perfectly lovely after the dull monotony of this place: I should do my very best at the language . . .

The truth is, I long to be really *doing* something, and not merely getting through a certain amount of Latin & Greek & other stuff . . . I think the time has come to do something else, and it will be the happiest day of my life when I feel I can really be earning my own living and not wasting your money—for that is what it comes to—in plodding round on circles already traced over and over again . . . I do not on any account want to go to the 'Varsity especially as that would mean at least another year here.[69]

On receipt of this letter his mother wrote almost immediately to his housemaster, Brinton, for advice and received the following interesting and perceptive comments on her son and his somewhat over-critical personality:

He is getting, in a way, old-minded. He never was a typical boy & he gets further from the type, I think, as time goes on. He has a considerable facility for work & does it well, but without apparent enthusiasm & he seems glad to get it done. He reads grown-up books & thinks partly on their lines & partly for himself, & his criticisms of things are so usually adverse that I feel my young enthusiasm quenched. I have even, in more than one of our brief chats . . .

urged him to find something to *like* in everything that he does . . . He has ability & thinks more than the ordinary boy. But his thoughts are, in my opinion, very much too critical of existing things . . . let him find something to *admire uncritically* in everything & his judgment will form on right lines by combining critical faculty with large-heartedness.[70]

By May, Edith Buckley Jones had finally given in to Philip's request. Elated, he wrote saying that he could not thank her enough for allowing him 'to follow this perfectly delightful plan . . . you may rely on me to do my utmost to prove to you that it is the right and best one.'[71] She also agreed to his having a motor cycle, a decision which Brinton thought a 'brave' one. Throughout his life Philip would have an interest in these machines and much of his early correspondence contains references to them, both to various purchases and ensuing mechanical problems.

Philip's final report for his last term at Eton, though generally praising his work and conduct in a rather stereotyped way, strangely makes no mention of his passionate interest in music. Such an omission speaks volumes about Eton's values and the general attitude to music at British public schools at that time:

I have no words of praise too high for his work and conduct all through the Half . . . he could not have ended his school-life with a better record. He evidently has a good memory, and his English papers have shown a command of style, as well as an intelligence of thought, that is quite remarkable. His weakest point is Greek prose, but even this is not at all bad. I think he takes a greater interest in English subjects than in Classical, and I am of the opinion that he will always be more successful in them. It has been a great pleasure to me to teach him.[72]

It is, however, in his moving letter of thanks to Taylor, written in July 1911 as he prepared to leave school, that we catch a brief glimpse of Philip's real love and all-consuming interest:

Just a few lines to say good-bye and a few inadequate words to thank you for all your kindness to me during my time here. I cannot possibly tell you how grateful I am to you for all that you have done for me, and for your influence in making me know and love modern music, which has become the greatest joy in my life.[73]

FRIENDSHIP WITH DELIUS
(1911–1913)

AFTER THE ECSTASY of the Delius concert in June, his meeting with the composer, and their ensuing correspondence, Philip's thoughts turned more and more towards a career in music. His mother was, however, determined that he should follow in the family footsteps and go to University to prepare either for a career on the Stock Exchange or in the Civil Service. Philip's sojourn in Germany was therefore to be a kind of compromise: he would acquire the knowledge of another language, which would be useful in his future career, and at the same time he would be allowed to satisfy his urge to further his musical studies. So in October 1911 he set out for Cologne accompanied by his mother who, no doubt, wanted to see him happily settled in with his hosts, Professor and Frau Bussius. *En route* mother and son spent some time with Uncle Joe in Marlotte. Among Joseph Heseltine's other visitors were the brother of Sir Leander Starr Jameson (of the famous 1895 raid in South Africa) and an American by the name of Thomas.

Soon after Philip had arrived in Cologne, Uncle Joe wrote to him apologizing for the fact that, because there had been so many people around during his visit, there had been no opportunity for them to have a quiet time together. He had also been immensely amused at his other visitors' conversations with his sister-in-law, 'because I suppose four people so utterly incongruous never met together & I could see not one of them understood the other & when Thomas asked Jameson if his brother was acquainted with [Cecil] Rhodes, my joy was immense.'[1] Uncle Joe also promised both to have the piano tuned before Philip visited him again, and not to sing any more songs. During the detour to Marlotte, Philip had also been able to see some of the neighbouring countryside, cycle to nearby Nemours, do a little composing, and, most important of all, go across to Grez to renew his acquaintance with Delius. This visit resulted in a subsequent row between Philip and his mother on account of his staying away until ten in the evening. As he later recorded: 'She was so angry at what she called my "rudeness" to my host at Marlotte that she would scarcely speak to me for two days! Of course, Uncle Joe didn't care two straws, so it was entirely due to her ridiculous ideas.'[2]

Once settled in Cologne, Philip enrolled for lessons at the Cologne Conservatoire where the head of the piano department was Carl Friedberg (1872–1955), a distinguished pupil of Clara Schumann. Philip was placed with Frau Lonny Epstein, one of Friedberg's pupils and assistant teachers. It was an unfortunate choice, for she made him concentrate on finger exercises to the exclusion of everything else. Philip's attitude to music was in many ways still very romantic and, lacking a natural aptitude for the piano, he was certainly not prepared to slog at building up a technique. The result was that his enthusiasm waned, for he felt that he would soon grow to loathe music if he had to grind at it in this way. He was also finding problems with his conversational German and confessed to his mother that he had to screw up all his courage to go into a shop and then would often find that he had forgotten his carefully prepared sentence.

But even as his enthusiasm for playing the piano waned, so did his interest in other aspects of music increase. He corresponded with Delius, telling him about all his activities in Germany and showing an intimate knowledge of one of Delius's scores:

To my intense joy I managed to hear a performance of 'Brigg Fair' yesterday in Coblenz! . . . it is absolutely *marvellous!*—and it was a very great additional pleasure to me that I knew the score, although the actual performance entirely shattered my preconceived notion of the tempi: I am probably wrong, I expect, but I should be very interested to know whether your direction 'With easy movement: dotted crotchet = 66' is best carried out by beating a rhythmical *one* in-a-bar, or by *three* beats in a bar: the conductor at Coblenz[3] adopted the latter method, and I am *quite certain* his tempo was considerably slower than dotted crotchet = 66: anyway, it seemed to me that by beating *three* the 'easy-going' of the movement was seriously impaired. But of course I do not know, since I have never heard the work before. The second 'easy movement' (section 22) seemed much nearer the proper time, but the next movement suffered, I thought, from a fault in the other direction:—the conductor just doubled the time, making a crotchet of 3/4 = a quaver of 4/4, which, since the preceding movement was taken fairly fast, did not seem to carry out your direction '*Slow*—with solemnity', and the 'Maestoso' sounded positively hurried! The return to 3/8 was treated in much the same way as the first 3/8 movement. The orchestra, however, was good, except for some very shaky playing of the wind in the introduction. Of course, I ought not to criticize the conductor, being no musician myself, but I hope you will forgive my doing so, since I am so *very* anxious to know all that I possibly can about your music, down to the correct *interpretations* of the scores. I would give anything to hear the work under Mr Beecham's direction: I could then be quite certain as to the right reading of it. . . .

Life here continues to be quite heavenly for me, the more so by contrast to the dull monotony of Eton and the depressing effect of being surrounded there by people whose chief ideal in life is to excel at football or some such thing!!

I am hearing a perfect deluge of music: the opera performances are very good indeed. 'Der Rosenkavalier' is played regularly once or twice a week to crowded houses! I have heard it twice: it is very amusing and interesting musically in parts, but I must confess that three hours and a quarter of Strauss (*exclusive* of intervals between the acts!) is rather more than I altogether care for! Hearing 'Heldenleben' last night after 'Brigg Fair' filled me with disgust . . .

The last Gürzenich concert, consisting of French music, was exceedingly interesting: the programme contained Berlioz's 'Queen Mab', which I love, and a quite wonderful 'Image' of Debussy:—'Ibéria', which I thought magnificently impressionistic and 'Stimmungsvoll'. The audience *hissed* at the end of it! . . .

I have just lately finished the scoring of a Suite of six numbers from Ingelbrecht's 'Nursery',[4] and so I have at present no *interesting* musical work, for I do not count piano finger exercises as music! I should very much like to make another piano arrangement of one of your works, since I found copying 'Brigg Fair' so very interesting and instructive. I am thinking of getting the score of 'In a Summer Garden' to do, as I do not know the work at all, but since you were kind enough to say that you thought my transcription of 'Brigg Fair' was not altogether bad, I venture to ask you first whether there is any other work I could do, either copying or arranging, that could be of use to you also, for I should consider it a very great honour to do the smallest service to you. If not, I shall get a copy of 'In a Summer Garden' and make a two-piano arrangement. We have two pianos in one room here, and it is much better than four hands on a single instrument. I found orchestration a very interesting study, especially after the very valuable advice you gave me at Grez. I cannot tell you what a difference that made to me: I *felt* that the work was quite different, after you had corrected the number I brought to you, and I re-scored all the numbers I had done previously. I am afraid, however, they are still very bad, as a beginner's work must inevitably be, but it gives me such pleasure to do—it is, I suppose, the next best thing to composing, which I *cannot* do, except by finding *every* chord at the piano, which is far from satisfactory! I hardly like to take advantage of your exceedingly kind offer to look over some of my work, when I have only such poor stuff to shew for it, but since you were good enough to say you would look over some, I should be overjoyed if you would allow me to send you perhaps one or two numbers of the 'Nursery' suite and a song or two—they are all very short, and you can burn them as soon as they arrive, if you like—I shall be quite content with the privilege of being allowed to send such nonsense to you. . . .[5]

I am having piano lessons, but for five weeks now I have been given *nothing* but finger exercises to practise, which, I am sorry to say, bore me horribly, since I have not the slightest wish to become proficient on the piano![6]

Even in these early days the rebellious Philip was picturing to Delius an enlightened Conservatorium 'where the teachers expounded the use of whole-tone scales theoretically, and harmony students were required to do exercises in the art of *not-being banal*— the reverse process, I take it, from the present system of teaching "harmony" and "*counterpoint*"!!'[7] In his replies Delius continued to give advice and encouragement:

I return you by the same post your transcription of 'Brigg Fair'—I have looked at it carefully again & find it exceedingly well done—In several places there are notes missing—& at times you might have made it rather fuller— With 2 pianos one need make no restrictions. One ought at times, I think, to interpret rather freely in order to try & regive the orchestral effect—Let me know how you are getting on & what the professors give you to do—I sup- pose they are still teaching in the old, old fashion—Never lose your own criti- cism & dont be *imponirt* [(over)impressed] & above all write as *much as possible.*[8]

Thank you so much for your warm & sympathetic letters which gave me the greatest pleasure—I am so glad you like the sound of *Brigg Fair*, & am sorry you did not hear it conducted in a better way—What you say is perfectly cor- rect—One must beat one in a bar—3 makes me shudder—Then again the slow section can scarcely be taken slow enough—The maestoso section must be taken solemly [*sic*] & not hurried—In other words it seems to have been a mis- erable performance! . . . I do not believe in any music constructed knowingly on any Harmonic Scheme whatsoever. All the people who write about the Harmonic system or try to invent other systems quarter tones etc. Dont seem to have anything to say on Music—Systems are put together from the compo- sitions of inspired musicians Harmony is only a means of expression which is gradually developing—I dont believe in learning Harmony or counterpoint— There is no piano score of the 'Summer Garden' as yet or of the 'Dance Rhapsody' Do one of them for 2 pianos—& I will hear it when I next come to Germany—perhaps in March—Send on the pieces you have orchestrated & I will be very glad to help you—You have a great talent for Orchestration—that I could see from the 2 pieces you showed me—We should be delighted to come & see you in Wales & we will try and arrange it for next September—or August—I should just love to see Wild Wales again & of course you must be there to shew it me—I think it absurd that your teacher only gives you finger exercises—I would simply tell him you did not come to Cologne for that pur- pose—If I were you I would go to the best Theorist in Cologne & learn what you can from him—As a writer & critic it may be of some use to you, as a composer none whatever—It is of no importance whether you write at the piano or not—As long as you *feel* you want to Express some emotion—*music is nothing else.*

. . . You must have thought very much about Brigg Fair—on the 25ᵗʰ I was quietly reading in my room when, suddenly, I could only think of Brigg Fair & I was obliged to get up & play it thro & the rest of the evening it quite haunted me—Telepathy? Write me soon again.[9]

By now, however, Philip had become completely depressed by his piano studies. This must surely have been a great disappointment to him as he had previously enjoyed his lessons with Taylor who had made every effort to encourage and interest him. By the end of January 1912 he was writing to Taylor to tell him that he had abandoned piano lessons as he could stand them no longer. After a great deal of thought on the subject he had, by the beginning of December 1911, more or less made up his mind as to his immediate future. He wrote to his mother saying that, 'as regards "musical talent", like dear "Old Father William"—"I am *perfectly* sure I have none", so I have definitely decided to waive the idea of music altogether'.[10] He had now come to the conclusion that, as he would not really enjoy working on the Stock Exchange, he would begin preparing himself for a career in the Civil Service, adding that he could easily learn the requisite amount of Latin and Greek necessary for the Oxford entrance examination.

So instead of practical music-making, he made the most of other musical opportunities by attending concerts and operas during his remaining time in Germany and of becoming acquainted with 'the divine works of Delius, and others'.[11] His letters from this period are full of perceptive and sometimes amusing comments both about composers and the music he had heard. On hearing Debussy's *Iberia* conducted by Fritz Steinbach (1855–1916), the city Kapellmeister and director of the Cologne Conservatoire, he wrote that 'next to Delius, this is the *finest* orchestral work' he had ever heard. 'It is perfectly *marvellous* in its subtle impressionism'.[12] In this same letter to Taylor he described Berlioz's *Requiem* (a work which was to hold a special place in his affection) as 'absolutely *thrilling*'.[13] A friend of Frau Bussius had a permanent box at the opera-house, where he found things 'splendidly done—acting, singing and staging being alike excellent'.[14] There he was able to attend Mozart's *Le nozze di Figaro*, which he enjoyed, Wagner's complete *Ring* and *Die Meistersinger von Nürnberg*, Strauss's *Der Rosenkavalier*, and Meyerbeer's *L'Africaine*—'pure "hogwash" . . . which is attracting enormous audiences because of its elaborate staging'.[15] Occasionally one hears the voice of a rather priggish adolescent speaking, as for example in his description of Puccini's *Madame Butterfly* as 'the most hysterically morbid and *unhealthy* thing'[16] he had ever seen and his dismissal of Thomas's *Mignon* on 2 December as the 'very *worst*, most absolutely uninspired and banal music of any kind'.[17]

It was in January 1912 that an article written by Philip first appeared in print; not on a musical subject, surprisingly, but one entitled 'The Van Railway' (a defunct Welsh branch line) in a magazine *The Locomotive*; Philip described this article to Delius as 'miserable . . . quite the reverse of anything artistic!'[18] He possessed a remarkably detailed knowledge of railways in Wales and in this article he described a railway in central Wales up the Severn Valley, a short way from Cefn Bryntalch. Philip's first serious efforts at composing also date from round about this time. During 1911 he had composed three songs, 'A Lake and a Fairy Boat', 'Music when Soft Voices Die' (the manuscript of this song is dated 21 September 1911), and 'The Wind from the West', and in July that year had first mentioned his compositions in a letter from Eton to his mother. Colin Taylor had evidently agreed to go through the songs with him and give him a few hints for alterations with a view to sending them to a publisher. Although the last-named song shows some melodic inspiration in its opening few bars, neither of the other two is particularly distinguished or remarkable and both are largely influenced by the songs of Roger Quilter (1877–1953) and Delius, Philip's two musical heroes at the time. Despite the fact that it was Delius who had now become his major musical obsession, his admiration for Quilter continued for a number of years. In June 1910 Quilter, an Old Etonian himself, had accompanied some of his songs at a concert at Eton and the young Philip had evidently been greatly impressed by what he heard. Even as late as October 1913 we find him extravagantly claiming Quilter the most perfect lyric song-writer in the world: 'His setting of Shakespeare's "O Mistress Mine" is the most exquisite and entirely lovely lyric I know . . . one feels absolute perfection in its three brief pages.'[19] Some years later Philip sent a copy of one of his songs to Quilter with the inscription: 'To R. Q. without whom there could have been no P. W.', an open acknowledgement of his debt to the older composer.

Philip's letters to Taylor during this period are full of enthusiasm about his early attempts at composing and in one of these he describes in some detail, albeit rather apologetically, his early method of writing music:

My 'composition' is rather ludicrous: the only way I can produce anything at all is to strum chords at the piano until I light upon one which pleases me, whereupon it is imprisoned in a note-book. When a sufficient number of chords and progressions are congregated, I look for a short and, if possible, appropriate poem to hang them on to. This found, more strumming has to ensue, until there is about the same quantity of music as of poem. Then the voice part is added, and the whole passes for a 'composition'! I should call it a 'compilation'![20]

It seems particularly ironic that ten years later Philip would write harsh and critical words about such methods in an article entitled, 'A Note on the Mind's Ear', for the *Musical Times*: 'The fact remains that a great deal of music, especially at the present time, is either extemporized at the keyboard or else is built up of fragments discovered, more or less fortuitously, at the pianoforte and afterwards unskilfully glued together.'[21]

These early compositions are largely undistinguished, dismissed by Gray as 'songs in which the interest was almost exclusively harmonic, with complex blocks of chords for the piano through which a mournful and sluggish voice part drifted, like the waning moon through a bank of clouds. It was, indeed, very moony stuff altogether: clotted dream music . . . the predominant influence that of Delius.'[22] To that might be added the influence of Wagner and some late English Romantics with, as Copley writes, 'a considerable harmonic vocabulary of the sensuously chromatic sort', the 'accompanimental textures . . . overloaded and ponderous, and his voice parts (he stipulates a tenor voice in each case) sprawling and ungratefully written'.[23]

Philip returned briefly to England to spend Christmas as usual with an enormous house party of relations at his Uncle Evelyn's large mock-Tudor house, The Goldings, in Warley, Essex, an annual event which he came to dread more and more. In 1912 he cynically told Delius that he hated most of the people who attended these annual gatherings and had 'to pretend to love them. They are all very religeous [*sic*], and the chief occupation of most of them is fox-hunting.'[24] It was doubtless memories of these stifling family gatherings which in later years contributed to his intense dislike of the Christmas season. On his return to Germany in January 1912, after a brief holiday in Wales and the four days in Essex, there was a spate of creative activity. This was probably sparked off by the fact that he had given up piano lessons and the consequent need to exercise his musical imagination. Once again he sent Taylor 'a little ditty . . . just a strumming-product . . . to know if you think it a *waste of time* if one can do no better!'[25] But whatever Taylor thought of these compositions, Delius was encouraging. He pronounced them 'beautiful' and, although he made a few alterations and suggestions, he reassured the young composer that it was of no importance whether he composed at the piano or not as long as he had the urge to express some emotion, adding, 'music is nothing else'.[26] Philip was, however, pathetically unsure of himself, telling Delius in a sudden outburst that:

. . . my little songs, whatever their intrinsic merits or demerits might be, are worthless in the one (to me) essential point—namely, that they should be (and are not) spontaneous expressions of the composer—in my case 'manufacturer' would be a more correct word! I have positively *no* ideas in music—I cannot think in music, and if I could, my thoughts would never assume definite shape—that is, I could never write down, or even play, what I wanted to, though I cannot tell you how I *long* for some medium of personal emotional expression—any kind of medium, through music, writing or even personality— But I have none: thought I *feel* so much,—the more, I am inclined to think, because my feelings must be for ever pent up, and can find no outlet in expression from this horrible *person* that encases them! In words, spoken or written, in music, I can positively *get nothing out*! In this way, I often long to be a 'disembodied spirit'—so as to be rid, once and for all, of an apparatus for expression which *does not work*![27]

As their correspondence continued, so the friendship between the two men blossomed—Philip telling Delius that he was his 'best friend in the world'[28] and Delius encouraging Philip to write to him as often as he liked: 'I love to receive your letters and assure you that they are never a bore to me . . . If you want some advice from someone who really likes you and feels real interest in your welfare you can come to me without the slightest restraint.'[29] In one of these early letters we even find Philip recommending to Delius a cure for biliousness: 'a mixture of apple, prune, almonds and oatmeal, put through a mincing machine and moistened with a little water, to be taken every morning before breakfast'![30]

Philip's sojourn in Germany was suddenly cut short when it was discovered that, to comply with the age-limit regulations, he would have to take the Oxford entrance examinations very much earlier than previously supposed. So, resigned at last to a non-musical career, Philip quickly settled down in March 1912 to cram Latin and Greek with the Reverend Clarence Rolt, the vicar of Chadlington, who soon moved, first to Hemel Hempstead for a short while in June and then on to the parish of Newbold Pacey, Warwickshire, in August, accompanied each time by his pupil. Philip did not care much for him and called him 'miserable' and 'erratic'—'the result of feeding on nuts and vegetables, and dabbling in Mysticism—his favourite pursuits'.[31] His dislike was no doubt also fuelled by what he considered to be gross interference in his personal affairs. For Philip's obsession with Delius's music had by now reached

proportions of absolute infatuation. Every time he heard a work of
Delius it seemed more and more appealing, 'more *absolutely perfect*
. . . I know no other music that appeals to me anything like as
much as his does, and knowing Delius makes it even more lovely—if
possible.'[32]

Obviously flattered by the young man's adulation, Delius was
now beginning to enjoy playing mentor and adviser. Perhaps he
already sensed the youthful disciple's potential for propagating his
art, but whatever his motives, Delius seemed also to be taking seriously the father-figure role into which he was being drawn. His letters cover a large number of subjects, including radical views on
religion which must have proved most attractive to the rebellious
and individualistic Philip, whose anti-establishment views were now
beginning to emerge. In March 1912 he told Delius that his 'private
views' were 'completely agnostic' and that he believed that socialism
was the only scheme which could save England 'from the present
entirely rotten state of affairs'.[33] Delius, who positively delighted in
his own anti-Christian views, was only too happy to respond:

. . . your letter gave me the greatest pleasure & I am so glad that you look
upon me as a real friend . . . You are just going thro' what I have also gone
thro' & I own that until I had become an entire disbeliever in any Life here-
after I was constantly in a very unsatisfactory state of mind—Read
Nietzsche—the 'Anti Christ'—'Beyond good & evil'—Christianity is
paralysing—If one is sincere it utterly unfits one for Life—If hypocritical one
becomes hateful to oneself . . . The moment you chuck all this rot over board
Life becomes interesting—wonderful—& one gets a great desire to make something of it—*to live it to its full* One enjoys things more thoroughly—*one feels
Nature*—there is no reason whatever for any doctrine or religion . . . Be free—
believe in Nature—it is quite enough & by far the most satisfactory standpoint
. . . When I come to see you in September we will talk about these things—I
am but a poor writer . . . Music Criticism is another fraud—Our critics are
nearly always composers who have failed & who have become bitter—Every
musician of genius brings something which belongs entirely to himself & cannot be criticised by miserable failures who have stuck fast & crystalised [*sic*]
Write to me soon again. I love receiving your letters . . . Perhaps you will
come over here in the summer we should be delighted to see you here again.[34]

In the letters that followed Delius pursued the same theme and
continued to give both advice and positive encouragement:

. . . should I come to see you before the [Birmingham] Festival or After?
Which would suit you best? Sea-drift is on October 3rd & I must no doubt be
in Birmingham about the 30th of Sept or Oct 1. for the last rehearsal—
Referring to your last letter I want to tell you that Jesus—Nietzsche & Co are
really the same natures—Earnest, ardent & sincere natures protesting against

human fraud & humbug: & destroyers of doctrine—Neither of them had any system; both were destroyers . . . I do not find it depressing at all to look upon death as complete annihilation It harmonises perfectly with my outlook on Life & I am an optimist & I love life in all its forms What do you believe? I dont mean—what do you want to believe—but what you *really* believe . . . try to be yourself & live up to your nature—Be harmonious—Whatever ones nature be one ought to develop it to its utmost limits & not be constantly trying to become someone else or be constantly trying to cork up ones nature: this leads to continual dissatisfaction & to failure.[35]

Meanwhile, unbeknown to Philip, Rolt had been writing to Edith Buckley Jones criticizing Delius's influence over her son:

I am beginning to understand his character better than I did, I think. He has the artistic temperament & hence is naturally sensitive, retiring & apt to dislike conventions. The rough & tumble of a great Public School, though necessary, was not congenial. His tastes were different from those of most of the boys, & he knew that, in the possession of these tastes, he was endowed with something better than the ordinary schoolboy ideas. And so far he was right. But there is a danger in such a position. He learnt to dislike Eton & hence to feel antipathy for all existing institutions. And this is a great loss to him. The higher nature of man can not thrive on mere antipathies. Moreover this antipathy makes him search for solace in such writers as Mr Bernard Shaw who . . . cannot be regarded as altogether healthy influences. Again Philip's admiration for Delius is not without dangers. Mr Delius is, I have no doubt, far better than his theories (or he could not write good music) but the intimacy of a Nietzschian cannot be a good thing for a boy of his age.[36]

Rolt would, no doubt, have been horrified to learn that during this period Philip was writing to Delius: 'Thank goodness I have completely thrown off the shackles of Christianity—"the Church"'[37] and by December he added that he hoped to wash his mind 'absolutely clear of all the Christian muck'.[38] Rolt's reference to the danger of Philip's admiration for Delius sent up the intended danger signals and an anxious Mrs Buckley Jones decided to visit Rolt and discuss the matter further with him, at the same time imparting some information which she had gleaned about Delius's personal life. There is no definite evidence as to what this information could have been. Possibly it was something to do either with Delius's Bohemian way of life in Paris in the 1890s, his brief involvement with the occult, or the fact that he had lived with Jelka at Grez for some six years before they had eventually married. Strongly influenced by Delius's religious views, Philip had written to him in July 1912 saying that he could not understand how anyone could get married in a church. 'For what is "getting married", I should like to know? It seems to me that, whatever it is, any third party is wholly superfluous, more especially if he be a canting priest with a book of formulae and directions!'[39] In another letter, written the next month (August), Rolt continued his denunciation of Delius in somewhat conspiratorial fashion:

I have been thinking much of what you told me at Hemel Hempstead about Delius—about his private life I mean & feel more & more anxious of his influences on Phil. Nothing can be more utterly disastrous to the development of a boy's character than that he should grow up with low ideas, or rather none at all, of that which is the very foundation of all that is sacred in human life. Phil does not mean to say outrageous things, but occasional remarks he has made would suggest not so much any conscious & direct antagonism to the Christian conception of marriage but rather an almost complete unconsciousness that such a conception exists. In fact Phil's theories in many matters (or at least in some) are quite unlike himself; & this is, I believe, due to the fact that he has imbibed them from Delius. . . .

I am not necessarily blaming Delius for hating Christianity . . . But I do say that the harm which may be done by his influence to Phil now that the boy's mind is in a plastic state (& he has a very receptive & quite acute mind with, of course, absolutely *no* experience of life) is quite incalculable.

At the forthcoming Birmingham Festival there is to be a work of Delius performed & I suppose Delius will conduct it. Phil will, of course, want to go, & if he goes will probably want to see Delius. If Phil goes from this house I shall absolutely forbid him to speak to Delius nor will I let him go unless he first promises to fall in with my wishes on this matter. And I shall explain to him that my sole reason is not theological prejudice but the fact which I have learned about Delius' private life.[40]

Whether there was ever a confrontation between Philip, Rolt, and his mother over Delius and his alleged bad influence we shall never know. If there had been, Philip would surely have written about it at great length to Taylor or Delius himself. From that moment, however, his mother was on the alert, poised and ready to strike, and it was surely no mere coincidence that she decided to accompany her son to the Birmingham Festival that October.

On 21 September 1912 an article Philip had written on Schoenberg was published in the *Musical Standard*. Although it was compiled chiefly from portions of Schoenberg's book *Harmonielehre*, Philip was already showing signs of contempt for the Musical Establishment, telling Taylor that parts of the article were directed against the critics of the Frederick Corder type, 'who consider their judgment infallible, and dub new music, which their limited intelligence cannot grasp with much the same words as they dubbed "Tristan and Isolde"—"the climax of cacophony"'.[41] This article of over 2,000 words is a quite remarkable piece of writing for a 17-

year-old, notable also in that it is one of the first articles on Schoenberg to appear in English. In it Philip did not attempt a critical assessment of Schoenberg's work but wrote rather of his theories, his aims, and the 'chief peculiarities of his style', as well as listing his compositions to date. In the course of his discussion he neatly summarized Schoenberg's style: 'The chief peculiarities of his style consist . . . in the total absence of any definite tonality . . . His rhythms, too, are very free, bars being of no consequence whatever.'[42] Delius, who was sent a copy, described it as 'very good & fair'.[43]

The publication of this article resulted in an unexpected exchange of correspondence in the columns of the *Musical Standard* between the author and one who signed himself 'S.O.G.' and who declared he hated the music of Schoenberg because he was convinced that it was 'essentially ugly, brutally ugly'.[44] Although Philip wrote a long and confident reply in the issue of 12 October 1912,[45] pointing out that his article was designed as information, not as criticism, he clearly panicked when 'S.O.G.' wrote yet again asking Philip to explain what he actually meant by 'chromatic harmony'.[46] It was then that he wrote to Taylor in urgent tone, asking for help in providing definitions of words as basic as key, scale, and tonality. One has the distinct feeling that, although very much out of his depth and perhaps a little nervous about this whole affair, Philip was rather enjoying his public sparring match with 'S.O.G.'. It was to be the first of many such encounters in the press.

Despite Rolt's avowed intention of preventing Philip and Delius from meeting that October, the Birmingham Festival in fact afforded an opportunity for the two men to get to know each other even better. This festival was the final one in a tradition that had lasted for nearly 150 years and, with Sir Henry Wood as principal conductor, included a feast of music in eight concerts spread over four days. Besides the choral 'regulars' such as the *St Matthew Passion*, *Messiah*, *Elijah*, and the Brahms and Verdi *Requiems*, there were premières of works such as Elgar's *The Music Makers*, Granville Bantock's symphonic poem *Fifine at the Fair*, Walford Davies's *The Song of St Francis*, and Sibelius's Fourth Symphony, all conducted by the composers themselves. Delius had declined an invitation to conduct the performance of *Sea Drift* himself because of his previous lack of success in conducting his works in England. There was also a galaxy of distinguished performers, including the singers Dame Clara Butt, John McCormack, Aino Ackté, and Gervase Elwes, the pianist Moriz Rosenthal, and the cellist Pablo Casals.

The orchestra numbered some 140 players with 351 singers in the choir.

Although during the Festival Philip stayed with a solicitor friend in a suburb of Birmingham, Edith Buckley Jones had booked in for three nights at the same hotel as Delius. As Philip had to spend a certain amount of time with her, this gave him the opportunity to see a good deal of Delius. He had promised to bring copies of Schoenberg's three piano-pieces (Op. 11) and Bax's *Enchanted Summer* to show Delius and there was even time to play through Philip's two-piano arrangement of *Brigg Fair* on the day before the concert which included *Sea Drift*. Needless to say an enthusiastic Philip had much to tell Taylor about the music he was hearing at the Festival:

Last night's concert was a most extraordinary hotch-potch. First came an overture by Beethoven called 'Coriolan' which bored me to distraction: then a quite delightful Brandenburg concerto [No. 3] by Bach: then some monkey-tricks by Moriz Rosenthal [Liszt's Piano Concerto No. 1], after which the 'piece de resistance' of the evening—Elgar's new choral work [*The Music Makers*]. I did not like it at all: it all seemed to me 'sound and fury signifying nothing'.[47] The enormous number of quotations from his own works, and the obscure references to persons and things which do not in the least matter struck me as being quite absurd.

Elgar himself looked ill and care-worn, and conducted in a very listless manner, though at times a sort of nervous energy seemed to come over him for a minute or two. I can't imagine how people can follow his beat. Scriabin's 'Prometheus' had to be abandoned, because Elgar wanted so many rehearsals for this wretched work!

Sibelius' new symphony [No. 4] was by far the best event of the evening: it is *absolutely* original—quite in a class by itself and uninfluenced by anything, save Nature! . . . it is very strange and mysterious, but at the same time, a work of great beauty, which one would appreciate more and more on repeated hearings.[48]

In his comments about Elgar, Philip showed perception, for Elgar was to write to Alice Stuart-Wortley on 7 October 1912, six days after the concert: 'I was really ill all last week & you must forgive much to a sick man.'[49] Philip predictably found *Sea Drift* perfectly wonderful, though he thought the programming of the concert unsatisfactory: 'We had to sit through *1½ hours* of Verdi (Requiem) before "Sea Drift"! I thought the Verdi appalling.'[50] So did Elgar. After the performance he went into the artists' room and said to the contralto soloist, Muriel Foster, 'in a voice loud enough for all to hear: "That is the worst performance of Verdi's *Requiem* I ever heard."'[51]

At the Festival Philip also had the opportunity of meeting the wealthy and generous composer Balfour Gardiner (1877–1950) who promptly took a liking to him. Philip found him extremely pleasant, very cheerful, and 'hearty', and Gardiner, no doubt impressed by the young man's intelligence and good looks, promptly asked him to make a piano score of Delius's orchestral work *Lebenstanz* which he was going to perform at one of his concerts in February the next year. Although Philip found it something of a challenge, he completed the task in ten days, reporting to Taylor that the score was frightfully complex and adding: 'I am not surprised that B.G. wants a piano version, if he has to read such a score!'[52] On receipt of Philip's arrangement in late October, Gardiner wrote him a letter of thanks describing his arrangement as 'almost indispensable',[53] at the same time offering him tickets for his next series of concerts. They kept in touch and Gardiner occasionally entertained Philip at his home at Ashampstead, some 22 miles from Oxford, and also visited him when he was at University there. It seems likely that it was through him that Philip was eventually able to meet Roger Quilter in November 1913. Philip perceptively noted that 'for all his geniality and good nature' Gardiner 'seemed very discontented about his music, and seemed restless and worried, fundamentally . . . He seems to spend his time making other people happy, to the neglect of himself and his own happiness.'[54] Philip appreciated Gardiner's kindness and encouragement in those early days and not only did he later offer to write programme notes for the projected set of Gardiner concerts in 1919, but he also dedicated his second set of songs entitled *Peterisms* to Gardiner when they appeared in 1924.

Delius's parting words to Philip in Birmingham had been 'Think more of your music than of your Latin',[55] and it may be that this advice precipitated some kind of confrontation between Philip and his mother. On 2 November we find him writing apologetically to her:

The less said or thought about Wednesday last the better: I am, of course, as sorry, if not more so, (though you would never believe that) than you are yourself that the events of the day were what they were, but they are over and done with, and will very certainly not occur again: blot them out of your mind.[56]

He had now to settle down to make his final preparations for the Oxford scholarship examination which was to take place at the beginning of December. In due course his mother received a letter

from the Christ Church authorities saying that, although Philip had
unfortunately not been elected to a scholarship, the examiners had
reported very well on his work and he would be accepted in October
1913 without further examination provided he passed Responsions
(a form of entrance examination which required a basic knowledge
of Greek and Latin). A note from one of the examiners stated that
'he was much interested in the English work your son did . . . and
said "I suppose he is a musician", and I agreed. He told me he had
written in an interesting way, and showed extensive but rather curious reading in modern books: Nietzsche and his like.'[57] Mrs Buckley
Jones was advised to send Philip for additional coaching to the
Reverend Hubert Allen (1856–1950), vicar of Didbrook, a little village at the foot of the Cotswolds, 10 miles from Cheltenham. Allen,
a former schoolmaster, was an older man and Philip preferred him
to Rolt, admiring his somewhat unconventional approach. He
thought him 'very exceptional: he wears a soft collar and tie, a green
coat, riding breeches and brown gaiters on weekdays . . . and apparently has no beliefs or dogmas whatever!—is most amusing, and
hates all forms of athleticism.'[58] Allen was also much loved by his
parishioners and in Didbrook parish church there is a memorial
commemorating his ministry there.

   Several of Philip's letters written at this time give further interesting insight into his developing views on religion, and on Christianity
in particular, views doubtless influenced by his adolescent reaction
to schoolboy religion, his discussions with his clergymen-tutors, and
especially through his correspondence with Delius. These he
expressed in a letter to Taylor:

The P[riest] believes that some sort of religeon [sic], no matter how stupid and
preposterous its dogmas, is necessary for some of the lower classes and crimi-
nals: Christianity *represses* people's will and instincts: if they have weak minds,
it terrorises them into accepting its tenets: it *denies* Life, and this prevents certain low and undesirable types from *living* their lives to the full. This view the
Priest shares with Nietzsche, and it seems to be fairly sound, though personally I could not bring myself to such a degradation as to pretend—even for a
moment—to ally myself with 'Jaggers Chraggers'[59]—though, if one holds the
P's views, to do so repulsive an action is undoubtedly a piece of supreme self-
sacrifice—which carries in its train a convenient emolument—verily a Christian
equation![60]

   As time passed, Philip began to feel an increasing sense of apprehension at the thought of what the immediate future actually held in
store for him. He poured out his anxieties at great length in an
almost desperate letter to Delius in January 1913:

I don't know what you will think of me for plaguing you with so many letters full of trivialities when you are busy with the greatest matters in the world, but you have been so good to me and I think perhaps you will forgive me if I ask your advice before taking or not taking a step which will be of the greatest importance to me: for there is no-one to whom I feel I can turn at the present moment, sooner than to you, though I hope I am not making a nuisance of myself, with my petty affairs. It is this: I simply cannot go on with my present humdrum slavery to Latin and Greek for the next five years, for the sake of a possible post in the Civil Service, where I could vegetate complacently for the rest of my life on a large salary and pension thrown in . . . Enthusiasm seems to me to be a factor of the highest importance for success in any work. . . . There is only one thing I have a burning enthusiasm for, only one thing I feel I could work for, come what may of adverse conditions, and that is, vaguely,—Music: I say 'vaguely' because I have absolutely no confidence in myself, or that I have the smallest ability to do anything in any specific branch of Music. At the same time, if I could but attain the meanest position in the world of Music, I would sooner die like a dog *there* (if need be) than attain to a comfortable and conventional position in the Civil Service, or the Stock Exchange. . . .

When I was with you in Grez, nearly a year and a half ago, you advised me to abandon all other pursuits, and to devote myself to music. I was a fool not to do so at once, I suppose, but at that time my ideas of what I was going to do were so utterly confused that I had not the courage to take any decisive step. Do you still advise me to do so? Can I rely on my enthusiasm—the greatest I have for anything in the world—for the necessary energy to make something of my project? Having no definite talent in any particular branch of Music, I am not particularly hopeful: my chief hope is that if I devote the next five years seriously to the study of music, instead of wasting my time at Oxford, I may be able to develop whatever slender ability I may have to some degree of proficiency.

. . . If I felt I could ever do anything worthy of the name of composition, I should have no hesitation whatsoever . . . I frankly admit, I am rather taken aback by my *present* lack of ability to do anything whatsoever, and by the consequent lack of confidence in myself . . . But, apart from composition, I would rather do anything in the way of musical work than submit to the life I seem about to enter upon—Perhaps I demand too much from Life, perhaps my castles in the air will fall with a sudden crash: still, I simply cannot help building them up, even if they are built in vain.—At the present moment, what I really have my eyes upon is—do not laugh at me too much!—musical criticism!! With five years general study of music, I think I could do that as well as some of the men whose columns one reads in the Press. With this, I also include the writing of books on musical subjects, and as many other musical tasks as I can combine with it.—Failing that, I might even be able to scrape along by copying orchestral parts, or even make piano transcriptions of orchestral works. I might learn some orchestral instrument, and so get to know the orchestra from the inside—that is, if I could get into an orchestra at all: at least, I could thrash the big drum! Or perhaps, after years of patient study, I might attain to the position of pianist to a cinematograph theatre. . . . I do not anticipate any very serious opposition from my mother, though there will be very likely a fearful row at first. I have not, of course, breathed a word to her on the subject: I cannot discuss things with her, for, except superficially, we are too far apart in all matters.

. . . Please forgive me for inflicting all this on you, but I cannot help asking your guidance at the present time. I am, so to speak, at a crossroads: I must make a decision, one way or the other, within the next few days. At the end of next week or the beginning of the week after that, I am supposed to be going to live with *another parson* (!!) and read Latin and Greek, Greek and Latin (world without end, Amen!) until I go up to Oxford in October. The whole prospect revolts me: I must get out of it somehow, if it is possible. . . .

. . . I do hope you do not mind me writing to you like this. I cannot tell you what a help, what a relief it is to be able to turn to you and ask your advice at a time like this. If you still advise me to devote myself to music, I can assure you that nothing on this earth shall prevent my doing so.[61]

Delius reacted promptly and a few days later a letter arrived which would precipitate a decisive turning-point in Philip's life. In it Delius 'strongly and unreservedly'[62] advised him to devote himself entirely to music:

You ask me for advice in choosing between the civil service—for which you seem to have no interest whatever—& music, which you love—I will give it to you—I think that the most stupid thing one can do is to spend ones [*sic*] life doing something one hates or for which one has no interest—In other words it is a wasted Life—I do not believe in sacrificing the big things of Life to anyone or anything—In your case I do not see why you should sacrifice the most important thing in your life to your mother: you will certainly regret it if you do later on—Children always exaggerate the duty they have to their parents— Parents *very seldom* sacrifice anything at all for their children—In your case your mother has certainly not; since she married again—In other words followed her own feelings—&, of course, did entirely right in so doing & I should advise you to do the same . . . One has every chance of succeeding when one does what one loves & I can tell you that I personally have never once regretted the step I took. The greatest pleasure & satisfaction I have experienced in Life has been thro' music—In making it & in hearing it & in living with it—I should advise you to study music, so that you will be able to give lessons in Harmony, Counterpoint, and orchestration. You can always become a critic. I think that you are sufficiently gifted to become a composer—Everything depends on your perseverance.[63]

It is interesting to read of Philip's response as he reported it to Taylor:

I had a most kind and encouraging letter from Delius about 3 weeks ago: he advised me strongly and unreservedly to devote myself entirely to music . . . I had an immense row with my mother, who, however, seems to be becoming more amenable at time goes on. The only question that remains is—how am I going to earn a living? I find that the £100 a year of my own, which I mentioned to you in Birmingham, may possibly be withheld altogether. My ambition, of course, is to become a critic, though whether I shall ever achieve that I have no idea. I am not sanguine about composition!! However, I think my mother will agree to my having a proper musical education, for I have explained to her (1) that one must devote oneself properly and thoroughly to the subject if one is to do any good, and (2) that I absolutely refuse to entertain any further ideas of working for the Civil Service, or going on the Stock Exchange.[64]

It was as if scales had fallen from the young man's eyes. After some deep soul-searching, he sent this highly emotional and frank reply to Delius:

. . . I never stood on my own feet, never woke up to life beyond the nursery and my mother's apron-strings until a year or so ago—that is, exceptionally late. I suppose I woke up comparatively suddenly, with a rude shock, so to speak, being quite incapable of standing on my own legs at all—as though all previous foundations had suddenly collapsed. They were thoroughly rotten, I admit. I am never thankful enough to be rid of them: but the unavoidable fact remains that I am, virtually, but three or four years old: my first fifteen years might almost as well never have been lived: and I find this lack of experience and accomplishments of living quite appalling. I struggle hard to develop now, I am trying my very best to live so as to redeem a part at least of the lost years: but I am constantly being dragged back—at least, I am always feeling the drag, though I do think I really am becoming harder and a little stronger at last. At the present moment, I cannot but feel that I am an absolutely useless specimen in every branch of life—only fit, as I am, for a lethal chamber—: hourly, do I curse the name of Jesus with a loathing too bitter for expression: his blasted doctrines are at the bottom of all this kind of thing. But for you, and a very few others—just one or two—I should have slept through life until the last and final sleep. Now, I am just about as fit for life as one who has only just woken up in the early morning, at the period when one is, perhaps, more inert and incapable of anything than at any other time, is fit to begin the day's work immediately. Though, alas, in my case, it is not quite early morning—so much of that has gone. The mood, however, is very amply outweighed by a passionate hope that something—perhaps unknown and inconceivable to me at the present time—will happen or develop. My strongest joy lies in *expectation*—in looking forward to things, especially if they are unknown, mysterious, and romantic, full of possibilities. That is what keeps me going: perhaps it is a vain illusion, a dream—but it is all I have. I have often felt myself to be a mere *spectator* of the game of Life: this, I know to my sorrow, has led me to a positively morbid self-consciousness and an introspectiveness that almost amounts to insincerity, breeding as it does a kind of *detachment* from real life. Lately I have tried passionately to plunge into Life, and *live* myself, forgetfully, if possible of this horrible aloofness: I believe I am just beginning to succeed a little, perhaps, though I know only too well that complete success now will be long and difficult, if not impossible, of attainment— Those fifteen years cannot be shaken off: I was formerly lonely, and shunned the healthy animalism of private and public schools, holding aloof, clinging to the atmosphere of home. Now that I can no longer endure *that*—though I have found, in part, a far better and more congenial atmosphere, though I would not exchange the nature of the typical English public-school animal even for my present unsatisfactory state—I know that I have been too much, too foolishly and fruitlessly alone, and at home now, I am far more lonely than anywhere else. As a result of this I have become morbidly nervous—even down to a physical 'nervous stricture'—which fact is a terrible hindrance to my having free, happy and healthy intercourse with my fellow-creatures—specially strangers, and those of great 'accomplishment' (so-called) in those rather trivial yet, from a social point of view, important things—games, of various kinds, indoor and outdoor, and an easy, natural, unaffected and un-self-conscious manner in general. Though I loathe athleticism, a mild proficiency in the elements of certain of these games is of great use to one, in helping one to opportunities of intercourse with others. Yet all this I would gladly have sacrificed if I could fall back for consolation to dreams which I felt one day I could create into realities. But I have, at this present moment, nothing at all—I said just now, I was three or four years old: in reality I have only just been born. The great fact that Life is before me, to make something of, is all that I have to live on—but surely it is enough to begin upon, with all the bitter, though useful, experience of those other years to look back upon, as upon a nightmare. The fears of my mother as to my relations with females . . . makes me almost break out into bitter laughter. I *feel* as much I *cannot express*—and no-one knows how much that is . . . I *feel*, as I say, so passionately sometimes, and yet can *never* express myself . . .

As for the opposite sex, and my mother's prudish fears,—the situation is truly ironic. I am acutely sensitive to sex, and to all the beauty and romance associated with it, both in Idealism and in Reality: but, as a matter of fact, I know practically no females at all:—absolutely none of my own age—for whose mere society I positively hunger—I know this is a morbid symptom, but that is what it has come to with me: I have never in my life experienced the 'kiss of passion'—and I am not strong enough—(or is it really—not *unnatural* enough!) not to desire it. Is this but a reaction from Christianity?—I suppose I ought to dance—what an almost ludicrous conclusion!

The long and the short of the matter, however, amounts to this—that now, at any rate, I am determined to *live* my life, to drain its cup to the very dregs, to live each day, each hour, feverishly perhaps just now—I am absolutely *ravenous* for Life: what I do matters not so very much, so long as I live![65]

As Gray pointed out, 'the importance of this as a psychological document cannot . . . be over-estimated'.[66] The last sentence amounts to Philip's moment of truth and is absolutely crucial both to the understanding of the whole development of his personality over the succeeding years and also as to what motivated him in later life.

Some people have expressed doubts as to whether the friendship between Delius and the young Philip was entirely beneficial to either party. Gray felt

that such a complete absorption in the music of Delius . . . was definitely harmful in certain respects; not merely because such a highly personal and idiosyncratic art must of necessity constitute a dangerous influence upon an aspiring composer, but also because its inner spirit and emotional content are fraught with perilous consequences to any who are insufficiently provided with the necessary antidote to it.[67]

Sir Thomas Beecham, an ardent champion of Delius's music who knew Philip, had this to say in 1959:

Upon me the letters from both sides have always made an impression that is far from agreeable. The trouble began in 1913 when an anxious ex-schoolboy, beginning to look upon Frederick as an infallible guide, sought advice as to his immediate future. Frederick . . . advises his young friend to do exactly what he feels like doing, and to stick to it. If he considers that music is the only thing in the world which interests him, he should take it up to the exclusion of everything else. But he adds that everything depends on perseverance, for 'one never knows how far one can go'. This reads very pleasantly and would be harmless if there had not been a world of difference between the two men. Frederick, once he had escaped from Bradford, not only realized that music was everything on earth to him, but had the iron will to pursue his way towards a definite goal, without hesitations, misgivings, or complaints. By the time he had arrived at full manhood both his mind and character had hardened into moulds that nothing changed until the day of death. Philip was of quite a different type. At that time barely nineteen years of age, and of a mental development which he himself admitted was distinctly backward, he vaguely desired a career with all the intensity of a great longing and a fruitful imagination, but was entirely incapable of either following a fixed course, or doing some of those things which might have expedited the close of a long period of vacillating apprenticeship.[68]

Beecham, however, could hardly be called impartial. As we shall see, Philip felt let down by Beecham on several occasions and expressed his disappointment and displeasure in no uncertain terms. Also, in a letter to Delius in 1916, Philip referred to Beecham's operatic productions as 'becoming more and more inferior and artistically valueless'.[69] Beecham would certainly have been sensitive to such criticism and also to the fact that Philip had that same year discussed with Delius an ultimately unsuccessful rival opera season, 'diametrically opposed to those of Thomas Beecham',[70] as Philip put it. Small wonder then that Beecham's words on Philip are far from complimentary. In the following extract it becomes apparent how patronizing and pompous Beecham could be:

. . . when I formed the English Opera Company which included most of the best singers in the country . . . I offered Philip a position on the musical staff. Here he would have had the opportunity of meeting a group of able and experienced persons, which after a while would have knocked some of the nonsense out of his head . . . He declined the offer. . . .

. . . I always recognised his undoubted gifts, and I did something on more than one occasion to help steer them towards some definite goal. He had a genuine gift for composition, but this did not manifest itself until several years later, when he produced a handful of songs and small choral works, in many ways equal to anything being turned out by his contemporaries in England. This side of his development, however, is not that with which I am at present concerned. It is the string of letters from him to Frederick beginning in 1913 and continuing until 1919, most of which contain a repetitious story of self-impotence, self-distrust and wandering intention. . . . The real culprit, if culprit there be in this tangled affair, is Frederick, who should never have committed the psychological blunder of preaching the doctrine of relentless determination and assertion of will to someone incapable of receiving it. It is hard to resist the impression that Philip's whole life would have been smoother, better ordered and increasingly rational if he had not devoted it wholly to the service in many forms of one art alone . . . The result was that for most of the time he did not really know what to do with himself, and worked off his self-discontentment by vilipending diatribes against nearly everyone around him. That he had quite another side to his disposition which abounded in humour (many of his limericks are deservedly still in currency), a more than occasional streak of practicability, and a rousing enthusiasm when his interest was excited, I am happy to bear testimony; and this aspect of him arose more and more to the surface, after the assumption of the second facet of his dual personality as Peter Warlock.[71]

What is beyond doubt is the marked emotional intensity of the correspondence between Philip and Delius. Sometimes the letters read like those between father and son, at times almost like those between parted lovers. It is as if Delius saw in Philip the son he never had, while Philip displayed every sign of adolescent infatuation with the older man. From then on, increasing references to immense rows with his mother indicate quite clearly that she was becoming more and more unhappy and impatient with the direction in which her son's ambitions were now moving, and possibly also with Delius's influence over him. Philip now described her as 'totally irrational', 'very impulsive', and 'embedded in Christianity'.[72] Correspondence between mother and son became more and more acrimonious, especially when it dealt with the touchy subject of money:

I hate coming to you like this for money, more especially as you have several times expressed to me your conviction that I regard you solely as a convenience from which to extract money: which grieves me more than I can say. During the last two or three years there seems to have arisen between us an inseparable barrier of misunderstanding . . . so that I feel doubly guilty whenever the subject of money has to be turned up, knowing what you think of me, and knowing, too, that owing to this seeming lack of understanding between us of late, it is impossible to convince you of the baselessness of your supposition.[73]

He was, however, allowed to accept an invitation to stay with Delius at Grez in March. Mr and Mrs Buckley Jones had gone to the south of France on holiday in February 1913 and *en route* had lunched with the Deliuses. Perhaps they made the detour to Grez to implore Delius to talk the young Philip out of a career in music. Philip spent eight days with Delius and five with his Uncle Joe and, soon after his return, wrote in detail to Taylor to tell him all about the trip to France. He had discussed at great length his future plans with Delius, who now advised him to work for a musical degree at Oxford which he thought would be a great help. Philip wrote anxiously to Taylor: 'Is it frightfully difficult? How long do you think it would take me to mug up all the stuff one has to do? . . . Can you recommend me the best book to begin with by myself?'[74] In the meantime he continued with his Greek and Latin cramming, and besides finding time to transcribe Delius's *In a Summer Garden* and practise some score-reading, managed to pass the Oxford entrance examination that April, despite having mistakenly prepared one of the wrong set-books.

During the time spent studying with his clergymen-tutors, Philip continued his sporadic song-writing, often sending his latest efforts to Taylor or simply asking for advice and suggestions. He was, however, still lacking both confidence in his ability and belief in what he was writing and he confided in Taylor that, as he still could not *feel* any of 'the absurd little ditties' he had written, 'he could not bear to think of their horrible little insincerities trying to impose on other people'.[75] Some of these songs were sent to publishers but, as Philip expected, they were rejected outright. This seemed to put something of a dampener on his creativity and for a while he seems to have given up composing.

In September 1913 Philip received an intriguing letter from his Uncle Joe inviting him to come across to France. He had staying with him at the time a young American poet, Alan Seeger (1888–1916), who he was sure his nephew would like very much. Philip needed no persuading and a week later was in Marlotte, where he stayed for a fortnight enjoying himself immensely, though he complained to Taylor that his uncle and his works of art were 'wilder than ever: the nude males in such abundance are most depressing'.[76] It may be that Uncle Joe had a streak of latent homosexuality (the 'very decided *kink*' that Philip had made mention of?) for we find Philip commenting about a sailor sleeping on a sofa in the studio, 'a great friend of the old boy's, who used to pose naked as a shipwrecked mariner—awful reminders of the fact, placed in conspicuous positions, must make him rue the day he did so'.[77] Philip was soon on excellent terms with Seeger, describing him as 'a young American vagabond-poetaster . . . interesting, well-read, and, above all *free* in his outlook on life'. A promising poet, Seeger was killed in the war in July 1916, a collection of his poems being published in New York the following year. Philip greatly enjoyed the young American's company, describing him as 'an erotic waster' who professed to fall in love with every pretty woman he saw. They soon discovered two 'amazing' American girls at the hotel in Marlotte, one a divorcée in her early thirties and the other a 'most charming creature of half that age I have ever seen . . . a delightfully naive child with absolutely no intellect whatever'.[78] During their time together they went on a bicycle trip to Nemours and back, Seeger escorting the older girl and Philip the younger. Uncle Joe, however, soon tired of his American guest and was relieved when he eventually departed early in October: 'He very nearly brought here one night a most dangerous little "apache", the cousin of a whore he was going with, but the scarlet lady had so many wealthier persons after her I fancy he did not score much although he says he will see her in Paris where I presume he is going to a house of ill fame.'[79] Philip and Seeger met again the next year, when the latter visited England in an attempt to interest a publisher in some of his poetry. On this occasion Seeger took Philip to a London night-club, an experience he did not enjoy, describing it as 'the dullest *soi-disant* "entertainment" one could possibly conceive'.[80] Whilst in France, Philip also spent some time transcribing Delius's *Dance Rhapsody* and composing—'the vicious habit of thumping out songs at the piano',[81] as he described it to Taylor. Captivated by Grez and the surrounding countryside, Philip wrote a fuller, almost poetic account of his visit, to a girlfriend he had met in Didbrook that spring:

I have been here one whole week—it seems more like the mere shadow of a day. I love being here, and all my surroundings are wonderfully soothing and peaceful, though I have an immense deal of interest that more than fills every day: I am working, with fitful energy, at a piano duet arrangement of a large orchestral work of Delius, called 'A Dance Rhapsody' . . .

The big studio is enormous . . . picturesquely built, with a first-floor balcony overlooking a strip of garden, a few white houses with tiled roofs of a redder brown than Cotswold hue, and a vast expanse of open country—very flat with no hedges at all, patchily wooded, mostly with small clumps or solitaries, though the distance promises wider tracts of woodland. . . .

Just outside the village begins the Forêt de Fontainebleau, an immense area of pine and beech woods, interspersed here and there with open spaces covered by enormous rocks and boulders. Two miles in the opposite direction is Grez, a wonderfully picturesque village on the Loing, a fine broad river whose banks are plentifully covered with fine trees and a wild profusion of undergrowth. . . .

On Sunday I walked over to Grez and saw Delius . . . he is working hard at his magnificent 'Requiem'[82] (which will be the first atheistical requiem in musical literature): the text is a wonderfully lovely prose-poem by a modern German poet [Friedrich Nietzsche], and, in the section devoted to Woman, contains some of the most beautiful things I have ever read . . . I wish you could know Delius: he is so wonderful.[83]

Meanwhile, between the two trips to France, another article of Philip's had been accepted, this time by the *Musical Times* who printed it in the October 1913 issue. Entitled 'Some Reflections on Modern Musical Criticism', it was inspired by a letter to the March 1913 *Musical Times* by Frederick Corder (1852–1932), a professor of composition at the Royal Academy of Music, for whom Philip had scant regard. The article was basically a plea for critics not to be so dismissive of modern music and, when reading its Delius-inspired quotations from Nietzsche and the references to Skryabin and Schoenberg, one has constantly to remind oneself that it is the work of a mere 18-year-old. He was paid 10s. 6d. a column for the article, telling Taylor that he hoped 'to clear about £2. 2. 0.',[84] an amount which he put towards buying a motorbike, one in a succession of many which proved unreliable and gave constant trouble.

One of the results of the article was a most enthusiastic letter from the young composer, Kaikhosru Sorabji (1892–1988, at that stage he still called himself Dudley Sorabji Shapurgi), sent to Philip care of the *Musical Times*, in which he congratulated him on his 'splendid courageous article—it is in the ultra-moderns that I am in my musical element . . . much of Beethoven's music is absolutely repellent to me.'[85] The son of a Parsee father (a structural engineer) and a Spanish Sicilian mother (an operatic soprano), Sorabji was a largely self-taught composer who from 1914 onwards produced a number of works noted not only for their eccentric complexity but also for their inordinate length. Even Philip, destined later to become a supporter and champion of his music, once wrote that 'looking at Sorabji scores does boggle the mind!' He resembled Philip in many ways, 'displaying a fearsome mix of encyclopaedic knowledge, warmth and sensitivity, an all-consuming intolerance of insincerity and dilettantism, restless energy and a barbed and excoriating wit exploding in all directions and guaranteed to hit its chosen targets with devastating infallibility'.[86]

It would appear that, although Philip found him amusingly interesting to begin with, he soon sensed that the homosexual Sorabji
might be developing too much of a personal interest in him. He
informed Taylor that he considered Sorabji was becoming 'more and
more queer, every letter he writes, but it is getting much too personal: I am "the most sympathetic person he has ever met", etc, etc
(although he has never *met* me—for that, at least, I am thankful!)
Moreover he is convinced that in a former incarnation, I must have
been closely related to him!! What funnys these Parsees are!'[87] The
two men corresponded and eventually met at a concert in 1914,
establishing a friendship which was to last throughout Philip's life.
Sorabji remained a loyal and staunch admirer of Philip, appreciating
his generous attempts to promote performances of his own music.

In the meantime, Philip continued his adventurous concert-going
whenever he had the opportunity of getting up to London. In early
July, for example, he attended a performance of Mussorgsky's opera
Khovanschina, part of a Russian opera season at Drury Lane which
included amongst the singers the legendary Russian bass, Fyodor
Chaliapin. The Mussorgsky opera predictably 'bored him to distraction', though, as an 'historical pageant', he had found it 'exceedingly
interesting'. A performance by the Russian Ballet of Debussy's
L'Après-midi d'un faune and Balakirev's symphonic poem *Tamara*,
on the other hand, made a great impression on him and, as a result,
he ordered several pianola rolls of Balakirev's music and added his
name to the list of his latest enthusiasms.

Philip had, however, badly miscalculated the strength of his
mother's determination as to his future career. Despite his resistance
to the idea, and the personal intervention of both Delius and Taylor
on his behalf, he entered Christ Church, Oxford, as an undergraduate on 10 October 1913.

THE OXFORD YEAR
(1913–1914)

A NEW CHAPTER now opened in Philip's life as he began the Michaelmas Term at Christ Church. During his year at Oxford he was assigned to room 4 (staircase 7) of the mid-Victorian Meadow Buildings, situated in an out-of-the-way corner off the main quad. His accommodation consisted of a large and well-furnished sitting-room, with plain, dark red wallpaper, a padded window seat, and a large 'stoney-kind' of fireplace, surmounted by a shelf and a large mirror, as well as a bedroom which he found 'dark but roomy'.[1] As these rooms were on the top floor and reached by a steep, stone spiral staircase, Philip was assured of a certain degree of privacy. Although the Morris motor works had opened the previous year in nearby Cowley, the peacefulness of pre-war Oxford had not yet been shattered, and from his window he would have had a rustic view towards the river across Christ Church meadow where cattle were and still continue to be grazed. As he had opted to read Classics, during his first year he would be expected to prepare for the preliminary examination known as Pass Moderations (Greek, Latin, and Logic). His tutor was the noted Latinist, Sidney George Owen (1858–1940) who spent thirty-five years at Christ Church and who was an authority on the poet Ovid. Needless to say, Philip was one of the few new students that year who chose not to join the Amalgamated College Clubs which, for a fixed subscription, brought membership of the Boats, Cricket, Tennis, Athletic, Hockey, Football, and Beagles. He did for a brief time, however, join the Mermaid Club, a play-reading society of some twenty members. It seems that he only attended three meetings (one of which was a reading of Shakespeare's *Twelfth Night* in which he took the part of Feste, the Clown) before his interest in the society fizzled out early in 1914.

Philip unfortunately left no record of his opinion of the Oxford academics with whom he came in contact during that year, though he seems to have had some respect for Ernest Walker (1870–1949), musical director of Balliol College and one of the most distinguished Oxford musicians at that time. Walker had a reputation for honesty and integrity which 'made him specially effective with the sensitive, sceptical, or rebellious type of young man. There were not a few of this kind who found, like Philip Heseltine, a sympathetic under-standing in Walker which they did not find elsewhere.'[2] Philip evidently showed him some of his early songs 'which [Walker] found a little advanced, and strongly under the influence of Delius'.[3] Philip also had a high regard for the Dean of Christ Church, Dr Thomas Strong (1861–1944), and told his mother that he found him as 'a charming man', though adding that he was 'somewhat embarrass-ingly gushing and affectionate'.[4] Strong described Philip as 'sensitive, courteous and gentle'[5] and Philip dedicated his 'Corpus Christi' carol to him some years later, by which time Strong had become Bishop of Oxford. It was Strong who was to help and encourage the young William Walton (1902–83) when he was a choirboy at Christ Church.

Whilst cramming with the Reverend Mr Allen in Didbrook, Philip had made friends and soon become infatuated with Olivia ('Viva') Smith, one of four sisters who lived in the village and who Philip facetiously referred to as 'that long-nosed woman of Gloucester-shire'.[6] This was the period when he was going through a major motor-bike craze and one of his first references to Viva is in a letter where he related to his mother how he took her to Stratford-upon-Avon and back on 1 March 1913. During the course of the outing he taught her to ride and she evidently drove him part of the way home with great skill. He even went so far as to have his bike regis-tered with the Greenock Borough Council in Scotland so that Viva's initials could be enshrined in a VS 316 number plate. Throughout Philip's year at Oxford they continued to meet, usually at weekends on their bikes somewhere between Didbrook and Oxford, and many of the letters written at this time include accounts of the breakdowns and other problems experienced with these somewhat unreliable machines.

Unfortunately, not a great deal is known about Viva Smith, but Philip's friendship with her was a particularly lively one and over a hundred of his letters to her between 1913 and 1918 have survived. Almost ten years older than Philip, she was evidently an intelligent and highly independent young woman who seemed always to be in control during the time of her relationship with Philip. This lasted until the summer of 1914 when, as Viva later recorded, 'to the great joy and satisfaction of their relatives and friends',[7] they fell out of love. In another letter written at the same time (1934) Viva made the interesting, though enigmatic, comment: 'I always felt that I had a terribly bad effect on him at a time when he would have been better to have had no women near him. I understood this and made several efforts to break with him. All the way through I realized that his good was of more importance than my personal feelings.'[8]

Philip, on the other hand, had fallen in love for the first time and for a while seems to have been overcome by an all-consuming passion. By July 1913 he was writing to her that she was 'all in all, everything in life' to him. 'I am so transcendentally happy, I can find no words to tell you: but I feel as though new life and an infinite source of new power and ability has been bestowed upon me.'[9] In October he was telling her that she had simply transfigured his whole life and by the beginning of November his feelings had become even more intense: 'How madly, how passionately I love you and how fiendishly well you know the way to make me! All that you may be, never that you are, I know: yet, did I know you as the siren of sirens, a female tarantula, I should still be yours, blindly, madly, absolutely.'[10]

During the course of the Oxford year this friendship developed to an intensity which eventually began to prove unsatisfactory for Philip: 'Dear one, do you remember how you have often told me that you look forward to the time when you can give yourself to someone, freely and passionately? Tell me, frankly and plainly, dear heart, can you feel this with me . . . can you look forward to giving yourself—to me?'[11] Philip's letters to Taylor at that time give details of a number of books that he had been reading on various aspects of sex, a subject in which he now suddenly began to show an enormous and understandable amount of interest. It was a matter very much on his mind and, in his anxiety, he turned to Delius, writing frankly and in great detail about his affair with Viva and his sexual frustrations:

I remember your saying to me at Grez that perhaps she wanted to keep me at a safe distance until I could marry her: I satisfied myself that this was not the case with her. Moreover it is not, as I thought before, and as I think I gave you the impression it was, when I was at Grez, the inherent timidity and cowardice of the traditional English person in sexual matters. You told me that the only thing for such people was to be *taken* by a strong man: it may be in some cases, but here it was out of the question, and I am not the one to do it. To me, it savours too much of mere prostitution: and I have said just now that unless the relation be perfectly mutual and spontaneous, it is nothing to me: to my mind, the physical relation, though intensely necessary, is nothing, intrinsically, but rather a symbol of complete sympathy and unity in everything . . . No, it is not timidity or cowardice with her: it is simply she does not love me: and yet, over and over again, she has lain in my arms and given me such kisses as only real passion could inspire:—one night, when I was staying there in the autumn, we lay together, naked, by the fireside—and yet, and yet—what does it all mean? Why is it that, having reached a turning point, we can progress no further and explore together the limitless possibilities that Love opens up for us?[12]

Philip then proceeded to discuss various discoveries in his recent reading on sex, discussing, amongst other things, the technique of Karezza. Quoting from his source, he described it as 'copulation, without crisis or emission', a technique reputedly 'having surprisingly psycho-physiological influences'. He also referred to some recent opinions on contraception, asking Delius for the name of a work in which he could find 'a rational account of the diseases incurred by women through prolonged virginity'. It would seem that Viva had what Philip described at 'a slight nervous affection of the eyesight' for which an oculist had told her the only cure! Philip unfortunately gives no details as to whether this cure was supposed to be sex or abstinence! Philip received an equally frank, if somewhat chauvinistic, reply from Delius:

I thank you for the confidence you bestow upon me in writing me so thoroughly & frankly all about your life, thoughts & doings—It is a letter from a real & loving friend—I shall be just as sincere and frank with you—Not everyone falls really in love—only few men & few women are capable of a great and real passion—But in my opinion it is of enormous importance for an artist to have had a great passion—It is that which gives that extraordinary depth of emotion to his work . . . Your friend knew you loved her a good deal sooner than you did . . . My opinion of your friend is the following—She does not love you but is flattered at being the object of such a great passion & wants to make it last as long as possible—Most women have the idea when they do not love—that as soon as they let the man obtain what he wants—or satisfy his desire—His love will stop & the whole thing will be over—The only possible way of bringing her to the point is the one you have taken—to see her no more—If she wants you *she* will come to you & then you might enjoy the one thing that is absolutely necessary between a man & a woman before they can be true friends. I am afraid your friend is cold—all you tell me about her lying naked with you before the fire points to a very self-possessed & cold nature . . . It is very cruel—If she meant well by you she ought not to exasperate your senses when she does not intend to satisfy them—Indeed if she had real tenderness for you she would behave quite differently—It is unhealthy & enervating & no wonder you feel depressed & in an unsatisfactory state of mind—The whole affair is much simpler than you imagine—You see everything now thro' those wonderful eyes of love—such wonderful colors & it really does not matter a bit who you do love, or wether [sic] she is worthy or not of your passion—for me the important point is that you are *capable* of a great passion; that sets a mark on you which elevates you greatly in my eyes. She is of course afraid of getting a child like all women who are not in love are—This touches, of course, on the old question of convention & Society which I will not touch on here—Everybody must settle that for himself—You have done well in fleeing & getting out of that atmosphere for the present . . . Love is a thing one must snatch at & hold & keep & enjoy as long as it lasts—for *it does not last*— but friendship does & that very often follows on love & gives place to something more lasting & gentle & more sure & healthier. A man who is in love can never be brutal & take a woman by force—Only a man who is not in love can do that—But the sort of woman you speak of is destined either to never get a man—or be forced by a man she does not even like—or get married to a perfectly indifferent person who can support her in a so called respectable way. When she writes to you that at the right time her love will be active enough it really means that she is incapable of a love sufficiently great to become active. If a woman has not loved before 27, or 30 I very much doubt whether she ever will . . . The world will presently be obliged to adopt methods to prevent over population & also the procreation of children by diseased people. A good syringe never hurt anyone & is used by every clean woman on the continent— Cundums [sic] are not as healthy for the woman—I have already heard of 'Karezza' but do not agree with any of those methods—That sort of thing might be all very well for the woman but for the man it would be very unhealthy & would shatter his nerves ultimately—The one real natural & healthy way to enjoy a woman is the natural one—with emission—& even this not to be abused especially when one is doing brainwork—Prolonged virginity for women is always very bad—they simply dry up & often become entirely sterile at a comparatively early age—30. 35 . . . Ignoring sex & the very source of life & Bringing forth generations of onanizing men & woman: both becoming hysterical & impotent & disatisfied [sic] . . .[13]

Often addressing Viva as 'darling little mouse', Philip was not only very candid when writing to her but also expressed some unusual theories, gleaned no doubt from the books he had just read: 'What a curious mixture of sexes you and I make! . . . the feminine in me responds so often to the male in you: and do you not see how I should be the mother of the fantastic children of our union?'[14] To her, as to no one else during this emotionally turbulent time, he exposed his vulnerability and innermost, passionate feelings, often in an almost prophetic manner: 'I feel that it were better to fling all caution and reactionary thoughts to the winds and perish, if need be, in one wild Bacchanalian orgy, than to live prudently and carefully to a ripe old age.'[15] After having resisted his persistent and often verbosely impassioned approaches for almost a year, Viva seems eventually to have succumbed to his sexual advances on

1 February 1914, for on the evening of that day we find Philip writing to her in a more relaxed and contented vein:

> . . . all the beauty and the wonder of my day with you, and the glory of it that utterly surpassed my farthest dreams, has not yet soaked in and saturated me enough, through and through: it all seems still so wonderful, too much of a distant, shadowy dream for me to realize—it's so much more than ever I desired even . . . oh, the joy if it, the deep-down lasting sense of peace . . . I cannot utter it now, it simply overcomes me: to-night I feel I can only sink down at your feet, in perfect content, perfect happiness, and worship you, my own dear, dear one.[16]

Philip's letters to Viva also furnish further evidence of the hostile relations which were developing between mother and son. In October 1913 Philip had confided in Viva that his and his mother's 'natures, temperaments and whole outlook on life' were 'entirely antipathetic to each other' and had been for a long while.[17] These feelings also succeeded in increasing Philip's feelings of guilt even more and by December he was writing to Delius that he was 'almost horrified by his own thoughts . . . there is something pathetic . . . about her fondness for an unworthy son, who has, perforce, to feign an equal affection, which honestly, from his very heart, he does not feel'.[18] By now it was evident that Edith Buckley Jones did not approve of Philip's relationship with Viva, doubtless regarding her both as a threat to her son's progress at Oxford and as a rival for her own affection. Philip, however, was hopelessly in love with Viva and was writing even more ecstatically: 'I still seem to feel your dear breasts under my lips'.[19] Significantly, he now wrote of her letters as he had about his mother's some ten years earlier: 'I kiss them all as they come.'[20] He was no longer the apologetic and defensive schoolboy and was fast learning how to manipulate his mother. He informed Viva that he was writing more civilly to her, 'keeping at a safe distance as far as intimacy is concerned, mentioning never a word more of the subject [i.e. Viva] than she does—no tags of sentimentality, no slops—cold, distant politeness, but with reserve on ordinary topics, such as motorbikes and the weather'.[21] On some occasions he simply resorted to confusing her: 'the position is too complex for her to unravel it with any chance of success, and I have just written her an obscure letter, which I don't understand, in order to make the affair a little more knotty.'[22]

Winifred Wood, one of Viva's sisters, recorded in her diary some rather interesting comments on both Philip's personality and his affair with Viva:

He is at Oxford, still very young, probably about 22 but he appears to be years older. All his life he has spent reading, never playing games, and thinking—he has read every book one has ever heard of and millions that one hasn't. . . . Music and poetry he practically lives for and he has only two other subjects. Sex and motor biking—the latter really is entirely a phase of the former as it is all for sensation that he does it. Add to this that I think he is not quite a man. Anyone reading this diary might think that I had a mania on that subject but the truth is we attract sex cranks and he is certainly one. Put this character in a beautiful young body 6 feet high, absolutely fit, as thin as a lath, hands rather ugly and red but a white face of the clearest skin, brilliant blue eyes, long fair hair brushed straight back from the forehead with never a hair loose though it is nearly 8 inches long and the curved lips and highhead carriage of a young Greek God. Add to this a charming Oxford accent and an emphatic manner and there he is.[23]

Her comment 'I think he is not quite a man' is most interesting. Winifred was not the only person to notice this trait in Philip, and Cecil Gray, later to become one of his closest friends, noted 'a streak of something akin to effeminacy' in him.[24] It is also significant to note that, according to Basil Trier, one of his close friends from the Oxford year (and the dedicatee in 1926 of the song 'Jillian of Berry'), Philip 'had a deep fear of impotence and anxiety'[25] when Trier first met him—a curious fear for a young man of 19 in the middle of what appears to have been a highly passionate undergraduate love affair. Although Bruce Blunt (a friend in later years) claimed Philip had no homosexual inclinations, he did add that Philip had confided to him that 'he regretted he had not tried buggery'.[26] Such comments perhaps hint at a touch of unacknowledged homosexuality in his make-up and his listing of works by authorities such as Edward Carpenter, Havelock Ellis, and Krafft-Ebing in letters at this time also suggest a degree of interest in the subject, a possible manifestation of some slight sexual ambivalence. As early as 1911 he had been corresponding with his Uncle Joe on the subject and a postcard sent to Philip that year contains his uncle's brief comments:

People say, a man is this & women are that, but this is not & they are talking round their hat. Because they forget it takes both sexes to make a male or a female & some males are nearly all female & vice-versa . . . some men prefer men to women, because the female predominates in them. I do not believe it is always their fault. It is a freak of Nature. I can write you a longer letter soon but the subject is very inexhaustible.[27]

The next year (1912) Uncle Joe was recommending to Philip 'a very good book on sex *What a young man ought to know* by Sylvanus

Stall'.[28] One can only hope that Philip did not read the book which, amongst other horrendous things (likely to give its readers sexual hang-ups of undreamt-of proportions), suggests that an over-enthusiastic indulgence in masturbation can lead to idiocy and even death!

Ten years later Philip was still discussing the subject with friends. In April 1922 Sorabji wrote to tell him that he had an article on sexual inversion from the October 1921 *Medical Times*, written by a very distinguished and enlightened doctor, which he wanted to show Philip: 'It has been very highly praised by other medical men as well which is also highly useful and edifying.'[29] It is also interesting to note the form of endearment in Sorabji's greeting in this particular letter, 'Belovedest and Bestest Thee', as well as the final sentence, 'I hug you & send much love'. It seems that by then Philip had happily accepted Sorabji's homosexuality and was quite at ease with his openness and frankness. Although Philip may have been exposed to homosexual practices at Stone House, Eton, and Oxford, there is no evidence of his having anything but a theoretical interest in the subject. He is recorded as having shown in public on at least one occasion an unsympathetic attitude towards homosexuality. His friend, the author Douglas Goldring (1887-1960), described an incident at the Café Royal when Philip, approached by an obviously gay young man, snarled at him, 'Go away, you dirty little joy boy!',[30] a seeming over-reaction which might have its explanation in possible feelings of recognition or sexual insecurity.

One of the more positive aspects of Philip's time at Oxford was his meeting and ensuing long friendship with an undergraduate at Trinity College, Robert Nichols, whose poetry was some of the first he successfully set to music. Having left Oxford after only a year, Nichols served in the Royal Field Artillery on the Belgian-French front in 1914-16 and gained early recognition through two volumes of war poetry. During the course of a colourful career he found his way to Hollywood as a filmscript-writer and in 1921-4 occupied the chair of English Literature at the University of Tokyo. Sir Arthur Bliss (1891-1975), who knew Nichols for many years, wrote of him as 'a complex personality compounded of many warring elements. Sometimes he would be wildly exuberant and excitable, at others he would sink into black depression and self-pity';[31] not unlike Philip himself, in fact. Nichols later contributed a chapter, entitled 'At Oxford', to Gray's memoir, in which he gave his impressions and memories of Philip, mostly culled from their student days together.

His early recollections of the young Philip were of one 'slightly above middle height, very neatly and quietly dressed . . . his face was pale and his hair, a little long, of an ashen blond [and] blue eyes'.[32] Nichols also found in his fellow student a kindred spirit, one with whom he shared enthusiasms for music and literature, discussed Nietzsche (a 'common admiration') as well as holding forth on the futility of war. 'Sex, literature (particularly Elizabethan literature) and music were our great subjects.' It is from Nichols that we learn something of Philip's early efforts at composition and in his recollections he records that on the occasion of his first visit to Philip's rooms at Christ Church he noticed a manuscript setting of a poem by Yeats. The two of them would often take walks together and it was during these that Nichols would observe in his silent companion someone supremely sensitive to the beauties of nature, a gentle, generous friend with 'a sharp and quick mind' who loved 'earthy words for their own sake';[33] one who vacillated between moods of excitement and 'a sort of reverie which was perhaps the only true happiness he knew in love'. Nichols also noted that although he found Philip innately gentle, from time to time the extrovert side of his personality was already beginning to manifest itself:

Philip had all the feelings of a poet—he was peculiarly sensitive to the most 'poetical' poetry such as . . . that of . . . Yeats . . . [but] he had another rhyming talent . . . he could write better rigmarole, nonsense verses and limericks, Priapian and other, than any man I have ever known. Such of his prose as I have read—and I have read much—was always sound, frequently excellent and on occasion brilliant . . .

There is usually some element which while the friend is with us especially appeals to us, and the memory of which we most cherish when he or she is absent for a while or for ever. For me that element in Philip was and is the extreme gentleness hidden in his heart of hearts. Those who knew him only as a combative spirit in the world of music may be astonished at that statement. Yet I hold this gentleness to have been absolutely fundamental in his character and that no few of his troubles were attributable to continued and exasperating outrage of it.[34]

At Christmas 1913 Philip had managed to escape the dreaded annual family get-together at his Uncle Evelyn's home in Essex, telling Delius that he had been every Christmas for the last ten years, but that year was determined 'to go on strike doubtless giving great displeasure in the family circle'.[35] He spent Christmas Day with his mother's sister, Constance, who was married to the Reverend L. W. Richings, vicar of Whitney-on-Wye in Herefordshire. Although it proved a peaceful break from his family, there was little to do in that isolated part of Wales in winter without either pianola or motor bike. Philip's mood was particularly bleak at this time and on Christmas Day he wrote to Nichols complaining that his mother was 'the most unsympathetic, the most utterly antipathetic person in the world'[36] to him. His personal life was in a state of turmoil and in his letters he described himself as being in a hopelessly unsatisfactory state and fearfully confused. Besides the rows with his mother about wanting to leave Oxford, there were ongoing problems in his relationship with Viva Smith. Both Delius and Taylor had advised him not to see her any more, advice he chose to ignore. Philip's Christmas Day letter to Nichols continued in a depressed mood: 'I am haunted by a myriad, fantastic variations on the one, old theme, and everything is so strange, everything so different: it influences everything, pervades everything in an extraordinary manner: I cannot get away from it, and—a thousandfold worse—can express not a particle of it.'[37]

As time passed, studying at Oxford seemed to Philip a complete waste of time and energy and he became increasingly unhappy and depressed. He felt trapped in 'this blasted colony of Hell',[38] realizing more and more that it was a life of music that really attracted him. Early in December 1913 Sorabji was already sympathizing with him: 'I feel very sorry for you in Oxford. You must feel like a fish out of water—musically in that Toriest of Tory towns.'[39] Unfortunately, the more Philip implored his mother to let him leave Oxford, the more determined and unrelenting she became. Further rows ensued as she tried everything in her power to discourage his ever-increasing interest in music. She even went so far as to hide the Cefn Bryntalch pianola, leaving Philip with the impression that it had been sold. When he eventually discovered it in the attic under sacking almost a year later there was an ugly confrontation as she tried to defend her action by saying that the pianola had been removed because it was spoiling the main piano, took up too much room, and made too much noise. She then accused him of being unjust to her and that his 'warped mind'[40] was always suspecting sinister motives.

During Philip's Oxford period Delius continued to play the role of mentor and father-figure, regularly advising him about future plans. He had now perhaps begun to realize that he was Philip's one secure emotional anchor and was feeling his responsibility more than ever. He was not particularly enthusiastic about Philip's idea of wanting to become a music critic and warned him that 'to become a music critic is to become nothing at all—the only possible attraction in music is to be a musician . . . But *critic* is no career.'[41] He felt that Philip perhaps needed to work in an office for a while to make a bit of money, studying harmony and counterpoint part time. There was, however, no work to be had and one of Philip's stockbroking uncles told him bluntly that there were no prospects of his finding 'any sort of job in the stockbroking office—or, as far as he could see, anywhere else'.[42]

Performances of Delius's music proved a welcome distraction at this time and Philip managed to attend the first English performance of the two tone-poems, *On Hearing the First Cuckoo in Spring* and *A Summer Night on the River*, conducted by Willem Mengelberg (1871–1951) at a Philharmonic Society concert in Queen's Hall on 20 January 1914. These had been a revelation to him and once again his words of praise to Delius were extravagant:

. . . the first piece is the most exquisite and entirely lovely piece of music I have heard for many a long day—it almost makes one cry, for the sheer beauty of it: I play it often on the piano, and it is continually in my head, a kind of beautiful undercurrent to my thoughts. For me, the deep, quiet sense of glowing happiness, and the mysterious feeling of being at the very heart of nature, that pervades the piece, is too lovely for words . . . it is simply perfect.[43]

He was, however, still at a loss as to what to do in the immediate future; as he wrote to Delius, 'I simply cannot continue to drift along in my present aimless fashion',[44] though his thoughts were still moving in the direction of trying to find work in a London office to make some money. His stepfather evidently highly approved of this idea and was doing his utmost to help. During his spare time, Philip took the opportunity to read widely and generally expand his intellectual horizons, even though his chief concern was how he could persuade his mother to let him leave Oxford.

In March 1914, while Philip was in London for two weeks attending concerts, Balfour Gardiner introduced him to Ernest Newman (1868–1959), the famous music critic, who had begun his career as a bank employee. When Philip asked his advice he suggested that he study music scores and write articles in the hope of getting them accepted, thus becoming well known enough to secure a permanent engagement with a newspaper. Newman evidently considered an ordinary academic training of small use, strongly advising Philip to take up some other profession until he was able to stand on his own two feet in the musical world. Although this first meeting between Philip and Newman seemed cordial enough, it would not be long before the two men would clash bitterly.

That March, at the first opportunity, Philip entered the preliminary University examination for Pass Moderations. He was unsuccessful, which was not surprising considering how little work he had done and how ill-prepared and unenthusiastic he was. Shortly before the examinations he had nonchalantly written to Viva saying that he 'really must do a little towards passing the ridiculous exam . . . true, it doesn't matter much, but failure to pass would perhaps only incense the parental mind unnecessarily!'[45] This set-back, however, put him in an even greater state of anxiety and he wrote to Delius saying that he was desperate to find some means of escape from the appalling, enervating, and depressing atmosphere of Oxford:

the place is just one foul pool of stagnation—I simply cannot stand it, and I am getting no good, and any amount of harm, from staying there. Yet *nothing* can I find to do elsewhere: I would do anything to get away from the place, and, if possible, make a little money. But it seems hopeless, and my people suggest nothing. Oxford leads nowhere—and it is fearful to wander on through life, aimless, objectless, and—what is worse—moneyless.[46]

Dean Strong, too, was of little help in solving his problems and, writing to his mother, Philip dismissed him with the words: 'he offered no advice and told me nothing that I could not have told him months ago.'[47]

In April Philip decided to take up an invitation from Delius to spend some ten days in the idyllic setting at Grez, arriving to find everything beautifully green in the warm, bright spring weather. He immediately set to work translating the text of Delius's work for chorus and orchestra, *An Arabesk*, as well as helping correct the orchestral parts of the opera *Fennimore and Gerda*, which was scheduled to receive its first performance later that year. Philip now sought further advice from Taylor. He had poured out his troubles to Delius, Gardiner, and, at Taylor's suggestion, wrote to the composer and musicologist Cecil Forsyth (1870–1941) as well, and was now considering the options, including the final desperate one of running away. He had come to the conclusion that the real reason why his people wanted him to stay at Oxford was because it saved them the trouble of making a positive decision regarding his future career:

Forsyth, as I think I told you, seemed to think that an Oxford degree was of great use for a critic or anyone bent upon journalism of any kind: do you really think that this is so? Delius and Gardiner are both very strongly against Oxford, which they regard as complete stagnation. Forsyth was very kind, and more encouraging than anyone else I have talked to on the subject: of course he could not (nor could anyone) give one any definite prospects, but he said that, if one devoted oneself to music and lived in touch with musical people, there was every chance of getting something good to do after a year or so, in one branch or another—either criticism, or orchestration (which he said was very useful, as it lead [*sic*] to good things in the way of conducting in theatres, etc), or transcriptions, etc. Delius also suggests studying accompanying, with a view to being engaged at an opera house to teach singers their parts . . . This might be a good thing to look out for . . . Now what I propose to do is simply to tell my people that I am not going back to Oxford, and point out that it is quite useless, and, in the matter of prospects, far less hopeful than music. I shall then propose that I go to London and seriously study music—not merely theoretically, but practically also, (i.e. so that I have time to go to concerts and study all kinds of music by myself, at the piano, so as to become thoroughly acquainted with all sorts of music, ancient and modern, which as Newman says, is the only real equipment for a critic). As regards the details of this scheme, I should be immensely grateful to you if you would tell me, more or less, how to set about doing so—i.e. whom to go to, in London, etc. I should like, if possible, to go to someone like Vaughan Williams, rather than any of the real academics—though he is academic enough, in his compositions at any rate—but as I know nothing whatever about this part of the business, it would be of the greatest possible help if you would tell me some of the details of it—what to study and where to study it . . . Please forgive all this tedious stuff about myself: I dislike inflicting it upon you, but as I am due back at Oxford on April 19th, I want to find out these things soon, so that when I see my mother, as I propose to do about four days before Oxford begins again, I can lay the matter quite plainly before her. Incidentally, it will cost her far less than Oxford, so I am sure that, in the end, she will not be averse to it, though I foresee that it may be necessary for me absolutely to refuse to return to Oxford, and possibly to disappear for a week or so—a rather hateful course, but what is one to do, after all, if people *will* be guided by prejudice and not by any sort of reason?[48]

Needless to say, confrontations between mother and son continued and in his desperation Philip managed to confuse her as to the exact date of the start of the new term in April and was thus able to spend a few extra days at Didbrook with Viva. The next month he push-biked 30 miles in sweltering heat to visit Balfour Gardiner to show him some of his latest compositions. He found Gardiner in a very genial mood and he was also most encouraging about the songs, a fact that pleased Philip greatly, since he knew that their views on song-writing were widely divergent.

In the Trinity Term, June 1914, Philip retook the Pass Moderations exam. This time he was successful and his tutor (in all innocence) wrote in his mark-book: 'Through. Didn't need to Viva'.[49] For this exam he had been required to study Pliny's *Letters*, Plato's *Apology* and *Meno*, as well as the *Agricola* and *Germania* of

Tacitus. He spent most of the summer holidays back home in Wales. For some of the time he wandered about the country on his motor bike, staying a few days at Didbrook, and for a short while on the Herefordshire border of Wales, which he thought 'a glorious district'. He also spent time at home saturating himself in Delius's music and vaguely planning some kind of book on the subject. One of his outings involved an enormous cross-country excursion: first of all by push-bike to his aunt in Whitney-on-Wye (53 miles) on 4 July, to Didbrook (another 56 miles) on the 6th, and then finally to London (on a motor bike borrowed from Viva Smith) to hear the all-Delius concert on the 8th.[50] It is easy to imagine his delight at managing to get to the concert that afternoon, especially as the composer himself was present. He later wrote telling Delius that it had been 'a wonderful and overwhelmingly beautiful experience' and that it had transcended everything, 'not only all other music. . . . it is the greatest thing in life'.[51]

The declaration of war on the 4 August 1914 decided Philip's immediate fate. Shrewdly seizing the moment, he managed to convince his mother that, because of the resultant financial scare, it would be cheaper for him to live in London rather than Oxford and that his annual allowance could thus be considerably reduced. In this he was aided and abetted by an Oxford Indian friend, Shahid Suhrawardy (1893–1963), who further convinced Mrs Buckley Jones of the wisdom of such a plan.

Another Oxford friend staying at Cefn Bryntach on this occasion was Brian Lunn (b. 1893), who in his autobiography, *Switchback*, gives yet a further dimension to the strange mother/son relationship:

The relations between his mother and Philip were different from what I had been led to expect from his manner of talking about her, for it was obvious that she admired him, and though a strong-minded woman, even seemed to wish to conciliate him. And while his remarks at meals were often provocative and contemptuous he treated her with a sort of humorous charm. One evening when I returned from a bicycle ride I happened on them in the garden. Philip's head was on his mother's lap and she was stroking his hair.[52]

By now Philip had decided not to devote himself entirely to music but to pursue some other course of study, once settled in London, for he badly longed for new enthusiasms and incentives. His relief was immense and he wrote to Taylor saying that 'the very thought of being completely free of Oxford brings a breath of new life with it!'[53] Owing to what he described as a 'lack of funds', he was forced to spend nearly the whole of July, August, and September with his family in Wales which, in a way, he now found worse than Oxford. He complained to Delius that he had never been 'so utterly depressed and "embougré" [the hell in] in his life'.[54] He did, however, manage to spend a happy week in September together with a friend, G. T. Leigh Spencer, in the Lake District, where they visited Wordsworth's cottage at Grasmere and 'walked six or seven hours every day, whatever the weather . . . and were rewarded, not only by magnificent scenery, but also by the most wonderful sense of physical well-being'.[55]

LIFE IN LONDON AS A
MUSIC CRITIC
(1914–1915)

Although he did not realize it at the time, the war was to have a catastrophic and destructive effect on Philip's life. On his return from his brief holiday, he lost no time in moving to London and by October 1914 was happily settled in colourful new surroundings in Cartwright Gardens, Bloomsbury, near St Pancras station, where he rented a ground-floor bed-sitter for 17s. 6d. a week. He described the area to Delius as 'a very jolly part of London . . . the neighbourhood is thoroughly *alive*—which is essential, for my liking—and unrespectable: at night the streets swarm with whores and hot-potato-men and other curious and interesting phenomena: and the darkness which the fear of hostile aircraft has enforced upon the city, makes everything doubly mysterious, fascinating and enchanting'.[1] He also had a great deal to say about patriotism, the war, and the chances of his being conscripted:

I have never been able to understand the sentiment of patriotism, the love of empire: it has always seemed to me so empty and intangible an idea, so impersonal and so supremely unimportant as regards the things that really matter— which are all the common heritage of humanity, without distinction of race or nationality . . .

But for my 'nervous stricture', which of course renders me 'physically unfit for service; (thus runs the phrase: the crude mind of the militarist has never yet dreamed of the mentally unfit!) the general public pressure would probably have driven me to enlist myself: hideous though a soldier's life would be for me, it would be less so than a life marred by the cheap sneers and dismal attempts at wit of the vulgar, blatant and exasperating Jingoes who, at a time like this, carry all before them. Fortunately, in my present condition, I escape both courses . . .

Music is, of course, at a low ebb, and I fear it will suffer greatly during the next few years: though there will be some consolation for the flood of patriotic filth that will be poured forth, in the fact that those composers who resist the force of the mob's passion will stand out in the greater relief and pre-eminence . . . I have been to various Promenade Concerts, but as a whole the programmes have been worse than usual, and the audiences—as a result— proportionately larger. It is difficult to escape Walford Davies' 'Solemn

Melody' or Gounod's 'Hymne à Sainte Cécile', or some such tosh, which invariably gets encored. Whenever the organ is used, the Britisher applauds: presumably because it reminds him of Church! [Sir Henry] Wood mangled your two little pieces in the most execrable way: the strings played just any-how, and the cuckoo came in at the wrong moment nearly every time: as for the rendering of the second piece, one can only imagine that both conductor and orchestra were reading the music for the first time! . . .

In the absence of Colin Taylor (as 'Private Taylor'!) I have become conduc-tor of a little amateur orchestra in Windsor—1 flute, 1 oboe, 1 clarinet, 1 horn, 2 drums, and about 20 strings. I took the first rehearsal last night: never having conducted before in my life, and knowing nothing about either the art of conducting or how the work (Mozart's G minor Symphony) should be played, I was very frightened, but managed to get through an hour and a half's stick-waving without a breakdown: my right arm, however, is dreadfully stiff to-day! It is very good experience for me, and I hope to improve with more practice. There is plenty of good material in the orchestra to work upon. When I know the scores better, I think I shall be able to do a good deal with them. If it is possible to get hold of the material of the 'First Cuckoo-note in Spring' without great expense, I want to make them do that: it would be so good for them, after many years' surfeit of Mozart, Haydn and Beethoven![2]

The 'nervous stricture' mentioned in this letter was, in the words of Dr Edwin Ash, a Harley Street doctor who had examined Philip, an 'inability to micturate when mentally excited, and especially in the presence of other people, with the consequence that he has had occasional prolonged retention'. In the certificate for his exemption from military service Ash added that Philip 'also complained of undue mental fatigue after moderate effort, and inability to carry out consistent daily work without distress, having to work in an irregular manner'. On examination Ash had found 'no sign of organic nervous disease', but was satisfied that he was of 'the neurasthenic type, due to an obstinate functional neurosis'.[3] All of which makes one suspect that Philip was somewhat of a malingerer.

Although still anxious to improve his theoretical knowledge of music, Philip felt very keenly the need of a somewhat wider educa-tion, 'a kind of mental foundation', and therefore he enrolled at University College, London, as a student of English language and literature, philosophy, and psychology. He wrote to tell Delius about his current musical aspirations:

In a few weeks I hope to begin lessons in composition with Gustav von Holst, whom Balfour Gardiner recommends as the best man in London for this pur-pose: apparently, the Royal College and Royal Academy of Music are so effete and antiquated that it is merely a waste of time to study there.

In music, as in other affairs, I feel very strongly the need of a master, and a thorough course of instruction, in matters of technique. In composition, I am stuck fast: I simply have not the means to express what I want to: it takes me hours to evolve a single bar. During the whole three months of inactivity in Wales, I only managed to do four or five little songs—the making of which could not have occupied more than a week at most.[4]

The planned lessons with Holst never materialized, which was probably just as well judging from Philip's later attacks on Holst and his music. The *Planets*, for example, was one of Philip's special dislikes and he wrote critically about it on several occasions, notably in *The Sackbut* and to his composer-conductor friend, Fritz Hart (1874–1949). A former Westminster Abbey chorister and later a student at the Royal College of Music, Hart had emigrated to Australia in 1909, eventually becoming the director of the Conservatorium of Music in Melbourne in 1915. Hart was a prolific composer (his enormous output included amongst other things 22 operas and 514 songs, as well as 23 unpublished novels!) and, on seeing some of his music, Philip had written to him in enthusiastic and encouraging terms, trying to find ways and means of securing performances of his music in England. This was the beginning of a warm friendship and correspondence which continued spasmodically for a number of years and Philip's letters to Hart contain much entertaining and often amusing news and gossip about the London musical scene. Even though Hart numbered Vaughan Williams, Ireland, and Holst amongst his friends, this did not deter Philip from his attacks on the latter's music:

Nobody has yet presented me with a copy of the score of Holst's *Planets* (which Sorabji calls 'the macro-cosmo-hydro-cephalic universe of Holst) and I am certainly not going to pay three guineas to buy one, but I should dearly love to . . . give a list, with parallel quotations in music-type, of the instances of sheer cribbing that occur in that God-forsaken work. . . . Where in fact is the exiguous body of Holst when you take away his Oriental garments, his ecclesiastical vestments, his folk-songs from Somerset and his bag of orchestral tricks from France and Russia—(to say nothing of what seems to me his most disgraceful exploit, namely his pilfering from his own gifted friends, for the indebtedness of his *Hymn of Jesus* to Vaughan Williams is surely a flagrant violation of the respect that is, or should be, due to one's friend's property)? I do not think it could be descried without the aid of a powerful microscope; in fact it would task the combined ingenuity of a modern Adams and Leverrier to discover it, as these did the planet Neptune, by mathematical calculation. Anyway, until this is done I shall continue to regard the little man as a charlatan who is only saved from detection by the fact that music, unlike words, is not actionable at law.[5]

Holst was lucky not to end up a victim in one of Philip's notoriously scurrilous limericks about composers and critics. Such a fate would doubtless have befallen him had Holst's name not been 'too hard to rhyme',[6] as a defeated Philip later confessed to Hart.

Back in the swing of London musical life and now sharing a small furnished flat in Maida Vale with Shahid Suhrawardy, it was not long before Philip was drawn into a heated controversy in the pages of *The New Age*, sparked off by a series of articles—a rather chauvinistic look at British versus German Music—written by the composer Joseph Holbrooke (1878–1958). Philip's letter, which appeared in the December 1914 issue, took Holbrooke to task for his insular attitude and contained such highly provocative sentences as: 'Not *all* British composers have yet sunk into the mire of sordid commercialism, wherein Mr Holbrooke would have them fellow-wallowers with himself.'[7] In the course of his letter Philip quoted the name of Delius, describing him as a cosmopolitan composer who had no need to stress his nationality to promote his music. The following week an enraged Holbrooke replied, attacking Philip with the words: 'Mr "Heseltine" is obviously out for trouble! He must be, from his writing, one of the parasites of Mr Delius. I succeeded in getting rid of mine!'[8] This was the first of many set-tos in which Philip would be involved in various journals. Some years later Philip guiltily felt he had perhaps done Holbrooke an injustice and in 1922 wrote to Fritz Hart telling him that

Some months ago I met Holbrooke and had several drinks with him and found him so pleasant a bird that I wondered if I had done him some injustice by disliking his music so much. So a few days later I borrowed his operas and one or two choral works from a library and not only carried them home—no small task when one considers the potentous size and weight of the vocal scores (the full scores I didn't tackle!) of the operas—but fell to studying them with an eye somewhat prejudiced in the composer's favour.

But in several hundred pages I found nothing—absolutely nothing. A dreary jungle of notes, that is all. . . . the music is a dismal failure—as bad as any fourth-rate German Kapellmeister's attempt to ape the grand manner of Strauss.[9]

Enthusiastic to launch out on his own, Philip now had plans to collaborate with one of his wealthy Oxford friends, Thomas Earp (1892–1958—he would later become the art critic of the *Daily Telegraph*), to edit a magazine to be called *The New Hat*. It was to be a modest issue of eight double-column pages with Earp agreeing to bear the cost of publication. Writing to Viva Smith on Christmas Eve 1914, Philip outlined a scheme which reads rather like a summary of his life's ideals:

I am collaborating . . . in the editing of a new monthly magazine 'The New Hat', devoted to Poetry and Music from a revolutionary standpoint—i.e. war on all the old-hat conventions, superstitions and humbugs with which effete professors and obsolescent pedagogues have long deceived a public too timid to contradict them. . . . its aims will be truth-telling and the plainest of plain speaking.—But, in addition to criticism, as much creative work as possible will be included—six pages of new poetry per month, at least. Also, one article per month by a distinguished outside contributor, and for the rest, articles by ourselves and our colleagues. . . . The first issue will appear on Jany 7th, and will contain an article by one of the greatest musicians in the country—the rest by the editors. For the succeeding numbers, we invite as many and as varied contributions as possible. No payment. . . . There will be *nothing* remotely connected with war-news or politics, and nothing shoddy or 'old-hat'.[10]

But no issue appeared on 7 January. Instead, a letter to Viva written that very day explained that Thomas Beecham felt that, under present conditions of both arts in England, poetry and music could not share a paper with any degree of harmony:

Consequently 'The New Hat' has been bashed in, and a much larger venture set on foot. This will take the form of a bi-monthly paper, entitled (probably) 'The Sackbut', which will be devoted exclusively to Music, from a very revolutionary and progressive standpoint. Beecham will be the proprietor, and I shall be the editor. There will be contributions from many of the most eminent musicians in Europe, and we hope to inaugurate a reign of terror for all the old-hatters, pedants and professors in this country. The paper is only a part of a very big musical campaign of T. B.'s, which will be revealed later.[11]

Despite all Beecham's plans and promises, no paper materialized and by October Philip would be writing to his mother to tell her that there were both difficulties with Beecham and more uncertainty about money.

By now it was evident that Philip's studies at London University were fated to be even more short-lived than those at Oxford. In February 1915 he was offered a position as music critic on the staff of the *Daily Mail*, an appointment which Lady Maud Cunard (1872–1948), the wealthy and brilliant hostess and patron of the arts, helped him secure. American-born, she had in 1895 married Sir Bache Cunard, Bt., a grandson of one of the founders of the Cunard line, and was for a time Beecham's mistress. Her Grosvenor Square salon soon became an important centre for London society and many an aspiring musician, author, poet, and artist cultivated her, succumbing to what was variously described as her 'frail Dresden china' beauty and 'bird-like charm', though Virginia Woolf dismissed her as 'a ridiculous little parakeet-faced woman'.[12] Having set up a meeting with influential *Daily Mail* personnel, Lady Cunard wrote to Philip on 3 February, begging him not to be 'proud or difficult' at his interview but simply to say 'you can & will', at the same time requesting him to write a review of a performance of the Delius Piano Concerto to be played by Benno Moiseiwitsch with Beecham conducting the London Symphony Orchestra in Queen's Hall on 8 February: 'You *must* make it short but wonderful . . . It is the thin edge of the wedge. If they pay you *tant mieux* if not at first, it does not matter. You must get in.'[13] It was indeed a 'wonderful' review. Philip described the concerto as 'a magnificent work' and Delius the greatest composer England had produced for two centuries. Lady Cunard must have been pleased to read in the final sentence that Beecham had 'surpassed himself, and secured the most superb orchestral playing that has been heard in London for many a long day'.[14] As a result of his interview and first effort he was offered the post at a salary of £2 a week, and immediately withdrew from his studies at the University to begin his new career in Fleet Street.

During Philip's time on the staff of the newspaper some thirty reviews appeared under the initials P. H. and were, by and large, limited to short factual reports of concerts and operas of about two or three column inches in length. In comparison with his later critical writings these early efforts seem almost dull and bland but, as we shall see, Philip was not entirely to blame for this state of affairs. Besides writing newspaper reviews he also occupied himself with more substantial musical journalism and early in 1915 produced an article, 'Some Notes on Delius and His Music', for the March edition of the *Musical Times*. It was the longest he had written to date and the first time that this journal had featured any significant writing on Delius. His essay of over 5,000 words began with two paragraphs of background information in which he drew the reader's attention to various characteristics of Delius's music, notably that 'one of the most striking features . . . is the almost complete absence of any other composer's influence'.[15] In the remainder of the article he summed up Delius's achievements, discussing some of the major works in detail and describing him as being

pre-eminently a harmonist . . . his harmonic effects are obtained vertically and not . . . horizontally, by the interweaving of several contrapuntal threads. He does not, however, limit himself to any fixed scale or system . . . consequently he avoids monotony and mannerisms alike, and gains considerably in freedom and range of expression. One cannot pin Delius down to a fixed harmonic scheme, although his harmonic idiom is quite unmistakably his own. The most one can say is that there is a certain harmonic aroma, as it were, which one can always recognize.[16]

It is somehow predictable that Philip should have ended his pane-gyric with the sweeping statement that there was 'no composer in Europe to-day of greater significance . . . nor any whose work seems more likely to outlast that of his contemporaries'.[17] The publication of this article was in a way also symbolic for, although Philip was not to realize it at the time, it marked the end of a period in his musical and intellectual development. Up until then his whole musical outlook had been dominated entirely by his obsession with the music of Delius. Within a year the situation would change completely.

Needless to say, the energetic and articulate Philip soon found work at the *Daily Mail* unrewarding and extremely frustrating, and once again, he became restless. His critical reviews were often sup-pressed and severely edited if, indeed, any space could be found for them in a newspaper operating under wartime conditions. By March he was already expressing his frustrations in a letter to Delius:

The Daily Mail people are becoming quite impossible. Last week two of my three notices were altogether cut out, for no discernable [*sic*] reason. My notice of the Classical Concert Society—which was full of praise, inciden-tally—was omitted, but space was found for a paragraph recording the doings of a military band on the pier at Felixtowe [*sic*]!! In addition to this, I was made to write a puff paragraph for a quite preposterously idiotic song about knitting socks for soldiers . . . If this kind of thing continues, there is no hope of doing any good for music by means of the Daily Mail and I am really ashamed to be receiving money for such degrading work.[18]

Delius attempted to help by writing to Lady Cunard, later reporting to Philip that she had written 'a long letter to Lord Northcliff [*sic*][19] telling him to give you a free hand otherwise it was no good what-ever having a musician there as critic—Probably that will help—Write just as you feel & dont take the slightest notice of their blue pencil.'[20] The situation, however, did not improve and, finding that there was little opportunity to develop his musical writings in this kind of journalism, it is not surprising that Philip resigned his post after a mere four months. His unpleasant experiences as a music critic in these early days soured his feelings towards this profession for the rest of his life. However, despite his unfulfilling daily work, Philip had evidently managed to enliven his free time, as a letter to Viva Smith reveals:

It has been particularly wicked of me to keep you so long without a letter, more especially since you have probably been thinking bitterly that preoccupation with the little French harlot we discussed together had banished every thought of you from my mind!!—which is far from being the case, since the damsel in question, though quite attractive *in* bed, proved equally tedious when out of it: and the appearance of symptoms which could only be those of either (1) inflammation of the urethra or (2) 'that most distressing and almost universal complaint', the clap, clinched the matter. Nous n'avons encore parlé, l'un à l'autre! Not that either of these complaints is in the least as alarming as influenza or a bilious attack, in reality. However, the advent of one or other of them has served as an excellent excuse for choking off a tiresome and rather expensive onhanger![21]

He had also spent a brief holiday in early April with two friends, the painter Adrian Allinson (1890–1959) and another of his Indian friends, A. K. Chanda, in a farmhouse on top of the Cotswolds at Upper Coscombe. Although the setting, some 900 feet above sea-level, overlooking the Avon Valley, the Malvern Hills, and the Forest of Dean, was superb, Philip complained to his mother that 'the wind blew hurricanes all the while . . . I have never slept in so cold a bedroom, or on so impossible a bed. One woke every hour or so in the night, either from cold or soreness caused by the bed. Chanda preferred sleeping on the floor, to his!'[22]

By May Philip was in a bad way. 'In the lowest depths of depression and utter lifelessness and hopelessness to which I have ever sunk . . . My mind is in an utter fog, so that I cannot think or describe or write anything whatever' was how he portrayed his state to Viva. Delius had already sensed his condition and had written in late March saying: 'You seem to be in a pretty unsettled state of mind . . . Why dont you try your uncle's office to see how you like it?—for breathing space—& continue writing your articles at the same time.'[23] An anxious Philip was now beginning to realize that he perhaps needed medical help and told Viva that he intended visiting a Harley Street doctor 'at great expense. Have already obtained the cash from a generous mamma, but haven't the energy or the initiative to rise up and make the effort . . . It is solitude (or what is worse, grisly company) that is killing me off by degrees.'[24]

After leaving the employ of the *Daily Mail* the awful truth gradually began to dawn on Philip: he was now out of work with no alternative prospects ahead and, more seriously, no qualifications for any kind of employment, least of all in the musical profession. That August, still restless and in a dissatisfied state of mind, he joined a group of friends on a summer holiday in Gloucestershire, in a bungalow on the slopes of Crickley Hill, overlooking the Vale of Evesham. In her short story, 'Till September Petronella',[25] the novelist Jean Rhys (1894–1979), wrote autobiographically about the few days she spent as a member of that party. This was the first of the many times Philip would become the basis for a character in fictional writing. Here he is portrayed as Julian Oakes, whilst Adrian Allinson appears as Andy Marston. Allinson was a handsome, talented, and intelligent young man, a fine pianist, a vehement pacifist, and had also been declared unfit for military service. Later, through an introduction from Philip, he designed sets for Beecham's productions of a number of operas, including Delius's *Village Romeo and Juliet*. Sometime earlier, in the Café Royal, he had introduced Philip to a beautiful and popular young artists' model, Minnie Lucy Channing (nicknamed 'Puma' on account of her fiery temperament), who is introduced in the story as Frankie Morell. Jean Rhys cast herself as the central character, Petronella Gray. Allinson had invited Jean Rhys to join the party and both Philip and Puma, who were just beginning what was to become a torrid and ill-fated love affair, had taken an instant and violent dislike to her, possibly because of her pro-war sentiments, refusing even to eat in the same room. The story is interesting because of its portrayal of the brittle relationship between Philip and Puma, while the picture Rhys paints of Philip himself has a faintly disturbing quality about it. It was evidently a disastrous time for all four members of the party. As Carole Angier writes in her biography of Jean Rhys: 'The "ensuing weeks" were "sheer hell" (Allinson), "nerve-shattering" (Heseltine), a "funny time" (Jean) . . . Heseltine and Puma made noisy scenes of sado-masochistic love . . . "When the situation had reached breaking point", two gentle and tactful Indian friends arrived and resolved it. Heseltine and Puma apologised.'[26]

For a time another member of that holiday party was Eugene Goossens (1893–1962), a promising young composer whom Philip much admired. Years later, in his autobiography, Goossens also wrote briefly about that particular summer, when he and Philip explored the neighbouring countryside on 'a decrepit motor-cycle'[27] to sketch old parish churches and to sample the local Cotswold beer. Philip must have written to Balfour Gardiner telling him of the holiday in lighter vein, for in September Gardiner replied, saying he had 'laughed heartily about Allinson, the three Indians and the panther-like mistress . . . I am glad that you have at last had the satisfaction of sowing a goodly number of wild oats.'[28] In his description of the holiday Goossens makes a brief but intriguing reference to Philip's 'East Indian mistress (whose dusky charm caused considerable comment among the neighbours)'[29] but does not elaborate further. Was this one of 'the three Indians', or 'the panther-like mistress'?

For the unsettled Philip this was a time marked by extreme swings of emotion: from listless, enervating depression to extrovert cavortings which included extravagant dancing in public and naked midnight motor-bike rides through village streets at great speed, significant manifestations of an almost pathological inability to grow up, a kind of extended adolescence. In his memoir Gray describes how Philip would break into 'extravagant displays of acrobatic dancing and *pas seuls* in all places and on all occasions, whenever he happened to be in a state of elation—in public houses, on restaurant tables, in the middle of Piccadilly Circus, even in the austere precincts of the Queen's Hall itself, to the stupefaction of concert goers'.[30] It seems that Philip was also developing a penchant for 'streaking', as the Australian-born author and editor, Jack Lindsay (1900–90),[31] with whom he was later to collaborate, related: 'He had acquired the habit of stripping all his clothes at a certain stage of drink and running about in the street . . . ladies still peeped through their midnight curtains in the hope-fear of seeing his white form speed along the pavement, chanting snatches of some relevant hymn or ballad-refrain.'[32] John Goss (1894–1953), the singer who promoted many of Philip's songs in later years, used to relate a story of how Philip, spotting a Salvation Army lady coming up the street with a begging cup, swiftly undressed and, when she knocked at his door, appeared completely naked, imitating her gesture with a chamber-pot in his hand!

Judging by a long letter written to Delius during this strange summer holiday, it was not a particularly happy time for Philip. A few months later he described it to Taylor as 'fearful, nerve-racking and entirely horrible', adding that he was 'trying to drown the memory of this period in much musical work of divers kinds. Composition is entirely impossible—but in December I am going to begin a long and strenuous course of lessons with Goossens, in the hope that I may be relieved of the fear which is haunting me, that I have no musical bowels at all!'[33] But no lessons followed with Goossens, nor with anyone else; instead it was a period of intense soul-searching for Philip as he contemplated his none-too-promising future. The letter to Delius in August reflects feelings of deep despair and depression:

. . . my outlook has daily become more confused and trance-like . . . something seems to have died—or gone out—and there is no peace, but only a weary restlessness. My head feels as though it were filled with a smoky vapour or a poisonous gas which kills all the finer impressions before they can penetrate to me and stifles every thought, every idea before it is born. . . . It is a feeling that has been enveloping me little by little for many months past, and although there are times when I think myself rid of it it always returns after a while more virulent than ever. . . . Creative thought or work—or anything remotely approximating thereto, is entirely impossible, and the chances of their becoming so seem every day more remote—yet without them existence— for all who desire them—is void and desolate—Hence those tears . . .

Forgive me—I have inflicted this kind of thing on you so often before, but as time goes on, I feel more and more that you are almost the only person I can confide in without the very smallest fear of a misunderstanding.[34]

At this point in the letter he refers to Beecham's earlier promises of appointing him as editor of *The Sackbut*. Nothing had come of Beecham's promises and by March 1916 Philip was considering legal action to make Beecham pay 'a couple of hundred' on the strength of their three-year 'Sackbut' agreement: 'I think his signed document is binding.'[35] A journal bearing that name would, in fact, eventually materialize five years later, but not under Beecham's aegis. Given such a background, it is not surprising that, although they were to co-operate years later, from then on a certain degree of mistrust existed between the two men. This is apparent in Philip's letters while, as we have already seen, forty years later Beecham would write about him in less than complimentary terms in his biography of Delius. But to return to Philip's letter to Delius:

. . . you are greatly to be envied living amongst the mountains that will never re-echo with the sounds of even the news of war. Here the war-cloud looms over one like some great sinister bird, poised and ready to pounce upon its hapless prey. The black influence alone is enough to quench every artistic impulse in all but the very strongest. It is very hard to escape it—in London impossible . . . My plans are very vague. It took three long letters, separated by intervals of a fortnight, and two reply-paid telegrams to extract from the elusive Thomas [Beecham] any information about the future of the 'Sackbut' and, incidentally, my quarterly allowance—I dislike intensely taking money for nothing done but under the present agreement, I am neither completely free to do my own work nor am I definitely given anything to occupy myself with, outside of my own studies—The 'Sackbut' is shelved from month to month— it is now postponed till next January at the earliest, and then, if we're all still alive there'll be still another postponement . . . I have to remain in London, the one place of all others where the war-fever rages most violently and where its effects oppress and depress one the most. If one had some continuous, all-day occupation, one could live there, but that alone could make life tolerable in such a place at the present moment.[36]

The constant background of the horrors of the war raging in Europe is absolutely essential to any understanding of Philip's fitful and at times bizarre development during this period. In London 'the fearful gloom of the war' was everywhere and these constant reminders added to his growing sense of anger, depression, and aimlessness. As he continued in a letter to Taylor:

The agglomeration of horrors of all kinds that this war has brought about makes me so sick and fills me with so much impotent rage against the barbarous conditions of human life in this the 20th century of the Christian era that I have absolutely no room and no use for any sentiments about patriotism, or nationality or national honour, or anything of the kind . . . if there were no such thing as patriotism and no such thing as national pride or honour, the world would have been spared this unspeakable and soul-shattering devastation.[37]

It was a time when there seemed no hope, no future at all and certainly not in music. All this was further compounded by Philip's own feelings of guilt and implied cowardice. As early as November 1914 he had written to Viva Smith dramatizing his mother's imagined reaction to his pacifism: 'she is badly infected with war-fever, and is evidently mad with jealousy when she hears of other women's sons being killed or maimed, when her own . . .—what a sickening disappointment it must be to her, to have suffered all the agonies of childbirth for—THAT CREATURE.'[38] Brian Lunn records how when Philip was 'molested in the streets by officious patriots he used to retort with a favourite quotation from Samuel Butler, "Thou callest trousers pants whereas I call them trousers, therefore thou art in hell-fire, O brother-in-law of Mr Spurgeon's haberdasher."'[39]

Back in London, and still without any prospects of employment, Philip turned now to the past, to the studying and editing of early music in the British Museum,

delving deep into the origins of keyboard music, and receiving daily delights and surprises from the works of Byrd, Gibbons, Tomkins, Farnaby, and many other astonishing master . . . which is exceedingly interesting from an aesthetic as well as an antiquarian point of view—a fact entirely ignored by most of the old fogeys, who have taken the trouble to do this in years past.[40]

In a few years' time this would become one of his most important musical activities and establish him as a pioneer in one of the century's most significant developments of musical knowledge and practice.

With his move to the cosmopolitan life of London, Philip gradually began to meet a number of people who would slowly usurp the position hitherto occupied by Delius. The first of these was one of the most significant English writers of this century, whose novels and anti-war sentiments had been attracting a certain degree of notoriety and not a little suspicion.

FRIENDSHIP WITH LAWRENCE
(1915–1916)

Whilst still at Oxford, Philip had been introduced by Robert Nichols to D. H. Lawrence's first three novels, *The White Peacock*, *The Trespasser*, and *Sons and Lovers*. The intensity and quality of Lawrence's *Love Poems and Others*, published in 1913, had so impressed him that he wrote to Viva Smith saying that he was sending her 'some of the most wonderful love poems in the world'.[1] He also sent a copy of these poems to Delius, adding that he considered Lawrence's novels unrivalled both in depth of insight and beauty of language. Writing to Viva about *Sons and Lovers* he used words such as 'superb', 'amazing', 'a real masterpiece . . . The style is most uncannily sure: every word rings true, every adjective, every phrase is so startlingly apt and precise. I hope to meet Lawrence soon, as I have discovered people who know him. No meeting could afford me greater pleasure or interest.'[2]

When possessed by an obsession there was no stopping Philip's single-mindedness and, just as he had engineered his youthful meeting with Delius during the interval of that momentous concert in 1911, so he contrived to meet Lawrence at a dinner party on 15 November 1915. Lawrence indicated his immediate fascination with Philip, telling Nichols two days later that he liked Philip very much: 'I think he is one of the men who will count, in the future. I must know him more.' Lawrence went on to encourage Nichols who was at the time recovering in hospital, imploring him not to go back to the front:

You must *never* go back. . . . There is so much hate and destruction and disintegration: let it all go, and do not belong to it any more. . . . I think you are a poet: take care, save yourself, above all, save yourself: there is such need of poets, that the world will all perish, without them. You have a mission to be a living poet.[3]

The next month Lawrence wrote once again in enthusiastic terms about Philip to his close friend, the author and critic John

Middleton Murry (1889–1957). Philip was no less impressed, as he indicated in a letter to Colin Taylor a short while later:

> Last week I met D. H. Lawrence, whom I have long venerated as the greatest literary genius of his generation. He has an outstanding philosophy of art . . . He is against conscious self-expression, introspection and reducing, analytic methods in general. 'I believe' he writes to me, 'that music too must become now synthetic, metaphysical, giving a musical utterance to the sense of the whole' . . . The outlook is so novel and startling—it is positively terrific—and needs a great deal of pondering.[4]

Here Philip was quoting from a letter which Lawrence had written to him on 22 November 1915. They had obviously seen each other again soon after their initial meeting. Judging from Lawrence's letter, which pursues matters as yet half-discussed, a clear emotional and physical affinity had already been sparked between the two men. Significant are Lawrence's comments and advice on being careful not to lose 'the power to love really and profoundly, from the bottom of your soul, to love a woman—not men'. His interest in such matters had already been expressed some years before as in the following letter to the free-lance journalist and essayist, Henry Savage: 'I believe a man projects his own image on another man, like on a mirror. But from a woman he wants himself re-born, re-constructed. . . . And one is kept by all tradition and instinct from loving men, or a man—for it means just extinction of all the purposive influences.'[5]

Clearly their conversation the previous night must have included the subject of homosexuality, with Lawrence possibly having suspicions as to Philip's sexual orientation. It is perhaps significant that Lawrence was soon to lend Philip the manuscript of a philosophical work, 'Goats and Compasses'. Details of this work are rather uncertain, but the unsympathetic Cecil Gray claimed to have read it and dismissed it as 'a bombastic, pseudo-mystical, psycho-philosophical treatise dealing largely with homosexuality—a subject . . . in which Lawrence displayed a suspiciously lively interest at that time'.[6] After this second meeting Lawrence wrote to Philip:

> I hope you didn't mind the holding forth of last night. But do think about what we were saying, of art, and life.
> It is so important that now, the great reducing, analytic, introspective process, which has gone on pure and uninterrupted since the Renaissance;—at least since Milton—should now give way to a constructive, synthetic, metaphysical process. Because now, reduction, introspection, has reached the point when it has practically no more to reveal to us, and can only produce sensationalism.

One must fight every minute—at least I must—to overcome this great flux of disintegration, further analysis, self analysis. If it continues, this flux, then our phase, our era, passes swiftly into oblivion.—In physical life, it is homosexuality, the reduction process. When man and woman come together in love, that is the great *immediate* synthesis. When men come together, that is immediate reduction: those complex states, the finest product of generations of synthetic living, are *reduced* in homosexual love, liberating a conscious knowledge of the component parts. This is like Plato. But the *knowledge* is always contained and included within the spirit, the process, of reduction, disintegration.

This may sound wild, but it is true. And it is necessary to overcome the great stream of disintegration, the flux of reduction, like a man swimming against the stream. Otherwise there is nothing but despair. This is why I am going to Florida. Here the whole flux is deathly. One must climb out on to a firm shore.

If we can pull Nichols out, then he will be a living poet. But I don't feel very hopeful about him.

Above all, be careful about losing the power to love really and profoundly, from the bottom of your soul, to love a woman—not men. Otherwise you will only feel despair. And I believe that music too must become now synthetic, metaphysical, giving a musical utterance to the sense of the Whole. But perhaps I don't know enough about it.

I am glad you are happier about the girl: and that she is happier. Don't be afraid of being sentimental: it is healthy to be a little sentimental at times. Only don't be cynical and self-sufficient: your face shows traces already.

I shall ask Lady Ottoline Morrell to invite you to Garsington. She is a sister of the Duke of Portland, wife of Philip Morell, radical M.P. for Burnley. She has crowds of artists at her house: often unfortunately. But she is a big woman, essentially genuine and religious. Only don't stick at the outside queernesses. You and Chrustchoff must go and see her.[7]

In all likelihood the girl mentioned in this letter was Dorothy Warren (1896–1954), the beautiful 19-year-old niece of Lady Ottoline Morrell. Lawrence had invited both Nichols and Philip separately to meet her at his house in Hampstead, in the hope of marrying her off to one of them. An ever-loyal disciple of Lawrence, she would gain a certain notoriety in 1929 when an exhibition of his paintings at her London gallery was raided by the police.

The flamboyant and somewhat eccentric Lady Ottoline Morrell (1873–1938) wielded considerable social power in literary and artistic circles at that time. She has been rather unkindly described as 'extremely tall and striking, with dyed red hair and jutting jaw, nasal voice and neighing laugh, and wore extravagant costumes that resembled the plumage of an exotic bird'.[8] As an enthusiastic and generous patron of the arts she had succeeded in gathering around herself a circle of artists, writers, and poets, creating an almost legendary milieu at her beautiful Tudor manor house, Garsington, near Oxford. Built of grey stone sometime in the late sixteenth century, the house was remodelled internally in the 1620s, the main downstairs rooms being panelled in oak, decorated with friezes, and featuring an imposing oak staircase.

Besides Lawrence, other regular visitors included Virginia Woolf, Lytton Strachey, Aldous Huxley, and E. M. Forster. As Ottoline herself summed it up: 'Garsington was a theatre, where week after week a travelling company would arrive and play their parts.'[9] Married to a Liberal Member of Parliament, Ottoline had a number of affairs, including ones with the painter Augustus John and the philosopher Bertrand Russell; consequently a good deal of intrigue revolved around her and her circle of friends. Although enjoying her considerable hospitality and generosity, some of these friends were not past ridiculing her and gossiping behind her back. Lawrence would later satirize her and her set in his novel, *Women in Love*[10]— which caused her much distress. At this stage, however, Lawrence still hoped that she would assist him financially in his plans to establish a Utopian community of 'about twenty souls', his 'Rananim', in America—his disillusioned reaction to the war and the persecution he now felt in England. Ottoline was a loyal supporter of Lawrence but no admirer of his wife, Frieda, whom she once described as a devil, saying: 'If only we could put her in a sack and drown her.'[11] Frieda's opinion of Ottoline was not very different: 'inside those wonderful shawls there is cheapness and vulgarity'.[12] This tension was soon to flare up through the agency of the as-yet-unsuspecting Philip.

Disillusioned by their older friends' lack of enthusiasm for their 'colony of escape', Lawrence and Frieda now saw the young Philip and Nichols as possible recruits for their scheme. This was the 'new, young generation' to whom Lawrence now turned. Swiftly setting his plans in action, Lawrence wrote to Ottoline almost immediately:

Yesterday I saw the sick poet [Robert Nichols] in his hospital . . . He jumped for joy at the thought of coming to see you. I like the other man, the musician, even better . . . I wish we could all have come down together: perhaps we might. At any rate, if you ask Nichols—he is rather seedy yet, very nervous—ask Heseltine along with him . . .

I am waiting now to hear from Delius, through Heseltine, about *his* place in Florida.[13]

Philip, enthusiastically assuming the role of the admiring disciple, had immediately written to Delius suggesting that the proposed Florida colony be established on the orange-grove where Delius had worked from 1884–5. Delius's reply proved anything but encouraging. California, he thought, would be a far better choice than Florida where, after twenty years, the orange-grove would be overgrown and the house tumbled down. Not only that: the place was isolated and life there was frightfully expensive. To let Lawrence go to Florida would be 'sending him to disaster'.[14] Delius's reply, however, hardly succeeded in quenching Philip's naïve enthusiasm. Now, completely under Lawrence's spell, he saw a chance to break with his stultifying past. In his next letter to Delius he wrote:

For myself I feel that I am—and have been for years past—rolling downhill with increasing rapidity into a black, slimy cesspool of stagnation—and with every day the difficulty of pulling up and reversing become more apparent. A big effort is needed—and lately my eyes have been opened to a clear and terrifying vision of this necessity, and I am filled with devastating fears lest it be already too late to do so. Four years ago you warned me of all this, and I was not ripe for understanding it and paid no heed. Now I am determined to follow not only your advice but your example too; casting all cautious fears to the winds, I am going away, to the uttermost parts of the earth, to *live*. Does this sound wild and vain? I don't care much if it does, nor if I perish in the attempt—This living death I can endure no longer.

Here have I been for years, lamenting the barrenness of my life, waiting for my seed to flourish in a desert soil—worse than fool that I am. I have never yet lived at all—and that is why I am going away—to Florida, Tahiti, anywhere—to have at least a year or two of real life to try and make something out of.

. . . I myself have at last obtained from my late doctor (now a colonel) a certificate of my unfitness for military service, so the passport difficulty will be considerably lessened for me. Of course, all prospect of money-making vanishes—but my £3 a week remains fairly steadfast—that is to say, if my mother proves amenable, and now I am of age she cannot cut me off on any account.

Now do write, when you have time, and tell me more about Florida, and about Tahiti—which I myself favour personally, though the others are inclined to the west coast of Florida—Fort Myers way. Is the orange grove entirely impossible? Couldn't we by any means rejuvenate it with the aid of niggers? . . .

This all sounds utterly wild—an irresponsible adventure, unthinkable to the cautious. But, good God, one must plunge, even if one never comes up again—

I am in a state of flux—my mind is a whirlpool of alternating excitement and depression.[15]

The tone of Delius's reply was still one of discouragement, though he took the opportunity to dispense good advice to Philip:

I would not advise you to go to America or to Tahiti except for *adventure* & to get out of a groove—You are only 21. I went to Florida at your age & and had not yet become a musician—Dont get despondent & desperate—The conditions of art in America are far worse than in England—If you dont feel sufficiently gifted to become a composer why not become a powerful writer—not a critic—but a writer on artistic things—on music . . . You must have a real fight with life before you give at [sic] up & there is some satisfaction to be got out of surmounting difficulties—By force to overcome the bourgeois! To lift oneself by degrees over the mob & feel ones powers—Dont let yourself be crushed by masses of inferiority & phrases of catchwords.[16]

The promised visit to Lady Ottoline eventually materialized and a party consisting of the Lawrences, Philip, and Shahid Suhrawardy ('a lineal descendant of the Prophet',[17] as Lawrence called him) was invited to Garsington on 29 November 1915. As Philip was drawn into this new circle, he found himself there again some two weeks later, this time with another friend, the Armenian author Dikran Kouyoumdjian who, under the name of Michael Arlen, would write a number of successful popular novels. In the meantime Lawrence had written to Ottoline, giving his own frank opinions of the two men: 'Heseltine is a bit backboneless and needs stiffening up. But I like him very much, Kouyoumdjian seems a bit blatant and pushing: you may be put off him.'[18] For her part Ottoline was not entirely impressed with what she saw and wrote in her journal with typical forthrightness. The descriptions of her new guests are enlivened by apparent prejudice, racial ones in the case of Kouyoumdjian and Suhrawardy and veiled innuendos of homosexuality about Philip. Such remarks were not typical of the normally tolerant Ottoline, who numbered among her friends both Jews and gay young men, the latter often openly discussing their problems and love affairs with an apparently sympathetic listener:

What strange creatures Lawrence and Frieda attract to themselves. He is enthusiastic about both Heseltine and Kouzoumdjian, but I don't feel attracted to them, indeed quite the reverse. Heseltine is tall and blond, soft and so degenerate that he seems somehow corrupt. Kouzoumdjian is a fat dark-blooded tight-skinned Armenian Jew, and though Lawrence believes that he will be a great writer, I find it hard to believe. Obviously he has a certain vulgar sexual force, but he is very coarse-grained and conceited. He and Heseltine seem to pollute the atmosphere, and stifle me, and I have to escape from their presence—also I get very tired of the continual boasting of what they are going to do. They flatter Frieda and pay her more attention than they do Lawrence, so naturally they are both geniuses in her eyes, and she is enthusiastic about them—they are going down to Cornwall when the Lawrences go there. I do not understand the Indian Sarawadi. He is extremely anti-English, but like all Indians quite foreign and remote, though he seems more substantial and self-confident than most of his race.[19]

It was during one of these visits to Garsington that Philip met and fell madly in love with a beautiful, young French-Swiss girl,

Juliette Baillot (b. 1896). Born in Neuchâtel, Juliette was at the time governess to Lady Ottoline's daughter, Julian (1906–89), and in 1919 married Julian (later Sir Julian) Huxley (1887–1975), the eminent biologist. Ottoline later described her as tall, slim, very pretty, shy, and severe, with plaits of fair hair done into two buns: 'I can never forget her lovely slim figure as she dived into the pond, her yellow hair making her look like a water nymph or a picture of a silvery saint by Crivelli.'[20]

In her autobiographical book *Leaves of the Tulip Tree* (1986), Lady Juliette Huxley recalled a large Christmas party held at Garsington, at which Lawrence and Frieda, Middleton Murry, and Katherine Mansfield were among the guests:

After dinner, Katherine Mansfield organised some tableaux vivants including Cophetua and the Beggar Maid. I was the Beggar Maid with a dark frayed tunic lent by Ottoline. Who was Cophetua? I think it was Philip Heseltine, and he was also the Beast, wearing on his head a wickerwork waste-paper basket and glittering clothes, to my 'Beauty'. I remember bending over his reclining 'dying' form and releasing my impromptu 'love-chant' and the waste-paper basket flying off to reveal his red sweating face.[21]

Juliette was of the opinion that Katherine Mansfield had arranged the scene to throw Philip and her together and it was not long before they began 'a strange correspondence' (as Juliette later described it) which at first 'flattered and bewildered' her. '"Tread softly, for you tread on my dreams"—but his letters were so divorced from reality that a deep instinct warned me of danger.'[22] In one of these letters Philip had also somewhat tactlessly referred to Ottoline as 'the Ott' and this had outraged the loyal Juliette.

In his letter of 21 December 1915, Delius had sensed this new infatuation when he wrote to Philip: 'Dear old pal! you are on the brink of being in love again—a phrase in your letter seems to tell me so'. Philip himself, however, wrote less discreetly to his Russian friend Boris de Chrustchoff (variously referred to as an anthropologist and bibliophile—according to Gray he was the 'greatest living authority on edible fungi').[23] Philip had met him in 1914 at Oxford during his dealings with members of the Society for Psychical Research. De Chrustchoff claimed that for many years he was Philip's closest friend and for a time the two men shared flats in Chelsea and Maida Vale:

Suddenly as I looked at the exceedingly charming little Swiss girl this evening, it struck me that I can NEVER return to Puma—it has become quite impossible. She has soiled my whole life—I can no longer imagine that I loved her the

tiniest bit, when I now passionately love the Swiss girl with my whole heart—
as no one ever before, God, but she is out of this world—Puma must away—it
must be—how can it be? Ah, my friend, it must, must, it *must* be! Ah, if I
only had courage—to send that one far away and to receive this one for eter-
nity!!

I beg you and Shahid—if he is with you—to do something—[24]

Lawrence soon involved himself in this *affaire de cœur*, proferring
advice to Philip:

. . . If you are very fond of Mlle Baillot, then marry her. I think it would be
best. Have enough of the other, then marry the little Swiss, properly, and she
shall come too. I think probably she will suit you better than any English
woman you can find. Since I have been thinking about it, I think you are right
to be fond of her. She is probably your woman.

Excuse the interference—I do want a few of us to make a good thing of life,
a new start. And I think we might do it together.

But always do that which you want most to do.[25]

For a while Philip and Juliette saw something of each other, meeting briefly in London where Philip took her not only for her first
walk on Hampstead Heath but also, at Juliette's request, to the Café
Royal. At this stage, however, she became 'frightened' and broke off
the relationship, 'not gently but finally. A little later, Ottoline questioned me about it, and I learnt he had a mistress who was pregnant
with his child. We never met again, and I burnt all his letters.'[26]
Juliette's account implies a gap in time between the breaking off of
her relationship with Philip and hearing of the existence of Puma,
presumably from Ottoline. There is unfortunately no evidence as to
why Juliette should have become 'frightened' but, judging from the
many complications in Philip's life during this particular period, his
resulting strange behaviour could certainly have been confusing,
even frightening, to a young Swiss girl living in a foreign country.
Writing about him all those years later she remembered him as 'an
unusual young man, unsure of himself and wasting himself in many
pursuits', significantly adding that he was 'perhaps part angel and
part demon'.[27]

Although his affection was not returned by Juliette, the whole
incident was crucial in his resolve not to return to Puma, the 'other'
girl mentioned by Lawrence. Born on 12 August 1894 in Chiswick,
Puma was the fourth daughter of a mechanical engineer, Robert
Stuart Channing[28] and Fanny Channing (formerly Fleming). With
black hair and olive complexion she was of striking, almost classical
Mediterranean beauty, a fact confirmed by surviving photographs.

David Garnett (1892–1981), a novelist member of the Lawrence circle, recorded that at the Wembley Exhibition of 1924 or 1925 the 'twelve most beautiful women in history' were displayed in cages, with Puma playing Cleopatra.[29] Hot-blooded, forthright, and vivacious, there was, none the less, an element of naïvety in her makeup. Paul Delany rather unflatteringly described her as 'a hanger-on of the bohemian set that frequented the Café Royal, a pretty and wayward opportunist who hoped to get some lasting advantage out of the floating world in which she lived'.[30]

Meanwhile, having learnt that he would not be allowed to leave England without official exemption from military service, Lawrence had impulsively gone to a recruiting station at Battersea Town Hall. After waiting two hours he suddenly fled, revolted and humiliated by the whole situation. Subsequently, at the end of December 1915, he and Frieda left London and moved down to Cornwall, where their novelist and architect friend J. D. Beresford (1873–1947) had lent them his house at Porthcothan near Padstow, a quarter of a mile from the sea. Lawrence wrote of it as 'a nice old house with large clear rooms, and such wonderful silence—only a faint sound of sea and wind';[31] Cornwall he found 'remote and desolate and unconnected: it belongs still to the days before Christianity, the days of Druids, or of desolate Celtic magic and conjuring'.[32] Despite his relief at having left London behind, Lawrence was ill and depressed, telling Murry that he was 'absolutely run to earth, like a fox they have chased till it can't go any further, and doesn't know what to do . . . I am beaten—knocked out entirely.'[33]

Within two days they were joined by Philip, who was also anxious to escape from London. The fact that he felt an overwhelming attraction towards the fascinating and beautiful Juliette Baillot was now being further complicated by the fact that Puma had fallen pregnant sometime in October 1915 and was expecting his child. Philip had discussed the matter with Delius and now elaborated:

I have found my Vrenchen—I hinted this in my letter from Garsington, but even now I can't write about it. I have not seen her since Garsington, where she lives, but she has written me long, wonderful letters—and I am more sure of her than I have ever been of anyone. She is Swiss . . .

Meanwhile, I am still worried to death by the little model I took away in the summer in sheer desperation of loneliness. I never really liked her, but she has been staying with me a good deal during the winter, because she had no home and little money, and, as I told you in London, she is going to have a child. Fortunately, I had a legacy of £100 the other day which I can draw upon to supply her needs, but I have no idea what is to become of the child.

She cannot possibly afford to keep it, and I have far too little liking for her to want to help her afterwards. As it is, I reproach myself for having been too Christian, too weakly compassionate towards her.[34]

Once settled in Cornwall, Philip began preparing to throw his energies into a new venture, this time to promote and publish Lawrence's books, a scheme already tentatively discussed by Lawrence and some of his older friends. His contribution towards the household expenses from his private income, though modest, would also have certainly been welcomed by the Lawrences. Philip, in fact, showed his usual generosity and Lawrence remarked to Lady Ottoline that he was 'always paying more than his share'.[35]

Soon after his arrival, Philip had written at length to Delius. Niggling doubts about Lawrence were already beginning to surface:

The past months have been full of anxieties and small nagging worries, each petty in itself individually, but en masse powerful and wearing to one's nervous vitality. At the moment I am completely exhausted, as though I had been dragged, insensible, out of the sea. . . .

I asked Lawrence to write you a few days ago, to give you his exposition of our plans. However, I don't want to identify myself with him in anything beyond his broad desire for an ampler and fuller life—a real life as distinct from the mere mouldy-vegetable existence which is all that is possible here. He is a very great artist, but hard and autocratic in his views and outlook, and his artistic canons I find utterly and entirely unsympathetic to my nature. He seems to be too metaphysical, too anxious to be comprehensive in a detached way and to care too little for purely personal, analytical and introspective art. His views are somewhat at variance with his own achievements. But he is, nevertheless, an arresting figure, a great and attractive personality, and his passion for a new, clean, untrammelled life is very splendid. . . .

I wish so much that I could have come over to you at Grez this New Year, but it appears to be quite impossible to get a passport.[36]

Delius replied, hoping that Philip would indeed be able to come across to Grez if his passport problems could be solved. Having seen yet another of Philip's compositions, he once again encouraged the young man to apply himself to music: 'Turn to music, dear boy. *There* is where you will find the only real satisfaction—Work hard at composition—There is real emotion in your song . . . My most earnest advice to you is to turn to musical composition at once & for good.'[37] Philip's reply was full of beautifully descriptive, poetic language:

Your splendid and encouraging letter cheered me immensely—It is hard to have faith in the progress of oneself when one's forward movement is so slow that is almost imperceptible. Yet there is always the little smouldering fire of confident hope at the bottom of one's heart and a letter like yours makes it leap into joyous flame. . . .

This Cornish coast is strange and sinister . . . There is a wealth of sombre colour in the landscape. The bare branches of the trees and hedgerows have all a kind of winter coat of a reddish tint which they put on to protect themselves from the excess of salt in the damp air. At this time of year this dull red is the predominant hue—it is emphasized by the redness of the soil which is just now being ploughed up. And at sunset (on clear evenings one sees the sun sink right into the sea) everything becomes burning red—even the grass seems to have a lair [sic] of red over the green. On the greyest, dullest days, a faint bluish-red comes filtering through the cloud-masses. All the roads, for some curious reason, are cut very deep down in the rock, below the field level—and on the rock, at the level of the field, grows the high hedges of evergreen tamarisk—so that one is always overshadowed. On the uplands, there are scarcely any shrubs or trees—the hedges are replaced by stone-walls, built in an intricate and very beautiful herring-bone pattern. It is all stark and elemental, rather cheerless and repelling, if one wanted to assimilate it, identify oneself with it, but for a while invigorating, cleansing—essentially a country for deliberation at a turning-point rather than for settled work. . . .

While this war lasts, one feels that 'sauve qui peut' is the only safe rule of life—if one does not want to throw one's life away. It is so difficult to keep one's head above water at all. But if one can weather *this* storm![38]

But a new anxiety had now manifested itself for Philip. Soon after his arrival in Cornwall a bill to make military service compulsory for single men had been introduced in Parliament on 5 January 1916, and was due to receive its third reading on 24 January. Lawrence, in the meantime, was keeping Lady Ottoline fully up to date with all the news:

Heseltine is here also. I like him, but he seems empty, uncreated . . . [he] seems as if he were not yet born, as if he consisted only of echoes from the past, and reactions against the past. But he will perhaps come to being soon: when a new world comes to pass. Meanwhile conscription hangs over his head like a Sword of Damocles.[39]

Kouyoumdjian now arrived to join the party on 10 January 1916. Lawrence's initial approval of the young aspiring Armenian author was to be short-lived and, in his depressed and sickly state, he soon began to find his young guests an oppressive intrusion. Kouyoumdjian had brought with him the loathsome atmosphere of London and the combination of the two young men was proving a source of irritation:

I think Heseltine will go first, back to his Puma (the girl, the model). He says he despises her and can't stand her, that she's vicious and a prostitute, but he [will] be running back to her in a little while, I know. She's not so bad, really. I'm not sure whether her touch of licentious profligacy in sex isn't better than his deep-seated conscious, mental licentiousness. Let them fight it out between them. Kouyoumdjian is trying also. I think he is in love with Dorothy

Warren, and not at all sure that she will reciprocate. So he is a little more assertive than ever, and tiresome. It is such a bore, about these young people, that they must be so insistently self-sufficient, always either tacitly or noisily asserting themselves. Heseltine silently and obstinately asserts himself, Kouyoumdjian noisily and offensively. But why should they want to assert themselves, nobody wants to obliterate them, or mitigate them. They are quite free: then why assert themselves. They spend their time in automatic reaction from everything, even from that which is most sympathetic with them. It is stupid, it is crass. . . . Why can't they be simple, fallible like other mortals.
    Still, one must be patient, and not dislike them. They will get all right.[40]

A few days later Lawrence wrote agreeing with Lady Ottoline's original opinion of Kouyoumdjian 'I dont care for him. I shall ask him to go away. . . . I will say that we want his room',[41] but added that he still liked Philip. There had perhaps been fun to begin with. In high spirits they had all started writing a play, 'a comedy for stage about Heseltine and his Puma and so on. It will be jolly'.[42] This play, however, was never finished—although some of the material may well have later found its way into the novel *Women in Love*, though no longer in a spirit of such jollity. Before having finally to be ejected by force from the Cornwall commune,[43] Kouyoumdjian, with Philip's assistance, had effected an ugly confrontation between Frieda and Ottoline. The two men had confirmed Frieda's suspicions that Lady Ottoline had, to put it mildly, not always said the kindest things about her behind her back. On discovering Philip's role in the affair Ottoline wrote to him in highly critical terms. Philip's reply, somewhat self-righteous in tone, included a melodramatic quotation from Homer:

I am not the real cause of offence—mine was merely corroborative evidence: though I must plead guilty to answering truthfully various questions that were addressed to me, because I believe that consistent plain-speaking alone can pave the way towards a just and honest relationship with others.
    You remember the Homeric motto Butler chose for 'Erewhon Revisited'?

> [Him do I hate even as I hate Hell fire,
> Who says one thing and hides another in his heart.]

I am certainly tactless, because I am convinced that tact, so far from providing a cure for misunderstandings, merely suppresses them for a while, after which they break out with renewed virulence.
    After living with the Lawrences for several weeks, I have come to the very definite conclusion that Mrs Lawrence has been most unjustly maligned behind her back, in several quarters. She has known this for some time past and, very naturally, she is unhappy about it. Am I, therefore, to blame for trying to help her mend matters?[44]

During his time in Cornwall Philip continued his efforts to set up a scheme for privately printing Lawrence's novel *The Rainbow*, which had recently been officially banned as obscene. A long letter to Viva Smith gave full details and attempted to enlist her support:

I am getting a circular printed . . . we suggest that the only resort is private publication by subscription. Those who agree with our attitude—and there must, after all, be a large number—must come together and form a nucleus— those who love the truth must support it. So we invite subscriptions for such books or musical works as would be either rejected by publishers or overlooked when thrown into the public trough along with the hogwash this country devours as literature and music. We shall have no capital—save perhaps a few pounds for the printing of our circulars. When enough subscriptions have been promised to pay the bare cost of publication, we shall print each book and send it to those who want it. Any profit that may be made will go to the author, or towards the printing of another book. But the object of the scheme is *not* money-making, but the mere desire that fine works should be accessible to those who desire them. . . . The first book will be a reprint of 'The Rainbow', unexpurgated, from the original MS. This, of course, cannot be publicly advertised or offered for sale in the booksellers' shops in this fair and righteous country, but for £120 an edition of 1,000 copies can be printed. The price will be 7/6, post free. Afterwards, will follow a sequel to 'The Rainbow' and a philosophical work 'Goats and Compasses' (a veritable soul-bomb, a dum-dum that will explode inside the soul!) by Lawrence, and a novel by Middleton Murry—This is preliminary announcement. Of course we shall discover new writers hitherto entirely submerged. Above all, there will be no committee—since committees are only the public on a small scale. The scheme is anonymous, an impersonal project for the propagation of fine, living works of art. Lawrence will select the books and I the music—but no names are associated with the scheme except mine, and that only of necessity, in my capacity as Secretary, since someone must receive the subscriptions and despatch the circulars and manage the actual affairs. If you can distribute some circulars, I will send over a consignment next week—say 50—you could easily discriminate 50 possible sympathisers. Attached to the circular is a form to be signed and sent to me at Cefn Bryntalch (the only stable address I have at present), by which the signer *undertakes* to subscribe for one or more of the works offered. No money need be sent until it is asked for, i.e. until enough promises have been received to enable us to start printing. . . . Do be interested and try and help—I see a rosy vision of a large house in London *full* of wonderful books and music, stacked up ceiling high, waiting to be despatched to enthusiasts all over the world![45]

The final prospectus read as follows:

THE RAINBOW BOOKS AND MUSIC

Either there exists a sufficient number of people to buy books because of their reverence for truth, or else books must die. In its books lies a nation's vision; and where there is no vision the people perish.

The present system of production depends entirely upon the popular esteem: and this means gradual degradation. Inevitably, more and more, the published books are dragged down to the level of the lowest reader.

It is monstrous that the herd should lord it over the uttered word. The swine has only to grunt disapprobation, and the very angels of heaven will be compelled to silence.

It is time that enough people of courage and passionate soul should rise up to form a nucleus of the living truth; since there must be those among us who care more for the truth than for any advantage.

For this purpose it is proposed to attempt to issue privately such books and musical works as are found living and clear in truth; such books as would either be rejected by the publisher, or else overlooked when flung into the trough before the public.

This method of private printing and circulation would also unseal those sources of truth and beauty which are now sterile in the heart, and real works would again be produced.

It is proposed to print first 'The Rainbow,' the novel by Mr D. H. Lawrence, which has been so unjustly suppressed. If sufficient money is forthcoming, a second book will be announced; either Mr Lawrence's philosophical work, 'Goats and Compasses', or a new book by some other writer.

All who wish to support the scheme should sign the accompanying form and send it at once to the Secretary,

PHILIP HESELTINE,
Cefn Bryntalch,
Abermule,
Montgomeryshire.

On receiving a copy, Delius immediately agreed to subscribe, encouraging his American neighbour, the writer Alden Brooks (b. 1883), to do so as well. But for some the tone of the prospectus was unpleasant. Lady Ottoline thought it odious: 'It makes me angry—I hate desdain [*sic*]—and contempt'.[46]

Now, to complicate an already volatile situation, on 2 February 1916 another guest arrived: Philip's pregnant girl-friend, Puma, who would stay for almost a month. Lawrence took an immediate liking to her and found her 'a quiet, quite nice little thing really, unobtrusive and affectionate. He [Philip] is fond of her, as a matter of fact, in spite of what he says.'[47] He was soon analysing and describing to Ottoline the dichotomy of Philip's love-life in typically Lawrentian terms:

About H[eseltine] and Mlle.[Baillot]—I tell him he ought to tell her. I suppose he will. It is queer. He declares he does not like this one, the Puma, but he does really. He declares he wants her to go. But he is really attached to her in the senses, in the unconsciousness, in the blood. He is always fighting away from this. But in doing so he is a fool. She is very nice and very real and simple and we like her. His affection for Mlle. is a desire for the light because he is in the dark. If he were in the light he would want the dark. He wants Mlle. for *companionship*, not for the blood connection, the dark, sensuous relation. With Puma he has this second, dark relation, but not the first. She is quite intelligent, in her way, but no mental consciousness; no white consciousness, if you understand, all intuition, in the dark, the consciousness of the senses. But she is quite fine and subtle in that way, quite, and I esteem her there *quite* as much as I esteem him.

Perhaps he is very split, and would always have the two things separate, the real blood connection, and the real conscious or spiritual connection, always separate. For these people I really believe in two wives. I don't see why there should be monogamy for people who can't have full satisfaction in one person, because they themselves are too split, because they act in themselves separately. Monogamy is for those who are whole and clear, all in one stroke. But for those whose stroke is broken into two different directions, then there should be two fulfilments.[48]

By now Lawrence was delving dangerously deeply into the psyche of his young guest. He had referred to Philip variously as 'empty, uncreated',[49] 'disintegrated'[50] and now, in a perceptively prophetic phrase, was suggesting him perhaps 'very split', though admittedly in his confused love-life rather than in his still unformed and still somewhat immature personality. He wrote to Lady Ottoline:

Heseltine is in a great state of (unjustly) hating the Puma, and looking on Mlle [Baillot] as a white star. He will swing from dark to light till he comes to rest. I believe if he stayed long enough with Mlle *exclusively*, he would hate her: but perhaps not. We can but let him oscillate violently. He is really very good and I depend on him and believe in him. But he is exasperating because he is always in such a state of mad *reaction against* things, all mad reactions. It is a terrible cyclonic state, but he will be worth having with us, oh, very much.[51]

At the end of February Philip, accompanied by Puma, returned to London to obtain medical exemption from military service and to further the promotion of the publishing scheme. He then hoped to be able to rejoin the Lawrences a 'free' man. There had been unfortunate repercussions with regard to the scheme. Lawrence's friends, Murry and the novelist Katherine Mansfield (1888–1923), who had been involved in the initial discussions, were angry when they discovered that Lawrence had allowed Philip to go ahead with these plans without first telling them. Frieda wrote in early March 1916: 'The Murry's wrote very indignant that Heseltine started about these Rainbow books without *them*, saying Lawrence was treacherous'.[52] Lawrence, however, quickly attempted to pour oil on the troubled waters, referring to Philip and his usefulness in a detached, almost impersonal way, though still without any suggestion of an impending rift. He had already written to Ottoline patronizingly describing Philip as 'one of those people who are born to be the conveyors of art: they are next to artists and they convey art to the world'.[53] He now tried to put Murry's and Mansfield's minds at rest:

Now don't get in a state, you two, about nothing. Heseltine was mad to begin it [the publishing scheme]—he wanted to get *The Rainbow* published. I felt, you don't know how much, sick and done. And it was rather fine that he believed and was so generously enthusiastic. He is the musical one: the musicians he likes are Delius, Goosens [*sic*], Arnold Bax, and some few others. I believe as a matter of fact they are good, and we are perhaps, outside ourselves, more likely to have good music and bad books, than otherwise.

. . . it is Heseltine's affair so far. I feel that he is one of those people who are transmitters, and not creators of art. And I don't think we are transmitters. I have come to the conclusion that I have no business genius. Heseltines family have just got that curious touch of artistic genius which will make them perfect dealers in art, I believe. His uncle had one of the best collections of pictures in England—Rembrandt Watteau etc—and he was a stockbroker and very rich. That is the style. Heseltine isn't rich. He has £150 a year of his own: his mother gives him something. He will have £600 a year or so when she dies. He is 21 yrs old, and I must say I am very glad to have him as a friend. He has lived here for seven weeks with us, so we know. Now don't think his friendship hurts ours. It doesn't touch you. You will like him too because he is real, and has some queer abstract passion which leaps into the future. He will be one with us. We must treasure and value very much any one who will *really* be added on to us. I am afraid he may be conscripted . . .

This is my declaration, now let it be enough. As for this publishing business, the whole of the work remains yet to be done. We will fight together when you come. Meanwhile let Heseltine take the vanguard.[54]

Lawrence's parting letter to the London-bound Philip was friendly and supportive. He sent him some literature from the No-Conscription League saying that while he was away he would curse the enemy: 'That is better than praying for you. . . . Come back soon, free. . . . I feel a new life, a new world ahead, for us—down towards Lands End there. We will be a centre of a new life, a centre of destruction of the old.'[55] But a fortnight later Philip had suddenly changed his mind and told Nichols that he would not be returning to Lawrence: 'He has no real sympathy. All he likes in one is the potential convert to his own reactionary creed. I believe firmly that he is a fine thinker and a consummate artist, but personal relation with him is almost impossible.'[56] As Nichols later recalled, Philip had dismissed Lawrence as 'quite the little Jesus Christ and, between you & me, at times a bloody bore determined to make me wholly his & as boring as he is'.[57] Unaware of Philip's real feelings, a concerned Lawrence was writing to various London friends, telling them to be 'nice to him. He is in a very overwrought and over-inflammable state.'[58]

What caused the sudden rift is not known and we can only speculate as to what might have happened. It may well have been that

Philip had sensed an attempt on Lawrence's part to manipulate him and Puma into a reconciliation or even marriage. It is also possible that, during a visit to Garsington, Ottoline showed him some of Lawrence's less than flattering letters. But when the rift came it was appropriately dramatic. Philip's letter has not survived, but Lawrence's cool and slightly pathetic reply gives a good idea of what its tone and content must have been:

Thank you for the Dionysos [sic, a drawing made by Lawrence for Lady Ottoline Morrell], which came this morning. By the same post came Frieda's letter to you, returned by Puma, with a note to the effect that we were both beneath contempt.

I forgot to ask you, when sending the Dionysos, if you would send also the MS of my philosophy. I should be glad if you would do this. Yesterday your hat turned up: I think it is the last thing I have to send you. My old hat that you took I do not want.

I shall be glad when I have that MS., and this affair is finished. It has become ludicrous and rather shameful. I only wish that you and Puma should not talk about us, for decency's sake. I assure you I shall have nothing to say of you and her. The whole business is so shamefully fit for a Koujoumdjian [sic] sketch.

Please send me the manuscript, and we will let the whole relation cease, and remove the indecency of it.⁵⁹

On 22 April Philip wrote to Delius telling him of the split:

The 'Rainbow' scheme fulfilled your prophecy and died the death. I got about 30 replies to 600 circulars. . . . My sojourn with Lawrence did me a lot of good, but not at all in the way I had anticipated. Lawrence is a fine artist and a hard, though horribly distorted, thinker. But personal relationship with him is impossible—he acts as a subtle and deadly poison. The affair by which I found him out is far too long to enter upon here. I will tell you about it one day, and we shall laugh together over it. The man must really be a bit mad, though his behaviour nearly landed me in a fearful fix—indeed, it was calculated to do so. However, when I wrote and denounced him to his face, all he could say was 'I request that you do not talk about me in London'—so he evidently had a very bad attack of guilty conscience.⁶⁰

But it may be that it was Philip who 'had a very bad attack of guilty conscience' for there is evidence that Lawrence had at some stage seen fit to confront Philip about his ungentlemanly treatment of Puma. As Murry wrote to Ottoline Morrell: 'Heseltine has been knocked into limbo. I can't quite gather what was the nature of his offence . . . He appears to have behaved like a blackguard to some woman or other (Puma is her name?) and Lawrence has rooted him out of his soul.'⁶¹ The break-up between Philip and Lawrence was in many ways prophetic of what was soon to happen between

Lawrence and Murry himself, for there are echoes of Philip's sentiments in a letter from Murry to Ottoline written in May 1916:

> . . . he [Lawrence] is really weakened by our being here, instead of gaining the
> strength he sought . . . Some where, he is gone all wrong. . . .
>   I neither agree with his ideas, nor am I stimulated by my opposition to
> them. In almost everything he consciously and deliberately says or does, I
> detect a taint of illness or hysteria . . .
>   . . . Other things have had their part—the war—and above all this cursed
> hybrid intellectualism that has warped his real and purely sensitive nature dur-
> ing the last year. . . . because I have loved him very much (I still do) . . . I
> know I shall desert him sooner, simply because he would kill me.[62]

Instead of returning the 'Goats and Compasses' manuscript as
requested, Philip sent Lawrence a collection of particularly cruel
'prophetic reviews' that he himself had written. One can easily imagine their effect on Lawrence, a sick man feeling abandoned by his
friends and still smarting from *The Rainbow* scandal and the accompanying bad press. Philip gleefully gave a full account to Delius:

> So I replied with a page of prophetic reviews of a future book 'D. H. Lawrence,
> a Critical Study by P. H.,' of which the 'Times' will say:—'Reveals the distorted
> soul of this unhappy genius in all its naked horror', and the 'Spectator' will gloat
> over 'A monster of obscenity tracked down to its secret lair'; 'John Bull' alliter-
> ates with 'Personified perversity pitilessly portrayed', while the 'Christian Herald'
> is 'grateful to the author for his scathing indictment of the immorality of the pre-
> sent generation—The book is a veritable sermon and should be in the hands of
> every Sunday school teacher', etc., etc. Lawrence was quite comically perturbed
> at the prospect of my 'revelations'. He has practically no friends left—The last
> one to drop off before me was an Armenian who published in the 'New Age'
> directly after the quarrel a most scathing and amusing satire on a 'brilliant
> young author, whose work was too good to be published' discovering his sub-
> conscious self in the middle of the night!![63]

Cecil Gray wrote about the incident years later:

> I do not know exactly what the immediate occasion of the rupture with
> Lawrence was . . . Philip was always reticent about the details, but from cer-
> tain remarks that he let drop on various occasions, and from what I know of
> Lawrence from personal experience, I have no doubt whatever that the latter
> had been attempting to interfere gratuitously, and to an unwarranted extent,
> in certain intimate matters concerning Philip's personal relations with other
> people . . .
>   The truth is that Lawrence was always inclined to treat his friends and
> acquaintances as if they were characters in one of his novels, and sought
> accordingly to mould their characters and direct their actions as he desired.
> When he failed in this—and he invariably did fail—he took his revenge by
> putting the said friends and acquaintances, recognizably, into his books, and
> there worked his will upon them.[64]

But Gray could hardly have been expected to be impartial in this matter having himself fallen out with Lawrence and been lampooned in the novel *Aaron's Rod*. The ill-fated 'Goats and Compasses' was in fact never published. Lady Ottoline Morrell was one of those who had read the manuscript but had found nothing good to say about it, dismissing it as 'deplorable tosh, a volume of words, reiteration, perverted and self-contradictory. A gospel of hate and violent individualism.'[65] Its fate is uncertain but Gray later claimed that there had been two copies and that Lawrence had destroyed one and Philip the other, using it contemptuously sheet by sheet as toilet-paper.

FRIENDSHIP WITH VAN DIEREN
(1916–1917)

PHILIP'S LIFE was about to take another new direction. He now returned to Chelsea, where he rented a small two-roomed flat at 14 Whitehead's Grove on the top floor of an old house surrounded by beautiful lime-trees just bursting into bud. He described it as very light and cheerful, 'discreet and pleasant, quite un-English or at least un-Londonish with its queer-shaped rooms, full of nooks and crannies and secret cupboards, its casement windows and innumerable, gorgeous cats'[1] who dined with him daily. It was scantily furnished with rows of books, two paintings by Adrian Allinson, a Tibetan devil, and a West African carving, features which Lawrence (having doubtless heard of them) would later incorporate into his description of Halliday's flat in *Women in Love*, where 'there were several negro statues, wood-carvings from West Africa, strange and disturbing'.[2]

At this time one of London's most popular meeting-places for artists, musicians, and writers was the Café Royal. Since its opening in 1865 it had been the haunt of people as famous and as diverse as Oscar Wilde, Whistler, Beardsley, Max Beerbohm, Bernard Shaw, and Aleister Crowley. In 1916 it was still furnished with red, plush seats and marble-topped tables, the floor covered with sawdust, the glitzy, gold decorations, the supporting caryatids, and 'shamelessly gilded walls, with their romanticized ornamentation that ran the gamut of French decorative art from Louis XIV to Louis Philippe'[3] reflected in the numerous, bevelled mirrors. As one of its regular clientele Philip had met many of the leading figures of the day including the painter Augustus John (1878–1961) and the sculptor Jacob Epstein (1880–1959). Years later both men were to write about Philip in their autobiographies. Augustus John's memories were of

a tall blond young man, usually accompanied by two or three young females bearing portfolios and scrolls . . . This young man's pale handsome face always wore a smile . . . and made one feel rather uncomfortable . . . He

displayed remarkable conversational powers and a fund of curious knowledge
. . . [his] delicate and vulnerable sensibility was carefully hidden under 'Peter
Warlock's' armoury, but it was impossible to remain unaware of the deeper
side of this man's nature, try as he might to dissimulate it under a show of
uproarious wit and effrontery.[4]

If Philip's ribaldry and violence of language could be at time disconcert-
ing—Socialism and the problems of over-population particularly inciting him
to the most lurid invective—this and his sense of the comic which was both
colossal and elaborate could not by any means conceal the fundamentally
romantic nature which was his. . . . I was often struck . . . by his emotional
response to the changing beauties of nature; and . . . his unceasing intellectual
alertness was to me a source of continual admiration.[5]

Robert Nichols later recalled that John had once told him that
Philip was one of the best talkers in England: 'Their conversation
must have been both incisive and deep: John's moody, penetrating,
sporadic & trenchant, Philip's discursive & analytic'.[6] According to
Eric Fenby (b. 1906), Delius's amanuensis, Delius was critical of the
powerful influence he felt Augustus John had over Philip. Years
later, in an interview, Fenby also remarked that 'Philip got mixed
up with models of John. There were all sorts of scenes and love-
affairs.'[7] Epstein, unlike John, was far less complementary, describing Philip as a restless and discontented character: 'His mentality
was . . . warped by a very crude and childish streak, and practical
jokes of a stupid sort satisfied him.'[8] This description, however, may
have been somewhat biased, for Philip and Epstein evidently had a
violent quarrel some years later.

It was in the Café Royal that Philip met a young Scottish composer, Cecil Gray (1895–1951), who had recently settled in London.
Gray came from a wealthy background, his father's family having
owned an iron foundry, and, like Philip, he was a product of the
Establishment. After an unhappy time at school, he had spent a
year at Edinburgh University studying History and French before
eventually persuading his parents to let him pursue his increasing
interest in music at the Midland Institute in Birmingham.
Disillusioned by the 'anarchical methods and outlook'[9] at the
Institute, he lasted there for only one term and then got his parents
to agree to let him move to London. He installed himself in a flat in
Cheyne Walk, where, living the life a virtual recluse on his private
income, he spent 'several months composing, writing, reading, and
trying—unsuccessfully—to learn to play the piano'.[10] A painter
friend finally introduced him to a wider circle of friends and to the
Café Royal, where he met a number of important people. In his

memoir Gray describes his first meeting with Philip: 'a young man of striking appearance and an indefinable charm of manner and bearing' came up to his table, 'tall, slender, pale, with bright blue eyes and longish fair hair, dressed in a neat black suit, soft black hat, and orange-coloured shirt'.[11] Gray became one of Philip's close friends and soon they were sharing in 'a queer barn-like studio' in Battersea with Old Mog,[12] a large black cat (which 'shared with its master a veritable passion for the music of Delius')[13] and generally living 'an enjoyably uninhibited bohemian existence.[14]

In a BBC radio broadcast in 1964, Elizabeth Poston (1905–87) was critical of their friendship and particularly of Gray's memoir of Philip. Somewhat caustically she referred to Gray as 'the unhappy satellite of a planet about whom he revolved pointlessly, obsessed, until in later years that orbit failed him and he faded out. . . . the friendship that started as an undergraduate link was not of a kind to mature.'[15] Although not part of the immediate narrative, this would seem an appropriate moment to refer to the rumours that at some stage Philip had an affair with the youthful Elizabeth Poston, rumours which seem to have originated from Miss Poston herself. To date, no letters nor, indeed, any other evidence, have come to light, though it might be significant that she left instructions that, after her death, a packet, presumably of letters and papers, was to be burnt. However, until some positive proof can be presented, the importance of the rumoured relationship should be viewed with a certain degree of scepticism and regarded as a purely platonic one, although there were certainly signs of an almost adolescent infatuation on Miss Poston's part. In the meantime, her role in the Warlock story will long be remembered on account of the fact that, having acquired Philip's letters to Delius at a Sotheby's auction in 1967, she then refused anyone access to them. Warlock scholars had to wait until 1993, six years after her death, before they eventually resurfaced, happily in the British Library.

Once settled in their new lodgings, Philip and Gray enthusiastically began planning a number of grandiose schemes by which to bring about a 'regeneration of music in England', which included the launching of a musical journal and a subscription scheme for cutting modern works for pianola. They also hoped to secure a large studio where weekly free concerts of all the best contemporary music would be given and where new works by aspiring young composers could be auditioned. There would also be very simple and non-technical lectures on music, 'addressed to those who have been gulled by financially-interested pedants into believing that music is an esoteric mystery which they cannot hope to understand without invoking the aid (*and* paying exorbitant fees) of the said pedants'. Finally, each year they would publish an anthology of songs or short pieces, 'representative of the real tendencies of *to-day*, by young composers who have never before appeared in print'.[16]

At about this time Epstein introduced Philip and Gray to the Dutch composer Bernard van Dieren (1887–1936), a largely self-taught, enigmatic composer who had emigrated to London in 1909 with his wife, the pianist Frida Kindler. Although influenced to a certain extent by Schoenberg and Alban Berg, van Dieren had evolved his own highly personal style characterized by contrapuntal complexity and a very individual harmony. In describing his music, Philip was later to write that van Dieren, 'having progressed further than any of his contemporaries . . . has been able to disentangle all the component strands of the modern harmonic complex, and . . . to weave them together into a clear filigree tissue. Melody emerges from the harmonic welter with added richness and still fairer potentialities.'[17] Van Dieren himself admitted that his music was not all that easily accessible to listeners, 'rather it is music that waits proudly as might some aristocrat until our mood is attuned to it'.[18] From all accounts he was a quite remarkable character. Sir Arthur Bliss thought him to be 'the most potent personality' he had ever met: 'He was a man of artistic perfection and remarkable will-power. . . . There was something complete about him . . . so that one felt humble in his presence. He could talk glowingly and creatively on every subject that fired him.'[19] Cecil Gray went even further, calling him a modern Leonardo and adding that

apart from his gifts as a composer he was a talented writer not merely on musical subjects but on all branches of art . . . an amazing linguist, speaking, thinking, and writing with consummate ease in English, French, German, and Dutch, and able to read fluently in Italian, Spanish, Portuguese, and Danish; a trained scientist, acquainted more than superficially with almost all branches of the vast subject, from chemistry to higher mathematics, and with an expert knowledge of medicine; a master of many and varied crafts, ranging from carpentry and bookbinding to rifle and revolver shooting; a learned bibliophile, a connoisseur of food and wine.[20]

Yet there were those like Herbert Howells (1892–1983) who were, frankly, sceptical and who considered van Dieren to be 'not a composer at all, it was all make believe, and the Oxford Press took him up and gave him a sort of smear of respectability'.[21]

Debilitated by a persistent kidney ailment, van Dieren had many major operations and was often forced to remain in bed for long periods and was thus seldom seen about in London. He remained such a shadowy figure that Vaughan Williams is reputed to have asked whether 'van Dieren' was 'another of Heseltine's warlockian tricks along the lines of the resurrection of Prosdocimus de Beldamandis!'[22] The friendship that ensued between Philip and van Dieren was to last for the rest of Philip's life and was to have an enormous influence on both him and his music. Philip's composer friend, C. W. Orr (1893–1976), even went so far as to remark that he suspected that many of Philip's opinions were little more than echoes of the older musician's pronouncements.

The afternoon after their first meeting, Philip and Gray visited van Dieren in his Hampstead home where he played them some of his compositions, the first they had heard. The impact of this new music, with its complex polyphony and individualistic harmony, proved a shattering experience. Quite bowled over by the meeting and the music, both men wrote independently to van Dieren soon afterwards. Philip's letter of 8 June marks the beginning of the second important musical influence in his life—an influence which was to propel his musical and creative energies for the next fourteen years and to eclipse to a large degree the previous influence of Delius:

I was so utterly overwhelmed by your music this afternoon, that all words failed me . . . And so I feel I have to write and tell you—inarticulately enough—what a profound impression my visit to you has made upon me. It has brought me to a turning point, opened out a vista of a new world; it has brought to a climax the dissatisfaction and spiritual unrest that have been tormenting me for months past, in the last few days more acutely than ever. . . .

Your music—(those fragments of the Shakespeare Sonnets and the Symphony that you played today)—is nothing short of a revelation to me. I have been groping about aimlessly in the dark for so long, with ever growing exasperation—and at last you have shown a light, alone among composers whom I have met; for neither Delius nor any other has even so much as suggested a practical solution of the initial difficulties of musical composition . . .

Is it too much to hope that, even without the establishment of a new conservatorium, you may set some of the younger generation in this country upon the right path? It always seems incongruous that a mature composer should be expected to spend his time instructing any but a chosen few of quite exceptional promise—but in England there is no teacher to whom we can look with any respect, and our need for such a one is greater than ever it has been in the past.[23]

An elated Philip quickly wrote to tell Taylor of his discovery of a composer of works even more 'advanced' than those of Schönberg, but 'at the same time of an amazing new beauty and strangeness that makes an instant appeal, almost reducing one to tears of joy'.[24] His account has something of an air of secrecy about it, almost as if, right from the outset, he wished to build a certain mystique around van Dieren, the 'Master', as he dubbed him. Thus inspired, Philip now considered himself called to bring about a revolutionary change in English musical life, which he felt was in a hopeless state on account of what he believed to be a fundamental and almost ineradicable lack of taste and discrimination in the British public. At the bottom of it all, he claimed, was the music profession, 'the greatest enemy of music', a phrase borrowed from the writings of the seventeenth-century English composer, Robert Jones. Both Gray and Philip jumped at the opportunity of being able to involve a man like van Dieren in their plans to remedy this 'colossal disorder' and to further the cause of contemporary music. Their first move was to commission him to write an opera. Robert Nichols was pressed into producing a libretto in a fortnight. Van Dieren immediately began work on the opera, *The Tailor*, and by 1917 had already produced a sketch of the piece.

Philip, completely under van Dieren's charismatic spell, had now found a new object for his obsessive, almost schoolboy-like, hero-worship, his search for a father figure. He was beginning to feel the need to break free from Delius's influence in his own compositions and van Dieren seemed in every way to be the perfect replacement. Here was a self-taught man who had not come out of the usual Establishment system and whose feelings about modern music corresponded closely with his own. Moreover, unlike Delius who lived in France, van Dieren was close at hand and was prepared to give him some lessons, the only tuition in composition that he would ever have.

Filled with enthusiasm and energy, he and Gray were determined not to let the grass grow under their feet. Two months later they were planning both publication and performances of van Dieren's music, Nichols being one of those approached for a contribution towards the publication of his First Symphony (Op. 6), the so-called 'Chinese' Symphony. Optimistically, but not very realistically, they also hoped to see van Dieren appointed conductor at the next Beecham season of opera, as well as at some orchestral concerts. Although Gray was unable to persuade the trustees of his own income to part with any money for the proposed opera season, they eventually agreed to give him enough to sponsor a concert of van Dieren's music in the Wigmore Hall on 20 February 1917, at which the composer would conduct his *Overture* and *Diaphony*, music described by Philip as 'epoch-making'. The programme notes were to be written by Gray, while Philip would produce the advance publicity in the form of a manifesto to appear under the pseudonym Prosdocimus de Beldamandis. Gray criticized it as 'somewhat aggressive and pontifical' and copies of this 'mysterious and sensational' leaflet were sent to every artistic and social notability they could think of, even including fashionable society beauties. It contained an extravagant paragraph which ran

without hastily acclaiming Bernard van Dieren as 'the great leader' . . . I think I am justified in saying, after a thorough study of his work, that he is the only contemporary composer to whom Dr Walford Davies' words 'the counterpoint of Palestrina, the harmony and counterpoint of Bach, the harmony and form of Beethoven await their consummation. Towards this musicians work while their expectation is set upon another great leader. If we may judge from the past he will not be fully understood when he comes, *and he will certainly be a great master of counterpoint*' could reasonably be applied.[25]

If Philip's manifesto was 'aggressive' and 'sensational', it was mild compared to Gray's programme notes which, as Philip correctly predicted, proved a veritable 'bomb'. Instead of modestly introducing van Dieren as an interesting new composer worthy of attention, Gray pronounced him a genius, at the same time ill-advisedly attacking established composers:

It is equally evident that he [van Dieren] has no connection with the neo-classicist schools of Franck or Reger, or with pure reactionaries such as Brahms, who are content to go on repeating what has already been said much better by the great masters. Such mechanical imitations, though psychologically interesting, are of no greater significance than the artistic efforts of the anthropoid ape known as the Unko or Hybolates Rafflesii, who has been heard to sing chromatic scales and melodies with perfect intonation and great intensity of feeling. . . .

After the debauch of romanticism in the last century, the music comes like a cool clear draught of water. It is good to be sober after so long a while— nearly a hundred years—even if it is only to enjoy getting drunk again.[26]

In short, the notes contained 'matter so ludicrous as to offend even the well disposed. The war, his [van Dieren's] foreign origins and unknown status . . . all mitigated against him; moreover, Heseltine had enemies, anxious to denigrate any of his activities. From then on van Dieren was something of a marked man.'[27] Gray, in fact, seemed almost to delight in the fact that the concert caused a considerable stir in London musical circles: 'Seldom had critical and enlightened opinion achieved a more impressive unanimity than on that occasion. Practically without exception the representative leaders of musical opinion of every tendency and persuasion, from extreme left to extreme right, burst out into a solemn howl of execration.'[28] The critic of the *Daily Telegraph* condemned both manifesto and programme notes as being misjudged:

Bernard van Dieren . . . is somewhat unfortunate in possessing friends who have made him the victim of the puff preliminary. A foreword to the programme implied that in his music the evidence would find the consummation of the art of Palestrina, Bach and Beethoven; and in later and more definite statements this music was made a theme for indiscriminate eulogies, in which it was apparently raised above that of Strauss, Debussy, Schoenberg, Stravinsky, and Irving Berlin.[29]

The critic of *The Times* launched into attack:

As Schönberg was the harmonic crank, so Mr van Dieren is the contrapuntal . . . just as Schönberg does not trouble about counterpoint, so Mr van Dieren accepts any harmony. A good many of the chords are quite intelligible in themselves, but in their context they make to our uninitiated ears nonsense . . . A voice, Mr George McDonald's,[30] sang, at intervals in the hour and 10 minutes of the 'Diaphony', two and a half sonnets of Shakespeare . . . His voice rose and fell at the proper declamatory moments, and he must be complimented on the skill with which he found what we must assume to have been the right notes . . . that is all that could be made of a first hearing; it is improbable that many of those in the room would wish for a second.[31]

The review which appeared in the *Musical Times* was equally uncomplimentary:

We have to confess that we were so dazed by the new music that we cannot pretend to offer a criticism. The 'Diaphony' went on without a pause or a cadence for nearly an hour, and to such beginners as ourselves it seemed that the players again and again missed their entries, but we are assured that this was not so. Now and then the voice emerged weirdly with the Sonnets. . . . The Overture, too, was very long, and although somewhat more intelligible than the 'Diaphony', was puzzling and dull . . . Perhaps some experience of van Dieren's earlier efforts . . . might lead us on, but at present we are unconverted and inclined to blaspheme.[32]

The fact that all the London critics condemned the concert outright, and that the takings amounted to a mere £5 compared with the expenses of £110, sounded the death knell of the second concert planned for April. In a perceptive article on van Dieren, Heseltine, and Gray, Hywel Davies suggests that, as a result of this concert,

any chance that van Dieren had of being widely accepted by the musical public was now gone, Gray and Heseltine having provided those who wanted to ignore him with good reasons for doing so. Their good intentions had backfired and simply turned van Dieren into something of a novelty and little more than a diversion from the war.[33]

Philip replied to his critics in the March edition of *The Palatine Review*, hitting back with well-chosen, cutting phrases, such as 'mediocrity instinctively recognises genius as its worst enemy'. Bitter and cynical comments such as these no doubt aroused further hostility and alienation among the London musical fraternity and Philip's growing number of enemies:

When the van Dieren concert was given, not one critic in London had ever heard a note of the composer's music: yet; although all were given a fortnight's notice of the impending concert, not one asked for any information about him beforehand, or manifested the slightest interest in his work. One who was specially invited to come and hear some of it any day he liked was unable to undertake the quarter-mile walk which this visit would have involved. During the concert, two groups of critics gibbered and giggled so incessantly, that neither they nor their immediate neighbours could properly hear the music; and scarcely one reporter stayed for the second item on the programme . . . the gossip column of a penny illustrated was honest in expressing concisely what all wrote in periphrasis—that the music was 'all futurist and funny'.[34]

Besides the meeting with van Dieren, another highly significant even took place in 1916. In November an article by Philip on Eugene Goossens's chamber music was published in a journal, *The Music Student*,[35] and for the first time he used the pseudonym 'Peter Warlock', telling Goossens that 'for very important reasons'[36] it was necessary to conceal his true identity from the editor, Walter Wilson Cobbett (1847–1937), an enthusiastic musical amateur and concert promoter. Philip obviously did not care much for Cobbett, referring disparagingly to him in an article in *New Age* in June 1917 as 'Mr Cobbett, with his galaxy of mediocrities'.[37] The reason for his choice of this particular pseudonym is not known. He once told the prominent ballet critic and bookseller Cyril Beaumont (1891–1976) that he had found it on a 'sampler' in the window of an antique dealer's.[38] Bearing in mind all its various associations, the choice was highly significant. 'Warlock' comes from the Old English *waerloga* and the Middle English *warloghe* and *warlach*, meaning one who breaks faith, a scoundrel, the Devil; synonyms include conjurer, demon, enchanter, magician, magus, necromancer, sorcerer, witch, and wizard. Copley has pointed out that this dictionary definition might later have had some significance for Philip, particularly in the choice of a woodcut of a 'Magus' on the title-pages of the early songs published by Winthrop Rogers.[39] One must also remember that this

was a time when the influence of the notorious occultist Aleister
Crowley (1875–1947) was being felt and a considerable amount of
interest was being shown in black magic and the occult. Although it
would be some time before Philip would embark on a serious study
of such things, his subconscious would seem to be leading him in
that direction.

Throughout his life Philip was fascinated by curious, humorous-
sounding names, many of which he used as alternative pseudonyms
in his writings, and in the British Library one of his notebooks contains a list of highly improbable names assembled at some time or
another.[40] He signed some of his early manuscripts Huanebango Z.
Palimpsest or Prosdocimus de Beldamandis; later articles were variously signed A. Whyte Westcott (a white waistcoat), Apparatus
Criticus, Jerry Cinimbo, Obricus Scacabarozus, Bagwaller, Q. Yew,
and Barbara C. Larent (a play on *Barbara Celarent*, the mnemonic
for classical formal logic syllogisms). Some of his later controversial
letters to the *Musical Times* were signed Mortimer Cattley and
Cambrensis (a Welshman), while Rab Noolas was a popular one in
more light-hearted writings. The story goes that Philip was sitting in
a pub one day when he suddenly noticed an intriguing name, RAB
NOOLAS, written on the smoked glass. It was, of course, SALOON BAR
viewed backwards.[41] He even once suggested that Taylor might consider using the pseudonym, Roger A. Ramsbottom, a play on the
letters RAM (the Royal Academy of Music), full of *double entendre*.
Philip himself, in fact, later used this very pseudonym as the signature to the highly entertaining preface to a series of largely unprintable verses.[42] Also among Philip's papers are to be found numerous,
strange jottings containing some extremely lewd verses and names.
There is, for example, a list of 'composers with fantastic names':
Asola, Johannes Bacfart, Johann Fux, Andreas Crappius, Giuseppe
Maria Po, Scheidt, Schytte, Nicolas Ponce, Bermann Pys, John
Blockley, Philip G. Clapp, and Antoine Pierre Piis.[43]

A letter written to Nichols in September 1916 also saw the
appearance of one of Philip's first recorded limericks on a composer.
It was a form that he would perfect and employ on many future
occasions:

> Gesualdo, the Prince of Venosa,
> Was a great and astounding composer.
>   But as soon as I hinted
>   His works should be printed
> My friends said, with emphasis, 'No, Sir!'[44]

In this same letter he told Nichols of his forthcoming plans 'to start on the very big task of collecting and printing the works of the old English virginal composers—astounding fellows'. Besides this and all his activity on behalf of van Dieren's music, Philip had continued composing in a desultory way. In the winter of 1915 he had set three Yeats poems, one of which was later to become part of *The Curlew* song-cycle, and had sent them to Delius for comment. Delius sent an encouraging reply, stating that this particular song, 'O curlew, cry no more in the air', was his favourite of the three, though he noted that there were beautiful things in all of them: 'Keep pegging away at your work . . . send me all you compose—I will, if you like, send you back a comment on the things I do not like.'[45]

Philip was now busy with another scheme, this time to hire a small theatre to present a four weeks' season of opera and concerts, 'with a definite artistic policy and no compromise with the mob'. As their first offering he and Gray somewhat ambitiously intended to present Delius's *A Village Romeo and Juliet* without scenery, 'possibly a suggestive back-cloth or two—nothing more—Costumes of extreme simplicity. . . . The interest must be centred entirely in the play and the music; and as regards the setting, *the imagination of the spectators must take an active part.*'[46] This was just a start. Eventually they hoped to include other neglected masterpieces such as Monteverdi's *Orfeo*, Purcell's *Dido and Aeneas*, Pergolesi's *La Serva Padrona*, Mozart's *Der Schauspieldirektor*, and Gluck's *Orfeo*. He wrote to Goossens as well, attempting to enlist his support and giving more details of the scheme, some of which were decidedly eccentric. There would be 'no "stars" but everyone efficient in an unostentatious way. *No vibrato singers*! You *must* help us: there are many more points (such as the robing of the orchestra in black cassocks with hoods, by which a very disturbing illusion-spoiling element will be eliminated) but these must wait for explanation till we meet.'[47]

When he was informed of this scheme, Delius was caught entirely off guard. He had always tried to encourage Philip's enthusiasm, which he had found refreshing, but now he could not conceal his apprehension at the idea, particularly as the intention was to perform the opera with accompaniment on two pianos:

To tell you the truth I have no desire to have any more of my dramatic works given in England for some years—*There is no public*—mark my words—Even if there were—I dont think that anything ought to be undertaken before the

war is over & the people have calmed down a bit. . . . *Wait a bit*—prepare—
gather works—look out for singers & teach them to act & then open up a
small theatre a highly artistic & original repertoire—you may form gradually a
public . . . Why not begin by a series of concerts in a small hall with a small
orchestra—giving only rare & excellent works—Some of which you have
named . . . When you start your Scheme you must absolutely make it a success or it will again fizzle into nothing like all artistic attempts in London—
including Beecham's & that makes the public more & more sceptical—Practise
conducting—if possible, take an engagement at any theatre simply to get a
little routine—even if you have to conduct musical comedy.[48]

Although Delius was highly intrigued by Philip's reports of van
Dieren as 'a man of miraculous genius', the notion that Philip and
Gray might actually go ahead with their operatic scheme began to
give him cause for a great deal of anxiety. A few weeks later he
wrote more forcefully, actively discouraging if not actually forbidding the staging of his opera:

Don't you see, dear Phil, that you are all going towards disaster with the best
intentions possible . . . With no experience whatever you are going to undertake one [of] the most difficult of tasks & you want to begin at once with one
of the most difficult works . . . It would be better & less harmful for the future
of art in England not to begin this undertaking than to do it badly & fail.[49]

When asked for his opinion of this ambitious scheme, Balfour
Gardiner, too, was mainly negative, as well he might be, given his
own unhappy experiences in promoting concerts in London. He told
Philip quite plainly: 'You had better—or rather, may just as well,
work out your own—damnation.'[50] When Delius finally wrote to say
that he did 'not want the *Village Romeo* to be given again except
under the best and most favourable auspices',[51] Philip eventually got
the message and the scheme was abandoned. Gray's trustees were at
any rate insisting that the whole thing be postponed until after the
war, which, given Philip and Gray's lack of experience and the likelihood of the project succeeding, was probably just as well.

In the meantime, Philip's personal life had become even more
complicated. Although his girlfriend Puma had given birth to their
son on 3 July, Philip took no interest in the boy, showing a contempt for children which was common among followers of Nietzsche
during that period (Albert Einstein, Wyndham Lewis, and Ezra
Pound had all given children away). It seems that Puma handed
over the baby to either her relatives or friends very soon after it was
born and had little, if any, contact with him from then on, though
she did make provision for him in her will of 1934. To begin with,
the baby was called Peter, though he was soon named Nigel, for rea-

sons which have not as yet been satisfactorily explained. Resuming correspondence with his former girlfriend Viva Smith in May 1917 Philip made brief mention of his ten-month-old son:

Do write and tell me about yourself . . . Shall you still keep dogs when you come back—or would you like my Peter for a present—with his private income and a' and a'? I believe he has been lent to somebody, but I have had no particulars of him since his dear mamma tried to blackmail me—without success, I am glad to say! But, really, one shouldn't have dealings with vampires at all![52]

It seems that for Philip women were often synonymous with vampires. Writing to Gray in August 1918 about the fact that Hilda Doolittle, with whom Gray had had an affair, was four months pregnant with Gray's child, he included the following warning little verse:

> *Then* you will know whom you must choke
> Before they get beyond a joke.
> To love a flower, a bird, a beast,
> Is to enjoy a spiritual feast.
> But do not keep a vampire bat,
> For love of Nature, in your hat,
> Nor take the accompanying sensation
> Of loss of blood for inspiration.
> I tell you this because I knew
> A wretched man it happened to.[53]

Yet, despite all his reservations and misgivings, Philip married Puma in the Chelsea Register Office on 22 December 1916. They were both only 22 years of age at the time. The marriage seemed doomed from the start. By April the next year Philip was writing to a friend he had bumped into, Phyl Crocker, about the marriage and of Puma as his 'nightmare'. Philip had fallen in love with Phyl, a Cornish doctor's daughter, during his stay in Cornwall. He later introduced her to Boris de Chrustchoff and was shattered when the latter had an affair with her and eventually married her. Some six years later Philip took crude revenge and, when both men were drunk, and despite his problems as regards urinating in public, emptied his bladder over the unconscious Boris. Phyl Crocker later left de Chrustchoff and committed suicide in 1929.[54] The despair, tortured emotion, and dark, Lawrentian symbolism shows Philip's highly troubled state of mind at the time:

I do not (and you do not) want to spend life with dead things, with ghastly, animated puppets, hopping about on a dark stage in artificial light. God, but how few *living* things one meets with! Everywhere, everything is dead, or merged with the forms of death, of destruction and darkness. Only live long enough in a tomb, with corpses and the stink of corruption, and you'll think *that* and that alone is life. The sun and the sea and open country will seem nothing at all. I have spent too much precious time already in a coffin, wallowing in death and corruption—in London which is *the* charnel-house par excellence. . . . I am intensely intrigued by the strange fact and occasion of our meeting . . . Strange—and then, to crown all this strangeness, you must needs meet with my principle [*sic*] nightmare—the nightmare which, while one sleeps, seems the most terrifying and when one wakes, actually *is* the most ridiculous of all! I have some idea of the impression of me which this nightmare would give you—but I am no doubt represented as more incredibly monstrous than any monster my own poor imagination could devise. If I am a monster, I would rather be hated for the monster I am than for the monster I am said to be—even if the former proves *more* monstrous than the latter! So that if one is an alligator, and a good (that is, from a human point of view, an objectionable) alligator, it is better to be known as an alligator rather than as an uncomfortable kind of griffin . . . In the Café Royal, which is the very vortex of the cesspool of corruption, you have heard something of me from the intelligent being who seems so proud to boast herself the wife of a monster. Now: are you satisfied with the witness of the darkness? If so, read no more. If you are not satisfied, convinced beyond possibility of doubt, read no more: it is enough. If not listen. It won't hurt you to hear—The purely animal relation— the relation of darkness, which is the only possible relation for some people, most people—is not only disappointing and unsatisfactory in itself, but leaves behind it a long procession of phantoms which one must either destroy or be destroyed by. This is inevitable, whether the relation is 'licensed' by marriage or not: it is all the same: institutions like marriage have *nothing whatever* to do with human relationships of any kind: they are *merely* external, superficial, unnecessary and, in *reality*, NOTHING at all, just nothing. In my own case I was insane enough (being a child of darkness) to let the phantoms I had raised devour me for a while, giving them—in the name of sentimentality, Christian morality and God knows what other superstition of darkness, concession after concession to feed upon. Finally, getting tired of being devoured, I was fool enough to make a pact with them to trouble me no more (instead of slaying them as I should have done), making a last concession—which cost me least of all—and fondly imagining they would keep their part of the bargain. This, of course, was supreme imbecility, to imagine that one can make pacts with the powers of darkness to one's own advantage!—But to be more direct: I have always looked on the institution of marriage as *the* supreme blasphemy—What have rude, official, or ecclesiastical, hands to do, meddling with the most subtle and wonderful of human relationships! The whole idea is filthy—and I, for my part, would never permit the paws of officialdom to mess about with *any* relation that really existed between me and any human being. So, when I was badgered by our mutual friend (with whom I had never had and could never have had any but a purely bestial relation) to make her a final present of forty shillings worth of respectability in a 'certificate of marriage', I made no objection, seeing that the ceremonial meant no more for me than to make a mock of what was already a mockery. Voilà tout! Such things are of less importance than a bruised shin-bone to anyone who is alive, unconditionally alive, to any-one who has the faintest glimmering consciousness of what a real human rela-tionship may be—These dead institutions and dead ceremonials—the sham flowers in a glass case on a grave—belong to the dead—or to the stage world of puppets. What have the living to do with them? What can the living do but laugh at them? Let us go out into the sun and laugh them out of their lives: on the moors under the sun they simply don't exist. I am a vagabond, not a domestic animal—What are you?—Now: this is the case as revealed in the wind and the sun. Do you like it better than the hot-air version of smoke and darkness—or not so well? Which? Don't reason: feel. Reason is nearly always wrong. But now if you hate me, you really hate *me*, not my shadow—And this is well. I am an alligator, not an uncomfortable griffin![55]

Philip seems to have shown nothing but contempt for Puma, hav-ing also written a poem about an animal with the same name in a collection of ribald rhymes entitled 'Unnatural History, Porno-graphic Poetry for the Private Perusal of Pure-minded Persons', which probably dates from about this period:

> You've heard of the promiscuous puma,
> She is of a most generous humour,
> She can't say no to anyone,
> Or rob a stranger of his fun.
> Because of this sad moral lack
> She spends her lifetime on her back;
> But, as she says, what one can use
> It seems so wasteful to refuse![56]

Despite the invective he directed at Puma, Philip seemed unable, or indeed unwilling, to make a complete break with her. Her name continues to appear in ambivalent references in his correspondence over the succeeding years. His troubled relations with both Puma and his mother would seem to indicate an immaturity in his dealings with women, particularly those with whom he sensed any kind of emotional tie or responsibility. Whenever he writes about either his mother or Puma there is often a paranoid quality, of guilt mixed with claustrophobia. His attitude to women seems, from all accounts, to have been chauvinistic in the extreme, unashamedly using them as it suited him. Jack Lindsay related how Philip vio-lently once denounced his preface to his versions of Sappho, accus-ing him of being a masochist, 'concerned with what women felt in bed'[57] instead of being interested in his own satisfactions. Eric Fenby in later reminiscences commented significantly on Philip's attitude to women, stating that he didn't think he cared 'that much [snapping fingers] about women really. He was using them—and the more the merrier. And some of them were very coarse. Oh, he was hopeless in that way! As soon as a pretty girl appeared, he was finished.'[58] Gray too made the interesting comment that, 'despite his innumerable love affairs', he doubted whether Philip 'was ever, ultimately, in love with any woman in his life' and that he treated women 'with complete cynicism . . . as rather inferior human beings'.[59] When Gray was busy writing his memoir on Philip, Nichols wrote a highly significant letter to him in which he remarked that he would like

to see Phil . . . drawn absolutely plain as he was, girls & all. But I guess that's impossible at present. It's a pity—because girls good, indifferent, & downright lousy were such large ingredients in his life & the interplay of their influences so largely determined his fate. . . . I feel he can't be understood if the girls are indicated only in the most shadowy way.[60]

By early April 1917, thoroughly disenchanted with life in what he described as the 'cesspool' of London, Philip had decided to return to Cornwall. Having been attracted by its Celtic associations during his earlier visit, it seems as if it was his intention to remain there for a while to rewrite the first sketches of the Delius biography he had been planning for some time and also to regain his peace of mind. He told Viva Smith that he had been on the verge of a complete collapse,

various forces, seen and unseen, material and psychological, combined with circumstances to bring a crisis—(a spiritual crisis not dependent on *facts*)—that there was no evading. . . . And so, just in time, I managed to get out of the mud which had almost swallowed me up, *just* managed to evade the whirlpool of sheer madness which had almost sucked me down—and then came here.[61]

He installed himself in a little wooden bungalow on a high ridge about two miles from Zennor on the way to Penzance near the small two-roomed cottage where the Lawrences had been living since the middle of March. Even though Philip's return certainly did not please Lawrence, he was still curious enough to ask for news of him and his doings in some of his letters to his friends. Once settled in at 'The Tinners Arms', an elated and refreshed Philip wrote enthusiastically to Nichols suggesting that he join him there:

Let us cut adrift and start anew! This stupendous spring is going to blow my head clean off, I am sure, and I shall have to go chasing it over the moors like a bit of dandelion fluff, from one sea to the other! Come and hold it on for me, do! It would be so good if you were here. The world has been reborn at Easter—everything is new and wonderful! . . . Let us have done with the past, once and for all. Oh, this spring! My head is dancing all day long.[62]

Outwardly at least, Philip attempted to resume cordial relations with the Lawrences, but for Lawrence the friendship was definitely over: 'I don't like him any more. It can't come back, the liking.'[63] What Philip did not know was that Lawrence was even then busy finishing *Women in Love*, in which he and Puma were being introduced as two rather unattractive minor characters, Halliday and Pussum. Gray, having read the manuscript, alerted Philip to the fact and, although angered, Philip did nothing at the time. Unflattering though the relevant passages may be, it is worth looking at them since they cast some interesting light on what Lawrence had perceived in the unhappy relationship between Philip and the pregnant Puma in early 1916. The following extracts cannot of course be regarded as a completely accurate reflection of what had actually happened that January, but they do appear to have a certain significance. In chapter 6, 'Crème de Menthe', Lawrence describes Halliday entering the Pompadour Café (a thinly disguised Café Royal) as 'a pale, full-built young man with rather long, solid fair hair hanging from under his black hat . . . with a smile at once naive and warm, and vapid',[64] and in the same chapter Lawrence gives a quite sensuous description of Puma as

a girl with dark, soft, fluffy hair cut short in the artist fashion, hanging level and full almost like the Egyptian princes's. She was small and delicately made, with warm colouring and large, dark, hostile eyes. There was a delicacy, almost a beauty in all her form, and at the same time a certain attractive grossness of spirit . . . Her appearance was simple and complete, really beautiful, because of her regularity and form, her soft dark hair falling full and level on either side of her head, her straight, small, softened features, Egyptian in the slight fullness of their curves, her slender neck, and the simple, rich-coloured smock hanging on her slender shoulders . . .[65]

Pussum proceeds to tell the assembled company about her relationship with Halliday:

'He made me go and live with him, and now he wants to throw me over. And yet he won't let me go to anybody else. He wants me to live hidden in the country. And then he says I persecute him, that he can't get rid of me. . . .'
. . . Gerald looked at Halliday for some moments, watching the soft, rather degenerate face of the young man. Its very softness was an attraction; it was a soft, warm, corrupt nature, into which one might plunge with gratification . . .
'You see he *made* me go and live with him, when I didn't want to,' she replied. 'He came and cried to me, tears, you never saw so many, saying *he couldn't* bear it unless I went back to him. And he wouldn't go away, he would have stayed for ever. He made me go back. Then every time he behaves in this fashion.—And now I'm going to have a baby, he wants to give me a

hundred pounds[66] and send me into the country, so that he would never see me nor hear of me again. But I'm not going to do it . . .'

A queer look came over Gerald's face.

'Are you going to have a child?' he asked incredulous. . . .

She looked full into his face, and her dark, inchoate eyes had now a furtive look, and a look of a knowledge of evil, dark and indomitable. . . .

'Yes,' she said, 'Isn't it beastly?'

'Don't you want it?' he asked.

'I don't,' she replied emphatically.

'But—' he said, 'how long have you known?'

'Ten weeks,' she said.[67]

In the following chapter ('Fetish') Lawrence adds to his previous description of Halliday. The choice of language, strangely reminiscent of Ottoline Morrell's diary entry of 3 December 1915, and the fact that at this stage Halliday and Maxim Libidnikov, a character possibly modelled on Boris de Chrustchoff, are both naked in front of the fire, gives the whole section a heavy homo-erotic overlay:

Halliday . . . had a rather heavy, slack, broken beauty, white and firm. He was like a Christ in a Pietà . . . the heavy, broken beauty. The animal was not there at all, only the heavy, broken beauty . . . Halliday's eyes were beautiful too, so blue and warm and confused, broken also in their expression. The fireglow fell on his heavy, rather bowed shoulders, he sat slackly crouched on the fender, his face was uplifted, degenerate, perhaps slightly disintegrate, and yet with a moving beauty of its own.[68]

In his final comments about the two in this chapter, Lawrence hits home hard: 'She [Pussum] had got her Halliday, whom she wanted. She wanted him completely in her power. Then she would marry him. She wanted to marry him. She had set her will on marrying Halliday.[69]

Lawrence was a shrewd observer of his friends, especially when he saw them as potential character material for his writing, and had no doubt quickly become aware of Philip's immature dealings with women, particularly with someone as sexually experienced as Puma—hence the significant comments about Halliday's character and his relationship with Pussum and the 'baby-faced girl' (suggesting Juliette Baillot) in chapter 8, 'Breadalby', which also bear mentioning:

He is really split mad. He wants a pure lily, another girl, with a baby face,— the good old chaste love—and at the same time he *must* have the Pussum, just to defile himself with her . . . She is the harlot, the actual harlot of adultery to him. And he's got a craving to throw himself away with her. Then he gets up and turns towards the lily of purity, the baby-faced girl, and so gets another thrill. It's the old game—action and reaction, and nothing between.

Although Philip had been deeply depressed earlier that year, the beauty of the Cornish surroundings now began to have a beneficial effect on him and in his letters there is an obvious appreciation of and real identification with the landscape around him. He expressed this in a poetic letter to Nichols:

All round, on all sides, nothing but open moorland and rock-strewn hills, mostly crowned with marvellous Druidic temples. Without leaving the house I can see the sun rise at five in the morning, and watch it sink at night into the sea. The sky never grows dark; the darkness seems rather to come welling out of the earth like a dye, infusing into every shape and form, every twig and every stone, a keen intense blackness . . . In the twilight, bushes, walls, roofs, and the line of the hills all seem to become rigid and sharp against the sky, like dark blades, while the upper air remains clear and bright and the sky becomes more and more luminous as the blue deepens to a marvellous purple setting for the first stars. The hollows and lower slopes of the hills are covered with the dazzling profusion of gorse and blackthorn—I have never seen such blazing masses of gorse. Tiny lizards dart about among the violets on the sunny banks and splendid gold-and-black adders often cross one's path on the moors. The other day, looking down from the cliffs into a clear, green sea-pool, I caught sight of a lovely young seal, gambolling about under the water. Up here on the moor all the birds and beasts come so near one, not suspecting any human presence. Foxes lollop leisurely along the road, bunnies hardly take the trouble to hop out of the way when one walks by. A chorus of larks makes the air ring all day long, and there are cuckoos innumerable, piping from far and near with delightful variations of pitch and interval . . . And on the edge of the pond near by an assembly of huge gulls holds colloquy (there is no other word for this strange croaking).[70]

At the same time, he wrote a grateful letter to Delius, expressing more fully the conflicting emotions that moved him:

. . . at the beginning of March I found myself on the verge of utter collapse, physically and mentally. Material and psychological difficulties combined with other things to produce a kind of climax, a decisive point at which it became imperative to break right away from old paths and choose a new direction—or rather to pull oneself out of the mud and regain the path one had slipped away from. The English capital, which our countrymen like to call the hub of the universe, is really a great cesspool—more especially where any kind of art is concerned: if one lives in it continuously for a year or so, one sinks deeper and deeper into the mire until one reaches such a pitch of blasphemy that one begins positively to enjoy one's wallowing. Then comes a horrible moment when the truth of one's position rises up against one—and then there is nothing to be done except to clear out of all the muck, or else sell one's soul to Satan for ever and a day. . . . The whole of the past year has been a nightmare for me—chiefly through my own imbecility—but it has also been a good cautionary experience. But now—in this wonderful country—this wild end of England which is not England at all—I feel a real regeneration, I feel the Spring in me as well as around me: this is a new beginning—but only a beginning. You were quite right—though I hardly appreciated the truth of your words at the time—when you wrote last winter that we—Gray and I— were as yet unripe for a big enterprise. I have now thoroughly understood how immature, how really *uneducated* one is—in every sense of the word— and, most important of all, how necessary it is to *be*, fully, before attempting to *do*. For one can only create out of the fullness of being—of this I am sure: it is no good building on the patterns of the past—which is all that the musicians of the present day are doing—not one of them has any real individual *being*. You have always been so very right in your estimate of them: and now I know what patience you must have exercised in tolerating my absurdly exaggerated and ill-founded opinion of the value of present-day artists! Really, when I consider what myself and my opinions have been during the last four years I am quite overcome with shame and confusion. You have been so good and so tolerant, and all the while so right![71]

Philip sang the praises of Cornwall to Gray in such a high key that it was not long before he too decided to move there, becoming quite ecstatic about Cornwall, 'the land of his dreams'. Here, near Gurnard's Head in a wild spot on the highest summit of the chain of cliffs stretching between St Ives and Land's End, he rented a house with the grand name of Bosigran Castle (for £5 a year) into which he moved that June. Gray soon met and became friendly with Lawrence, who now admitted that he felt more 'kindly'[72] towards Philip. He also went out of his way to make Gray feel welcome by helping him acquire some second-hand furniture and making the house ready for his arrival. It was not long before Gray became part of the Lawrence circle, in fact there is every indication that he and Frieda may even have had a brief affair during that period. But like so many of Lawrence's friendships, the relationship was doomed, and by November 1917 Lawrence was writing: 'I don't care what you accept or don't accept, either: it bores me a bit. But don't go throwing about accusations and calling me a liar gratuitously.'[73]

In the meantime, the astute Delius had sensed that Philip's personality was undergoing a change for the worse. He gently tried to encourage him to develop his own personality to the utmost: 'Never mind if you make mistakes—we have all made the most stupendous blunders—but keep your soul intact. By soul I mean your real bedrock self: that which you really are and not the trimmings or the adopted.'[74] Not surprisingly in these congenial surroundings, Philip's interest in composition was re-awakened and, on receiving Nichols's recently published book of poetry, *Ardours and Endurances*, which he extravagantly claimed 'the finest volume of poems issued by any of the younger men',[75] he immediately set several of the poems to music. Apart from one not particularly appealing song, 'The Water Lily', these 1917 settings have not survived.

It was during this period that the nationalist revival in music began to show its influence on Philip's compositions. Just as, in Europe, composers such as Grieg and Bartók had rebelled against German influence and were exploring their respective folk-music, English composers like Vaughan Williams and Holst were busy rediscovering the musical heritage of their own country. It was therefore inevitable that at some stage or another Philip would be intrigued by the possibilities of introducing folk elements into his own compositions. In letters written at this time there are increasing references to experiments with Celtic folk-song which, in due course, resulted in the *Folk Song Preludes* for piano. He was, however, determined to treat each tune in a short and straightforward manner, 'without the usual idiotic harmonic restrictions that faddists like Cecil Sharp, V. Williams and Co. like to impose upon themselves'.[76] At this stage he was very critical of Vaughan Williams, writing in *The New Age* that he was 'one of those for whom mysticism means mistiness and vacuity rather than exceptional clarity of vision. Misty subjects have an irresistible attraction for him—London, the Sea, the Fen Country. He aims at the sublime by sheer ponderosity, as Handel did: but where Handel achieved a colossus, Vaughan Williams only manages a rather uncomfortable rhinoceros with flabby legs.'[77] That Philip was subsequently to change his opinion is born out in this quotation from Gray's memoir:

I well remember once in later years Philip pointing out 'V.W.' to me at a Prom., 'That big man there, standing by himself, who looks as if he ought to have straw in his boots!' On another occasion after a performance of 'V.W.'s' Pastoral Symphony he exclaimed, 'A truly splendid work!' and then, with a smile, 'You know I've only one thing to say against this composer's music: it is all just a little too much like a cow looking over a gate. None the less he is a very great composer and the more I hear the more I admire him'.[78]

At that time Philip had also written some light-hearted musical satire, which he referred to as 'César Franck rag-time', and which was actually played at Selfridges department store in London by a rag-time band consisting of violin, piano, two banjos, and 'the most marvellous assortment of "kitchen utensils"'.[79] This was 'The Old Codger', a send-up of the main themes from César Franck's Symphony in D minor in the currently popular 'rag-time' style and dedicated to Colin Taylor. It was one of a set of the so-called *Cod-pieces*, a title itself full of *double entendre*: a cod-piece being the ornamented flap or bag concealing the opening in the front of men's breeches in the fifteenth century, as well as a colloquial word for the penis. He called this piece 'No. 6 of Bulgy Gogo's Contingencies', having used the name Bulgy Gogo as early as 1905 in a schoolboy play. The other *Cod-pieces* also have fascinating titles: 'Orientale (for a Tahiti Timbuctoo scene)' and 'Beethoven's Binge (Der Beethoven-Bummel) (or the Bard unbuttoned vide Sir George Grove passim)', an amusing send-up of themes from the Fifth Symphony. Copley suggests that Philip intended some of these pieces to be used 'in a theatrical context, for occasional stage-directions are included, together with suggestions for lighting and hints for suitable lyrics'.[80] According to Arnold Dowbiggin, a research chemist and amateur singer who came to know Philip in the late 1920s through corresponding with him about his songs, Philip had considered writing a revue during the mid-1920s—'of which only a typically Warlockian stage-direction, "Enter villagers, muttering, they throw shit at the Rectory windows", survives'.[81]

In mid-1917 a strange couple, whom Lawrence described as 'herb-eating occultists', suddenly appeared on the scene: Meredith Starr and his recent bride, the 'half cast' daughter of the Earl of Stamford, Lady Mary Starr (née Grey) (1881–1945). Lady Mary's father, the Reverend Harry Grey (1812–90), an Anglican clergyman, had been a remittance man who lived in Wynberg near Cape Town and who had married a black woman, Maria Solomons (1838–1916), in 1880 and had unexpectedly succeeded to the title of the eighth Earl of Stamford. The Starrs had moved to Cornwall and taken a cottage a mile from Tregerthen at Treveal. Lawrence found them faintly amusing. He told Lady Cynthia Asquith that 'they fast, or eat nettles: they descend naked into old mine-shafts, and there meditate for hours and hours, upon their own transcendent infinitude', though he was obviously slightly irritated by them: 'they descend on us like a swarm of locusts, and devour all the food on the shelf or board.' The Starrs even gave a concert in St Ives on 22 August, in aid of the Red Cross, when they made 'the most dreadful fools of themselves'.[82]

Possibly influenced by his meeting with the Starrs, Lawrence himself for a time showed a renewed interest in the occult (as a young man he had attended meetings of the Theosophical Society in Nottingham). On 14 June he wrote to Gray: 'It is raining in wild torrents here, the air is full of dark omens, and surcharged with Starr's destructive electricity. I feel as if bad things were on the wing, a doom, huge and dark, flying towards us. . . . I feel as if bad things were abroad, and hide in my cottage as it were a refuge.'[83] In a letter on 27 July to the American novelist and essayist Waldo Frank (1889–1967), he said that the esoteric doctrines were 'marvellously illuminating' and that magic had interested him a good deal. By 24 August 1917 he was corresponding with the early Freudian psychoanalyst Dr David Eder (1865–1936) on various occult-related matters. Here Lawrence begins by referring to a book by the enigmatic founder of the Theosophical Society in New York, the spiritualist Helena Petrovna Blavatsky (1831–91):

Have you read Blavatsky's *Secret Doctrine* [1888]? In many ways a bore, and not quite real. Yet one can glean a marvellous lot from it, enlarge the understanding immensely. Do you know the physical—physiological—interpretations of the esoteric doctrine?—the *chakras* and dualism in experience? The devils won't tell one anything, fully. Perhaps they don't understand themselves—the occultists—what they are talking about, or what their esotericism really means. But probably, in the physiological interpretation they do—and won't tell. Yet one can gather enough. Did you get Pryce's [*sic*] *Apocalypse Unsealed*?[84]

This was a reference to *The Apocalypse Unsealed: Being an Esoteric Interpretation of the Initiation of Iôannes* by James Morgan Pryse (b. 1859), who had introduced both George Russell ('Æ') and Yeats to magic and initiation rites, a book in which Pryse expounded the theory that a latent power can be liberated through the controlled awakening of the seven principal nerve centres ('chakras') which are situated along the spine.[85] It was a book over which Philip himself would soon be enthusing.

In the preceding years, the subject of the occult had gradually been more and more in Philip's own mind. As early as December 1911 he had written to Delius about telepathy, saying that he believed in it 'very strongly, as also in many other occult and, at present, undeveloped sciences, though many people laugh at them, because *they cannot themselves understand them*'.[86] In 1912 Delius had written a letter to Philip in which he mentioned 'table-turning & spirit rapping',[87] while in September 1913 Philip told Viva Smith that Delius had been 'greatly interested in various occult séances'.[88] During his time in Paris Delius had indeed showed a considerable interest in such matters and in the 1890s had specialized in astrology and the casting of horoscopes. He had even collaborated with the notable French physician and occultist, Dr Gérard Encausse ('Papus', 1865–1916), to produce a booklet entitled *Anatomie et physiologie de l'orchestre* which appeared in print in 1894. It is more than likely that at some stage he would have discussed his opinions and experiences with the young and impressionable Philip. In April 1914, whilst still at Oxford, Philip reported to Viva Smith that he had been invited to join 'a little society of Psychical research' and that he was 'keen to go into this subject fairly deeply' and had ordered a catalogue of 'Occult, Psychic and New Thought publications'.[89] Early in May the same year he had a long discussion on the subject with a tutor at Corpus Christi College, Dr Ferdinand Schiller (1864–1937), an Anglo-American philosopher who was president of the Society for Psychical Research in London. It is significant to note that, as early as 1887, Schiller had written about experiments in the phenomenon of automatic writing; a process whereby, without the control of the conscious self, scripts are produced. The potential of automatic writing in the field of musical composition was something which would soon fascinate and influence Philip.

Now he again became interested in the occult through his discussions with Lawrence and his meeting with Meredith Starr, who had written a letter to the *St Ives Times* (31 August 1917) claiming Aleister Crowley to be 'by far the greatest living artist in England', citing also Epstein and Augustus John who, as has been noted, were two of Philip's friends. In fact, Philip was now so impressed with Starr that in June 1917 he wrote to Nichols urging him to visit him. Nichols, however, remained unimpressed and later dismissed Starr as a charlatan, relating how he quickly

fled from the presence of an imbecile with hair hanging over his shoulders & a snake ring on his finger. This ass had a bedizened wife or concubine prophetess with him: all black and bilious complexion & muddleheadedness. They were a couple of blithering piebald donkeys & no mistake & damned pretentious at that. It was characteristic of Philip that in his Faustean search for truth he should interrogate such oracles as these.[90]

For a while Philip kept in contact with Starr and there are two references to him in letters written from Ireland early in 1918, in one of which he asked Gray to contact Starr in connection with what appears to have been a telepathic 'experiment of considerable interest'.[91] But whatever the background or reasons, Philip's interests were now moving more swiftly in the direction of the occult.

By June, Philip was back in London, living at Anhalt Studios in Battersea, once again busily trying to promote van Dieren's music. Whether he was hoping to organize another concert or not is unclear, but on 26 June he wrote to Gray saying that Waldo Warner (1874–1945), the violinist of the London String Quartet, had guaranteed that the quartet would meet 'no less than ten times . . . for the purpose of rehearsing quartets that are both futurist *and* funny',[92] a bitter reference to one of the reviews of the disastrous concert of van Dieren's music that March. In July, however, Philip suddenly and impulsively decided to abandon the Anhalt Studios which, possibly as a result of some disturbing occult experience, he now found 'tomb-like and nightmarish'[93] and moved briefly back to Cornwall. Although he had been violently anti-Puma in April and May that year, there seems to have been at least a temporary reconciliation and she joined Philip on this trip. Lawrence made a brief reference to them in a letter to the American part-time journalist and artist, Esther Andrews, dated 23 August: 'Puma and Heseltine came down: wan and unhappy she, crazy he; stayed a fortnight in the bungalow, she hating it; now have disappeared utterly. Starr says mysteriously "Mum's the word." It is all the sheerest nonsense. Gray is at Bosigran, painting his cupboards. The Starrs are at Treveal . . .'[94]

But by now the war situation was becoming critical. The House of Commons had been stunned by the news that two million tons of shipping had been lost to German U-boats and that England had only three to four weeks' supply of food in stock. The economy had also taken a downward plunge and by the end of March 1917 food prices had risen to 94 per cent above July 1914. Philip's anxieties about the military now proved to have been well founded. In the summer of 1917 there was a revision of all previous exemptions from military service and, as his case automatically came up for review, he accordingly received a summons to appear for yet another medical examination. Although Philip had 'a certificate of complete and absolute exemption from any form of service',[95] he made an impulsive decision to ignore the summons and he and Puma fled to Ireland. A letter written to Nichols at this time provides further evidence of Philip's pathological instability and swings of mood. Here he writes at some length about the change in his feelings towards his wife:

For years I have been looking for love to give me the key of my own being, of reality. What I have actually been doing has been to pursue a phantom of my own too-self-sufficient mind, up to the moon and down again—or, if you will, consciously pursuing my own imaginary tail . . . it has prevented me from seeing anything outside the vicious circle, it has prevented me from getting anywhere or doing anything. Now, at the moment of complete uncertainty, a strange inner voice has prompted me to throw over all my apparent certainties as illusions and fall back upon quite inexplicable realities . . .

At least I have found one certainty, I have found a direction, and a peace that passeth, not the understanding but certainly the mere reason. What I have hitherto sought as love has proved the most ridiculous of vain illusions: love has been with me all the while and it is I, and not love, that has been blind . . . I have found, for the first time in my life, reality in the one place of all others where I was most certain that it could not be found—and if this is not real, nothing in my life ever could be. I have found in Puma and my babe a greater and realer love than I have ever been able to imagine. In seeing them as they essentially are—as I can do now—instead of regarding them through the bleared spectacles of my own foulness, I can see at last, and clearly, the way, and the only way, to the fulfilment of my own being. All that I have hated and cursed in Puma has been myself—my foul old self—and that is dead now, once and for all. . . . Forgive me this incoherent confession, but I want to try sometime to make this clear to you, since I had hitherto made it impossible for you to see anything in Puma but my own foulness projected into an unwilling other.[96]

So August 1917 found Philip with Puma in Dublin about to embark on a new phase of his life. With the 'foulness' of London and the threat of conscription now safely on the other side of the Irish Sea, Philip set about picking up the pieces of his shattered life. He was not yet 23.

THE IRISH YEAR
(1917–1918)

Away from the pressures of life in London and the fear of conscription, Philip was now able to devote considerable energy to his many varied interests. As Jack Lindsay wrote: 'Ireland gave him a sense of escape from corruption',[1] with which he now associated London. The novelist, playwright, and editor, Douglas Goldring (1887–1960), recorded his first meeting with his friend Philip when he called at his rooms soon after his arrival in Dublin. Philip was suffering from an appalling cold and, in typically eccentric fashion, was passing the time by reading aloud a translation of the works of Appolonius of Tyana to Puma, whom Goldring described as 'extremely beautiful'.[2] Goldring's first impression of Philip was one of 'abstemiousness' when, offering him some alcohol at a subsequent meeting, he refused even a glass of sherry. They met again later at another party, where Philip was introduced to the Irish writer, J. M. Hone (1882–1959, who wrote biographies of both Nietzsche and Yeats) and to Hester Dowden (Mrs Travers-Smith, 1868–1949), a 'highly cultured professional medium'[3] as well as a fine musician. She conducted Ouija board experiments, for which she had become famous outside Dublin, and was also considered one of the best English automatists, well-known for her successful experiments in automatic writing. She claimed that the words came through so quickly that it was almost impossible to read them and it required an experienced shorthand writer to take them down when the traveller moved at its maximum speed. She and Philip soon became great friends and it was not long before the impressionable Philip was himself caught up in her occult experiments, probably especially in those involving automatic writing. It is highly significant, as we shall see, that some of his most famous early songs were composed in her house and at her piano. Over the years she continued to hold Philip in high regard and it is interesting to note that she was one of the financial supporters of the concert given in memory of Philip in the Wigmore Hall on 23 February 1931.

In the meantime, however, he and Puma were beginning to settle down happily in their new environment and in early October Philip wrote to his mother thanking her 'a thousand times' for a pair of beautiful, golden pyjamas and saying that they were 'having lovely sunny days, though I have been too busy to be out much. Dublin suits us both, and I have seldom found any place more congenial to work and study.'4 This letter also contains brief mention of their small son (at that time still called Peter, not Nigel) whom Edith Buckley Jones had now agreed should be moved to Cefn Bryntalch and brought up under her care: 'I hope Peter will be happy with you and you with him: I am so glad to think that he is going to live in decent surroundings at last. Of course Mrs Fisher took care of him well enough, but the atmosphere of surroundings *is* important, even for babes.' On the same day Puma wrote in her rather immature handwriting to Edith Buckley Jones thanking her for an amount of £26. 10s. It is the only letter from Puma known to have been preserved and is particularly interesting in that she addresses her mother-in-law in a rather impersonal way, suggesting that up until that time the two women had not actually met:

Dear Philip's mother,

. . . I will leave it to you about Peter's shoes, I expect you know best anyway I suppose he will have to wear shoes sometime, and Phil's feet don't look as if they have ever suffered from cramped shoes and that is all I care about that they should not be made tender by them . . .

P.S. I am longing to know that Peter is safe with you.5

Puma stayed only a short while in Dublin. By February 1918 Philip was writing to Gray implying that the 'muliercula impudica' (the shameless hussy) was now in Wales, staying at Cefn Bryntalch with his mother (whom he dubbed the 'fons et origo pecuniae', the fount and source of the money), adding a brief and cynical comment: '2 Persons!!! 1 Room!! No peace!'6 Unpleasant disagreements regarding the fate of their furniture now ensued, and by June Puma had angered Philip even more by claiming £30 of his money from his mother, for repayment of what Philip described as 'the fictitious-furniture loan of last July'.7 This had particularly annoyed him as he had intended sending the money to van Dieren. In May, Philip had written to Nichols, regretting the fact that he had abandoned his old friends on account of Puma, quoting an original Latin poem

in the style of Catullus: 'You alone have not been repelled by my
fits of madness, my fits of intolerable weakness, my imbecility: one
after another I have driven my good friends away from me. To you
also I can say, as I wrote—I fear fruitlessly—to Cecil Gray some
while ago':[8]

PROSDOCIMI DE BELDAMANDIS AD FRATREM PROBINBALNEUM PALINODIA

Vere insanus eram (negare nolo)
Qui propter mulierculam impudicam
Dilecto potui nocere amico . . .
Detestabilis usque erasque erisque
Cunne, heu, tot scelerum nefasta causa!
Cunne, in te latet omnium malorum
Semen: to quoque litium est origo:
Te vaginam habet universus ensis! . . .
Tristis, Prosdocimus Beldamandis
Luget se, subito furore raptum,
Excordem simul occupasse amicam,
Jam solum sedeo ad focum (puella
Nequaquam esse viro potest sodalis),
Nec fert amphora Bolsiana pacem.
Cunctorum at mihi pessimum malorum est
Illo uno comite unicoque egere
Quocum 'despicere in loco' solebam,
De mundo et furibunda cantitare,
Res et commemorare suarianas
Docto colloquio bonas per horas . . .
Quid prodest aliquid? dolere vanum est:
Me ipsum follibus irrumare oportet!

Nun, en! hendecasyllabis Latinis
Formosam palinodiam peregi.
Peccavisse pudetque paenitetque . . .
Nonne ignoscere tu potes amico
Quondam, Prosdocimo de Beldamandis?[9]

RECANTATION BY PROSDOCIMUS DE BELDAMANDIS TO HIS BROTHER
TRY-IT-IN-YOUR-BATH

I really was crazy (I won't try to deny it) to find it in me to hurt a cherished
friend, all because of a girl without any morals . . . Cunt, you always were
loathsome and always will be. In you, cunt, lies the seed of all evil: you are the
fount of strife: everyman's sword has you as its sheath! Prosdocimus de
Beldamandis, contrite, bemoans the fact that, carried away by sudden madness,
he simultaneously took possession of a silly girl and lost a cherished friend.
Now I sit beside a lonely hearth (a girl cannot possibly be a companion for a
man), and Bols gin cannot bring relief. But for me the worst of all evils is to be
without that single unique companion with whom I used to fool around, chant
satirical verses about the world, and while away pleasant hours chatting about
matters alligatorial[10] in learned conversation . . . What use is anything? It is
pointless to feel sorry: I ought to suck myself with a pair of bellows!

Look now, I have composed an elegant recantation in Latin hendecasyllables. I am ashamed of having done wrong, and I'm sorry. Just this once, can't you forgive your friend Prosdocimus de Beldamandis?[11]

From this time on Puma becomes a somewhat mysterious and shadowy figure. We do not know when she and Philip actually decided to separate or even if they eventually divorced. Apart from a few brief mentions in one or two of Philip's letters, she now practically disappears from the story. It seemed to be fairly common knowledge that the marriage had been a disaster and by December 1918 we find Jelka Delius gossiping in a letter to a friend that 'Little Phil Heseltine' had made 'such a terrible mess of his life he's gone and married a model who got a baby, which he thinks is his—if he liked the girl—but he doesn't—there he is in a small flat a-quarrelling with her—pitiful'.[12] Jelka even added that she suspected he was taking drugs as he looked 'so pale and miserable'.

Despite his references to 'work and study', the irresponsible side of Philip's character gradually began to emerge and Goldring's first impressions of abstemiousness were soon dispelled when he heard rumours that 'this pale and studious Heseltine had been seen "on the spree" in the streets of Dublin, in the company of some English painters . . . The change was said to be due to the discovery, on Philip's part, of the virtues of Booth's gin, a discovery which he insisted on sharing with some of his Dublin friends.'[13] Philip was also composing again and, in a letter to Taylor, discussed his earliest surviving orchestral work, *An Old Song*, which he had begun in Cornwall. Although he referred to the tune as Gaelic (it is in fact based on a Scottish folk-song, 'There was anes a May'), he added that the piece was very much inspired by the Cornish moors:

The tune should emerge, as from afar, chiming in with one's thoughts while walking. The curious way in which it seems to end on the supertonic gives the impression that it fades away into the distance, unfinished. One stands still, attentive to catch another strain, but there is only the gentle murmur of wind—and only fragments remain in the memory—and a mood half-contented and half-sad.[14]

All the same, Philip still had reservations about his potential as a composer and told Taylor that 'except in moments of conceit, I don't regard myself as a composer at all—as yet. Perhaps, at the age of 35! . . . the more clearly I see the foundation principles of music and of composition, the further off do I seem myself from the possibility of attaining anything whatever'[15]—ominous words which show a degree of self-deprecation which was already becoming an almost fatal flaw. *An Old Song* is scored for chamber orchestra of flute, oboe, clarinet, and horn, with strings (violins occasionally divided into four parts), and divisi cellos. It was published in 1923, after some slight revision of the scoring, and was dedicated to Philip's conductor friend Anthony Bernard (1891–1963). Gray thought it 'an exquisite little miniature . . . full of delicate atmosphere and haunting fantasy. Some wit has dubbed it, "On hearing the second cuckoo in spring", and there is certainly sufficient of the Delian influence to justify the joke.'[16]

Soon after establishing himself in Dublin, Philip pursued his interest in early music. He told Taylor of his projected plans for transcribing 'William Ballet's Lute Book', a seventeenth-century collection of English lute and viol music, including 'Greensleeves' and 'Sellinger's Round', in the Trinity College Library, if he could obtain access to the manuscript room. He would no doubt have been amused by the little graffito written in an early hand on the flyleaf of this 'collection of priceless Elizabethan tunes':

> God made man and man made muny
> God made bees and bees made honny

He jokingly told Taylor that

It occurred to me the other day what a wonderful theme for a set of variations would be provided by the old tune of 'Walsingham'—Bull and Byrd between them pissed around it a great deal but by no means in their best manner.

Piano figures are entirely beyond me so I send you the little tune hoping you may set to work at it. It is, incidentally, superb to 'rag', not only in the simple syncopations suggested immediately by bars 5 and 6, but also in complex figures like this:—

I bethought me of this grisly variant as the climax of a stupendous version of 'De Camptown Races' for vast orchestra with dozens of banjos which I am contemplating: the irrelevance of its entry is a great joy! . . .

P.S. . . . Why not make a waltz out of Liszt's 'Liebestraum'?!! Also a ragtime chorus to be sung to a lamp post by a 'drunk': (to the tune of Hymn no. 266) ['Lead, kindly light'].[17]

At the beginning of October Philip wrote to Taylor again, this time to express sympathy on hearing that the latter's close friend, Hugh Sidgwick (1882–1917), had been killed in the War. He had been reminded of the extract from the poem, 'Heracleitus', by the Greek poet, Callimachus (fl. *c*.260 BC), which Sidgwick had quoted in his dedication to Taylor in his book, *The Promenade Ticket*: 'I wept as I remembered how often you and I had tired the sun with talking and sent him down the sky',[18] and 'immediately it seemed to fit itself to music, so I am sending you the outcome which I hope you may like'.[19] This setting has a strong van Dieren influence for, besides having no key signature or barlines, there are no definite tonal centres. The voice part, with the strange instruction 'the voice murmuring to itself', is highly chromatic and extremely difficult, whilst the accompaniment is markedly contrapuntal in style. When the song was eventually published in 1923 (as no. 3 of the *Saudades*), it was dedicated to Taylor—*saudades* being a Portuguese word meaning 'that haunting sense of sadness and regret for days gone by . . . a word which has no equivalent in the English language'.[20] Another song which Philip sent Taylor was 'Along the stream', later destined to become the first of the three *Saudades*. This setting is also heavily influenced by van Dieren, but Philip has made the style totally his own and, although the vocal line is at times cruelly taxing, there are haunting phrases which foreshadow those found in the later songs. In references to these compositions Philip showed merciless self-criticism and agony, saying that it cost him a great deal of trouble and anxiety, and begging Taylor to criticize every point of which he disapproved,

however small—as I am anxious to let nothing mediocre appear under my own name, especially as I shall never make a penny out of publishing music. Everything that is even suspicious must be sternly suppressed! . . . As it is, there are long periods when music recedes quite away from me and I bury myself deeper and deeper in other studies, of necessity—but there is no joy like working day and night at a composition, even if one only keeps a couple of bars at the end of it all![21]

Another work he described at this time was a *Chinese Ballet*, writ-
ten in either 1916 or early 1917 to a scenario by his painter friend
Adrian Allinson, who also designed the scenery and costumes.[22]
Philip, however, seemed to have thought the work of dubious merit:
'I felt guilty of indulging in a real debauch, filling page after page
with the bastard offspring of Chappell-Boosey and Puccini! If it
were literature, it would certainly not be passed by the censor.'
Together with his first letter of the new year, 1918, Philip sent
Taylor a greeting (with the inscription: 'A happy new year!') in the
form of the manuscript of a new song, 'I asked a thief to steal me a
peach', a 21-bar setting of a short poem by William Blake. Copley
draws attention to the so-called 'gigue-figure' (though it is actually
more like a siciliano in character) in the piano accompaniment,
pointing out that this 'is sometimes used by Warlock when setting
texts of delicate (or, more properly, indelicate) dalliance'.[23] Two
manuscript versions of this song exist, the copy sent to Taylor
(dated 31 December 1917) and an undated copy with numerous revi-
sions, retitled 'A poem with a moral'. This second version also has
at the end a cryptic message to an unknown recipient: 'Come now,
tell me now, what's wrong with the penis?' Could the recipient perhaps have been Gray? In a letter to him on 30 May 1918 Philip uses
a very similar turn of phrase when he compares one of Gray's recent
remarks with a condom: 'at the risk of vulgarity I would expand: it
is a *vraie capote anglaise*: come now, tell me now, what's wrong with
the plain penis?'[24]

During his stay in Cornwall, Philip had become interested in
Cornish, a language no longer spoken and in danger of becoming
extinct. Determined now to learn the Irish language, Philip spent two
months in early 1918 on a remote and desolate island, separated from
the west coast of Ireland 'by a narrow strip of sea'.[25] Here he found
time to study not only Irish but some of the other Celtic languages,
Welsh, Gaelic, Breton, Manx, and Cornish, and was eventually able
to read, write, and speak fairly fluent Irish. On this unidentified island
('not a mile square') he had found a wonderful opportunity to
observe the inhabitants ('nearly a hundred') and their way of life,
which he found vastly interesting, but above all he was struck by the
barrenness and utter desolation of the place: 'It reflects into one's
very soul till one becomes chill and numb—such desolate lives in such
a desolate region—black wintry weather and the full force of the
Atlantic beating, always beating, almost at one's very door.' His host,
the island's schoolmaster, was evidently a charming man

of great versatility and strange experiences—the very embodiment of enthusi-asm—living only for the preservation of the Irish language. He is also a cham-pion bag-piper, and almost taught me to play that wonderful instrument! As a result of this long period of exile, I have come back to Dublin and to musical work with quite a new enthusiasm and new vigour—which I think I shall at last be able to turn to some *practical*—to some *dynamic* account![26]

During his stay in Dublin Philip did not forget van Dieren, who had been ill yet again. He had generously continued to lend him money, a practice of which his mother highly disapproved, especially as Philip on occasion asked her to send some of his allowance direct to van Dieren. In letters to Gray, Philip railed against her meanness: 'The sum total of her capital—not counting her husband's—is well over thirty thousand. I do hope she wrote nothing to the old man that would upset him.'[27] But upset him she had and van Dieren promptly told Philip that he had

a great fear of receiving any further moralizing communications from Cefn Bryntalch and in case you can actually obtain any funds I shall be very grate-ful if you could arrange so that they were sent to you because I could never feel pained or ashamed at receiving anything directly from you . . . The last two letters from that quarter however were quite as much as I care for to receive for the duration of my life.[28]

Philip's anger and frustration were mounting and he fulminated that

a sum approaching £25,000 should be actually entailed upon me and I am unable to touch a penny of it during my mother's lifetime. The thought makes me sick with rage—especially when I think of her house of fifty rooms and four or five servants!!—but I'll circumvent the blasted arrangement somehow, and meanwhile my mother shall have no peace till you have plenty. . . . there is no need for you to have the slightest compunction in asking me for as much as you want . . . Your friendship and your works are my greatest treasure—they have enriched my life beyond any possibility of repayment on my part.[29]

He also hoped that he could be instrumental in arranging another concert of van Dieren's compositions:

When Peace comes on the winds of the late Spring, I shall get to work upon several saurian schemes that simmer yet in my mind—and first of all, I have sworn a magical oath to Bagnigger, Bagwaller and Bantaballoo[30] (late Shadrach, Meshach and Abednego) that before all else the Chinese Symphony shall be heard—together with Delius' Songs of Sunset, on one great memor-able occasion in London. After which, we will abandon London for some less ill-favoured spot.[31]

The reference in this letter to 'a magical oath' is significant, for a more sinister aspect of Philip's year in Ireland, his increasing involvement with the occult, was slowly emerging. Goldring later recorded that Philip 'was greatly preoccupied with the study of magic and occult phenomena . . . At one of Mrs Dowden's séances, which Heseltine and his wife attended, the "control", as he entered the room, rapidly spelt out the message: "That man who has just come in is dogged by evil influences. Send him away." '[32] This message could very well have been from 'Eyen', the Egyptian control of Hester Dowden, who claimed to have been a priest of Isis in the reign of Rameses II and is reputed to have cursed and sworn in verse 'against a member of the circle who drove him out by hypnotic suggestion given to the medium'.[33] Gray mentions that a large number of Philip's notebooks from that period were

filled with extracts from and comments upon works dealing with every aspect of the subject, from the most highly scientific and elaborately technical aspects of astrology to the method of divination by means of the tarot, and from the purely philosophic and theoretical side of magic, as found in the writings of Eliphas Levi, down to its actual practice according to the formulas, rituals, and incantations contained in such works as *The Book of Abramelin the Mage* and the writings of Cornelius Agrippa.[34] From these activities Philip undoubtedly suffered certain psychological injuries from which, in my opinion, he never entirely recovered.[35]

In some disturbing notes made by Philip at the time he is reputed to have written: 'Awoke with a cry. Confused but startling dream, and I now very seldom start up fully awake. Later I woke again with a vampire sensation . . . I wrested myself from it.'[36] Gray also testified to the uncanny accuracy of Philip's power of divination by means of the tarot, adding cryptically that the results he obtained in the actual practice of magic itself were 'spectacularly unsuccessful . . . disastrous and catastrophic'.[37] Unfortunately, he does not elaborate further, and little is known about the full extent to which Philip involved himself in such practices. Gray's daughter, Pauline, suggests that her father and Philip were involved for a time with Crowley and his group,[38] but no convincing evidence of such a friendship exists. In two short letters from Augustus John to Philip (written in October and November 1924)[39] there are brief references to Crowley (whom John met occasionally in London and Paris) but neither is important enough for any conclusions to be drawn. Pauline Gray is also recorded as remembering, but 'without being able to provide details', that her father practised black magic, and that he was sympathetic to Heseltine's view that if

one were to make use of a certain magic formula believing in it implicitly, in order to obtain something which one knew to be otherwise unobtainable, that one's powers of attaining it would be increased and one could almost inevitably attain it. Gray and Heseltine usually created these formulae to inflict distress on an enemy, or help further an amorous adventure.[40]

Most of the sources of information on the subject are found in these few references. Philip himself wrote tantalizingly little about it, making only the odd, passing mention as in a letter to Nichols where he refers to an 'idiotic' letter written some four months previously, 'believe it or not as you like, I was suffering from the reaction that inevitably overtakes those who tamper prematurely with the science vulgarly known as Black Magic . . . If you have my Eliphas Levi[41] still, you might send it over to me. A great book, isn't it?'[42] A brief reference in a letter written to Viva Smith in November 1918, shows that by then he was well aware of the dangers associated with such practices:

Don't play about with what you call 'table-turning'—Either take the matter seriously and understand it thoroughly (and this will take up all your time for a good long while) or leave it altogether alone. I have done a considerable deal of work myself on these lines and I know the futility, not to say the danger, of tampering with such pursuits.[43]

Further evidence that Philip was affected by his experiences with the occult is to be found in the foreword to Gray's memoir, where Augustus John relates the following incident at Holy Trinity Church, Winterton, Norfolk, which took place sometime in the late 1920s:

It was that evening . . . that a thoroughly nerve-shattering event took place. Philip, his girl friend, John Goss and I were visiting the parish church—a fine example of Perpendicular. Philip had just given a rendering of Harry Cox's beautiful but profane song 'Down by the riverside' upon the organ, and we were about to leave the building, when, moved by a perverse whim, I proposed to revive the rites of a more ancient cult by there and then offering up Miss [Peache] upon the altar. My ill-timed pleasantry had hardly been uttered when, with a deafening crash, a thunderbolt struck the building, instantly filling the interior of the church with smoke and dust, and with electric cracklings on every metal surface and the screeches of a distraught charwoman adding to the general confusion, one received a vivid impression of Hell being opened and all its devils loose! Philip with his peculiar beliefs in 'Principalities and Powers' was the most shaken, especially as he was about to mount the tower of which a pinnacle lay shattered on the ground outside. I believe he composed, at the vicar's request, a hymn tune for the church 'as a thanks-offering for our providential escape'.[44]

In a letter written to Gerald Cockshott in 1941 Moeran stated that Philip did not, in fact, 'compose a hymn tune or anything else to mark the occasion'.[45] Cockshott later added to this story saying that, even if Philip had been momentarily shaken by this unnerving experience, he soon realized its commercial possibilities. After ascending the tower with the rector, the Reverend C. A. P. Porter, he is said to have remarked: '"There's money in this. We've got a celebrity with us." Whereupon he put through a call to a London newspaper, said he had a story and asked what the paper would pay. A fee of two guineas having been agreed, Warlock recounted the incident.'[46]

Despite his recent unpleasant experience with Lawrence, Philip was still magnanimous enough to want to help him. After reading his *The Reality of Peace*, four essays of which had been published in the *English Review*, he set about trying to interest a publisher in Ireland and, at his instigation, one of the partners of a large publishing firm in Dublin secured the manuscript of the whole book from which the essays were taken. Philip told Nichols that he considered the work to be 'the supreme utterance of all modern philosophy . . . it is impossible to exaggerate the book's importance. Lawrence can't get it published in England . . . But we must get it printed and we want to make a big thing of it.'[47] Besides these efforts on Lawrence's behalf, he had also sent him a gift of a reproduction from the historic *Book of Kells* in the Trinity College Library.

But all was not going as smoothly as it appeared. In late April Philip suddenly expressed acute anxiety in somewhat alarming terms and we find him apologizing to Taylor for not replying earlier: 'I have been away for nearly two months, on the verge of utter insanity, and no letters have been forwarded. I am quite incapable of writing a coherent letter: one seems surrounded in a cloud of nightmare.'[48] Was this perhaps the result of certain unfortunate black magic experiences or sheer anxiety over the financial mess ensuing from the existence of an unsupported family? Philip's interest in the occult did not, however, produce only negative or disturbing results. In fact it may not be an exaggeration to say that, without these experiences, the composer in Philip may never have successfully emerged at this crucial stage. His correspondence with Taylor and Gray during this year shows how his belief in his own gifts as a composer were gradually developing. Some of these letters are very prolix and the arguments convoluted and complicated, but it would seem that, through his reading of a number of books on religion, the occult, and occult-related subjects, he was beginning to develop a more confident personal philosophy regarding music and creative inspiration—a philosophy which hints at a kind of automatic writing. Mere technical equipment was not enough: the composer is the vessel into which a higher force pours the finished product—if the recipient is open to this flow. As he eventually summed it up: 'All art that is of any real value, must be the *overflow*, and not merely the *fullness*, of life. Music is the voice of the God in man.'[49] He wrote to Taylor of his slowly forming theories in language heavily weighted with religious imagery and quotations:

. . . the most important of all undiscovered countries is the 'Kingdom of God' which is within us.[50] . . . And since all music, all art of any kind that is of any value, must be sought and found in that inner kingdom and there alone, it is only reasonable that we should try and acquire some knowledge of its geography. But do we do so?—do we ever admit the necessity of doing so in this fag-end of an era of blasted materialism? For the majority of us, any knowledge we may have acquired of an inner or 'spiritual' life has been derived from one of the so-called 'Christian' churches, whose very foundation we have afterwards discovered to be rotten through and through. And in our repudiation of this rottenness, in our horror and disgust at the humbuggery that has beset us . . . for so many years, we have cast overboard everything that we have ever associated with it—including things of a value unsuspected by ourselves.

This at any rate was my experience and to judge from the evidence of the arts . . . it has been the experience of the majority of artists for several generations. The Christian churches are more remote in spirit from their Founder than the Jewish church was in his own day. The letter has again prevailed over the spirit,[51] the sign over the thing signified—the very same tendency for which the Scribes and Pharisees came in for so much censure. 'Woe unto you Lawyers, for you have lost the key of the Gnosis!' runs one passage which is rather obscurely translated in the Authorized version. Amongst the Jewish priests, there was a very real Gnosis,[52] or received esoteric tradition of inner meanings lurking in the words of what were to outward eyes only simple stories. *This is precisely what has happened to music.* It is all surface forms and surface ceremonial, uninformed—save in rare instances—by the *living* spirit. We have indeed lost the key of our Gnosis[53] through our childish attitude of superiority to what we consider to be old wives' tales . . .

I have realized—painfully, in myself—that no one can hope even to understand the messages of an art, much less to create anything of any value, until he is thoroughly educated—in the strict sense of the word: that is, until his real self with all its potentialities has been *drawn out* of its slumber into consciousness, until he begins to live as a human being and ceases merely to exist as an animal humani generis. . . .

But I have rambled a long way and probably bored you very much . . . these matters are so intensely personal that one can hardly speak of them to another with any coherence, and it is almost impossible to do more than drop stray hints that *may* be useful, and *may* be only so much gibberish—to anyone else.[54]

Here we also have a brief glimpse of Philip's latent spiritual side emerging, in a plea for true religion as opposed to an institutional-ized one. His frustrations with current attitudes of materialism, kindled by the hopelessness of war and what he perceived to be the perversion of religious values, are often characterized by outbursts of profanity. These frustrations may have been one of the reasons for his rebellious attitudes towards the Establishment (as symbolised by his family, Eton, and Oxford), which subsequently produced his unconventional, at time immature, behaviour. To have produced works of the religious and mystical intensity clearly apparent in many of his later carol settings, for example, he must have had somewhere deep down a real belief and understanding which he found difficult to express in terms of formal religion. It is perhaps significant to note that he had earlier told his mother that he had gone to Westminster Cathedral on Christmas Day 1915 'and enjoyed the Catholic ritual very much. The music, in spite of a fear-ful organ, was superb—The whole thing being infinitely ahead of any religious service I have ever witnessed.'[55]

Denis ApIvor makes some interesting speculations in connection with Philip's religious background and his subsequent behaviour, linking it to a large extent to his repressive Welsh background and the Nonconformist attitudes with which he would have been sur-rounded during the time he lived in Wales. Although Philip dis-played anti-religious feelings throughout his life, ApIvor draws attention to the 'religious' quality of his most significant work. He refers to Gray's description of Philip's 'emotional *volte-face*' on one specific occasion, 'when in the midst of a wild and riotous gathering, he suddenly rose saying, "One has only a short time to live, and yet one spends it like this," and walked out, not returning until the next day'. ApIvor notes that Gray's memoir 'does not refer to the episode in which Heseltine was seen lying on the ground in Westminster Cathedral with his arms outstretched like a crucifix'.[56] After Philip's death, Gray found a scrap of paper on which was scribbled the following: 'When I see, and smell, a crowd of Battersea children swarming round the doors of Stephenson's bakery, I am minded with disgust of a swarm of obscene flies hovering over a clot of dung in the roadway. but when I turn away there sweeps over me the unspeakable poignancy of the Good Shepherd and His Lambs.'[57] Strange as it may seem, particularly when one takes into account Philip's general behaviour and his earlier railings against Christianity and the Church, his son even suggests that in his later days Philip told his stepfather that he felt he might enter the church and become a clergyman.

Anxious to share his new discoveries with Taylor, Philip enthusiastically recommended four books which he considered to have been of particular benefit in his own personal development, one of which was Pryse's *The Apocalypse Unsealed* which Lawrence had mentioned in his correspondence with Eder the previous month. Philip adds a touch of mystery and intrigue with his secretive instructions in the final paragraph:

> . . . it would be well worth your while to read four books which *must* either seem to you mad and incomprehensible, or else full of the most astounding wisdom and illumination that has as yet been granted to man . . . The first is called *Science and the Infinite*[58] by S. T. Klein[59]—a simple little book that may seem full of airy nothings: for me it contains . . . all the old châtelaine's keys. The second and third are two books by J. M. Pryse—*The Magical message according to Iôannes*[60] and *The Apocalypse Unsealed* which consist of a literal translation, with a commentary, (but what a commentary!) of St John's Gospel and Revelation respectively. These two are without exceptions whatever the most illuminating and altogether wonderful books I have ever read. The fourth is Eliphas Levi's *History of Transcendental Magic*[61]—a book belonging to a far lower plane than the other three but none the less remarkable. Being a history, it gives one a digest of a certain line of thought through successive ages which could not be followed otherwise without recourse to a multitude of books in many different languages. . . . These books, *which are only introductory*, contain more that is of priceless value to the artist for whom art is fullness of *life*—real life—than any works written round their little 'special subjects'. The secret of art is 'Know Thyself'[62]—and through thyself the Universe of which thou art but an epitome—this is the secret message of one of the most despised of all the old wives! . . .
>
> Plato's theory that knowledge is to a great extent remembrance of a very dim, very remote past is by no means to be discredited.[63] I wonder if you feel, as I do often, that the very greatest manifestations of truth—whether in music or in literature—seem much rather *to awaken a responsive memory* that was asleep within us than to put anything new into us? . . . *Please do not mention the books I have told you of to anyone else*: this is important. When you have read them you will see that this kind of book must not on any account fall into unfit hands: this sounds queer but you will see that it is true. There are far more dangerous books than obscene novels, in existence!!—dangerous even to the scoffers themselves.[64]

Dangerous, indeed, some of them were. A study of Eliphas Lévi's *History of Transcendental Magic* reveals sections such as 'The Sabbath of the Sorcerers' and 'Infernal Evocations', with detailed descriptions of how to invoke demoniac powers. However, not everything was evil for, as he told Taylor, positive views on music were beginning to emerge from these studies:

... there is no room, no excuse even for music in the gospel of materialism—
and no amount of study of the merely material side of music will be of any
real avail, without the inner light. *This* must be sought *first*—and then the
purely material accomplishments will be added. The inner developments of the
soul are alone of real importance. There is no need to study how these may
'apply to' music: they will apply themselves, automatically, by a seeming mira-
cle. One should not live for art: but art, if one really lives with one's *whole* self
(and to find out what is one's whole self is no small matter for us Europeans),
will be added unto one. All this may seem strange to you, coming from me:
but I will not pretend to conceal the fact that I have been on a hopelessly
wrong track for years, completely fuddled, groping blindly in the dark for
something of whose very nature I was quite ignorant. I am only now beginning to see a glimmer of light, and this, to the best of my poor ability, I must
try to show to others.[65]

Right from his student days Philip had much admired the poetry
of W. B. Yeats and had begun setting his poems to music as early
as 1913. Now, having met the poet himself in April 1918, he wrote
of him in ecstatic terms saying that they had 'talked for several
hours about the moon—and the talk was as illuminating and as
beautiful as the moon of the fourteenth night itself'.[66] Within a few
years their association would end on a sour note, but for the present
Philip saw him as 'a golden and blessed casket'. In a letter to Gray
describing this meeting there are also significant and mysterious references to elemental spirits, controlling powers, and instruments of a
higher agency:

It is a strange thing, and a thing you will mock at but a thing that I know
very certainly, that for the last twelve months my life has been in the hands of
Elemental spirits—and if they have not been actually the controlling powers,
they have at least been the instruments of a higher agency. On this hypothesis
alone are certain events explicable in that positive manner that transcends
mere ratiocination. Some day I shall write an exhaustive analysis of their operations: and perhaps after all you will not laugh ...

I am writing with great enthusiasm two Cornish hymns: it is probably the
first time the old language has ever been musicked deliberately (assuming that
the folk-songs—of which Cornwall seems to possess practically none—gener-
ated spontaneously) but it is wonderful for singing purposes, containing many
sounds almost unknown in English (except in Cornish-English dialect) which
have a real musical value of their own. The hymns, which are set for a capella
chorus, bear no resemblance to the clotted and sepulchral works of which I
was guilty some eighteen months ago, being for the most part *vierstimmige*—as
are also certain songs with string quartet, not so wholly unsatisfactory as not
to give me an irritating sense of what might be achieved under decent conditions. But here, for one week when composition is possible, there are ten
wherein it is out of the question and at least one nightmare of a week when it
does not even seem worth while.[67]

He ended his letter by suggesting that Gray give his love to Lawrence and Frieda, 'if I did not anticipate too clearly that he would fling it back at you: and oh, how horrible it is to be bespattered with flung love!'[68]

On 12 May 1918 Philip delivered an illustrated lecture entitled, 'What Music Is', at Dublin's famous Abbey Theatre, a building which had a considerable influence on world theatre. Built in 1904 at the time of the Irish literary renaissance, with men such as Yeats, J. M. Synge (1871–1909), and Sean O'Casey (1880–1964) being influential figures in its history, it was destroyed by fire in 1951. Philip first made mention of an intended lecture after his return in April from the remote island where he would have had ample opportunity to make plans. The event was announced as 'a lecture followed by a short programme of music (Stalls 1/- and 6d.; Balcony and Pit 3d.)'[69] and, in his correspondence at the time, Philip wrote at great length about it. It was to prove highly significant in his musical and personal development, in that it gave him the opportunity to clarify and articulate his thoughts on music and to gain self-confidence in public. It was also a typical 'Warlockian' occasion, there being much youthful criticism of the music profession, as well as an attempt to expose what was wrong in current musical life and then provide all the answers. Part of the script of this lecture is in the British Library[70] and, although only the first three pages have survived, it makes interesting reading. There are also detailed descriptions of the lecture in letters to Taylor and Delius. Using these, as well as Gray's account of the lecture in his memoir on Philip, a good deal of information about this unusual event can be pieced together. The Abbey Theatre was practically filled, and dramatic, coloured lighting effects were used throughout—the auditorium itself being in complete darkness. The lecture took about three-quarters of an hour and Philip was quite pleased with it, describing it as 'strong and bitter'. The musical illustrations consisted of a group of piano duets by Paul Ladmirault, three piano pieces by Bartók, and four arrangements of Dutch melodies by van Dieren played by Philip himself. An Irish-speaking and an Indian singer sang some traditional songs, Philip hoping thus to demonstrate what he believed to be a striking similarity. The Indian singer was evidently superb and a great success, the Irishwoman nervous and not so good, but the comparison had proved interesting. The discussion at the end of the lecture, which Philip had hoped would be controversial, 'fizzled out' poorly: 'There was no indignation—

only a few fatuous and harmless questions. I think and hope that the "intellectuals" (who are more hopelessly clique-y and static here than in England even) were hurt and insulted by various remarks in the lecture.' Philip also had another card up his sleeve:

As a further blast against them, I induced the wonderful Old Man of the Mountains[71] . . . to come and make a short speech—which he did, with great effect, saying that to restore the ancient Irish tradition in music we must all go out into the mountains and live with the sun and the fairies, as the founders of that tradition had done. This was just the kind of speech I wanted him to make, and it was greeted with tumultuous applause.[72]

It is unfortunate that the surviving text ends so abruptly, just as Philip was getting into his stride and about to define what in his opinion music was, for the lecture is written in a lucid, direct manner, with clear logic, and employing images that would have been easily understood by the average layman in the audience. One of its most interesting features is the inclusion of one of his regular hobby-horses—that the worst enemy of music is the professional musician—an opinion which would later lead to widespread hostility among the London Musical Establishment. It is also important to remember that Philip was only 23 at the time and also to note the heartfelt plea for an honest and unprejudiced approach to music, something for which he fought all his life. A fortnight later he wrote to Gray, incorporating in his letter some of the lecture material, and referring to his emerging theories as to the nature of art:

I am driven day by day towards a purely mystical conception of the nature of art: I believe that creation is a wholly spiritual act for which this or that faculty may or may not be employed as a tool: the means and methods are matters of indifference. To some the intellect may be of use, to others it is a clogging impediment. If one has something to say, IT will—as you remark with literal truth—GET ITSELF said, sooner or later, whether one be mad or sane, willing or unwilling, conscious or unconscious. If one wants to assist, that is to accelerate the process, one can only aim at the realization of the central peace subsisting at the heart of endless agitation—for this is the *condition* of the central being which, I think, is not a 'thing' one has or has not but a state to be realized and attained—though God knows the path is difficult enough at Time's present stage—our generation is overlaid and shackled and half-buried by intellectual chains. Our first task is to resolve complexity and still our endless agitation.[73]

An enthusiastic letter to Delius about the same lecture, written in rather more serious and philosophical vein, resulted in renewed correspondence between the two men:

You will have thought this long year's silence very strange—some day I will explain it altogether. At present I can only tell you that I have passed through a year of dark and critical vicissitudes, metamorphoses of various kinds, follies and their consequences, from which I am only now fully extricating myself . . . for years my letters to you have been too full of petty personal complaints . . . Now, however, the skies are clearer, and I am no longer tempted to dilate upon the mere circumstances that have lately hedged me round . . .

I have not written much music during the past year—a few small works which are, I know, immeasurably better than the very paltry productions I have sent you from time to time—but I am still in only a very experimental stage, and do not expect to do anything of any real significance for another seven years. If I cannot come forward before the world with something I *know* to be better than anything of any of my contemporaries, I will not come forward at all—and, good heavens, one hasn't much to eclipse, anyway! At present there is only Bernard van Dieren who can even share the name of composer with you . . . [he] is a man of miraculous genius for whose music my love and enthusiasm grows by what it feeds on. . . .

It is wonderful how much more clearly one can think about music when one is right away from it than one can possibly do when in the whirl of a concert-season. I have done a great deal of work at the philosophy and history of music while I have been in this country. The wilderness is the best place for meditation—and I have spent a considerable time in the most desolate and solitary region of the West coast. I believe it is so necessary to be sure of one's first general principles before proceeding to formulate any ideas about particular examples in art that I have spent most of my time lately in attacking the most comprehensive question of all, in music—namely, *What Music is*—in all its aspects: and I really feel I have arrived at results which—at any rate as a beginning of new discoveries—are of some value.[74]

Delius was delighted to resume their correspondence:

I need not say how welcome your letter was . . . It would interest me enormously to hear all about your experiences and troubles, as I can assure you that there is no one who takes such an interest in you or is as fond of you as I am. So you have been in the wilderness—a wonderful place—and the only place to find oneself after a prolonged sojourn in towns; one gathers such a lot of dross that ultimately it smothers one's real self. . . . I was immensely glad to hear that you are writing music, and also that you had lectured in Dublin. What you say about art is so true: where there is no art whatever there is a chance for an original artist, but none where there are crowds of mediocre thrusters. . . .

You know my opinion on contemporary music. For me music is very simple: it is the expression of a poetic and emotional nature. Most musicians by the time they are able to express themselves manage to get rid of most of their poetry and all their emotions. The dross of Technic has killed it; or they seize upon one little original streak, and it forthwith develops into an intolerable mannerism—Debussy and Ravel.

I am seriously thinking of going to New York in the autumn to have my new works produced, and then go to California until the war is finished. Will you come with me?—seriously. You might lecture on music; you will find a better public than in London. I want also the *Requiem* produced; I don't think I have ever done better than this . . . Do write soon and tell me all your troubles, and don't keep your friend again so long without news.[75]

Philip replied the next month:

It was a very great joy to me to receive a letter from you again: there is nothing in the world I prize so much as your sympathy and interest and kind thoughts for me—without the help of which, I need hardly repeat, I should never have emerged as far as I have out of the Cimmerian darkness which for most of our race constitutes life! How gladly I would confide everything about myself to you if we could but meet again for a short while! But these personal difficulties, these psychological complexities are so difficult to set down on paper with any degree of coherence and intelligibility: and although I think I may thank heaven that I have at last managed to extricate myself from the particular network of complications to which I referred, I am still too near to the old circumstances to be able to write about them with that complete detachment which alone could frame them into a consistent narrative. . . . I should dearly love to come with you to America—indeed, were it possible for me to do so, there is nothing that would be at once more delightful and beneficial also to me than to make this trip, but alas, I fear it would be impossible for me to obtain a passport despite the fact that I am completely useless for military purposes. The atmosphere of these islands becomes more and more stifling and putrescent to anyone who cares for art above all things. To get away altogether, to be with you, to be able to hear and study your new works and to be able to carry on my own work, writing and lecturing, in surroundings which gave it a chance of having some influence—this would indeed be joy and a new impulse of life to me. Oh, what a curse has fallen on the world—and when will it be removed? . . .

It is the musical profession that is always the greatest enemy of music—chiefly because, in listening to music, they cannot view it as pure utterance, pure expression: they regard as real the purely verbal, and so—in cases of true expression—non-existent, differentiation between the thing expressed and the mode of expression: with the result that instead of giving their attention to *what* is being expressed, they concentrate always on the manner—the *'how'*—and thus is perpetuated the dismal superstition that technique, as a separate entity, exists as a thing apart from expression. It is this fallacy that lies at the root of all the rottenness in modern music. It is responsible for the prevailing view of music as mere sound-for-sound's sake—a kind of aural counterpart of sweet scents: and it is to this fallacy also that one must attribute the fact that certain sounds have come to be regarded as 'beautiful' and 'ugly' *in themselves*, quite without reference to their context or to what they are used to express: and so we have arrived—so far as the musical trade-unions are concerned—at a kind of static musical diction.[76]

As Delius was on holiday there had been some delay in his receiving Philip's letter. Needless to say, all the lavish praise Philip had heaped on van Dieren in his letter of 15 May had intrigued him no end:

All what you wrote me of van Dieren makes me wish to get there as quick as possible—So that he, himself may make me acquainted with his music & that I may yet be able to help him. I will certainly do all in my power both in England & America for this unfortunate genius—God help a genius without money & influence anywhere, but most of all in England . . .

How long shall you stay in Ireland? cannot we meet in London? I should love to have long talks with you & hear about all your experiences since we last met. I could also shew you my new works—I am looking forward to Van Dieren's Symphonie . . . Write me at once, whether we shall meet in London—I will write you again as soon as we have decided when we shall go.[77]

In his reply Philip still seemed to be beset by many psychological problems, though now there was a slight glimmer of optimism:

As for myself, I cannot tell whether we shall meet in England or not: but I think you know me well enough to understand that it will not be through lack of effort on my part if we do not. You can imagine how hungry I am for a talk with you after three long years. . . . It exasperates and maddens me that one's life is circumscribed with so many petty and idiotic restrictions in these evil times. For ten years now all my best strength and energy has been dissipated by the mere effort required, in these islands, to keep the flood of national bilge-water from surging in upon me and engulfing me completely: and when one bungs up one hole, it begins at once pouring in from another quite unexpected quarter. Just now, when I am bursting with fresh schemes and enthusiasms after my long sojourn in the wilderness (for artistically the whole of this island is a wilderness) there is no outlet for them or for any activity on my part . . . The past three years have been a real nightmare to me—not, perhaps, unbroken by flashes of light which, added together, do no doubt mean real progress, yet for their very brilliance the general gloom has only seemed afterwards to deepen and grow more intense. I have sunk to the very lowest depths, stuck fast in the mire and only lately realized, when on the very point of being wholly submerged, the supreme necessity of getting out of it even if I left my own skin behind—of throwing over the whole wretched past at all costs: and this, thank heaven, I think I have now succeeded in doing once and for all, though perhaps the costs are not all paid yet. Still, I believe in Destiny: one *does* what one *does* because one *is* what one *is*—and it is often necessary for the general plan of one's existence that one should have the most apparently absurd and profitless experiences. I have long ceased to imagine that anything one does has any connection with praise or blame, intrinsically, save in the minds of fools. You may hear all kinds of unpleasant things about me in England—but I know you are too good a friend to listen to these things before you have heard the whole truth from myself—for nobody else knows the whole truth. I have my sojourn in the wilderness to thank for the impulse that finally extricated me from the morass.[78]

As early as September 1913, Philip had written to Viva Smith telling her of his discussion with Delius on the question of artistic inspiration:

I was talking to Delius the day before yesterday about the question of artistic inspiration, and the conversation impelled me to read a similar meaning into many inexplicable things in the most fascinating and absorbing province of all research—the unexplored region of the human mind. . . . Delius, who has been greatly interested in various occult séances and has the telepathic sense highly developed, considers this 'substance' to be as elusive and intangible as the so-called 'inspiration' which enabled him to write well at some time and not at all at others. At the same time I elicited from him that this inspiration grows greater and more regular by constant practice and persistence in endeavouring to invoke it, that it does not come all at once, in a sudden frenzied moment, and that it is not in the least incompatible with orderly and regular hours of work—if, indeed, it is compatible with aught else, after a certain point of immaturity has been passed. This of course, is not to say that any inspired artist can be as great as any other: we are still faced by the immense riddle of the nature of comparative grades of genius, of the 'will-to-create' itself, even, if we go a stage farther back. At the same time, what more conclusive example could be required, of the necessity for the union of reason with energy, if any really satisfactory results are to ensue?[79]

These were obviously thoughts which had been evolving in his mind, for in mid-1918 he referred, in a letter to Gray, to his newly forming theories of composition and musical inspiration, all seemingly developed in some way from occult experience:

I do not believe that it is possible for utterance to be impeded by 'lack of technique'—or whatever you may call the mere craftsmanship. I believe that those who imagine themselves thus obstructed simply deceive themselves *because* the truth *is not in them*—that is to say they have not yet focussed that truth they would utter aloud within themselves . . . There is no one thing called Technique—it simply does not exist. *How* a thing is done is absolutely unimportant—what matters is to get it done. . . . I do not say that the conscious intellectual processes have no part in artistic creation—far from it—but what I *do* say is that the intellect is one tool among several—and a tool that may be dispensed with in many cases. . . . In any age of extreme materialism it is necessary to insist on the things of the spirit rather more strongly than would be needed by a more enlightened epoch. We I think, can take the material processes for granted—Art, we are agreed, is pure utterance—but I would add, at this point, an axiom that if we cannot acquire and use the language of art as naturally and spontaneously as we acquire and use our mother tongue, we had better leave it alone altogether (until we can!)—if we must learn the language of art laboriously like a foreign tongue, we shall only speak it as foreigners and our utterance will be at best artificial.[80]

Gray challenged these views and repeated his belief that a composer needed to have a solid theoretical background. He recalls in his memoir that he told Philip 'that in order to become a musician one could learn more from Fux and Albrechtsberger than from all the mystics who ever lived—a palpable absurdity, as I thought even then, but only thrown out as what I conceived to be a salutary corrective to his unduly mystical and unpractical bias at the time'.[81] Philip replied immediately, elaborating and expanding his theories:

Your proposition in its final form bids me believe that you seek to attain interior clarity by study of what is not only entirely exterior but—what's more—what never in the beginning sprang from any interior impulse . . . And if you argue from precedent and tell me that great men of the past have followed a similar course, I would ask you to point out a single essential . . . feature in any work of art that can be attributed to this theoretical study, as distinct from the study of actual works of art—to say nothing of what intrinsic genius has itself created. I do not and shall never believe that van Dieren derived anything of essential importance from this kind of study . . . I refuse so far to detract from the power of his own creative genius as to attribute any part in his music to the influence of such pursuits. . . .

There is, too, a somewhat mystical utterance of Mozart, of whom one would hardly expect such a thing, to the effect that he frequently conceived *instantaneously* a whole symphony in all its parts and detail, after which vision its composition was only a matter of *unrolling*, so to speak, into terms of time. And I remember the Maestro showing me one day a small sheet of paper on which were a few little pencil jottings, and saying that the whole work to which they related (I think it was the second string quartet) was now *already composed*—a statement which points to a similar conception or instantaneous vision having taken place in him as in Mozart.[82]

A few years later Philip still held the same views but had now further developed his opinions on the subject, and was able to express himself more confidently when he wrote in an article that

Musical technique is simply the ability to express oneself in one's own terms: all that can be *learned* of technique (and this is what constitutes 'musicianship' in the accepted sense of the word) is how to string together 'effectively' a number of tags and cliches culled from the works of other composers. For some this may be good exercise, for others it is no better than a dangerous drug.[83]

But his bursts of enthusiasm alternated with fits of depression. Again he was suddenly full of doubts and despair, telling Taylor that he could not write a note of music:

I am utterly desiccated: I shall have to shut up entirely for a good while in this department, though I have a good deal to do in others . . . I have no illusions about the value of such little works as I have already done: and I do know that the work I hope to do some day will be of such a very different nature that I would rather preserve absolute silence towards the world at large until I feel myself ripe for a real achievement.[84]

He had just completed two Cornish Christmas carols ('Kanow Kernow I and II'), possibly begun in Cornwall the previous year when he had first become interested in the revival of the Cornish language. The instructions to the singers at the beginning of the second of these carols, 'Kan Nadelik', gives a clue to the style: 'To be sung fairly fast, with sudden alternations of hardness and sweetness, of rude heartiness and tenderness touched with awe.' Despite the introduction of a quotation from the familiar carol 'The First Nowell', there is a certain austerity and hardness apparent in the setting. Philip felt strongly that these carols should be performed in the original language, as the music was inseparably associated with the actual Cornish words and that 'any translation would pervert the whole character of the works'.[85] With his current enthusiasm for the Celtic languages Philip had even written to Gray with ideas of reviving the Cornish language

for many most excellent reasons . . . All neo-Celtic nationalism is in effect anti-national, in the sense in which we detest nationality: it becomes almost an individualizing movement—a separating one, at any rate. What more effective protest against imperialism (in art as in other matters) could you or I make than adopting, as a pure ritual, a speech, a nationality, that no longer exist— for you to make your dwelling the centre of a Celtic rebirth—the rebirth of a something that never was born? . . . to have a *private language*!! What luxury![86]

Philip had sent copies of the carols to Balfour Gardiner for comment and was amazed and upset by his candid reaction that 'this sort of music . . . makes the same impression on me as a lot of 16th Century stuff that is declared, without a dissentient voice, to be excellent'.[87] To send his work to Gardiner had probably been a mistake, for the two men's musical tastes could hardly have been more different. When Philip sent him a copy of van Dieren's 'Chinese' Symphony the next month Gardiner confessed that, on his first two attempts to read it, he 'suffered acute mental distress' and, although he was 'much struck by the freedom, resource & beauty of the polyphonic parts',[88] he stated quite bluntly that in the harmonic aspects he found combinations that he could not imagine he could ever bring himself to tolerate, as well as evidence that van Dieren's sense of orchestral values was 'defective'. Needless to say, Gardiner's negative response to his own composition sparked off an angry reaction and Philip wrote asking Taylor if he thought there was 'anything 16th centuryish about it?—and, first of all, what is 16th centuryishness in music? I suspect always the people who speak of music by century-labels: one knows that when they come to the 20th century, they would explain themselves by adding—"Oh, like Debussy and Strauss, you know the kind of thing".[89]

But matters were now coming to a head. Feeling isolated and dissatisfied with his lack of direction and general aimlessness, Philip thought the time had at last come for action on van Dieren's behalf. Even though his occult experiences seemed to be telling him something positive and he still felt the urge to compose, a real belief in his own ability was lacking. His confidence in the 'Master', however, remained unshaken and was an important anchor amidst all his confusion and uncertainty. Therefore, before finalizing any plans to return to England, he wrote to Taylor asking for a favour.

AN INFAMOUS LETTER
(1918)

Soon after giving his Dublin lecture Philip had sent Taylor a copy
of ten of van Dieren's *Dutch Melodies* for piano, feeling sure that he
would love them. Now, on 13 June 1918, he wrote again, this time
asking him to try to find a publisher in London for these 'exquisite
works'. He felt that they were 'of so delicate a nature that the mere
dumb manuscript, left with a not over-intelligent or sympathetic
publisher, might easily fail to convey the frail and subtle beauty of
the music'. If, however, Taylor were to play them, Philip decided
they would then have the best of all possible chances. He hoped,
too, that Taylor would find an opportunity to visit the ailing composer and discover more about the man and his music. Although
still confined to bed, van Dieren was working at a new string quartet which he was composing without any preliminary sketches or
alterations, 'directly into a *fair-copy* score, without any rough notes
whatever'. In Philip's postscript there were also dark and cryptic
comments to the effect that he had 'just had a most astounding
communication through a mediumistic friend (who is entirely unmusical) concerning van Dieren and the immediate future of music'.[1]
These predictions had obviously convinced him that van Dieren was
dying and his next letter to Taylor was couched in similarly urgent
and mysterious tones:

Please keep *strictly* to yourself anything I may have said in former letters
about certain communications and predictions. These have developed into a
very serious and important matter which I will tell you fully one day. At present, however, you would be rendering me a very great service if you would go
as soon as ever you can to visit the Master . . . He may be too ill to see you
but you will see his wife. Say I sent you to inquire about him and do anything
he may want with regard to his works. I fear he has but a few more weeks to
live. Please let me know how you find him and *send me any messages he may
give you*. He is probably too ill to write. I have not heard from him for some
time and I am very anxious in view of these persistent predictions, which I
again beg you most strongly to keep entirely to yourself. I must see him again

before he dies—so that I shall probably have to cross over to England very
soon (though don't mention this to him either; the whole matter is very complex and singular—I dare say these references surprise you and seem confused,
but I will explain all before long) and this will mean, as you probably realize,
the extinction of all my activities for an indefinite period.[2]

The ever-dependable Taylor reacted promptly, visited van Dieren
as requested, and took the *Dutch Melodies* to the publisher
Winthrop Rogers, an unfortunate choice which filled Philip with dis-
may:

I did not know it was W. Rogers you were going to visit in London: he is a
perfectly frightful individual I think, and has already had the Dutch tunes and
turned them down, so it is sheer humbuggery if he pretends now that he is
'considering' them. This kind of man is infinitely worse than the publisher who
is openly and honestly nothing but a business man. Rogers must needs pretend
to be 'something more', a man of taste, refinement, culture etc, etc, but in the
end nothing comes of it but nasty water slobber which is far more unpleasant
than the good healthy hogwash of Boosey. Rogers 'composes' himself too!! . . .
Incidentally, he is not very rich as publishers go and would probably not
pay van Dieren anything like their real value for the Dutch tunes. Naturally
that kind of person would find any definite statement or theory of the function
of music profoundly disturbing. Being a publisher and, what's more, a composer into the bargain, he wishes to be approached with deference . . . These
are the very worst types of professional musicians.[3]

On the very day that Philip wrote this letter, Rogers replied critically to Taylor about the van Dieren piano pieces:

I took these little pieces home, because I have been so busy at my office that I
have very little time for looking things over here, and as it happened, I
showed them at separate times to John Ireland, Frank Bridge, Anthony
Bernard, and Roger Quilter. I made no comment or expression of opinion to
any of the above four, but they all felt exactly as I do about van Dieren's
work.
First, that his workmanship is shockingly bad.
Second, that the harmonic scheme is in bad taste, especially so because it is
impossible to hear the melodies in the midst of the errors of harmony.
Third, because the whole scheme is quite the opposite of what one under-
stands by 'the modern spirit', and is more in the musical class of the mediocre
Germans of the middle of the nineteenth Century.
One of the four said at once, 'This is the work of a sick man'.
I write all the above quite frankly, because it is no use to beat about the
bush in such matters. I appreciate your kindness both to Van Dieren and
myself, in suggesting that we get together, and I hope my decision in this case
will not deter you from making any other suggestions which occur to you.
I feel sure that we are not mistaken in Van Dieren's case. I know that great
talents have often been misunderstood, but the fact should not make one
timid, especially when one sees clear evidence of inferior musicianship.[4]

To say that Philip went berserk when Taylor forwarded the letter to him is to understate his reaction. His single-minded loyalty to, and admiration for, van Dieren unleashed a torrent of words, covering a wide range of topics and containing colourful imagery drawn from sources as diverse as Christianity, war, 'buggery', and his disillusionment with materialism. As he leapt to van Dieren's defence, his vivid imagination, fired no doubt by his recent experiences with the occult, saw van Dieren as a Christ-like figure, Rogers as Antichrist, music as 'a fair lady in distress', and himself and his friends as 'the very few champions that remained to fight her battles against an insidious and cunning horde of monsters'. His ten-page reply of well over 3,000 words in miniscule handwriting is one of the longest of his surviving letters. Here his words flow with an almost hysterical, paranoid quality:

I am very grateful to you for those letters. If they do not add much to one's previous knowledge of the writer and his associates, they at least give one the satisfaction of having from one's enemy's own mouth a more eloquent statement of the case against himself than one could have framed in his own words . . . I feel that in those letters we have the concentrated essence of the great poison that has for some while past been tainting music as well as the other arts, the chief force against which we and all who care for the true welfare of art will have to contend with all our strength during the next few years . . . these letters bring the matter to a head—they act upon me like a trumpet-call to battle. . . .

What Rogers defines as 'the modern spirit' in music is in reality the spirit of Antichrist. This is a word which is very much misused and misunderstood. It has of course no necessary connection with the Christian religion as understood to-day, nor with the historical Jesus. From your reading of Blake, James Pryse and others you will know what the Christ principle really is—the crown of human endeavour, spiritual attainment. Antichrist, however, is not the mere negative-opposite of Christ. Polarity and equilibrium are necessary to life, light is balanced on the darkness, darkness is the necessary complement of light. Failure to recognize this fundamental fact is the underlying weakness of all systems of moral values manufactured on this side of good and evil . . . This is a very important point and gives the key to the whole situation. It is not the mere neglect or negation of art that is art's worst enemy: it is as Blake said 'a pretence of art' that destroys art.[5] This is the monster we are out to slay—the perversion of the very function of art . . . It is when this true purpose is forgotten, when such things as these are done in the name of art, in the name of a spiritual principle of which they are themselves the embodied refutation that the supreme blasphemy takes place, that—relatively speaking—*evil* arises. . . .

The spirit of the present era is materialism: it is everywhere rampant and, despite all the seeming contradictions, as yet still dominant everywhere. . . . Now the 'modern spirit' being essentially materialism, how is it possible that any art can spring from it? Materialistic art—that is art that is in sympathy with and an expression of a materialistic age—is a contradiction and a lie. Art is the reconciliation of opposites, spirit and matter, an expression of spiritual things in material terms—this is the quintessence of art. But when no spiritual things are known? How can art exist? The answer is that it can not exist, and that if there exist something in these conditions which is called art, this is a counterfeit, a monstrous perversion and a lie. . . .

Let us now think particularly about music, reverting to the letter from Winthrop Rogers. . . . I have often reiterated to you that the worst enemy of Music is the musical profession . . . Rogers' letter is a magnificent corroboration of that dictum . . . One suspects at once that something indecent has occurred when one discovers a composer-publisher round whom petits maîtres revolve like satellites about a planet . . . Rogers is a very good example of this confusion which is the very root of all evil in art: one may take him as a symbol, a figure-head which sums up everything that is most insidiously, virulently hostile to the interests of art at this critical period which is the climax of the old order out of whose subsidence the new will gradually arise. Rogers is by no means the only, perhaps not even the best example in England: indeed nearly everyone is tainted with this spirit. But he is a very clear and definite embodiment of the modern spirit and in *smashing* him and all his crew we shall be striking a good blow on behalf of Music. It will not be so difficult as it may seem to you at first. But to recur for a while to the letter itself: observe the intense *personal* animosity behind it . . . note too what this implies: he and his crew *feel* something behind van Dieren: their hostility is a high tribute to his power which, even in its mildest manifestations, can move them to such an outburst. Mediocrity always recognizes genius by a kind of instinct—as its worst enemy of course, and gets on its guard accordingly: but it always *recognizes* genius—in its own interests of self-defence. No mediocrity's work would prompt a letter of such intensity and feeling. And then observe that, as happened after the concert, this *instinctive*, unreasoning hostility, as of a wild beast to a man, entirely overmasters the reasoning faculties of those in whom it is aroused: with the result that when they try to express it in terms of reasoned criticism, they come utterly to grief. Their criticisms simply do not apply to the works in question (save for that very penetrating remark, for which I will credit Rogers with far keener critical acumen than any of his colleagues, about the 'modern spirit')—for the most part they do not even make sense in themselves. The force of hatred that animates this man has made him inarticulate almost. (It is possible also that he remembers with some bitterness the association of certain *definite ideas* with van Dieren and feels that at all costs, whatever the nature of van Dieren's music, those ideas must be defeated). But what sense is there in the phrase 'errors of harmony' from a partizan of 'the modern spirit'? Why, it's a positive joke! And then remember it was Rogers' colleague Quilter who introduced and welcomed to London the prodigious 'futurist' Leo Ornstein!!!! 'Errors' of harmony, from such a man! Though I must say I am just a little surprised and grieved at the inclusion of Quilter's name among this crew. He is a man of far greater refinement and intelligence than most musicians, and although as a composer he had very little to say and has already said it several times over, that little was at first of a rare and exquisite quality and the best lyrics that he wrote ten or more years ago remain the sole examples of modern English music that one can hear over and over again with undiminished pleasure . . . As for the other 'meistersinger'—

well, I do not expect that if one blew up the house of Rogers with all its attendants and hangers-on, that any stray works of genius would perish with the dross. . . .

The *order* of Rogers' accusations is also significant. First of all comes *workmanship*. (Incidentally this is the biggest joke of all to anyone who knows van Dieren's work.) It is very characteristic of 'the modern spirit' to care nothing at all whether anyone has anything to say, so long as he mouths and gibbers in the approved fashion: the *means* entirely eclipses the *end* in importance!

'Bad taste' smacks of the herd again: it is the criticism of the slaves of fashion jealous of the free. As for its being 'impossible' to hear the melodies (etc)—one begins to wonder whether Mr Rogers was *really* sober when he read the pieces, since the only possible explanation of this judgment would seem to lie in the fact of his having contemplated the MS *upside down*—seeing that the pieces in every case consist of a plain tune—always in the treble part—accompanied by straightforward 4-part harmony! This is the kind of criticism that makes argument impossible and necessitates more forcible weapons . . . The phrase 'This is the work of a sick man' is also very contemptible, especially as everyone knows that van Dieren has lain for years at Death's door and it is apparently pretended that this fact was discovered by some miraculous process of divination from his work . . .

Rogers has got to be *smashed*, and—what's more—Rogers *shall* be smashed. As a preliminary move I have written a very full account of the whole case to Delius, who is shortly coming over to England—partly to acquaint him with this very characteristic illustration of the state of music in England, partly to warn him of the true nature of Rogers seeing that the latter might easily scent profits in some of the numerous new works Delius is bringing over with him (indeed I once heard Bernard express a keen desire that Rogers should secure some of his new songs), and partly because Delius has now a very considerable amount of influence and is not afraid to lay bare the naked truth about the enemies of art. I can assure you that Mr Rogers will bitterly repent him of his attitude towards van Dieren before we have finished with him.[6]

The original letter from Rogers, with indignant marginal comments in Philip's minutest handwriting was sent to Gray, with instructions to keep it 'carefully for future use'. Many of these comments repeat or echo those in his angry letter to Taylor but in more melodramatic terms:

Here is Antichrist in person, in person, in person! Although one already knew Messrs. Rogers, Bernard and Co. fairly well, this astounding document is something of a revelation: to us, I think, also a trumpet-call to action of some kind. It is always stimulating and satisfactory when one's enemy formulates the case against himself more eloquently and more concisely than any words of one's own could have done it. . . . You will observe the extraordinarily virulent *personal* hostility manifested in the letter: this is as usual emphasized by the utter irrelevance of all the particular charges to the particular music in question—this is the true Antichrist spirit. It is not the pure negation of truth—that is far cleaner. This is the overlaying of truth by the positive assertion of a lie—and this is the germ from which a vast and poisonous movement might well spring. Note the sinister symptoms:—commerce and art in an unholy (i.e. unequilibrated) alliance. Boosey and Chappell, Ascherberg, Hopwood and Crew—all these are harmless atheists—commercials, for whom art, qua art, does not exist. But one sees what's afoot here: British music—capture the enemy's trade—oh Lord, I can't write about it, no words can even approximate expression of the utter and inconceivable depths of filthiness revealed in this document—no, not inconceivable, alas, nor yet unable to conceive and bring forth monsters enough to devour every true work of art that makes its appearance in the world during the next two decades. 'The modern spirit'—my God! Here is the pretence of art to destroy art, with a vengeance. It is no longer the individual versus the herd—the herd itself becomes an individual and voilà—*the modern spirit*! . . . These things have forced upon my mind very insistently the fact that, for some obscure reason, you and I have been selected as almost solitary defenders of the faith during a period which will without a doubt prove one of the darkest in the whole history of music. The tremendous responsibility of caring for the Master and his work which has been laid upon us as a kind of a sacred trust implies a still larger responsibility for directing, as far as lies in our power, the whole immediate future of music—in England at any rate—and not only there. You too know this yourself, though you will probably consider my words somewhat exaggerated—but they are not so. At the moment I feel utterly inarticulate to express a tithe of what I would. But I tell you—our power is far greater than you suppose or suspect at present: it is practically unlimited in this direction, and I am waiting with the utmost impatience to hear finally from you that you have cast off the last remaining fetishes of the old life, in order that I may communicate to you what I already know concerning the great and marvellous work that lies before you. Remember, Antichrist is subtle as the serpent, able at times to deceive the very elect: *Satan cannot cast out Satan*—and all our strength will be required for the conflict that is to come. For the love of God do not delay longer. The Master has but a short while to live on this earth, and there is much that needs to be done and done quickly. I am coming to England for a few weeks.

But the Rogers affair seemed to have one good effect. Now passionately roused for battle, Philip suddenly became incredibly productive. He wrote again to Taylor a fortnight later:

During the last few weeks the solution of a psychological problem that has obsessed and baulked me and stifled me now for nearly three years has been revealed and I am sensible of a tremendous liberation of spirit. One is prone to effervescence in the celebration of such occasions, and I have written ten songs in the last fortnight—they are probably more fizz than actual stuff, but still such activity has hitherto been a thing unknown with me—and it is a great relief.[7]

The reference to an unidentified and mysterious 'psychological problem' that had 'obsessed', 'baulked', and 'stifled' him is infuriatingly enigmatic. If it had been a problem to do with his belief in himself as a composer then he surely would have openly articulated it to

Taylor. Is it perhaps that through his lecture on 'What Music is' he had discovered for himself that inspiration must lie in something truly felt within, not in mere technical facility? Or was it something more sinister connected with the occult, or the bouts of depression referred to in various letters during the preceding years, or maybe even something of a sexual nature which he found too difficult to mention to anyone?

At about the same time as the drama with Rogers was taking place, Philip had also corresponded with Gray about the medium's predictions: firstly that van Dieren was about to die and, secondly, that Philip had a highly important message for Gray which could only be delivered to him in person. It was evidently of such import that it could not 'fail to impart a new and profound significance' to Gray's whole life: 'I can neither trust myself rightly to deliver nor you rightly to receive.'[8] Understandably Gray was somewhat sceptical about the whole matter, with the result that Philip wrote more urgently:

I have been too profoundly moved and shaken by certain events of the past few days . . . I have considered long and carefully whether these things could possibly be communicated to you in any way that would obviate the necessity of your spending a week over here: but I have been driven to the conclusion that there is absolutely no other way . . . I know you will imagine that I am purposely making it seem obscure and mysterious . . . yet I swear to you that for every reticence and every precaution—however unnecessary they may seem to you now—there is an absolutely compelling reason, which you will fully acknowledge when you know the whole truth. I cannot even tell you the nature of these things unconditionally—if I were to do so without reserve I should only be doing you an ultimate injury . . .

I therefore send you in the enclosed envelope as much—and it is very little—as, with all the desire in the world, I can tell you in writing at the moment, *trusting you to burn the paper unread if you are not willing to promise me that no word or hint of its contents or any matter pertaining thereto be given to anyone whatsoever, so far as this lies in your power* . . .

May Heaven preserve you and lead you in the right direction! I am terribly anxious.[9]

Enclosed was the following dramatic note:

I have lately received, in the presence of witnesses, a series of direct communications relating to you from—what shall I say—the Unknown, the Unseen— all words are inadequate. These messages, which have already run into many thousands of words of precise and explicit narrative, are of an importance that I can only truthfully describe as overwhelming. As I wrote before, they cannot fail to impart a new and profound significance to your whole life. For this reason I regard them as too vital, as too sacred perhaps, to be communicated to you in any way that might involve the slightest risk of misunderstanding, or of the natural incredulity with which you could hardly help receiving them if they came to you merely from me. *It is therefore necessary for you to be present here so that the messages can be repeated directly to you in person: you will then be able to put any question you wish to the unseen authors thereof, and to subject them to any and every test your scepticism can devise.*

It would be quite useless, if not actually harmful, for you to hear these messages without conviction . . . If you have any faith in me at all, you will find some means of coming here at once. In doing so you may be able to save yourself and others from much suffering: in any case, a great light will be shed on your life.

I swear to you that this is God's literal truth.[10]

Gray stubbornly refused to take these predictions seriously and, in his reply, Philip assumed an air of chastening superiority:

When you stand utterly alone and utterly empty, when you have cast away all trace of any and every extraneous influence of other persons (save the Master [van Dieren] whom you could not and should not try to escape), as well as every personal attachment, when you are willing to accept, finally and without one waver of doubt, the condition of having no existence apart from art, let me know: for you will then be ripe for the great work you have the power to accomplish . . . when you are ready for it, this news will bring into your life a dazzling light which, were you not fully prepared for it, would only plunge you into darkness and horrible confusion . . .

The condition of absolute secrecy attaches also to this and any subsequent communication I may be authorized to make.[11]

Yet Philip's tone in his next letter to Gray suddenly became deflated and apologetic. In less urgent terms he now makes mysterious reference to 'the linking-up of a broken circle':

Forgive me if my last letters have seemed cold and curt and remote. I was in a state of nervous tension and irritation most of the last fortnight and this made me unduly cantankerous . . . I am really a very bad hand at writing letters . . . I am totally incapable of speaking *directly* in writing: whatever efforts I make to do so, it seems inevitable that when I try to speak intimately through my pen I must also talk through my hat—and a very old, worn-out hat, too. The grotesqueness of this situation has been slowly dawning on me for some time and it has now become quite unbearable—perhaps because for the *very* first time in my life it seems to me that I have a few things to say. . . . I am quite sure that the moment has come for the linking-up of a broken circle—if you can see what I mean: I can express it in no other way—As to what may follow upon *that*, who can tell definitely? I have my own speculations, but the one thing that is absolutely clear is that I must come over to you immediately. This is far more definite and clear than any idea as to the exact nature of the affairs whose instrument I am. All this will read like the most grisly gibber, so I had better cease, begging you as I do so to realize my miserable limitations of utterance and to be swayed rather by what I have *not* written than by what I have.[12]

Gray later explained the significance of this last portion of the letter:

And grisly gibber it certainly did seem to me, all these mysterious references to affairs of which he was the instrument, broken circles which must be linked up, and so on. The explanation, I discovered eventually, was to be found in certain occult experiments in which he had been engaged at the time, in accordance with which he had received what purported to be communications—astral, celestial or demoniacal—to the effect that he and I were destined to be closely associated in some epoch-making, earth-shaking activity or other. I do not mention all this merely in order to show how deeply immersed he was at this time in the quicksands and morasses of occultism, but because, under the surface absurdity of the whole thing there lurked a certain element of truth. It was not only that we were in fact to be associated with each other in various enterprises—though assuredly of by no means so important a nature as the otherworldly revelations would have had him believe—but also because we were in a sense two complementary aspects of one personality, two halves of one whole . . . . We were in fact, born collaborators, and I believe that we could have achieved very much more in working together than we did separately.

I laughed at it all then, but now I see that the oracle—or whatever it was— spoke more truly than I knew.[13]

It is also significant that during this period Philip grew a beard for the first time, his 'fungus', as he liked to call it. He explained to Taylor that he had cultivated it

for a purely *talismanic* purpose: as such it works, and this is more important to me than mere appearance . . . it *does* have a certain psychological effect on me: and seeing that now for ten years all my best strength and energy has been used up negatively in keeping out the tide of the world which wants to swamp me and prevent me from doing the only kind of work I *can* do with any success . . . it is necessary for me to make use of any little magical energy-saving devices that suggest themselves—and this is one of them.[14]

The beard was, in short, an attempt to create a more confident self-image with which Philip could face people, in the music world in particular, without the previous feelings of inadequacy. Gray, in preparing his readers for his controversial split-personality theory, describes it rather dramatically as 'the first decisive step towards the assumption of the elaborate mask which he was ultimately destined to adopt permanently, as a defence against a hostile world'.[15] Arnold Dowbiggin later gave a vivid portrait of the bearded Philip: a tall, handsome man with a 'neatly trimmed Van Dyke beard, grey shirt, red tie, wide-brimmed velour black hat and tall Malacca cane with a large silver engraved knob. In no sense flamboyant: it all seemed perfectly natural, and his urbane and friendly manner immediately put one at ease'.[16]

But to return to Philip's letter to Taylor of 22 August: Philip's comments that there had been 'a tremendous liberation of spirit' and that he had written 'ten songs in the last fortnight' are of the greatest importance. It was in these songs that Philip had at last found his own individual voice as a composer—all his theories of 'overflow' and 'pure utterance' seemed to come miraculously into effect. Gone is the self-conscious imitation of Delius and van Dieren. As Copley so neatly puts it, 'in place of laboured complexities of harmony and texture, ease, economy, and a certain inevitability and rightness in the use of constructional devices are to be noted. For with these settings of fifteenth- and sixteenth-century texts, six-teenth- and seventeenth-century musical influences had come to the fore, and from now on he had a mature style at his command.'[17] Elizabeth Poston also perceptively pointed out that Philip's work 'is whole, of a piece. Except for one or two recognizably immature works and the early vein he never returned to, his work has no development, no middle or late period. The songs he wrote at the beginning are those he was writing at the end.'[18]

These early songs are quite remarkable in all respects. Suddenly a new-found confidence and inspiration manifests itself in these minia-ture masterpieces—'the songs that made him', as Colin Taylor later described them. Even if the influence of Delius or van Dieren is occasionally discernible, in a song such as the plangent 'Take, O take those lips away', there is a passion and originality which belongs to Warlock and to Warlock alone. The Elizabethan-influenced 'As ever I saw' and 'Lullaby' ('Golden slumbers kiss your eyes') with their grateful melodies, contrapuntal accompaniments, and gentle, chromatic touches, contrast with the almost medieval 'My gostly fader' and 'The bailey berith the bell away'. The strange and puzzling symbolism of the text of the latter song is perfectly captured in the wistful, deliberate archaisms of the music. Indeed, it has an uncanny, eerie, and faintly disturbing atmosphere—an almost tangible evocation of the early origins of the words. Gray, too, had spotted this when he later wrote that 'the peculiar quality which dis-tinguishes these [works] . . . from all other music I know lies in the union of a vein of medieval mysticism with an acutely modern sensi-bility. The spirit of the ancient poems is perfectly caught . . . .'.[19] Were these inspired compositions in some mysterious way perhaps the result of his occult experiences with the medium Hester Dowden, who was particularly noted for her skills in automatic communica-tion?

Philip provides a few clues in a letter written to Taylor in August 1918:

... in my view individuals in artistic matters (as elsewhere) are but the tools of certain tendencies and forces. One is given certain talents, certain forces in order that one may play a particular part in the general operations. Things do not happen at random and powers are not bestowed upon one for no particular purpose. . . . One allies oneself with a certain force or direction and the more one effaces oneself, the more strongly can this force operate through one: that is the actual fact—yet it *appears* to the world that one's power is a *personal* thing . . . whereas in truth—in very literal truth in *all* matters of art and spiritual things—'every good and every perfect gift cometh from above'[20]—that is from within and yet from beyond one's self—he that loseth his life shall find it[21]—the truer, higher self, the force that works through the phenomenal puppet the world calls the person. . . . For years now I have been led by some power stronger than myself along strange paths of preparation for the work that has now clearly revealed itself to me. I have travelled in the dark, often ignorant of the end of my journey, often ignorant of the very fact that I was travelling at all. During the last few months the light has begun to break: I have had experiences which have brought me to the realization of things which seemed before incredible. . . . when we meet I shall tell you of experiences which will astonish you, which you will probably be unable to believe at first. But you will, whether you believe or not, at least be able to understand the surety and confidence which they have implanted in me. It is not for no purpose that I have been drawn to the study of the things that lie beyond the confines of our narrow sensuous world: and I will tell you, in strict confidence, that I have already received very definite and detailed communications *concerning music* from sources which the ignorant and unheeding world call supernatural: and that there is unlimited power behind these sources.

This suggestion is not as extraordinary as it might seem. Yeats, for example, had also been involved in the study of the occult and when, after his marriage in 1917, his wife began automatic writing, he believed that these mysterious communications had been sent to give him new metaphors for poetry.

Another of Philip's songs dating from this period, 'Whenas the Rye', could not, on the other hand, be in greater contrast to the introvert mysticism expressed in the two compositions mentioned above. Here there is a taste of the extrovert, harmonically daring Philip with difficult accompaniments which would characterize many of his songs yet to come. Besides these fine solo songs Philip also produced his first choral settings, the two 'Cornish Christmas Carols' (mentioned in Chapter 7), 'As Dew in Aprille' and 'Benedicamus Domino'. 'As Dew in Aprille', an evocative setting of an anonymous fifteenth-century text, is light-textured with transparent, occasionally chromatic writing, while 'Benedicamus Domino', in contrast, is more homophonic—vigorous and extrovert in character.

Still believing the predictions that van Dieren was about to die, Philip unfolded to Taylor a typically selfless and generous plan:

I am very much afraid van Dieren is dying—and my belief rests on communications both from the secret source of which I have hinted to you before and from the Maestro himself. . . . this crisis of health has exactly coincided with the worst pecuniary crisis that has yet arisen. The poor man has spent more than his little all on doctors and druggists, and now he is practically penniless. You will get some idea of how literally true this statement is when I tell you that his precious violin and viola are in pawn and Steinway's are threatening to take away his piano unless the bill for its hire be paid immediately . . . The other day he sent me a pathetic telegram for a few shillings. It is too monstrous and horrible that the greatest artist of his generation should be reduced to such a condition in this vaunted era of culture.

Now since it is a case of *all* contributions, however small, being most thankfully received, it has occurred to me that my ten songs, which are all light and simple like the two I enclose, might be turned to some account—despite my resolve to have nothing to do with publishers for the present. But still, the case is a desperate one and calls for desperate remedies. I therefore fling myself upon your kindness and beg you to tell me (1) whether such songs as the two I send you are saleable (2) and if so who is the most likely publisher to purchase them, (3) etc, etc—especially (3)! In fact, if you would go so far as to send them, with your recommendation, to some publisher with whom you are on friendly terms, I should be eternally grateful to you. Perhaps they are quite unsuitable, but still—one must try every expedient for raising money. Please tell me candidly how these strike you. If you like them, I'll send on some of the others. Forgive me for plaguing you thus, but you see what necessity prompts me to do, and you will realize, I know, that I cannot with a clear conscience neglect even the smallest opportunity of doing what little I can to relieve the stress of a friend to whom I owe such added joy and understanding of music as van D. has given me.[22]

As Taylor was still in the army, stationed at Newhaven, he was unable to take these latest songs to a publisher. Philip, worried about van Dieren's health and, less anxious now about the possibility of conscription at this stage of the war, decided to return to England in August 1918. He had, by this time at any rate, grown tired of what he called 'the dead, stagnant atmosphere of Ireland' and for the last few months had kept to himself, staying largely indoors, seeing no one and working steadily.

Although the armistice would be signed on 11 November and the war would at last be over, Philip was returning to an England very different from the one he had left, a society turned upside-down in four disastrous years. The Victorian and Edwardian way of life and its values were rapidly disappearing and a sense of aimlessness and hopelessness hung over those young men who had survived the horrors of the war. Between 750,000 and 950,000 British soldiers had been killed—a 'lost generation'—with the total number of deaths estimated at some eight and a half million. The war had also had a devastating effect on the British economy; income taxes had risen from 15 per cent in 1915 to 30 per cent, and the national debt had climbed to an unprecedented £8 billion. Little wonder that Philip returned home disillusioned, feeling himself very much a lone voice. His utter detestation of what the war symbolized had no doubt been compounded by the fear that the authorities might eventually catch up with him and also by feelings of guilt that others had paid with their lives. For him, materialism had been the cause of all this evil, slowly corrupting and destroying the artistic and spiritual life of England and Europe in its wake, at the same time poisoning his creative aspirations. Now he heard the 'trumpet call to action' and was ready to do battle with any adversary that might be awaiting his return from Ireland.

THE SACKBUT
(1918–1921)

THE MANNER of Philip's return to London that summer seems to indicate that he wanted it to be known that he had created a new image whilst in Ireland. Gray recalled meeting him at the station early one hot August morning. Philip was 'wearing a thick fur coat with the collar turned up, a large, sinister black hat, with the brim turned down, dark blue spectacles and a huge unkempt beard which, though real, looked as if it were false. He looked, in fact, like an exaggerated caricature of a Bolshevik and a German spy combined.'[1] If the military authorities had been on the look-out for Philip, they would have had little difficulty finding him arrayed in such garb, but by that time the war was practically over and deserters and draft-dodgers were no longer being hounded with any degree of enthusiasm.

Back in London one of Philip's first tasks was to put into effect a plan of deception that he had been busy plotting for some time. He gave an amusing account of this in his next letter to Taylor:

I have had a most excellent revenge on Rogers for his insulting letter about van Dieren and his insulting remarks about myself. I sent him a book of seven of my recent old English lyrics (including the two I sent you) under the name of Peter Warlock, asking if he would care to publish them. Some days later I received (or rather P. Warlock received) a note asking me to call at 18 Berners Street—which I did in my own proper person (without beard or other appendages), Rogers having not the faintest notion who I was!! For at least an hour and a half he talked most amiably to me about this, that and the other thing, and in the end offered to publish all seven songs in an album, paying me a royalty of 5d or 6d on every copy sold . . . isn't it an excellent joke?—and what would he say if he discovered it—what, indeed, *could* he say? . . . And just as I was leaving, he remarked that he had shown my MSS to Quilter who had expressed great admiration and a desire to meet the interesting new composer!!![2]

Philip's interest in early music was as strong as ever and within a few months of his return he was once again busying himself with man-

uscripts in the British Museum. It is also interesting to note his changing musical tastes, described in a letter to Taylor early the next year:

Not so very long ago I should have laughed if anyone had suggested that in
1919 I should go to a concert and be enchanted, overwhelmed by a Beethoven
Symphony after the performance of a new Delius work had left me cold and
disappointed! Yet this happened last Saturday at Queens Hall: and I do not
yet know whether my sadness at the decline of one whose earlier works have
moved me perhaps more than any other music, and indeed do still, is not
compensated by the intense delight that has followed upon my ears becoming
suddenly opened to the splendour of Beethoven! I am more than ever convinced that young people ought to begin with the moderns and work back
through them, through a surfeit of them, to the older masters.[3]

Even though Philip was here voicing outright criticism of a Delius
piece, he had certainly not dismissed Delius's music completely. In
the period following this letter he still continued to support Delius's
cause, making arrangements of his music, writing about him for
music journals, commissioning him to write two articles, completing
the first full-length book to be published on Delius, and also continuing to promote his music. He still considered works such as the
Mass of Life, *A Village Romeo and Juliet*, *Sea Drift*, *Appalachia*, *In
a Summer Garden*, and the pieces for small orchestra to be masterpieces of the first order. It was only in confidential letters to close
friends like Taylor that he expressed reservations. In his public writings he was unswervingly loyal. He was also critical of the *Requiem*.
As early as September 1913 Philip had written excitedly to Viva
Smith, telling her that Delius was 'working hard at his magnificent
Requiem'.[4] Now he continued his letter to Taylor in critical vein
saying that the new works of Delius made him sad, first because he
was a very dear friend who had always been exceptionally good and
kind, a sort of musical godfather; secondly, because Delius himself
imagined that he was still progressing and had even said that he had
never done better than the *Requiem* which, as Philip added, 'I must
most mournfully testify after making the piano score of it, hardly
contains one striking page . . . alas, this Requiem is doomed to
oblivion or ridicule, I am afraid.'[5]

Early in 1919 Philip again began planning the publication of a
musical journal to be called *The Sackbut*, a title that had been mentioned as early as December 1914. 'There is no time to be lost. Now
is the occasion for launching the paper, if it is ever to be done.'[6]
Brimful of enthusiasm he wrote to Gray in January, saying that he
felt the time was exactly ripe for such a venture, adding that he
would be only too delighted to undertake the whole administration

of the paper and also to provide or collect interesting material. But as was the case with Philip's earlier hopes of producing such a journal, these plans once again came to nothing, despite the fact that he had even gone as far as producing a circular publicizing it. Dejected, he wrote to Delius to say that '"The Sackbut", I am afraid, will never materialize. . . . the same fate overtakes all my enterprises—lack of funds, for which no earthly amount of good intentions can make up.'[7] On hearing this disappointing news Delius sent sensible and encouraging advice:

Don't begin to think, dear Phil, that luck is against you because the real reason is that you do not push your ideas to their materialisation with sufficient energy . . . You would succeed at anything you take up if you would concentrate on it & not diffuse your energies on so many things . . . Stick to one thing just for fun for 2 or 3 years & see if I am not right. I think you are admirably gifted as a writer—you would succeed either as a writer on music or as a composer if *you stick to one* & push it thro' regardless of everything. I vouch that you would have the most influential & powerful paper in London if you started one and stuck to it. Why not get Newman to join you I read his articles & they were splendid.[8]

Impatient and generally dissatisfied, Philip was now becoming more and more involved in a number of public and private quarrels which would mark many of his future undertakings. These, as often as not, took the form of bitter confrontations with music critics. As early as 1917 he had been involved in a dramatic incident in the Café Royal, when he struck the critic Edwin Evans (1874–1945) during a heated disagreement over the merits of the music of van Dieren and Bartók. Now, despite Delius's advice, it was Ernest Newman's turn to be the main target of protracted attacks. In May 1919 Newman had written a highly critical article in the *Musical Opinion*, after having seen the preliminary prospectus of *The Sackbut* to which he took exception, finding it 'gratuitously offensive to musical critics and journals'.[9] In a way one can sympathize with Newman, suddenly confronted with a paragraph which stated that it was 'common knowledge that the average newspaper critic of music in this country is either a shipwrecked or worn-out musician or else a journalist too incompetent for ordinary reporting.' Alas, such ill-judged and hasty remarks were all too typical of the headstrong and intolerant Philip, so often blinded by his own idealism and enthusiasm that he saw nothing but his own crusade. On receiving a letter from Newman rebuking him with the words, 'The truth is, my dear Heseltine, that you are getting very egoistic, very intolerant, and very unreasonable',[10] Philip immediately began a hostile feud. This later developed into a fierce campaign against Newman, with Philip accusing him of being unwilling to espouse the cause of new, unknown composers such as van Dieren and Sorabji. Angered by Newman's review of his double concerto for violin and cello and, forgetting his earlier advice, Delius egged Philip on, suggesting that he included in *The Sackbut*

a sort of review of the musical criticisms on a new important work—Especially to draw attention to anything especially inane or idiotic—Ernest Newman could be held up to great advantage every now & then—Some of his articles are really nothing but words—a sort of writing Diarrhoea . . . Newman wrote an especially stupid notice on my 'Double Concerto' as time will show.[11]

It was therefore inevitable that, in due course, the controversy would continue in the columns of *The Sackbut*, with Philip goading Newman on with remarks such as 'This is one of the most despicable exhibitions of vindictiveness and petty personal spite I have yet experienced—an offence against the first principle of justice and fair play which its perpetrator could not survive without discredit and ignominy in any department of life but musical criticism'.[12] He also retaliated with another of his favourite below-the-belt revenge tactics—a limerick composed at Newman's expense:

> Said a critic initialled E. N.:
> 'Why does my wife like young men?'
> A friend said: 'You fool,
> Don't you know that the tool
> Is mightier far than the pen?'

It is to Newman's credit that, in his notice of the memorial concert given in the Wigmore Hall shortly after Philip's death, he could forget the quarrels of the past and write that 'the young man who could conceive these exquisite things ["Corpus Christi", "As Dew in Aprille", and 'Balulalow"] and realise them so perfectly in music must have had the root of the matter in him; they are three gems that will keep his name alive as a composer'.[3]

Over the years Philip invested a great deal of intensity into his friendships and demanded a high degree of loyalty in return. He could be hyper-sensitive if he suspected an unequal commitment and the mere suggestion of rejection or even coolness on a friend's part could result in a cutting letter, such as the rebuke he sent to Gray in April 1919:

You may perhaps remember that some while ago you honoured me with an invitation to dine with you at the Cafe Royale [sic] on Saturday April 19th 1919 at 7 o'clock p.m.

Now it seems to me, from a series of indications which, I think no extant pachyderm could have failed to perceive, that you must have done so at a time when your customary caution and sure instinct of self-preservation had temporarily deserted you. This conclusion is, moreover, confirmed by the fact that my momentary apparition in the Restaurant European on Saturday last seemed to cause such acute distress to you and your vis-a-vis that neither you nor he were able to repress an exclamation of horror at so unpleasant a spectacle.

I, therefore, being on the whole well-disposed towards my fellow-creatures and not markedly less humane than the majority of my kind, should be very unwilling to take advantage on the one hand of your temporary aberration and on the other of the natural reluctance that you, with your retiring disposition, might conceivably feel in retracting the rash invitation it betrayed you into making.

So, as the saying is, I shall not inflict upon you to-morrow evening the quite intolerable suffering which the proximity of my person for a prolonged period would indubitably entail—unless in the meanwhile anything occurs to disprove the accuracy of my conclusions.[14]

The misunderstanding was, however, soon cleared up and by the next month their friendship and correspondence was back to normal.

On 13 May Philip was invited by the prestigious Musical Association (later the Royal Musical Association) to deliver a paper at one of their monthly meetings. With Winthrop Rogers's criticism of van Dieren's music and his remarks about 'the modern spirit' doubtless still festering in his mind, Philip entitled the paper 'The Modern Spirit in Music. A Criticism, in Relation to a Suggested Definition of the Function of Musical Art, and an Attempt at a New Perspective'. It is vintage Heseltine, containing ideas which had been formulated as early as the Dublin lecture. He once again railed against those who, when writing about music, discussed technicalities to the virtual exclusion of the essential quality of music. He also pointed out that if one wrote nonsense in words, one was quickly found out, but if one did the same in music, one could even be claimed as a genius by a certain section of the public that was always ready to accept as magnificent anything that it found completely unintelligible. It would seem that with this paper Philip had made an impression on musical scholars, for that September Edward Dent (1876–1957), a lecturer at Cambridge University and later to become Professor of Music there, asked for a copy, complimenting him as possessing 'that rarest of combinations, musical knowledge and literary style'.[15]

As he slowly gained confidence, Philip began to express his views more frequently and more aggressively in print. In June 1919, in response to a series of articles entitled 'Modern British Composers', he wrote to the *Musical Times*, arguing that it was almost impossible to define where 'serious' music ended and 'light' music began. One can only presume that he was being deliberately provocative when he proceeded to point out that 'the greatest composers have at times descended to trivialities', suggesting that

if any musician will leave all his prejudices at home and visit, say, the Comedy Theatre . . . he will hear a small orchestra whose ensemble it would not be easy to better, and scoring of a sureness and subtlety for which one might search in vain in some of those neglected native masterpieces for which the poor worn-out 'classics' are expected to make room in our concert programmes.[16]

The following month he became involved in another heated controversy, once again in the columns of the *Musical Times* and this time over the music of Stravinsky. Philip was one of those who had criticized the influence of the visit to London by the Russian Ballet a few years previously (1911) and, like others in the Delius set, saw little virtue in the early Stravinsky works (though he would later revise his opinion somewhat). In the June edition Leigh Henry (1889–1958), a music critic, author, composer, and conductor, well known for his efforts on behalf of contemporary music, had written a eulogistic article on Stravinsky. Under the pseudonym Mortimer Cattley, Philip wrote a letter which was published in July. Highly sarcastic in tone, the letter makes use of phrases from Henry's own article to belittle his pro-Stravinsky 'panegyric' as Philip mockingly dubbed it:

The music of 'Petrouchka' is marvellously apt and appropriate to the pantomime for which it was written, but, apart from a few small points of technical interest, has it any musical significance whatever? The evolution of Stravinsky, from the sentimentally Chopinesque pianoforte pieces of 1908, via the 'Firebird' (that pastiche so industriously compiled from reminiscences of Berlioz, Grieg, Rimsky Korsakoff, and the 'Casse Noisette' Suite) and the more original 'Petrouchka' to such soulless and consciously imbecile productions as 'Pribaoutki' and the songs for a cat, reveals the gradual elimination of every element that might be recognized as emotional or moving, in any but a purely physical sense. One feels quite sorry for his cat. It is more usual to try such things on the dog—but then it is just in these little details that Stravinsky's startling originality is most apparent.[17]

An angry Henry replied in August, saying that prejudiced people were incapable of analysing anything, even the writings of critics: 'It is not so much my article he dislikes, as the music of Stravinsky,

about which it is written.'[18] True, Philip was no admirer of
Stravinsky and his adherents, but in this instance he was primarily
attacking Henry's use of high-flown, technical jargon which he felt
made music inaccessible to the layman. He pointed this out in his
reply:

The propagandists of the Stravinsky cult should reflect that those who find
'Petrouchka' an agreeable evening's entertainment will be more likely to pursue their study of the composer's music on the strength of this pleasant
impression than as the result of reading articles *of* or *about* (or even *towards*!)
the 'unprecedented', if unphilosophical, things it is supposed to give utterance
to. If these things are not apparent in the music, still less are they apparent in
the propaganda.[19]

In the mean time it had taken Winthrop Rogers until November
1919 to discover Peter Warlock's true identity. Anthony Bernard,
one of the readers for Rogers, had recognized Philip's handwriting,
'roared with glee and then was full of chagrin' for fear he had made
a mistake in revealing to Rogers whose it was. Despite the animosity
and deception engendered by the 'infamous letter' the previous year,
Rogers seems to have taken the joke in good spirit and Philip
quickly gave up his anti-Rogers campaign. Rogers wrote assuring
him that he and Bernard would keep the secret for as long as Philip
liked: 'At all events, it is a gay secret, and the songs, so clear and
straight and true, are like fresh breezes on a sultry day. I am very
happy to have my name on the outside of them.'[20]
A delighted Philip wrote immediately to van Dieren in Holland to
tell him about this amusing incident. From the following extract one
can see just how diligently Philip was still working in his attempts to
publicize van Dieren's music:

It has been a source of enormous interest and delight to have your manuscripts here and to go through them again. I copied the score of the Overture
and took the copy to Busoni but did not see him as he was occupied when I
called. The autograph copy of this work is at present in the hands of Adrian
Boult, as it seemed that there was a remote chance of getting him to do it at
one of the Philharmonic Concerts . . . Hertzka, of Universal-Edition, went to
Frankfurt for the production of 'Fennimore' and Delius very warmly recommended him to publish your piano pieces;[21] and from Delius' letter I gather
than H. appeared very sympathetic towards the proposition. I despatched the
MS by registered post on October 30th, enclosing a beautiful letter to H. which
Frieda [sic] wrote for me, and took the precaution of writing to Busoni at the
same time, asking him to write a further recommendation of the pieces to
Herzka; which I am told he very promptly did.
I have given the score and parts of the 2nd Quartet, first movement of the

3rd Quartet, 'Cenci' and 'Levana' etc to one Arthur Bliss, a rich enthusiast who gives Sunday evening chamber concerts at the Lyric Theatre, Hammersmith, and seems eager to devour every piece of modern chamber-music he can lay hands on . . . He seemed very excited over the quartets and said that, since he would no doubt find himself quite incapable of reading the scores, he would have a private rehearsal of them all so that he might hear them and get a better impression of their character . . .

I enclose an amusing notice of Warlock and Wurricoe.[22] It appears that the reviewer rang up Rogers and asked 'Quis est ille Toad-in-the-Hole'? and the good publisher, having no evidence to the contrary, replied that he was no doubt the very person he appeared to be, to wit one Peter Warlock. It gives me great satisfaction to reflect what the 'Daily Telegraph' would have said about these same compositions had they been signed Philip Heseltine!

. . . I hear that Gervase Elwes, John Coates and Muriel Foster are studying the songs with enthusiasm, and I received a word of approval and kindly encouragement from no less a personage than (I tremble to write his exalted name) Frank Bridge!!!

Now however that the secret is out, as far as W.R. himself is concerned, I shall have the satisfaction of telling him, as I told Anthony Bernard to-day, that whatever is good in the workmanship of these little tunes is due to pro-longed study of the works of one B. van D. . . . But all these things are so utterly trivial that I feel more inclined than ever to go to Germany or Vienna at the earliest opportunity and *learn music from the very beginning,* as I feel so hopelessly incompetent.[23]

Philip also sent van Dieren copies of the songs which Rogers had recently published. The letter of acknowledgement is most movingly worded:

My dearest Philip,
              For days I have been taking up the two 'Warlock' songs, and after reading through them I felt a warm tear somewhere behind my eye running down to my heart. They are no monuments for our children to stand before in awe, but they are so sweetly sad and so infinitely lovable. Every time again I look at them I feel moved and impatient to write to you and tell you how clear a deeply loving spirit they reveal to me.

I told you already that I know what to think of it when you sneer at these songs. They may have a few affectations strewn on them here and there but these certainly are not flaws and matter so very little here where the whole thought is so beautifully maintained. I know this music and what one must have felt before one can write it. These are those things that come out of one as the precious substances out of the wood ooze out of the wounds made on the tree's trunk, your melody that 'weeps so gaily and smiles so sad' makes you the dearer to me. I feel your absence more than ever, I miss your good face and miss your good company. My thoughts are always round you and carry my best wishes.

I embrace you,
        vale et me ama
            Bernard VD[24]

Philip's oft-quoted reply shows just how much these words of praise meant to him:

I was greatly touched and not a little flattered by your kind words about my songs. You understand everything so wonderfully, even the most insignificant things in their minutest details. I could wish no higher praise nor for a juster appreciation of my little melodies. Sometimes I feel that this exiguous output of tiny works is too futile to be continued—though I have neither the impulse nor the ability to erect monuments before which a new generation may bow down. And then when I think of some of the 'monumental' composers in present-day England alone, I feel that I would rather spend my life trying to achieve one book of little songs that shall have a lasting fragrance than pile up tome upon tome on the dusty shelves of the British Museum. I should be more than happy if at the end of my days I could look back upon an achieve-ment comparable to that of Philip Rosseter who left behind him but one small book of twenty-one immortal lyrics.[25]

When van Dieren wrote again sometime early in 1920, he included in his letter a most perceptive comment on Philip's art and his con-tribution to music: 'I am vastly more impressed by these excellent little melodies than by many an original but rather helpless huge work for full orchestra which is the least young composers think they owe to themselves to put their thoughts into.'[26]

Philip was also able to assist his friend in another more urgent and important way. Van Dieren was writing a book on Epstein but further illness had delayed its progress and Epstein, egged on by his wife Peggy (the 'ever-diabolical Scotchwoman' as Philip dubbed her) had evidently complained about him to John Lane, the publisher. Van Dieren, fearful that he might lose the much-needed £75 fee, wrote a desperate letter to Philip, imploring his assistance in the completion of the book:

Need I say what I want you to do with the M.S. . . . . Correct the grammatical mistakes, and orthographical faults, substitute synonyms here and there where a word is unnecessarily repeated in too close proximity, rearrange the position of the words in the sentences where it is clumsy, or unidiomatic or too involved. Where the sentences are so long as to become too much for human breath and too vast for the field of human vision cut them up into three or more of the length English prose requires. They may of course in accordance with the pedantic trend of my character retain something of their Johnsonian complexion where they are at their best, but imperatively call for division where their length and complexity is obviously the result not of deliberation but of nonchalance and lack of previous plan in construction.
    . . . give it some of the colour of your own incomparably racy English and weed out what is obviously translated from the Thibetan language. Is it too much what I am asking?[27]

In typically generous fashion Philip immediately put the publisher's mind at rest, took over the whole project, and corrected and helped with each chapter as it was sent it to him from a nursing home in Holland where van Dieren was recuperating after yet another spell of illness. It must have given him a great deal of satisfaction to be able to review it at some length in the June 1920 edition of *The Sackbut* and describe it as a 'sumptuous book' which gave 'a most illuminating exposition of some of the darker problems connected with the creation and appreciation of works of art'.[28]

After his success with Rogers, Philip continued producing songs, some newly composed, others completed from earlier sketches. Amongst these are the beautiful 'Mourn no More', and 'Sweet Content' with its very obvious Elizabethan-influenced false relations, as well as the not-entirely-convincing 'Love for Love' (dedicated to Puma), though it is worth noting that in this song the melody of the third and fourth verses is an exact retrograde version of the other verses. It is dedicated to Puma which suggests that, at the time of the song's publication in 1920, he was possibly thinking of trying to salvage his marriage. 'Dedication' has an especially taxing vocal line and also one of the most flamboyant and difficult of Philip's piano accompaniments, while 'There is a lady sweet and kind', one of Philip's four settings of the same text, is redolent of the Victorian ballad with its rich harmonies and slightly sentimental melodic line. 'My little sweet darling', another beautiful and unjustly neglected song, with words originally set by William Byrd, skilfully blends Elizabethan and modern features.

At the beginning of 1920 A. H. Fox Strangways (1859–1948), the music critic of *The Times*, established a new quarterly journal, *Music and Letters*, for musicians to write articles about various aspects of their art. Philip contributed to the first three editions, his two articles taking the form of a general review of the London musical scene. In the first he referred somewhat critically to the Carl Rosa Opera Company, pointing out that the current season had 'no specially novel features', concentrating, as it did, on composers such as Mascagni and Puccini to the exclusion of new British operas, hitherto a feature of their programmes. After praising the Southern Syncopated Orchestra, a group of 'coloured musicians', for their skill in improvisation, he proceeded to criticize not only the form of the recent Promenade Concerts, but also the inclusion of 'too many undistinguished novelties, and too little of certain great masters—Haydn, Mozart, Berlioz, Liszt and Brahms for instance'. At the same time he put in a good word for the Elgar symphonies, which he claimed were 'still too rarely to be heard'.[29] In the next 'London Letter' he was more outspoken and acerbic in his remarks, declaring London to be 'still a comparatively unmusical centre' and the musical life of the city 'indeed no life, but a depressing struggle for existence'—words which seem almost to echo his own recent feelings about life in London. He then continues on a favourite hobby-horse already expounded in his Dublin lecture:

A man is not considered a fool for regarding a simple piece of music as though it were a treatise on the fourth dimension. Though he hold the most decided opinions on other subjects, he will be deferential when it comes to music, afraid to express any opinion, afraid to say Bo! to a Goossens. He will cheerfully confess to an ignorance of music of which he would be ashamed with regard to literature or politics, imagining that he is thereby absolved from the necessity of questioning anything a self-styled 'expert' likes to tell him. The 'expert' too often encourages this attitude, persuades him that music is an esoteric mystery to which he, the expert, alone has the key, and while feigning to enlighten him on the subject, carefully contrives to bewilder him more and more and to darken what little musical understanding he originally possessed.

His next complaint echoes his recent contretemps in the *Musical Times*, with its by now familiar attack on Stravinsky and the 'surfeit of musical propaganda':

Our concert-halls have become a dumping-ground for any and every musical experimenter 'regardless-like' . . . Now someone comes along beating the big drum and proclaiming Stravinsky one of the greatest composers that ever lived. For the past few months it has been impossible to pick up any musical journal without finding a long and verbose article (reminding one irresistibly of the closely-printed panegyrics in which patent medicines are wrapped) to the effect that music, after the painful and half-articulate labours of past ages, has at last come to fruition in 'Petrouchka'. 'Petrouchka' has indeed become a popular idol on whose altar many a young composer has sacrificed potential originality.

In his most waspish terms he finally proceeds to another *bête noire*:

There remains a Scryabin-epidemic to record. Scryabin is a composer whom the public has long been taught to regard reverentially from afar, through the cloud of dust raised by scribes and propagandists. . . . There is nothing at all difficult or obscure about the music. Harmonically it is very simple, once the un-common-chord basis has been realized, and very restricted, and while there are rhythmic figures which, in isolation, might have a certain independence and vitality, they all seem to be struggling painfully in the glutinous mush of the harmonic tissue, like flies in treacle. Though fully aware of the opprobrium and ridicule with which the 'saved' will greet the comparison, I cannot help remarking that Scryabin, with his luscious, languishing chord-clots, his pseudo-religious eroticism and naïve excursions, as of the unwilling-virtuous, into the realm of Satan, appears to be the direct apostolic successor of Charles Gounod.[30]

Philip's final article, for the third issue of *Music and Letters*, was entitled 'The Scope of Opera' and gave a brief survey from Greek drama through to 'Grand' opera in which he singled out Purcell's operatic masterpiece, *Dido and Aeneas*:

. . . Gluck and Mozart are still the supreme masters of operatic art, but before either of them were born there existed a work which, in spite of all subsequent 'reforms' and experiments, is yet as near an approximation to the perfect type of opera as anything that has followed it—Purcell's *Dido and Æneas* . . . Here if anywhere in opera we can find the true spirit of Greek drama resuscitated . . .

Purcell's opera is now more than two centuries old, but the interim development of the operatic form has not been in any sense an advance, and opera has still to determine its true direction.

In conclusion he developed ideas already expressed to Delius in late 1916 and prophetic of the later contemporary chamber operas:

. . . there is the far more hopeful prospect of the development of a form of 'chamber-opera' in which the most intimate and subtle subject may be dealt with in appropriate surroundings. . . .

A small curtained stage on which variety and subtlety of lighting will for the most part take the place of scenery, a small cast and chorus, and an orchestra of four to four and twenty players—these are the modest requirements of chamber-opera.[31]

Philip used some of these arguments again in the introductory paragraphs of an article on Delius's opera, *Fennimore and Gerda*, which appeared in the *Musical Times* the next month (April). Although the major part of this article was devoted simply to expounding the plot of the opera, Philip managed to include some cutting remarks about the inefficiency of Covent Garden and the fact that Delius would not allow the intended performance of *A Village Romeo and Juliet* at the end of 1919, as 'no full rehearsals had yet taken place, and . . . such preparations as had been made for the production were in a state of chaos . . . in consequence of which the public were given two additional opportunities of acquainting themselves with the master-works of Puccini'.[32] Early in 1919 Philip had also made an English translation of *Fennimore and Gerda* for the vocal score which Universal Edition were to publish. Although the full significance of the humour would not have been fully appreciated at the time, the printed score contained an amusing misprint when the hero, Niels Lyhne, exclaims, 'Oh, why did I not know you. All those years of hippiness [*sic*] I've missed.'

Strangways sent copies of the early editions of *Music and Letters* to Delius. The two men had met sometime earlier in 1919, and Philip wrote humorously to van Dieren about the meeting. Strangways 'in the jocular-schoolmaster-out-of-school-hours manner, with his interminable and pointless conundrums' had evidently asked Delius

whether the respective lengths of violin bows and cello bows affected the phrasing with regard to the sex of the performer, etc, etc—or something of the sort. After a few minutes Delius smiled benignly and exclaimed: 'I don't know what you're talkin' about. You might as well be talkin' *Chinese*'! Whereat the musical critic of London's leading newspaper (who I must add had previously enquired of Delius, with his usual amazing tact, *where his music was published*!) perceptibly blushed through his bronzed and assuredly pachydermatous hide and muttered something about 'Mere small-talk, you know: don't *you* ever use small talk?'[33]

It is therefore not surprising that Delius later commented cynically to Philip about the journals, saying that Strangways had sent him a copy of his magazine containing a long dissertation on Vaughan Williams, *'the Great English Genius. I had already judged him at the Concert where you introduced him to me. If he turns out anything interesting ever*, I shall be a very astonished person.'[34]

But by this time there was no further need for Philip to contribute to Fox Strangways's new periodical or, indeed, any other for that matter. In his reply to Delius he wrote excitedly about the long-awaited journal which he himself was at last to edit. Rogers had recently taken over a paper called *The Organist and Choirmaster* and decided to reorganize it into something better and of more general interest, suggesting that Philip should be its editor. Philip succeeded in persuading him that 'nothing could be made out of this rotten corpse of a paper and that it would be far better as well as more profitable to start a new paper on quite different lines'. So *The Sackbut* absorbed *The Organist*, starting off with the advantages of *The Organist*'s existing circulation, subscription list, and organization, including a very able and efficient business and advertisement manageress who had worked with Rogers for years and who knew everything about the commercial running of a paper. 'It will not take long, I feel sure, to make this the best musical journal in England. Rogers has given me an absolutely free hand in the matter of contributions . . . I want the first number to be very first-rate, to drop like a bomb into musical and pseudo-musical circles.'[35] In the agreement drawn up with Rogers, Philip was to receive £50 an issue, an amount which would, in fact, never be paid to him.

The Sackbut occupied Philip's time and talents for the next year, and though to begin with he enjoyed the challenge, the evidence shows that it proved something of a strain. Towards the end of August 1920, for example, we find him writing to his mother that 'running the "Sackbut" is beset with difficulties of many kinds and the first two weeks of the month are a perpetual nightmare of anxiety lest one won't be able to get in—or think of—enough stuff to fill the paper'.[36] Between May 1920 and March 1921 nine issues appeared, which included a vast and varied amount of material, much of which was of a deliberately controversial nature—exactly what Philip had always intended it to be. In May 1920 he had told Delius that in *The Sackbut* he wanted, above all, '(in addition to sound knowledge, sound judgment and enthusiasm) *brilliance*— a literary style with a generous ration of "nutmegs and ginger, cinnamon and cloves" in it . . . Above all the paper must be *readable*—without this, the finest and most intelligent criticism is useless.'[37]

So we find, for example, Philip writing to Gray about his own contribution in the June 1920 issue, 'my leading article, entitled "Ile Reporter" will I think make Newman (and a great many old men) sit up and take notice',[38] the purpose being essentially to fan the flames of the Sorabji–Newman controversy which he had started at the end of the previous year. To be fair there were a large number of serious articles by people like Gray, Nichols, and Sorabji, but Philip's controversial objectives are stamped on every article and review that he himself wrote. One moment, as Mrs Barbara C. Larent, he is attacking Holst's *Planets* as enough to make one utterly despair of the future of music in England, 'an anthology of musical platitudes, laboriously compiled from the pages of nearly all prominent modern composers',[39] the next, as 'Obricus Scacabarozus', he is humorously condemning theatricalism in the concert hall, imagining the day when the London Symphony Orchestra would be compelled to make themselves up as *moujiks* in order to perform a Russian work, and the smell of vodka be artificially instilled into the auditorium.[40] Then like quicksilver he suddenly re-emerges as Jerry Cinimbo hoping to shock his readers with a clerihew:

> Diodoros Siculus
> Makes himself ridiculous
> By asserting that thimbles
> Are phallic symbols.[41]

However, as we have seen, not everything was provocative. Besides the serious and erudite articles, *The Sackbut* regularly included musical illustrations from Gesualdo and Purcell to Bartók, van Dieren, and Sorabji, reproduced in Philip's own immaculate calligraphy. Hubert Foss (1899–1953), an admirer and friend of Philip and one-time head of the OUP music department, later described *The Sackbut* as 'a paper, of too short a life, which gave the opportunity for personal expression to several very able people. It was more than an admirably informed musical journal, more even than a paper with a wholly personal attitude; it was also a paper that was often alarmingly right'.[42] One of *The Sackbut*'s declared aims was the inclusion of all the arts and certain issues contained a great variety of non-musical items, from an article on Petronius by Arthur Symons (1865–1945), a drawing of four women by Augustus John, to 'some interesting poems'[43] by the young South African poet, Roy Campbell (1901–57), who for a time was one of Philip's drinking companions. Philip had been one of the first to recognize Campbell's genius and, on reading his early masterpiece, 'The Flaming Terrapin', had written to Campbell enthusing that 'the buoyancy and exhilaration of the whole thing' was 'immense, and practically unique . . . in this dispirited and half-hearted generation that knows not youth'.[44] Not all the subscribers, however, found the *Sackbut* selection of Campbell's poems 'interesting'. One, an irate Mr Herbert Hodge, wrote to say he did not wish to renew his subscription, as he had not 'yet entirely recovered his health'[45] after reading the three printed in the March 1921 issue.

Part of the policy of *The Sackbut* was also the promotion of concerts, two of which took place on 18 October and 2 November 1920. In fact, in an attempt to publicize the launch of the periodical and these concerts, Philip had even attempted to organize a parade of three 'curiously garbed' trombone players (the modern-day equivalents of sackbuts) around the streets of London, selling copies of *The Sackbut* and eventually coming to a standstill outside Queen's Hall just as a large audience was assembling for a concert, 'playing stentorian motifs from Wagner'.[46] At the October *Sackbut* concert van Dieren's String Quartet No. 2 (Op. 9, 1917) was given its first performance, other music in the programme including works by Purcell, Sorabji, Delius, and Ladmirault. Two more concerts were planned, but owing to inevitable financial difficulties, they had to be cancelled. This must have been particularly disappointing for Philip as both the British premières of Bartók's first two String Quartets and Schoenberg's *Pierrot lunaire* had been scheduled for these concerts.

Although not part of this series, there was also a recital in the Mortimer Hall on 6 October in which Gerald Cooper (1892–1970), a musicologist-singer friend of Philip and 'a budding London concert entrepreneur'[47] who he described as being 'fabulously rich', presented a number of songs. Included in the programme of works by Bach, Mozart, van Dieren, Arthur Bliss, and Frank Bridge, were five of Philip's songs accompanied by chamber ensemble, four of which would later be incorporated into *The Curlew* cycle. In September Philip had written to his mother about the concert, adding that he thought these particular songs his best work so far, though he predicted that the unusual combination of instruments for which they were written would prevent the cycle from ever becoming widely known. In the event he was not particularly happy with the performance, telling his mother that it had been 'a dismal affair'. Cooper's voice, 'never very thrilling, was in very bad form and most of the instrumentalists were simply incompetent. There were passages in my songs that sounded just like Pussy at midnight.'[48] A disconsolate Philip later told Delius that the piece had been murdered 'by some of the most incompetent performers ever let loose even in London—which is saying a deal'.[49] He would have to wait another two years before the work would be performed again.

Right from its inception Delius showed a keen interest in *The Sackbut* and in April 1920 told Philip that he was just the man to edit such a paper:

I am so glad that Winthrop Rogers has had the wit and intelligence and perspicacity to seize hold of this most excellent occasion. There is really no first-rate, unbiased musical periodical in England. The chief feature of *The Sackbut* ought to be independence and real criticism. The old clichés of fault-finding as a subterfuge for one's impotence and incapacity ought never to figure in your paper. Only then will it become a real live paper, and only then will it be read by the real music-lovers and enthusiasts. You have now a wonderful opportunity. I hope you will grasp it; I am sure there is a wonderful field open to you waiting to be cultivated. What is wanting in England. what is wanting in British music, is idealism and enthusiasm.[50]

In later letters Delius did not hesitate to give advice as to what he considered the aims and policies of *The Sackbut* should be. One senses a degree of manipulative self-interest when he suggested to Philip that he might very well have a column in *The Sackbut* of 'enquiries—for instance—We should like to know why so & so etc—

Let us say, as an example—"We should like to know why none of the works of Delius were included in the Programms [sic] of the so called British Music Festival".'[51] Philip even managed to persuade Delius to write two articles for *The Sackbut* (the first, entitled 'At the Cross-Roads', appeared in the September 1920 issue) and several letters show Delius's irritation at the non-arrival of the copies he was eagerly expecting. He very much enjoyed the article on Bartók by Gray but was anxious to hear how the October *Sackbut* concert (which had included some of his own songs) had gone and to see the second of his articles, 'Recollections of Strindberg'. He was even moved to send Philip a limerick he had composed on the subject of Philip's enthusiasms for Gesualdo:

> Why unearth old Gesualdo Venosa?,
> Or any old mouldy composer?
>   Let him rest in his grave,
>   Why these madrigals save?
> Enough rotten music we know Sir.[52]

It was about this time that a romantic drama took place. Cecil Gray had fallen in love with a certain young lady, Viva Booth (later Viva King), who did not seem to reciprocate his affections. A desperate Gray therefore decided to enlist Philip's aid in reporting her feelings back to him and consequently introduced them to each other in the Café Royal. Viva Booth soon found the handsome Philip irresistibly attractive and it was not long before the two had a brief affair. Feeling thoroughly uncomfortable about the whole situation, Philip openly confessed his betrayal in a letter to Gray in June 1920:

I meant to talk to you about it yesterday but the predicament—being one of those that arise unreasonably, automatically and, indeed, against one's will—seemed so preposterous that I was afraid of merely gibbering or perhaps of breaking out into a 'mirthless laugh' such as we know rather too well . . . I feel wretched, and mean—and yet the whole thing happened so inevitably, so automatically that I cannot conceive an alternative. I fear you will never forgive me. I hate to have to tell you all this, for I know it can only make you more unhappy—but I hated still more the thought that you might hear fragments of the story from other sources, and suspect me of deliberate deceit and underhand sinister dealings.[53]

The unsuspecting Gray was thoroughly appalled by Philip's actions and told him as much. Philip's reply showed how he had underestimated Gray's possible reaction to his confession:

I am dreadfully distressed about you. Your letter—surprising as it may seem to you—came to me as a shock; I had completely misjudged the intensity of

Plate 1. Edith and Walter Buckley Jones (*c*.1906–7).

Plate 2. Philip as a child (aged 2½).

Plate 3. Cefn Bryntalch.

Plate 4. The Goldings (Evelyn Heseltine's home in Essex).

Plate 5. Philip aged 12 (7 January 1907).

Plate 6. Eton Music Staff (*c.*1905). *Back:* Colin Taylor and Edward Mason; *front:* M. Clapshaw and Thomas Dunhill.

Plate 7. Colin Taylor (*c*.1914).

Plate 8. Frederick Delius.

Plate 9. Robert Nichols.

Plate 10. Olivia ('Viva') Smith.

Plate 11. Philip with Adrian Allinson (*c.*1914).

Plate 12. Philip in 1915.

Plate 13. Minnie Lucy
Channing ('Puma').

Plate 14. 'Puma' and Philip.

Plate 15. Eugene Goossens, 'Puma', Philip, and Hassan Suhrawardy (1915).

Plate 16. Unidentified waiter, Jacob Epstein, Philip, and the Hon Evan Morgan (later Lord Tredegar) (c.1915).

Plate 17. Dikran Kouyoumdjian (Michael Arlen), Philip and D. H. Lawrence at Garsington (1915).

Plate 18. Juliette Baillot (1915).

Plate 19. Cecil Gray.

Plate 20. Bernard van Dieren.

Plate 21. John Goss.

Plate 22. Eynsford Cottage.

Plate 23. E. J. Moeran.

Plate 24. Constant Lambert.

Plate 25. C. W. Orr.

Plate 26. Philip (1926).

Plate 27. Augustus John and Philip (far left) with John Goss, Barbara Peache, and E. J. Moeran (centre) in the garden of the Windmill Inn, Stalham (*c.* 1926).

Plate 28. Philip and E. J. Moeran with members of the Shoreham Dramatic Society (*c.*1926).

Plate 29. Hal Collins, E. J. Moeran, Constant Lambert, and Philip in the garden of the Five Bells, Eynsford (c. 1928).

Plate 30. Phyl Crocker, Philip, and Judith Wood.

Plate 31. Bruce Blunt.

Plate 32. Philip with Jelka and Frederick Delius at the 1929 Delius Festival.

Plate 33. 12a Tite Street, London.

Plate 34. Philip's grave in Godalming Old Cemetery.

your feelings and I fear that my last letter to you, in which I deliberately tried to make light of the matter, must have seemed very horrible . . . Your letter brought me to my senses with a jerk . . . For me no woman is worth the sacrifice of your friendship, and the few words in your letter which show me that I have not been entirely without significance in your life are far more precious to me than a woman's most passionate declarations of love . . .

Your dream and illusion is not shattered; you tried to embody it in something ready-made and the form did not fit—but your dream remains intact. It is only the misfit that grieves you and, no doubt, makes you despair of ever being able to embody it. How great a misfit it was . . . I alone know. I had no illusions about the woman before I met her.[54]

Gray, however, was not quite so ready to forgive what he regarded to be a treacherous betrayal by one he considered a close friend and Philip was forced to write yet again:

. . . in what respect have I spoiled your prospects any more than dozens of young men with whom the lady has indulged in mild flirtations—for that, I assure you, is all the little affair amounted to. I took no more liberties than anyone might have taken without blame, than dozens of others have indeed taken; and now even that is quite at an end. It seems so trivial a thing to have broken our friendship.[55]

The affair between Philip and Viva Booth lasted little more than a month and later she did, in fact, become engaged to Gray. But, tiring of her after a while, Gray broke off the engagement and in due course the two men forgot their differences and resumed their friendship. By the beginning of July Philip was able to send Gray a postcard saying how much he was looking forward to a promised article for *The Sackbut*. He thought the title superb: 'I itch for the article. This is going to be a brilliant number!!!'[56]

Philip had long been planning a book on Delius and for some time had been working at it in a desultory way. Now with the offer of £25 from the publisher John Lane ('more than I hoped for from this notorious skinflint'),[57] he was spurred into action. He proceeded to spend ten days in August 1920 at Grez, collecting material for the book and leaving Gray to edit *The Sackbut* during his absence. It would be, in his own words, 'simply a matter of looking it through, correcting proofs and "making up" the stuff for the printers'.[58]

As the paralytic sequel to a disastrous syphilitic contact made in his early years, either in Florida or Paris, Delius was finding it more and more difficult to write. He had recently been asked to compose the incidental music to James Elroy Flecker's play *Hassan* and during this visit he persuaded Philip to write out the full score from the pencilled drafts which would be sent to him in London. He also rather rashly promised to try to secure for Philip the conductorship for the run of *Hassan* though, in the end, Eugene Goossens conducted on the opening night and Percy Fletcher (1879–1932) took over the remaining performances. For Philip it was a happy summer at Grez as he occupied himself helping Delius, correcting proofs of the *Requiem*, and writing enthusiastically to Gray that 'the "Sackbut" is so excellent, nine-foot sunflowers beam down upon me . . . Delius is hugely pleased with your article and has talked of nothing else all the mornin'.'[59]

Unfortunately, on his return from France on 26 August, Philip found *The Sackbut* heading into troubled waters. Just as its success seemed assured, Rogers, nervous of the implications of all the contentious material (especially the attacks on Newman), withdrew his financial backing after only five issues. He wrote to Philip on 19 October telling him that, so far as possible, he had recalled the present edition of *The Sackbut*: 'I also feel that I must write to Mr Newman and apologise on my own behalf, and tell him that I strongly disapprove of the whole controversy.'[60] Philip was understandably incensed, writing angrily to Anthony Bernard late that October:

The Sackbut is in imminent danger, thanks to the anile imbecility of the proprietor who tried (without success, though) to suppress the current issue because I had replied, vigorously and without mincing matters, to the attacks made upon Sorabji and myself by that august and greatly-to-be-revered personage E. Newman. Mr W.R. also thought it fit and proper to write and offer E. Newman his personal apologies for the Sackbut's attacks on him! Naturally, neither I nor my friends can agree to a milk-and-water policy by which we are denied the right of free speech and self-defence. So now it is a question whether, before the 15th of next month, Rogers can find a new editor who will do the work I have been doing for the salary I have been receiving (viz. £0:0:0.), or whether I can find a new proprietor for the Sackbut. Meanwhile a great deal of litigation seems to be indicated. It is a horrible nuisance and I sincerely hope the old idiot will lose every penny he ever put into the paper, in order that he may learn the value of his pig-headed policy.[61]

After all his struggles to establish *The Sackbut*, Philip was not prepared to give up quite so easily. When Rogers withdrew he decided to act as sole proprietor and editor, telling van Dieren that a great effort would have to be made during the next few months to get the paper more widely known and increase the circulation and number of advertisers. He unburdened himself saying that the net loss was about £15 a month: 'This we must convert into a profit, by strenuous propaganda *and* by our intrinsic excellence! My chief

difficulty is in getting sufficient quantity and variety of contributors—*good* contributors, that is, for third-rate journalistic effusions
come pouring in.'[62] His mother was one of those who came to his
financial rescue and Philip wrote to thank her for her prompt and
generous reply: 'You are very kind—and the fact of having a little
capital behind us will enable us to bring out the next number without delay as soon as the necessary legal negotiations are
completed.'[63] A friend from his Eton and Oxford days, Evan
Morgan (Lord Tredegar, 1893–1949), had also volunteered to buy
Rogers out for £200 on Philip's behalf, a promise which came to
nothing.

For no apparent reason, Philip suddenly decided to visit France
again in December and once more the obliging Gray was left to edit
the magazine on his own. Obviously distressed and under some pressure, Philip had sent from Paris a mysterious and cryptic letter containing a few hasty instructions:

I can't come back—A calamity has befallen me which has made me even less
capable of thought or action than I was a week ago—if that is possible. I feel
utterly annihilated, broken up. I have tried hard to write something but nothing happens. If I can possibly make sense of what little I have been able to
scribble down, I'll send it off to-night with the cheque for the printers.
Otherwise, do the best you can—or reduce the number of pages . . . Open all
letters—answer as few as possible. I leave for Naples tomorrow, hoping never
to return. For heaven's sake try and get Miss V[oules] to sell the paper to
Paxton for £250—or as much as she can get. If it was worth his buying two
months ago it is still worth it . . .
    I enclose cheque for £50 to cover any immediate bills that may be presented.
In addition there ought to be money from November sales and advertisements.
    When Rogers sends the cheque for P. W. please post it off to Barclay's
Bank . . .
    I shall write from Naples, so you can communicate in case any difficulties
should arise. But I feel sure I have forestalled everything.[64]

However, as Philip was the registered proprietor of *The Sackbut*,
Gray was not legally entitled to dispose of it. Moreover, there was
no material for the next issue and, to add insult to injury, Philip's
cheque was promptly returned by the bank. An irate Gray nevertheless managed somehow to produce the December issue and, on
Philip's return at the beginning of January, wrote him an angry letter
refusing to associate with him ever again. Philip's icy reply, explain-
ing his side of the story, was couched in acidly sarcastic tones:

Your letter, I regret to say, exhibits but little of the equable disposition and
calm aloofness from mundane matters that might be expected from one so

profoundly versed in the mysteries of metaphysics, so admirably fortified by the consolations of philosophy as Mr Peter Gore.[65] Indeed, it is rather of Kensington Gore that I am reminded—the moral infallibility of S.W.7 expressed with a super-Ciceronian vehemence of invective—and still more of an old plantation ditty which proclaims that *Nobody knows de trouble I've had, Nobody knows but Jesus* with such emphatic iteration that long before the last verse is reached, everyone within earshot knows all about it only too well.

And if your experience of 'suffering' reached its maximum point in the sudden necessity of writing out in ink two very creditable articles which I feel sure already existed in the less durable form of pencil sketches, and of correcting a few proof-sheets, I can only congratulate you on having entered this vale of tears under a more fortunate disposition of starry influences than most mortals can boast of.

Personally, having no reputation to lose (except perhaps the kind of reputation which is lost on the Salvation Army's penitent stools) I have no objection to your fulminating against me, both publicly and, for that matter, privately also, amongst your large circle of friends (all acquired and retained, no doubt, by persistent acts of self-sacrifice and solid 'worthiness')—if it gives you any pleasure to do so. But I cannot refrain—out of sheer native malice, hatred and all (if not more) uncharitableness—from laying before you (if you read thus far) certain little facts . . .

On December 2nd ult. shortly before mid-day I received a communication which necessitated a hurried journey to Paris. I left London the same evening at 4.55, intending—and fully expecting—to return early in the following week. Three days later . . . an unforeseen occurrence placed me in an extremely difficult position—in fact, very seriously upset me and all my plans, and altogether threw me off my bearings. (Incidentally it formed the prelude to three of the most wretched weeks I have ever spent. But as it has been officially decreed that I was 'enjoying myself', I suppose this remark is quite useless). I was not at the time in a particularly logical and clear-headed mood and, without pausing to calculate whether, in terms of amiability, altruism or even £.s.d., I have proved myself worthy to make so portentous a demand upon your friendship, I rashly presumed that you would give me your not-wholly-grudging assistance, to help me tide over a time when I was even more than usually incapable of clear thinking or lucid writing.

But, alas, it is not always those who prate most loudly about the selfishness of others who are themselves conspicuous for their devotion to other interests than their own. . . .

It is true that the cheque for £50 made out to you was an oversight on my part, but if you had sent Rogers' cheque and my mother's to my bank, instead of retaining the one and returning the other (from motives I forbear to stigmatise in words) the printer's bill would have been more than met and there would be no deficit whatever.

If you are really so concerned about my financial morality, you may, if you like, come and examine the fag-ends of my cheque-book—but if you want to preserve in all its lurid colouring the picture you have painted of me as embezzler of my own mother's money, you had better stay away. It would be better still if you could get the better of your spleen and drown your ill-will in a gallon of Aquatic's best: but I am afraid you enjoy them far too much—more's the pity.[66]

Philip was bitterly disappointed at this turn of events and wrote despondently to van Dieren telling him that

unfortunately, after the December number, the poor Sackbut expired . . . although the net losses on the last few numbers were inconsiderable, we had no capital to go on with. Printers and paper merchants won't give credit to private individuals, and the revenue from sales and advertisements trickles in very slowly. Now, however, temporary assistance had arrived from another quarter—and if the financial result of the next two numbers is not too deplorable the paper may quite possibly be placed upon a stable basis of something aspiring, at any rate, to the condition of permanency.[67]

All this anxiety and pressure had brought on renewed bouts of depression in addition to which his mother had been writing nagging letters about money. His reply to her on 15 February 1921 seems tired, dispirited, and resigned:

I fear you entirely misunderstand me when I don't write frequent letters to you. It is not that I have become cold or indifferent towards you—very much the opposite, and it hurts me that you should suppose that to be the reason. It is simply that the depression and gloom that nowadays seem to hang perpetually over me like dark clouds reach such a pitch that I feel like going into a corner to hide myself. It is not that circumstances are against me as that some essential part of myself seems to be dead. Whenever good fortune comes my way and an opportunity presents itself, I am unable to grasp it. All my faculties seem to have deserted me. . . .

If only I had my old energy and enthusiasm, success would be well within my grasp, in several lines; but alas, I am—save on rare and short-lived occasions—almost devoid of either—I feel utterly broken down—and this is not a sudden, transitory feeling but one that has been steadily growing upon me for months—almost years now . . . If my imagination were not utterly sterile and dried up, outward things would matter very little. But I no longer have any ideas—the only faculty that remains unimpaired is that which shows me unerringly the futility of everything I do.

Please do not say that I cut myself off from you. I think that the reverse is the case. You imagine that I forget you because of my silence, and you cut yourself off from me. I am sorry—If I saw you more often it would comfort me a good deal and help me. But you are always so much occupied with other things and other people.[68]

Having completed the March 1921 edition, Philip suddenly left England again, this time on a more extended trip with Gerald Cooper. They travelled via Marseilles and Algiers to Biskra, spending three days in the Sahara and then moving on to Tunis, from where they sailed to Naples. It is interesting to note that their trip into Africa followed exactly the same route as that taken by the occultist Aleister Crowley and Victor Neuberg (1883–1940), Philip's poet-friend, in 1909 when they travelled from Algiers to Biskra through the desert. In an attempt to enhance their joint occult powers through sex-magic, Crowley had sometime earlier initiated Neuburg into homosexuality and during this trip the two men performed various occult rituals in the desert which involved certain homosexual acts.[69] Was it mere coincidence that Philip and Cooper took this same route twelve years later? Philip's letter to Delius from Biskra makes no mention of anything abnormal or untoward:

We have just returned from a three days' expedition in the desert, on horse-back, with two camels to carry the tents and provisions. The effects of light and colour in this country are wonderful, especially in the evening about sun-set; but there is a certain deadness about it that robs it—for me at any rate—of any emotional suggestiveness. And I found when riding in the Sahara that whenever I travelled in my mind to some other place, the vision seemed more intense and real than my own surroundings: the desert has a strange tendency to vanish suddenly and give place to whatever rises up in one's imagination.

The Arabs on the whole are a degenerate, depressing crew—ill-clad and evil-smelling, persistent beggars and inveterate swindlers. Most of the wares exhibited for sale here look as though they had been imported from Manchester. And as for the women, Leicester Square or the lowest pub in Limehouse has nothing so incredibly revolting to show as the 'Ouled-Naïls' or dancing girls who sit on the pavement in the evening and try to lure the unwary traveller into some stinking Café Maure where, as a preliminary to other things, the tedious Danse du Ventre is performed to the strains of a hideously strident tin-oboe and various kind of tom-tom. For glamour and poetical suggestive-ness give me the barrel-organ or the automatic piano! Only a Bantock or a Holst could find them in the street of the 'old nails'.[70]

After a short stay in Rome they moved on to Venice for four days. Philip thought it by far the most wonderful place he had ever seen, describing it as 'almost too good to be true', the mosaics at St Mark's impressing him particularly. The following visit to Vienna, too, was a great success. There Philip saw Hertzka of Universal Edition (whom he hoped to interest in publishing some early English music) and heard 'stupendous performances'[71] of Wagner's *Tristan und Isolde* and *Der Ring des Nibelungen* conducted by Richard Strauss (1864–1949). Philip finally reached Budapest where he was able to visit Béla Bartók (1881–1945), whose music he much admired and with whom he stayed briefly. For a time he even considered the possibility of spending some time in Hungary to study with Bartók, which he felt would do him 'a world of good'.[72] While he was there Philip also took the opportunity of visiting another Hungarian composer, Zoltán Kodály (1882–1967). Many years later,

Bartók's first wife's strongest memories about Philip's visit were his unusual appearance: 'pink shirt, lilac-coloured cravat, and reddish beard'.[73] With typical enthusiasm Philip wrote to Delius from the Hungarian capital: 'Bartók is quite one of the most lovable personalities I have ever met',[74] whilst he described him to Fritz Hart as 'a most beautiful personality and one of the half-dozen finest creative intelligences in the musical world of to-day'.[75] He later told Taylor of their meeting:

While travelling about last Spring I went to Budapest and made the acquaintance of Béla Bartók and Zoltan Kodaly and heard many of their works. They have both been for a number of years too much absorbed in their own work to pay overmuch attention to that of their contemporaries—which is a very healthy sign in these days when everybody's music sounds exactly the same as everybody else's. Bartók has done some stupendously great works—great in conception and idea, not in size—always multum in parvo. . . . Kodaly, a more striking personality, is a far inferior composer—though his new sonata for cello without accompaniment is a most remarkable achievement.[76]

Philip related to his mother the story of an amazing chance discovery and meeting in Budapest:

Looking at a theatrical advertisement I noticed a bill of the Moscow Art Theatre who are giving a season there, and in the list of the stage managers and régisseurs I saw the name 'Dr. S. Surawardi'. I rushed down to the theatre and found to my great delight and astonishment that it was indeed our old friend Shahid Suhrawardy whom everyone had given up for lost or dead these last five years.

It seems that all rumours circulated about him in England were quite untrue. He has been in Russia continuously from 1916 until last year [1920]—not, as one had been led to believe, for political purposes but in the capacity of professor of English at various colleges in Moscow. During the revolution he had a very hard time: it was impossible to leave the country and life was very difficult and precarious. Eventually he became régisseur to the famous Moscow Art Theatre and last year, while touring with one of their companies, managed to escape . . . He hopes to visit England this summer—and I hope he will come, for he badly needs a time of rest and quiet.[77]

On the whole Philip's letters to his mother written during these travels in Europe seem warmer and more affectionate and from Rome he wrote hoping that when he arrived back in England she would be there: 'I am so very anxious to see you and Nigel again. I think the time is very near when he ought to be with me permanently—if that is possible. In any case we must all see much more of each other than we have been doing.'[78] But these seem to have been merely words of nostalgia, tinged with a touch of homesickness, which came to nothing. In a few months' time, correspondence between mother and son would once again be tense and strained.

Philip stayed only a short while in England before leaving yet again for France, this time to spend some weeks in Brittany, at Camaret, finding much-needed peace and quiet amid the lovely cliff scenery, an 'ideal spot for work'.[79] Just before his departure he wrote to Delius telling him things had 'been just about as wrong' as they possibly could be. To this he added the highly significant comment: 'For the past few weeks my existence has been such a nightmare that only increasing belief in and fear of the something after death could have stopped me from putting an end to it altogether. . . . I have been nearly demented during the past days.'[80] At the end of May he wrote to his mother telling her that he had crossed over to France because life in London had proved once again altogether too much for him: 'I found I was spending too much time and energy over things that didn't really matter and my work was suffering in consequence . . . I shall probably remain here for some time as I have a great deal to do and the conditions for working are ideal.'[81] By now he and Gray had reconciled their differences, having met accidentally at a friend's house, and Philip sent him a typically Warlockian letter from Camaret:

[John] Curwen[82] has taken over the Sackbut and is going to run it—i.e., pay all expenses *and* contributors, giving me an entirely free hand as editor—I made it quite clear that I would not risk a repetition of the Stinkthorp [i.e. Winthrop!] business—for at least a year or so. If I can get any money out of him for the 'goodwill' and other attendant phantasmagoria, I shall send you some of the spoil.

I have been staying here on the Breton—and quasi-Cornish—coast for some weeks, working very hard—and really, for a change, getting on quite well—and drinking practically nothing. In fact I haven't been anything but strictly sober since the afternoon I left Paris when, staggering towards the Gare Montparnasse with a bag in one hand and a bottle of Calvados in the other, I fell prone before a tram-car and but for timely assistance might easily have missed more than my train.

Really, there is a fortune waiting for the first man who starts a Calvados trade in England. It is one of the purest and most potent drinks in existence. One can get blind in 10 minutes, unfailingly—yet it's not even imported to England—and it could be made by the gallon *in ea parte quae dicitur Westcuntre*, being but the spirit of that staple product cider. . . .

On the cliffs facing the open sea there stands a castle with eight little towers and a portico on which is inscribed: *La beauté est l'exaltation de la vérité*—one better than Keats. It makes me think of Tristan (and more particularly of Isolde), although it seems to be overrun by white cats and I have seen a goat sitting at night, yes—on one of the *window-ledges*. Tomorrow I am going down the coast to Quimper (nothing sexual about it) and hence to Carnac, the mystical centre of the Celtic world. . . . I shall probably stay some while in Paris, or thereabouts.[83]

It was possibly during this visit to France that, after one of his monumental binges, Philip ended up one morning in a police court. Gray relates how

he was found lying face downwards in the gutter of the Rue Blanche in the pouring rain, without a penny in his pocket, and removed to the Santé where he was next day stood in a row naked together with pickpockets and vagrants, and washed with a long mop dipped in cold soapy water while his clothes were baked under the assumption that they were verminous.[84]

At this time Philip also described himself to his mother as being 'entirely hairless, either on face or head'.[85] The visit to France ended disastrously and at the end of June Philip was stranded in Paris, living on a few borrowed francs in the Hotel Namur on the Rue Delambre. He realized he needed to get back to London to sort out the mess at the offices of *The Sackbut* but lacked funds even for the return fare. A telegram and a letter were dispatched to his mother who eventually forwarded him 800 francs as an advance on his allowance. Philip's letter to his mother was pathetic in the extreme:

I have been in great trouble ever since I returned from Vienna. I wanted to tell you about it but it seemed to make you angry. You thought I merely wanted money from you but it wasn't that . . . I needed your help so much when I telephoned you from London and ever since I have been floundering on and only making matters worse and worse. I can't explain it all in a letter but I can tell you that this matter—it is not really a matter, one thing or fact at all—seems to be at the root of all my purely material troubles.

I am sick and weary of wandering about, having no home and no certainties in life. I would, if necessary, abandon music altogether and take up something fixed and definite that brought in money steadily—if I were good at anything else or could find anything else that I could take up. Do you think you could help me in this respect? It was really this that I wanted to ask you about in London. . . . I want to settle down and feel secure in a material sense—I have too little confidence in myself to resign myself to music and poverty for the rest of my days—though, for myself alone, it would be no bad thing.

But my life will be simply a wreck of failure and dissatisfaction till I can put behind me the follies and miseries of the last few years, and make a home for Puma and Nigel. I know you are unsympathetic about this and think me mad. Perhaps I am mad, but I feel that while I am doing nothing for these two my life is useless and vain—that I can redeem all these years of selfishness, which has only led to more misery for myself in the end, by devoting myself to these two—for in spite of everything that has happened I cannot give up Puma and I can never live happily without her. You see, a great part of the reason for the failure of the past years with her lies in the fact that I have always been a sort of vagabond, with no real home, making no money and continually being hard up. Over and over again—even until quite lately—she has gone her own way and I mine after a quarrell [*sic*]. But it has nearly always been because we were unsettled and she felt she had no anchor in life and no security in me.

I feel so worn out and embittered by the kind of life I have been leading— and the kind of life I have indirectly driven her to lead, for no one can live on £8 a month in these days—that I should feel a new being if I could only find something—anything—that would bring in money and enable me to settle down in security, with *her* to begin with.

I know you wouldn't want to part with Nigel and I don't think it would be for his good that you should, at first. But you don't know how this sense of disruption and separation, where there should—and could be love and har-mony—hurts me like a long ache in my heart. And I know that—whether you call it love or whatever name you give it, there is something stronger than myself which holds me to Puma—and that I could never really love any other woman. I have died even as she has died. But now—I would give my life for a little peace and security. This probably sounds quite incoherant [*sic*] to you— the whole business is far too long to explain in a letter—but if you could put aside your aversion for a while and realize the *fact*—which has been ham-mered into me by one bitter experience after another during the last few years—that I can never really cut myself off from Puma—I could I think make it all clear to you.

Please do not think too hardly of me, dearest Mother.[86]

The references to Puma and Nigel are indeed puzzling. There is no logical explanation why, after having made an apparently complete and acrimonious break with his wife, Philip should suddenly have had this urge to return to family life again. It suggests a complete disillusionment with his whole life-style since 1918; or perhaps a state of oscillatory chaos, thinking that he could make a 'go' of his failed marriage and look after Puma and Nigel on almost no income whatsoever. Or was it really an exploratory move to see if his mother would provide a larger income if he were seen at last to be attempting finally to settle down with his family? Whatever the motive behind the letter, his mother had reached the end of her tether. On the back of the envelope she wrote these despairing words in her characteristic large, spidery writing: 'This letter was written the same day he telegraphed me for Aug. money to be advanced. I *wired* it *him* same day & have never had an acknowledg-ment. It cost me 10/- besides. I have not answered this and don't mean to till I hear of the money's safe arrival. What *am* I to say?[87]

There seems to have been a misunderstanding, for Philip *had* writ-ten a letter of thanks on 30 July, a few days after his return to London. He was still very worried and miserable: 'I hope to get my financial affairs straight at any rate this week. After that comes the problem of what I am going to do and where I am going to live. This unsettled existence is driving me perfectly mad.'[88] To add to his problems and anger, he had discovered that during his absence in France, without either telling him or forwarding any money to him, Miss Voules, *The Sackbut* secretary, had pieced together the June issue from some of his manuscripts. The end was as swift as it was unexpected: Curwen took over the publication of the journal and Philip was summarily relieved of the editorship. Extremely bitter about the way in which he had been treated, Philip wrote to Fritz Hart saying that, when one encountered such people, one longed for 'the powers of the black magicians of the middle ages!'[89] The accounts were finally arranged so that Philip received nothing; in fact he even ended up paying some of the contributors, including Bartók, out of his own pocket. When Curwen appointed the young Ursula Greville as the new editor (the *Daily Mirror* called her an 'editress at seventeen—London's youngest girl editor')[90] Philip nick-named her Miss UG, referred to her as Curwen's 'slut-like mistress', and promptly enshrined her in a limerick:

> One evening Miss Ursula Greville
> Was about to be raped by the Devil,
> But her bush proved so thick
> That it baffled his prick—
> So he sent for the Barber of Seville.

Curwen was obviously intent on furthering Miss Greville's career, for in the 1920 *Musical Times*[91] there is a review of a song-recital given by her on 15 October, 'at a concert organized by Messrs. Curwen', whilst in 1922 *The Times* announced that 'Messrs. Curwen have arranged, with the co-operation and assistance of Miss Ursula Greville, for a concert tour to be undertaken at their joint risk during March in Germany and Austria'.[92] Of such stuff are musical politics made. When Miss UG's first *Sackbut* appeared in September 1921, Fritz Hart wrote indignantly to Philip calling it 'a nasty smell'.[93] In this same issue Miss Greville published an angry letter from one of Philip's friends, Robert Lorenz (1891–1945), an amateur musician, writer on music, and broadcaster, in which he stated that 'the current number of the "Sackbut" represents in a small way one of the most squalid victories ever achieved by philistinism over art'.[94] He thereafter referred to the magazine as 'The Backslut'. Lorenz was clearly a typical member of the Heseltine circle. On several occasions at Queen's Hall he raised his strong and resonant voice in protest against some work of which he disapproved. He would wait until the applause had died down and then give tongue with startling effect, declaring that he had as much right to express his opinion as the rest of the audience had to express theirs!

There was also a brief note from the new editor to the effect that she had been 'very courteously reminded by Mr Philip Heseltine that the report of the Schoenberg Matinée',[95] which had appeared in the July edition, should have been acknowledged as 'a leaf from Busoni's Diary' reprinted from *Die Musikblätter des Anbruch*. Like Lorenz, Gray and van Dieren had also written letters of protest, but evidently in terms which rendered them quite unprintable!

RETURN TO WALES
(1921–1924)

In the autumn of 1921, after the *Sackbut* débâcle, an impecunious Philip moved back to Cefn Bryntalch. Apart from the occasional trip to London, often to negotiate with publishers, he would live there almost continuously for the next three years. During this time he applied himself to a large number of different projects, telling Taylor that the only way to escape intolerable boredom was to work from morning till night. Ian Parrott suggests that his possible routine was to go through the spacious drawing room of Cefn Bryntalch,

stepping out on to the broad lawn and right through the shrubbery until he reached a secluded arbour. Here he listened to nature, brooded and composed . . . Sometimes he would shut himself up in the drawing room in the mornings, working on an old Broadwood. His son, Nigel Heseltine, who was six in 1922, remembers the strict instructions not to go in![1]

A humorous letter written to Gray in November 1921 shows a relaxed Philip stoically accepting the enforced return to his mother's home. Busily working on Delius transcriptions commissioned by Universal Edition, he felt a great sense of relief after the upheavals of the previous few months:

I am being very abstemious here, rarely attaining and never exceeding half a gallon of innocuous bitter ale per diem. This more than moderation is, all the same, due rather to solitude and the lack of anyone to share one's potations than to any other cause. . . .

This is the kind of house that ought to contain rare old books and fine old wine. And it is true, there are rooms full of books and cellars full of bottles but alas, treasures are not to be found. I am making a gradual investigation of the cellars. There are dozens of bottles which have lain there untouched and forgotten for at least sixty years but unfortunately Time, low fellow that he is, has been and buggered most of them, and this operation has had its customarily degenerating effect upon their innards. Still, after I had spewed and poured down the sink several gallons of various liquids not recognizably anything between vinegar, mushroom ketchup, marking-ink and bile, certain shy virgines intactae came forward and proffered (a) madeira of unspeakably lovely mellowness and (b) a curious concoction which I believe to be a home-brewed raisin-wine, of a rich dark amber colour and prepotent properties. The said virgins were of a most peculiar shape and size and, all things considered, there seems to be little doubt but that they have chastely contained themselves for at least a hundred years.

But Wild Wales alone holds an enchantment for me stronger than wine or woman and intimately associated with music. In these admirable and tranquil surroundings I can work more quietly and steadily than I have ever been able to before . . . Congenial companionship alone is lacking—but I console myself with the reflection that if I had that also there would be more drinking and less working—and I have a great deal of lost time to make up. I have had a number of Delius piano scores to do lately, and several others to revise, make fair copies of and prepare for printing—and this has taken up most of my time, even though I work on an average six or seven hours a day . . .

My books and MSS recently arrived from Ireland and I have re-written several compositions I had forgotten. There was much more stuff than I thought there were among the MSS; I seem to have been quite industrious during my temporary exile. I have made, I think, quite a good thing out of that gloomy chorus by Nichols, retaining only the opening and closing bars of the original version. Apart from this I have done nothing much—two or three songs, including one good roaring one about beer, and a piece for small orchestra which is not yet scored. But as soon as the Delius book is finished and in Lane's hands, which I trust it will be before Christmas, I shall begin work seriously at composition, regardless of whether the result be good or bad. I feel sure that is the only way to set about it.

. . . Last Sunday, in response to a sudden and urgent request from the Rectum, I attended divine service, for the first time in many years and—in the language of provincial reporting—'presided at the grand organ', fully arrayed in cassock and surplice—to say nothing of the beard which of course has become quite profuse during my rustication! During the Communion Service in E flat by Mr Caleb Simper(!!)[2] I discovered three pedals each of which, when depressed, shot out half a dozen stops, whose names were quite unintelligible to me, with a roar, or shot them in again with a sound like an expiring bagpipe. It was almost as good fun as changing gears on a motor-car. However the strange sounds I produced were nothing compared with the caterwauling they were supposed to accompany—and I received the congratulations of the parish on my beautiful performance. I was persuaded to undertake this truly Tibetan task chiefly by the reason for the village schoolmaster's absence (for this individual usually officiates with, I am told, far less skill than even I can command, although he has done the trick every week for the last forty years); and this was—would you believe it?—utter incapability to move as the result of Saturday night! That my sobriety should be called in to assist another's incapacity seemed to me one of the best jokes of recent months. I celebrated the occasion by playing as a 'voluntary', as the congregation departed, that fine old Welsh tune entitled 'Ton-y-Bottel', with harmonies that must have seemed *most* appropriate to the villagers.

That stinking bitch Voules is still trying to make trouble over the Sackbut. She has never replied to the various charges made against her management, but is trying to get money out of *me* now to recoup herself for what she alleges she has lost over the paper—apparently quite regardless of what other people have lost and of all she has swindled me out of. However, she can bugger herself recte et retro[3] before she gets anything out of me.

I have just sent the unfortunate Bartók a draft on a Budapest bank to the value of £4. 7. 6. for his article which Curwen ought to have paid for.[4]

Philip was quite correct when he told Gray that he was being industrious during his temporary exile, for this period in Wales was to be his most prolific. The works mentioned in his letter to Gray are important ones: the 'gloomy chorus by Nichols', 'The Full Heart', begun during the 'Irish' year, is one of the earliest of the surviving part-songs and is dedicated 'To the immortal memory of the Prince of Venosa' (Carlo Gesualdo, later to be the subject of a book in which Philip and Gray would combine their talents). Unusual but startlingly effective, with chromaticisms and rich choral sonorities (mostly in six and sometimes in eight parts with occasional soprano solo), 'The Full Heart' is a remarkable but suitable homage to the harmonically adventurous Gesualdo. The 'good roaring one about beer', 'Mr Belloc's Fancy', is a companion piece to the famous and often-sung 'Captain Stratton's Fancy', a song composed in 1920 in praise of rum, which Philip light-heartedly described as 'Two True Topers' Tunes to Troll with Trulls and Trollops in Taverns'. With their 'rattling good tunes and full-blooded accompaniments',[5] these are typical of the extrovert Philip. Of an entirely different character is the evocative and atmospheric setting of Edward Shanks's poem, 'Late Summer' ('The fields are full of summer now'), also dating from this period. The sensuous atmosphere of this piece, captured in rich harmonies, lingers in a languorous Strauss-like postlude for the piano. Some seven years later (January 1928) Philip was to write disparagingly to Dowbiggin about this song, describing it as an early effort for which he didn't much care.

The numerous letters written to Gray during this period are brimful of good humour and gossip:

As for your abstinence from alcohol, the coincidence between the date of your giving up drinking and that of the departure from London of your evil friend Prosdocimus is most striking and will no doubt be used by your sister-in-law as evidence in support of her long-maintained moral strictures! Unregenerate, I have added a new tipple to my repertoire, having at last discovered a wine-merchant who supplies genuine Canary sack in flagons.[6]

Salacious comments abound, with frequent sexual innuendo and references which hark back to Philip's apparently 'delayed' adolescence and the kind of peculiar sexual hang-ups often found in the upper-class Victorian and Edwardian public schoolboy. There are post-scripts such as:

Another mystery. Vide *The Concise Oxford Dictionary.*

STIMY. n. and v.t. Lie of balls on green *such that player has other's ball between his and hole*; (vb; usu. in p.p.) (?)[7]

as well as the occasional outrageous limerick:

> Hear now, if your mind a good jest tickles,
> The true story of Origen's[8] testicles.
> Off he'd no sooner smote 'em
> When he popped in his scrotum
> Twin onions from Lazenby's best pickles.[9]

Philip's letters to Delius from this period tell of a renewed interest in composition despite the old feelings of self-doubt:

I would love to come over and see you and it is most kind of you to offer to pay the fare—but at present I feel that I daren't stop working and leave Wales. I have been travelling about so much this year that things have got very much in arrears—and for one thing I am determined to get this book about you finally completed this year; it has been already too long hanging about halfdone.

And I am also, with great difficulty and still greater diffidence, starting composition again—an orchestral piece this time. I don't know what will come of it, but I am driven ahead, in this as in other work of a less interesting but more remunerative kind, by a fearful feeling of having to use every hour to make up for lost time. Perhaps it is good for one, in a way; but I know that if I left Wales and stopped working even for a couple of weeks, as I inevitably should if I went away, I should find it very difficult to begin again.[10]

I feel ever so much better here than in any city and I have never been able to work so whole-heartedly before. There is great joy in turning out stuff regularly even though one knows that it is very bad! However I am trying to cease to care about that; excessive self-criticism leads to complete sterility which is a most horrible condition.[11]

His solitary life in the country gave him more than sufficient time to brood and in February 1922 he wrote a long letter to Fritz Hart couched in similar terms:

I work, alas, very slowly and with incredible difficulty. Days and weeks pass when I can do nothing, not even bad work. I have no facility, and I envy those happy people who, like you can go on steadily creating. It must be a great joy—and I should indeed thank heaven for the ability to work steadily, even though what I produced were of the most miserable quality.

I sometimes wonder whether my complete ignorance of the academic processes of composition has not perhaps made things more difficult for me. In one way I am sure it is an advantage to have no relics of the text-book in one's head, but at times I am equally sure that without having experienced that kind of training *at an early age*, one can only acquire technical facility after enormous and painful efforts. How I wish you were near at hand for I feel I could learn an immense amount of useful technique from you. It is so very seldom that a good composer and a good teacher are united in the same person, and I could never seek instruction in the matter of musical composition from anyone, however learned, whose original works I did not admire and respect. There is certainly no one in England I could go to with any confidence.[12]

Van Dieren had recently returned to London from Holland, where he and his family had moved briefly after the war, and Philip sent some of his 1919 compositions to him for comment. He received frank, constructive criticism. Van Dieren admired the tenderness of the declamation and the subtle sensitiveness of line in 'The Cloths of Heaven'[13] and found 'The fields are full' as 'sweet and fresh as a young green leaf', but for him the setting of Stevenson's 'Romance' was 'too damn English'.[14]

When in 1917 Gray had alerted Philip to the fact that Lawrence had included him as the unflattering character, Halliday, in his novel, *Women in Love*, he had chosen to do nothing about it. Now, in late 1921, on learning that Martin Secker was about to publish the novel, he decided that it was time for action. On completing the book in 1916 Lawrence had obviously felt a certain degree of apprehension and had sent a copy to his friend, the Scottish writer, reviewer, and critic, Catherine Carswell (1879–1946), asking her to find out from her barrister husband Donald (1882–1940), whether he thought any part libellous: 'Halliday is Heseltine, The Pussum is a model called Puma, and they are taken from life.'[15] By now, however, Lawrence was claiming that all the Halliday–Pussum scenes were purely fictitious: 'No shadow of a resemblance to them ever happened, as far as I know . . . Heseltine ought to be flushed down a sewer, for he is a simple shit.'[16]

On hearing from Philip's solicitor, Secker contacted Lawrence who was at that time staying in Taormina, Sicily. Lawrence was at first confident that Philip could be easily fobbed off and he believed the thing to do was 'to go quietly and let Heseltine get tired. He's a half imbecile fool.'[17] Despite his initial inclination to ignore the matter, he soon thought better of it and by the next month had agreed to Secker's suggested changes in the text. He told Donald Carswell that he had now given Halliday lank, black hair and Pussum yellow hair, adding, 'Heseltine is a thoroughly rotten sort, so is the woman. He is only doing it for blackmail and to advertise himself: chiefly the last. I think it's disgusting that such a person is allowed to air himself and preen himself in court. He's a foul sort.—But I hope Secker will be up to him.'[18] Philip, however, did not feel these changes to be significant enough and wrote indignantly to his solicitors. The high moral tone of his letter is not without a certain irony, particularly in the suggestion of an appeal to the National Council of Public Morals, a body for which, in normal circumstances, Philip would surely have only had contempt:

I should be glad if you would press the claim for damages in respect of the libels in copies already sold as far as ever you can without involving me in greater expense or embarking upon an actual case. I can't afford to fight them, but it will be as well to give Mr Secker and the author the impression that proceedings will certainly be taken if the matter cannot be settled out of court. I leave it to you to decide the proper sum to be claimed as damages.

. . . These (alterations) are ridiculously inadequate and make little difference to the libel. But surely the withdrawal of the book from circulation and the submitting of a proof (in Lawrence's handwriting) containing alterations in the personal descriptions, constitutes an admission of the charge of libel on the part of both author and publisher? This seems to me important and I should like to have your opinion as to how much the submitting of this proof implies, legally. If it constitutes an admission of the charge, as I suspect, then we may safely go ahead, not only in claiming damages in respect of copies already sold, but also in threatening further proceedings should the book be reissued even with the suggested alterations. If you look at these corrections you will see that they make no material difference. The circumstances and the situations remain the same.

I am inclined to accept the proposals as regards the alterations—because I fear that further demands for excisions might lead to a case in court which I could not afford—and partly because I am convinced that the second edition will be no less obscene than the first and can therefore be easily suppressed on public grounds . . . I consider that the libels are not removed by the suggested alterations and cannot be removed except by the omission of the characters altogether. Were the character of the book other than it is, I should press the demand for their omission, since the libel is now clearly admitted by Mr Secker. But as the second edition will without doubt provide a case for police intervention on general grounds of obscenity (there is almost enough evidence of it in the two chapters submitted in proof) I propose . . . to take such steps as may be necessary to get the book totally suppressed by the police when it next appears . . . Another reason for not pressing the matter of excisions further is that, if it came to a case, my wife would be an essential witness and I have not finally separated from her.

. . . I purposely left in certain passages which in other circumstances I should have insisted on getting omitted, in order that there should be no dearth of evidence of certain tendencies for which to get the book suppressed by the police. Will you please communicate with Scotland Yard again immediately. Every day's delay is bound to make a difference to the circulation of the book, and I am most anxious that action should be taken in the matter at the earliest possible moment.

Apart from the chapters containing the libels, this second edition does not differ in any way from the first, and if ever a book afforded grounds for prosecution on a charge of morbid obscenity in general and the glorification of homosexuality in particular, this one does.

. . . If Scotland Yard proves dilatory, could you not address a communication to the National Council of Public Morals, urging them to take the matter up and press for police action?[19]

In his reply Secker valiantly tried to defend Lawrence by saying that he did not admit that Philip had been grossly libelled, nor did he consider him entitled to damages, substantial or otherwise. He also attempted to call Philip's bluff: 'If your client is not satisfied with this I have no further proposal to offer, and he must now take such further steps in the matter as commend themselves to him.'[20] The whole affair was obviously festering in Lawrence's mind and his correspondence to friends at that time is full of angry, abusive comments about both Philip and Puma. He became more and more enraged, as he realized that Philip would most likely win the case. On 8 November he wrote to Secker: 'I should think the most likely thing is that Heseltine is trying to blackmail you. It is quite in character. And then he would like to draw some limelight on to himself. He is an impossible person. But money is at the bottom of it. And I'd see him in several hells first.'[21]

By handling the situation with tact Secker eventually achieved success. His conciliatory letters poured oil on troubled waters and the case was settled out of court. Philip received £60. 10s., £50 in settlement of his claim and 10 guineas for costs. Lawrence, however, hardly seemed appreciative of Secker's efforts on his behalf and wrote to tell him he was sick with rage to think that Philip had got the money out of him: '*Really*, one should never give in to such filth.'[22] His last words on the subject were to his friend, the South African artist Jan Juta (1897–1990), when he described Philip as 'that filthy rat', saying that he felt Secker would somehow manage to get the £50 hush-money' out of him: 'Curse them all.'[23] A triumphant Philip duly celebrated his victory by sending the following little poem to Gray:

> Come, fill a vial with vintage, *vieux et sec*
> Fit for the King of Thule's golden *Becher*;
> Get half-seas-over—swamp the blooming deck
> Swill swipes, swig swizzle, singing
> 'SUCKS TO SECKER'![24]

Besides composing new songs Philip was also busy rewriting and revising earlier works, principally in the hope of generating some much-needed income. He wrote to Taylor cynically asking him if he had kept the manuscript of some Scotch and Irish tunes that he had sent him from Ireland: 'I can't remember them and have no copy but recollect that they were sloppy enough to be likely to bring in a few pounds if published now—and I am so hard up that I leave no stone unturned which may have cash concealed beneath it.'[25] On receiving the returned manuscript Philip told Taylor that he intended keeping five of the 'little piano pieces' which he would offer, slightly retouched, to a publisher.[26] These reworked pieces, the *Folk-song Preludes* for piano are, however, not among his most inspired creations, a fact which Philip himself had already acknowledged. Copley described them as 'a rather laboured production' with 'very thick and clotted' textures and harmonies that 'often sound contrived rather than inevitable'.[27] When they were eventually published in 1923 the organist, composer, and writer on music, Harvey Grace (1874–1944), hardly enthused about them in his *Musical Times* review, lamenting:

Where is the Peter Warlock who delighted us all with such spontaneous songs a few years ago? He is not the same in the *Folk-song Preludes* by a composer of the same name, just published by Augener. There is an overdose of grinding discord and complication for mere complication's sake. . . . Some occasionally effective passages do not make amends for the crabbed and overwrought character of the pieces as a whole. We can only sigh for the return of the old Warlock.[28]

Among the many contrasting songs from this prolific period is the dialogue song 'Hey, troly loly lo', the folk-song-like 'The Bachelor', the gossamer-light setting of 'Piggesnie', the two sets of *Peterisms*, and the boisterous setting of 'Good Ale'. The local vicar evidently objected to this last-named song 'on the score of the poet's association of the Blessed Virgin Mary with Good Ale'. Philip, however, gleefully pointed out to him 'that the 15th century, when the poem was written, was a much more pious age than the present and clearly what was good enough for an age when people were grilled for blasphemy'[29] was quite good enough for 1922!

In addition there is the unique, impressionistic 'Autumn Twilight', two Elizabethan-inspired songs, 'Sleep' and 'Rest, sweet nymphs' (for some curious reason originally published as part of a series of unison choral songs) and the cheerful, extrovert setting 'In an Arbour Green'. Although Philip himself later dismissed 'Rest, sweet nymphs' as 'rubbish',[30] in these settings he shows himself to be a master in his inspired treatment of very varied texts. Particularly interesting is the group of five songs, *Lillygay*, settings of poems from an anthology edited and published by his friend Victor Neuburg at his Vine Press which he had established at Steyning in Sussex. 'Conceived during long walks among the Welsh hills which he loved so dearly',[31] these settings have a distinctly folk-song quality, though the material itself is entirely original. He dedicated them to his favourite cousin, Irene Heseltine, who had settled in South Africa and who was visiting Wales in June 1922, just about the time they were composed. He wrote to Gray about Irene's visit, fascinated by the fact that in South Africa she kept 'two tame secretary birds, for protection against serpents. These have been observed to devour one serpent between them, each beginning at an end. There is a ring of sempiternity about this procedure.'[32] In complete contrast to the songs of *Lillygay* is the masterly setting of 'Sleep', a unique amalgam of Elizabethan and van Dieren influences, and considered by many to be one of his finest songs. In all these settings Philip captures the atmosphere and every nuance of each poem with such skill that it is difficult to imagine the words being set in any other way.

This productive period in Wales also saw the transcription, editing, and publishing of over 300 early songs and part-songs. Philip's interest in the Elizabethans had come a long way since the early days at Oxford. His first tentative attempts at research in the British Museum in November 1914 had been followed up in Ireland towards the end of 1917. Now he was completely captivated by the music of this era, writing to Fritz Hart that the more he knew of this music, the more gloriously beautiful seemed 'the whole harvest of that period . . . the culmination of the most *perfect—technically* as well as aesthetically—periods music has ever known'.[33] When Canon E. H. Fellowes's edition of the English lutenists began to appear in 1921, Philip immediately recognized the immense value of what he was doing, but objected to his methods of scholarship and editing which seemed to imply that the original works were less than perfect. It was at this stage that the seeds were sown in Philip's mind to edit and publish this music himself, so as to rescue the Elizabethans 'from the besmirching paws of antiquarians'[34] as he called them. He summed it up neatly in a letter to Nichols: 'when one slangs a man for doing a job badly, the best thing to do is to go and do it well oneself'.[35] From then on he declared war on the

venerable Canon, whom he promptly dubbed the Reverend Horoscope Phallus. Fellowes was an obvious target for irreverent limericks and Philip included three in this same letter to Nichols:

> To old lute songs the reverend Fellowes
> Adds counterpoints, chords, ritornellos
>> But the shade of old Jones
>> Says, 'O friends, not *these* tones—
> And *you*—bugger yourself with the bellows!'

> The Reverend Horoscope Phallus
> Took a whore to the (hic) Regent Palace
>> When he got ½ seas-over
>> He said, 'I'm in clover!'
> And, stroking her knees, murmured, 'Shall us?'

> I leave you to guess what occurred,
> And next morning his reverend averred:
>> 'Though I've had a banana
>> With fair Oriana,
> *This* time I've indeed stuffed the Byrd!'[36]

Apart from some advice and help sought from the eminent choir-
trainer and scholar Sir Richard Terry (1865–1938), the organist of
Westminster Cathedral 1901–24, it would appear that Philip was
entirely self-taught in the art of transcribing and editing. The first
contact the two men had was when Terry wrote a letter of congratulations to Philip at the time of the second of the *Sackbut* concerts (2
November 1920) and a firm friendship and mutual respect was
immediately established.[37] Terry much admired Philip's work as an
editor, particularly his perceptive understanding of Elizabethan
music, as well as his brave, independent spirit. He was also appalled
at the way in which the Musical Establishment in England had
treated him and, in a short tribute which Gray included in his memoir, he drew attention both to Philip's remarkable skills as an editor
and his shabby treatment:

For Heseltine's rivals the contriving of a score of Tudor music (to say nothing
of their dreary comments thereon) appeared usually to be nothing more than a
matter of ink and paper. From the very first I could see that for Heseltine the
score meant vastly more. And he was able to convey that meaning to others in
the finished product. The music sprang to life on the page before him . . . his
mind intuitively leaped to the music's true significance—none of the aloof aca-
demicians that imagined themselves his rivals ever reached that goal. . . .
Heseltine made no parade of learning, but he *knew*. His knowledge was
equalled only by his modesty. Before he had grasped a thing thoroughly he
always professed entire ignorance of it, and accepted information on the subject from whatever source with childlike humility. . . .

. . . he was a scholar, but not a pedant; a consummate technician, but withal possessed of vision; a creative artist who could penetrate the minds of Elizabethan composers as no mere transcriber could ever hope to do. With his passing England lost an artist, a scholar, and, in the literal sense of a much-abused term, a gentleman.[38]

When summing up Philip's achievement in this field, one is constantly aware how far ahead of his time he was, as regards matters that are now taken for granted in this day of urtext editions and performances on original instruments. He believed primarily that this music was not of antiquarian interest only, but living music of the finest order. As he expressed himself more fully in an article in *The Sackbut* in 1926:

. . . music is neither old nor modern: it is either good or bad music, and the date at which it was written has no significance whatever. Dates and periods are of interest only to the student of musical history. . . . All old music was modern once, and much more of the music of yesterday already sounds more old-fashioned than works which were written three centuries ago. All good music, whatever its date, is ageless—as alive and significant today as it was when it was written.[39]

In the bibliography printed at the end of his book, *The English Ayre*, Philip also took great pains to explain his editorial practice, maintaining that the primary task of the editor was to produce in clear, modern notation a literal transcription of what the composer had written. His work as an editor is marked by an integrity rare at that time and many of the vast number of transcriptions and editions which he produced have not yet been supplanted.

In the winter of 1921 Philip's singer-friend, Philip Wilson, (1886–1924), visited him at Cefn Bryntalch, bringing with him copies of a number of Elizabethan lute songs in tablature. Wilson had been professor of singing at the State Conservatory in Sydney from 1915 to 1920 and, on his return to England in 1920, gave a number of recitals at the Wigmore Hall. One of these (in May 1923) marked the tercentenary of the death of the Elizabethan song-writer Philip Rosseter (c.1575–1623). Together the two men worked on these transcriptions and during his visit to Wales, Wilson (who Philip described as 'a really admirable and intelligent singer')[40] was able to sing through some of his latest original compositions. When early in 1922 Philip told Gray that he had been 'Cephasturbating',[41] he was referring to the completion of the first set of *Peterisms* which he thought were 'imbecile enough'[42] to make a little money. This first set consists of the songs 'Chopcherry', 'A Sad Song', and

'Rutterkin', while the second set (dedicated to Balfour Gardiner) comprises another three, 'Roister Doister', 'Spring', and 'Lusty Juventus'. The significance of the name 'Peterisms' was later supplied by Taylor. At that time 'a well-known firm of brewers had created an errand-boy character named Peter, who, from time to time, gave tongue to amusingly perky sayings (in their advertisements) which were headed Peterisms'.[43] The first song of the set, 'Roister Doister', is a particularly rumbustious and colourful setting of a sixteenth-century text about a country wedding which builds up to a crashing climax. At the end of the original MS there is the instruction: 'Stamping of feet, clapping of hands, pounding with pint pots and expectoration ad libitum but in strict time on the first beat of each bar'.[44]

Philip was a regular reader of the *Musical Times* for many years and from time to time his writings appeared in its pages. February 1922 was a bumper edition as regards contributions by Philip, for no less than three appeared: an article entitled 'A Note on the Mind's Ear'[45] and two letters to the Editor,[46] one headed 'Mr Yeats and a Musical Censorship', the other 'Scriabin's Music and the Three Choirs Festival'. Each of the three items was signed with a different name: the main article by Philip Heseltine, the first letter was signed Peter Warlock, while for the last he used the *nom de plume*, 'Cambrensis'.[47] The article, 'A Note on the Mind's Ear', amounting to some 2,000 words, filled almost four columns and dealt with the functions of the brain in the hearing and composing of music. It was a subject in which Philip was much interested and one which he felt had never been properly investigated. His article contains stimulating ideas, well-argued and well-expressed but, considering his description of his own methods of composing in a letter to Taylor some years earlier (24 January 1912), there is something rather ironic about the following critical comments:

The general public clings to the notion that composition is impossible without the aid of the pianoforte, or some other keyboard instrument. This belief was recently fortified by a pronouncement from Dr Vaughan Williams (whose methods of composition have, it is rumoured, led to complaints from his neighbours); and Mascagni has even made use of an ingenious instrument which notates automatically whatever is extemporized on the pianoforte to which it is affixed. The composer who cannot play any instrument, and the music-lover who claims to read a score, are still generally regarded with a certain scepticism and incredulous contempt. When Berlioz was found wandering about the mountains, note-book in hand, sketching his Overture to *King Lear* [Op. 4, 1831] he was arrested as a spy, and his protests that he was not making notes in a secret cipher were received with ridicule by the police. 'It is well known', they said, 'that music cannot be composed without a pianoforte'. Berlioz we know could not play the pianoforte. But his case provides no rule and the fact remains that a great deal of music, especially at the present time, is either extemporized at the keyboard or else built up of fragments discovered, more or less fortuitously at the pianoforte and afterwards unskillfully glued together.[48]

The first of Philip's two letters to the *Musical Times*[49] dealt with the copyright problems he had been having with Yeats's poetry. Yeats was unfortunately not very musical and had such strong feelings on the subject of his poetry being set to music that he appointed a special musical censor to consider all submitted settings. Philip's letter attempted to bring the situation to the attention of the public and to throw down the gauntlet before the poet and his musical censor. It is not without typical Warlockian humour for, in giving the background to Yeats's reluctance in allowing his poetry to be set to music, Philip relates that this was the result 'born of his horror at being invited by a certain composer to hear a setting of his *Lake Isle of Innisfree*—a poem which voices a solitary man's desire for still greater solitude—sung by a choir of a thousand Boy Scouts'.[50] In his letter Philip tells how, when some of his settings had been turned down, he wrote to the censor to ask in what respect his 'unfortunate little songs had offended', suggesting 'that much trouble and annoyance would be saved if the censor would reveal the principles to which musical settings of Mr Yeats's lyrics are expected to conform'. Needless to say, no satisfactory reply had been forthcoming. In the last three paragraphs, Philip pointed out that 'if the music of a song were so flagrantly at variance with the poetry with which it was associated, it would not be impossible for any capable critic to show the reason why'; he thought it not 'unreasonable on the part of composers to request that he [Yeats] shall appoint as his censor some competent musician who will be consistent in his judgments and articulate when they are called in question'. With this letter he enclosed two of his rejected songs, requesting that if the editor of the *Musical Times* found the 'general atmosphere and character of the music to be utterly unsuited to the poetry' they should not print his letter.

Gray tells of the 'acrimonious correspondence that ensued between poet and composer', resulting in the termination of 'the friendly relations which had hitherto existed between them'.[51] Philip had evidently tried to think up devious ways of circumventing the

ban: by printing the poems backwards, or in anagrams, or with nonsense verse substituting the original poetry. If such had ever
appeared, they would certainly have proved highly entertaining
given Philip's singular sense of humour. When *The Curlew* was
selected for publication under the auspices of the Carnegie United
Kingdom Trust, Yeats was more or less forced into giving permission for the publication of his poetry. Philip wrote to his mother on
I September 1923 hoping that, as he had obtained permission to
print four poems in *The Curlew* from Macmillan without any
difficulty, he would succeed in getting permission to publish one or
two of his other Yeats settings without having to approach the poet
in person. Yet again he seems to have met with opposition and no
other settings were in fact published nor, sadly, did Philip ever set
any of Yeats's poetry again. Sometime after Philip's death Yeats
wrote these rather regretful words:

Years ago he and I fell out because of his rudeness to a harmless, well-bred
woman who acted as a kind of musical agent for me. I hardly knew her but
felt I had to protect her. The result was that very regretfully, for I knew his
music was good, I forbade him to use my words in future and he was of
course enraged. He threatened to pirate my words and I called in the Society
of Authors. One thing led to another. I rather think he left unpublished music
to words of mine which I would of course gladly see published—one's quarrels
stop at the grave.[52]

As we have seen, one of Philip's particular dislikes was the music
of Skryabin and his letter to the February 1922 *Musical Times* criticized a proposed performance of the *Poème d'extase* at the forthcoming Gloucester Three Choirs Festival. The style of this letter is a
tongue-in-cheek send-up of the rather archetypal, pompous, and
outraged tone which people sometimes affect when they write to the
press:

SIR,—It is with considerable astonishment that I observe, in the preliminary
programme of the next Three Choirs Festival, that it is proposed to perform
Scriabin's *Poem of Ecstasy* in Gloucester Cathedral . . . It is thoroughly morbid, erotic and sensational in the worst sense of these terms, and its performance at Gloucester would create a most undesirable precedent. Music
performed at these festivals cannot fail to influence the general opinion as to
the style of composition that is fit and proper for use in our churches . . . The
admission to our Cathedral festivals of a composer whose influence . . . would
be even more destructive of good taste than that of the saccharine school of
the last century, might prove a serious hindrance to the success of devoted and
learned enthusiasts . . . who are now endeavouring to purge our worship music
of the impurities of this school—of whom Scriabin is a fitting successor—and
to reveal to us the more worthy treasures of our grand old English tradition.[53]

By February 1922 Philip had finally completed his book on Delius. As early as April 1914 he had written to Viva Smith mentioning his intention of writing such a work and he had begun making some preliminary sketches in 1915. But he had not found it an easy task and told Gray in December 1921 that it was causing him 'acute pain':

It is most unsatisfactory and I fear will have to be started all over again. I am feeling the effects of the spiritual debauchery of the last few years of my existence most terribly. To write a good book I feel I should have to spend a week over every sentence: at other times it seems equally clear that the only thing to do is to write the whole thing at a single sitting.[54]

He felt no better about it the following year when he again wrote a typically self-deprecating letter to Gray:

It is so miserably bad. I suppose I have really drunk myself silly. I am more ashamed of this dreadful production than of any little Peterism I have ever perpetrated. But having undertaken the job, I suppose I must produce something or other and I have already waited too long in the hope of being able to turn out something better.[55]

Eventually published by John Lane in 1923, the book includes a preface, chapters on Delius's life, his operas, his choral and orchestral works, and his music viewed as a whole. There is also an appendix listing his works (up until 1921) with details of their first performances. When it was reprinted in 1952, Hubert Foss added an introduction in which he wrote that 'the book itself is a work of art, a charming and penetrating study of a musical poet's mind. For itself alone, as a piece of English prose, it is worth reading and re-reading . . . Though Heseltine was 28 when he wrote the book and 29 when it was published, there hangs about it a delicious scent of youth and enthusiasm.'[56] Although conceding it to be a 'thoroughly sound and sometimes exceedingly brilliant piece of work', Gray thought the book 'occasionally pitched in too high a key' whilst he felt

certain pages . . . somewhat too florally ecstatic and vacuously mystical . . . On the other hand there are sections of the book which are among the finest things in English musical criticism, alike for soundness of aesthetic judgment and eloquence and grace of style. Particularly notable in these respects is the analysis and appreciation of *A Village Romeo and Juliet*, and the final chapter on the music of Delius viewed as a whole.[57]

A letter to Taylor written in February 1922 is of particular interest, for it reveals the intriguing possibility that Philip might have

joined the staff of the South African College of Music in Cape
Town:

I am immensely intrigued by your saying you nearly cabled for me two
months ago—but don't quite understand what you exactly meant. I should
hardly imagine that you would recommend me to the director of a
Conservatorium as a competent teacher or that, even on your own recommendation, the said director would engage anyone who has never taught anything
in his life before: and of course you know I could not afford to take a trip to
the Cape on the chance of picking up enough pupils to make a living when I
got there. But if by some extraordinary chance it was a question of a definite
job at a definite salary—which I can scarcely believe—I am sorry you didn't
cable or at any rate write me details. I am always open to offers—which I
never get!—and it would be very nice to join you in your work for a couple of
years or so.[58]

It is interesting to speculate what direction Philip's career might
have taken if he had indeed gone to Cape Town. Taylor evidently
thought it would not have been a good idea and some years later
wrote that he, personally, was extremely glad that this idea never
bore fruit, for he was quite sure that Philip would have been sadly
out of place in their 'somewhat restricted and perhaps rather prim
community'.[59] Considering his life-style and varied interests, it is
highly unlikely that Philip would have survived for very long in the
oppressive colonial provincialism of Cape Town in the early 1920s.

In February and March 1922 a two-part article by Philip entitled
'Musik in England' appeared in *Musikblätter des Anbruch*, a periodical published by Universal Edition of Vienna, who were Delius's
publishers at the time. Originally one long article, the publishers
divided it. Part I was entitled 'Rückblick' and Part II, appropriately,
'Frederick Delius'. These two brief excerpts give some idea of its
content and style:

. . . if a new composition shows the influence of Stravinsky or Ravel, the public
(including our totally inadequate music critics of the daily papers) will greet
the work with the greatest enthusiasm and praise its composer to the skies. . . .

[Delius] is primarily a harmonist and his richly coloured music is reminiscent of the beautiful dazzling hues of the evening sun in a tropical sky . . . His
music conveys pictures of overwhelming beauty in which the great endless
peace—the 'mystic peace amidst endless unrest'—is strangely penetrated by the
bitter pain of loss. It seems as if we see, for a moment, a paradise that we
remembered vaguely and from which we are now expelled by the angel with
the flaming sword . . . Nietzsche . . . inspired him to his greatest work, the
Mass of Life, probably the most outstanding work since Wagner.[60]

Having met Bartók during his trip to Europe the previous year,
and being a great admirer of his music, Philip was now even more

determined to promote his cause in England. Correspondence between the two men continued and in March 1922 the *Musical Times* published an article by Philip entitled, 'Modern Hungarian Composers',[61] a kind of preparation for Bartók's forthcoming tour of Britain, trying to make people aware of the unaccountable neglect of these composers in the contemporary English music scene. In a letter to Gray, Philip wryly commented that he had originally sent the article to the *Daily Telegraph* but that it had come back so promptly he felt sure that it had never even been read.[62] During Bartók's tour Walford Davies, Professor of Music at the University of Wales, invited him to play at a concert at the local University College at Aberystwyth on 16 March, where he contributed two groups of his own piano pieces. Walford Davies had evidently spoken at some length beforehand, but after the performance was heard to whisper, 'Baffling, isn't it?'[63] Returning to London after the concert Bartók broke his journey on Friday, 17 March, and spent a couple of days at Cefn Bryntalch. Although Philip, Gray, and Bartók met during the latter's subsequent visit to Britain in May 1923, it would appear that by then their friendship had come to a natural end. When Bartók made another tour of Britain later in 1923 there is no evidence that they met again, although Philip had made a point of especially praising Bartók's opera, *Duke Bluebeard's Castle* (1911), in his book on Delius which appeared the same year.

Even though Philip was busily working at his own musical projects, he still found time to help aspiring composers, a typically generous trait which has already been noted. Some years previously he had seen some of C. W. Orr's songs which the composer had sent to Delius in April 1917. Impressed by these pieces, Philip wrote to Orr expressing an interest in his compositions and the two men met at the end of 1918 in Delius's Hampstead flat during the latter's stay in England. Orr recalled that, when he arrived, Philip was busy playing some of van Dieren's compositions to Delius. It soon became evident that Delius was taking very little interest in the music. 'Instead, he kept up a running commentary of adverse criticism such as: "Not very original, this", or "Rather a banal passage, don't you think?" and so on, and eventually poor Philip gave up his attempts to persuade Delius that a new musical star had arisen in the shape of this unknown Dutch composer.'[64] When Orr later sent some of his songs to Philip, the latter generously negotiated with the copyright holders of the poems, copied out the songs, and arranged for them to be engraved in Austria. The rate of exchange at that time (7,000 crowns to the pound) made this an economically sound proposition and Philip also encouraged other composers such as Sorabji and Fritz Hart to make use of this advantageous situation. He then sent Orr's songs to J. & W. Chester who agreed to publish them on a royalty basis. The following year Orr sent him six more songs which elicited another enthusiastic response. Philip thought 'The Carpenter's Son' quite magnificent and was delighted that it had been dedicated to him: 'All the songs are beautifully made and show that your workmanship is at all times equal to the expression of your quite excellent ideas . . . the songs are a most remarkable achievement.'[65] Two years later Philip was to perform a similar act of kindness when he showed another batch of Orr's songs to the distinguished baritone John Goss (1894–1953) and sent the manuscripts to Foss, the musical editor of the Oxford University Press, with a very strong recommendation to publish them. Philip described the song 'With rue my heart is laden' as one of the loveliest songs any English composer had written: 'It is perfectly beautiful, especially the last line—the emotion of "where roses fade" could not be more completely realized or more perfectly expressed.'[66]

In the mean time Philip had sent some more of his own recent publications to Taylor in Cape Town: his transcription of Delius's *North Country Sketches*, the 'Corpus Christi' carol of 1919 (which the Oriana Choir, under Charles Kennedy Scott (1876–1965), had recently added to their repertoire), and two 'pot-house' songs. Constant Lambert (1905–51) claimed that the song-cycle, *The Curlew*, and the 'Corpus Christi' carol were the two works of which Philip thought most highly.[67] The latter setting of an early sixteenth-century poem has an almost uncanny atmosphere, Gray perceptively describing it as having a 'peculiar quality . . . the union of a vein of medieval mysticism with an acutely modern sensibility'.[68] For Foss, writing about it in 1924, it was 'a fine example of variety in unity, complexity in simplicity'.[69] Almost continuously throughout the work, the choir provides a wordless accompaniment to the soloists, evoking an atmosphere of restless sadness which matches the words perfectly. Philip was to use this rocking figure again both in *The Curlew* and in the later choral setting, 'Call for the Robin Redbreast and the Wren'. At the same time he was also putting the finishing touches to *The Curlew*, and in a letter to Gerald Cooper allowed himself a rare moment of self-praise, adding that, though not given as a rule to flattering his own works, 'I think it is by far the best work I have done yet.'[70]

As has been noted, Philip had written to the *Musical Times* earlier that year criticizing the inclusion of Skryabin's *Poème d'extase* in the Gloucester Three Choirs Festival programme. Now in August, as his family were going to Sutherlandshire for grouse-shooting, he wrote to Gray suggesting they both attend the Festival where a new Bliss work, the 'Colour' Symphony, and Goossens's choral piece, *Silence* (Op. 31), were also to be premièred: 'These new Mr.-pieces, as Lorenz would say, may provide good copy—especially as Bliss has already given out in the Daily Telegraph that although his previous works may have been merely "clever", they were only preliminary to *this* which is meant very much *au grand serieux*.'[71] If Philip did indeed manage to attend these performances, he left no comments, but he would certainly have been piqued to have discovered Skryabin's work had been included in the week's programme after all. Goossens later recalled Elgar's reaction as the *Poème d'extase* 'drew to a noisy, disorderly close, and the groined vaultings of the Cathedral turned the blare of trumpets into a shattering infamy' and 'finished in shocked silence': 'To think that Gloucester Cathedral should ever echo to such music. It's a wonder the gargoyles don't fall off the tower.'[72]

Although a number of his articles had been printed in various musical periodicals, Philip was having less success as regards the publication of his own compositions. Several songs were accepted by Augener but many more were rejected. Undaunted he returned to London briefly in October 1922, to transcribe old music and to supervise its publication, but by early December was back in Wales, telling Gray that he had not 'touched a drop of alcohol since leaving London. TT for the rest of the year. It's not a bit difficult in the country and I feel all the better for my long debauch. So much for the evils of drink.'[73] During this short stay in London his song-cycle, *The Curlew*, had been performed on 23 November. Even though Philip Wilson had 'buggered up the voice part completely . . . the instrumentalists were fine',[74] and he told Taylor that for the first time in his life he had felt really pleased with something he had written.

The Curlew, which held a special place in Philip's affections, is considered by many to be his finest work. He once referred to it as 'a kind of symphonic poem'[75] and of his other works only the *Capriol Suite* is conceived on as large a scale. Unlike many of his other so-called song-cycles (*Lillygay*, *Candlelight*, *Peterisms*, or *Saudades*), which are merely collections conveniently grouped under a title, *The Curlew* is unified by a number of themes or motives which appear throughout the piece. The work is in essence a song-cycle accompanied by chamber ensemble, though there are no breaks between the four songs; they are instead separated by instrumental interludes. To the basic string quartet is added a flute and cor anglais, the latter instrument ideally suited to the dark, melancholy mood of the work. The cycle is also characterized by economy of material and motivic unity (particularly in the use of the interval of a fourth) and Philip's own particular genius is apparent in the intensely felt and essentially vocal melodic line. With a constant awareness of the changing moods of Yeats's poetry, Philip's setting employs sensitive and subtle word-painting. Yet, as commentators have repeatedly noted, the abiding impression is one of almost unbearable melancholy and intense sadness (Foss referred to it as an 'ecstasy of sadness')[76] which hits unerringly at the heart of the poetry. Nowhere does Philip bare his tormented soul more openly than in this agonized *cri de cœur* which lasts a little under twenty-five minutes. Present-day listeners may not perhaps appreciate just how original this work was, both for its time and country of composition: not only in the choice of the particular instrumental accompaniment but also in its overall conception. It is a crystallization of all Philip's twentieth-century inspirations and ideals and it is interesting to note that, although the van Dieren influence is to a certain degree apparent, it is, in fact, the spirit of Bartók which hovers far more closely. Philip himself wrote somewhat cynically to Nichols in January 1923 that he was pleased with the work, 'it sounds the depths of desolation and despair, so of course people don't take it seriously but speak of pose and the "luxuriousness" of Celtic melancholy'. He added: 'I know my limitations and keep within them, and where people will class me among my blasted English contemporaries, for none of whom do I care one three-farthing fuck, is no matter at all.'[77]

Gray, to whom the work was eventually dedicated, described the mood of the piece as 'one of the darkest despair . . . I do not know of any music, in fact, more utterly desolating to hear.'[78] The work evoked similar feelings in Moeran, who thought it 'undoubtedly one of the most original things achieved by any British composer in recent years . . . a perfect expression of the poems round which it is constructed'.[79] When the adjudicators of the Carnegie United Kingdom Trust recommended its publication, they noted it 'a most imaginative setting of Mr Yeats' poem, of which, indeed, it may be regarded as the musical counterpart. It is pervaded by a keen sense of colour, which is here used to most appropriate effect.'[80] Its publication by Stainer & Bell in 1924 was not without incidental drama: originally dedicated to Gerald Cooper, some kind of contretemps between the two men resulted in an 'Eroica-like' action on Philip's part. Cecil Gray replaced Cooper as dedicatee and small strips of paper bearing Gray's name were pasted over Cooper's in the first published copies of the scores to obliterate the original dedication. Philip also vented his spleen in an inevitable limerick:

> So great is the wealth of G. Cooper
> That to own it would make any Jew purr;
>   But his gross personality
>   Has the sickening quality
> Of reducing his friends to a stupor.

Philip's letters at this stage of his career are filled with descriptions of a workload exhibiting an almost maniacal, hyperactive quality. He was also looking forward with eager anticipation to a second performance of *The Curlew*, in the fifth of a series of noon 'Concerts Intimes' to be given at the Hyde Park Hotel on 31 January 1923. John Goss was to be soloist, with the Charles Woodhouse string quartet and Leon Goossens playing the cor anglais. Despite all this there were still dark references in his correspondence to the ever-lurking spectre of 'grisliness', the depression which he so much dreaded. In his letters during this period there are also tantalizing references to 'a volume of 12 admirable but extremely bawdy songs' which, alas, never appeared. In the course of his transcribing, Philip had assembled the more indelicate and *risqué* songs and planned to print them in a private, limited edition of 180 copies. He had also corresponded with Havelock Ellis who Philip found 'a mine of information regarding both sexual and Elizabethan literature'.[81] The volume was to contain songs by Campian, Jones, Corkine, and others which, 'while being musically quite excellent, are associated with words unsuitable for drawing-room use'.[82] He told Nichols that these songs 'dealt with such pleasant topics as devirgination, dildos, putting it in, leading apes in hell (a curious conceit, this, for the reign of the *virgin* queen!)'.[83] He had planned to call the compilation 'Dildos and Fadings', although he carefully referred to it as a collection of 'Comic Songs' when asking his mother to advance the money to have it engraved in Vienna. In 1925 he wrote that the songs, 'though already engraved have not yet been published, negotiations having fallen through with two different publishers'.[84] The book remained unpublished and the plates have not survived, though the original typed preface containing what Philip hoped would be 'a mine of etymologicopornographical research' still exists.[85] The title, 'Dildos and Fadings', perhaps needs some explanation. Both words, of obscure origin, are used in the refrains of seventeenth-century ballads, often of an indecent character. Dildo has a double meaning, being either the refrain in a song or the colloquial name for a penis or penis-substitute; a fading is a type of dance of Irish origin, possibly originating from the Irish word 'feadan', a pipe or whistle. In his typed notes, also entitled 'Dildos and Fadings',[86] Philip quotes the following poem by Thomas Nash (1567–1601?) entitled 'The Choice of Valentines' or 'Nash his Dildo':

> A knave that moves as light as leaves by wind,
> That bendeth not, nor foldeth any deal,
> But stands as stiff as he were made of steel,
> And plays at peacock twixt my legs right blithe,
> And doth my tickling swage with many a sigh;
> For by Saint Runnion he'll refresh me well
> And never make my tender belly swell.

That Philip knew his Shakespeare is clearly demonstrated by the following quotation from *The Winter's Tale* (1611) where he had found the title for this intended compilation: 'He hath songs for women of all sizes. . . . He has the prettiest love-songs for maids, so without bawdry, which is strange, with such delicate burthens of dildos and fadings, "Jump her and thump her".'[87]

Christmas 1922 would have been a rather dull and solitary family affair had it not been for a visit from the poet Arthur Symons, who stayed at Cefn Bryntalch for a week. Symons had written an article on Petronius for the September 1920 issue of *The Sackbut* and Philip later set several of his poems to music. He found him 'an interesting old bird full of anecdotes and reminiscence. He seems to have met everybody that's been anybody for the last half-century.'[88] Philip much enjoyed the stimulus of Symons's company and the two of them went for long walks every day.

During 1921–2 Philip had also been working in a desultory way on a Serenade for string orchestra which he intended as a sixtieth birthday present for Delius. In December 1922 he had written to Taylor telling him that he was 'writing a Serenade for strings in three movements . . . which I think is going well'.[89] Perhaps the deadline which the birthday dedication imposed on the piece resulted in its eventual truncation to a one-movement work and there is no evidence of Philip actually beginning work on either of the other two intended movements. At the time of the actual birthday (29 January) the Deliuses were in Frankfurt, surrounded by 'delightful and friendly musicians, poets and [Max] Beckmann, a great German painter',[90] and on the day itself Delius was given a surprise chamber concert at the home of their close friend, Dr Heinrich Simon, proprietor of the *Frankfurter Zeitung*. Besides the Serenade Philip had sent a warm letter of congratulations, hoping that Delius would 'enter like Verdi upon a second youth and go on writing glorious works for another quarter-century'.[91] Percy Grainger (1882–1961) (who by then had become a close friend of the Deliuses) and Alexander Lippay, conductor of the Frankfurt Opera, played the Serenade through to Delius and 'they all liked it'. Delius himself wrote enthusiastically about the work, describing it as 'a very delicate composition of a fine harmonist. Composition is your true vocation and I cannot tell you how happy I am that you are now following it and have left the Polemic of the Sackbut behind you.'[92] As is to be expected, the language of Philip's early idol pervades a work written for such an auspicious occasion. From the very first bar of the opening phrase the listener is immediately transported into a typically English, quasi-pastoral atmosphere. This is largely created by the 12/8 rhythm, the rich Delius-like string writing, full of divisi and double-stopping, as well as the lush harmony which, even though it never strays far from the orbit of the D major and B minor tonality of the opening, more than nods in the direction of its dedicatee. For all this, it is no mere pastiche but a work which deserves far more frequent hearings and is worthy to stand alongside the other string works in the repertoire.

In 1922 Philip had composed five songs which were first published by OUP as unison choral songs and which included the carols, 'Adam lay ybounden' and 'Tyrley Tyrlow'. These had obviously impressed no less a person than Vaughan Williams, who subsequently wrote to Philip sometime in mid-1923, telling him that he badly wanted some carols with solo, chorus, and orchestra to conclude the Bach Choir Christmas concert in December. It is also about this time that there are a few brief references to Philip's friendship with Victor Neuburg, who had by this time broken with Crowley and had settled in Steyning in Sussex from where he operated his private press. In his *Confessions*, Crowley had generously describe Neuburg as 'extraordinarily well-read, overflowing with exquisite subtle humour, and . . . one of the best-natured people

that ever trod this planet'.[93] Nicknamed 'Vickybird', he had the reputation of being a generous and warm-hearted friend, and was also
a minor poet whose work had a mystical, lyrical quality. At the time
of Delius's sixtieth birthday, Philip had written to Gray saying that,
to celebrate the occasion of 'the diamond jubilee of Fritz Albert
Theodore Delius', he would in all probability 'go and soak' with
Neuburg, 'the author of "Sick Dick or the Drunkard's Tragedy"', at
Steyning.[94] Later, in August the same year, Philip certainly spent
another few days with Neuburg, commissioning from the Vine Press
a pamphlet which listed his compositions, transcriptions, and books
to date, at a cost of 5 guineas. During his second stay in Steyning
Philip also completed the set of *Three Carols* which Vaughan
Williams had requested. Philip used one of his 1922 settings, 'Tyrley
Tyrlow', and the 1919 carol, 'Balulalow', adding a newly composed
setting of 'The Sycamore Tree'. Sandwiched between its extrovert
partners and accompanied by muted strings only, 'Balulalow' comes
as a superb contrast being one of Philip's most inspired carol settings with a strange, other-worldly, mystical, and quasi-medieval
atmosphere.

This was also a period when Philip experimented with certain
drugs for a short while. In his memoir on Philip, Gray mentioned
this fact, taking care to point out that 'in those days *cannabis indica*
[Indian hemp] could be obtained at any chemist by merely signing
the book'.[95] Gray was of the opinion that Philip had such 'a perverse sense of humour . . . that he would often speak to people as if
he had tons of the stuff in his possession, merely to give them the
impression that he was a monster of depravity'.[96] In August 1922,
we find Philip reporting, in a strange letter to Gray, that he had
tracked down 'a certain pharmaceutician to his lair in a remote suburb and extracted cannibalistic indications[97] from him . . . Also the
possibility of a certain Crowleyian compound, which has not yet
arrived. If I come to Wales I shall bring them.'[98] In another letter to
Gray, dated January 1923, he included a weird extended limerick
with references both to cannabis and cocaine:

> There was an old sister of Binnory
> Who came to a chemist in thin array
>   Just like Monna Vanna. This
>   Great punk wanted cannabis
> And said: 'O my dear Mr Whinneray
> Give me some, and I'll pour all my gin away.
> What more can a sodden old sinner say?'
>   But *he* said: 'For a tanner, miss.

> I'll sell you a can o' piss—
> Nothing else—though the chemist at Pinner may.'
> 'But I need a stiff swig to begin a day—
> Can't you get one some coke before dinner, eh?'
>   '*No*', he said, 'these vile practices
>   Are the death of young actresses'—
> So she walked with a grisly grim grin away.[99]

Years later a contemporary from Philip's prep school days also recorded that, during a meeting with him in the early 1920s, Philip told him of the wonderful experiences he had obtained from smoking *cannabis indica*.[100] He also claimed 'he could have an orgasm in any part of his body—even his finger-tips'.[101] Occasionally, however, the effects were not so 'wonderful', as Philip related to van Dieren in a letter in February 1923. From then on he abandoned his experiments:

This is not to endeavour to make excuses for my quite unpardonable failure to turn up on Tuesday night, but to explain the cause and offer my very humble apologies. I really feel terribly guilty about it—but the fact is that on Monday night there were indubitable indications of cannibals who, I regret to say, attacked in such force and with such vigour that I was entirely *hors de combat* for more than 24 hours! Such a consequence has never occurred before and, I may say with certainty, will never occur again, for the experience is to say the least of it distinctly grisly.[102]

In this same letter to van Dieren we find the name of Puma briefly reappearing. Philip's anxious mother had evidently persuaded him to return to Cefn Bryntalch, having taken seriously a threat from Puma that she intended removing Nigel from her custody. Philip remarked that he supposed this simply to be a feeble attempt at blackmail on his 'dear' wife's part, but had nevertheless gone to Wales to pacify his mother. Puma's last recorded appearance in the story of Philip's life is really quite inexplicable. Later the same month (21 February 1923) Philip wrote to his mother telling her of 'an almost perfect performance' of a work of his (the orchestral piece, *An Old Song*) conducted by Anthony Bernard. There is a postscript at the bottom of this letter mysteriously adding 'Love from Puma'. Given the circumstances one can only presume that this was simply a black joke on Philip's part, knowing his mother's worried state at the time. There is certainly no evidence to suggest that Philip and Puma were temporarily reunited, even briefly. When next we hear of her she had married again, to Edward Sassoon (b. 1892), a member of the landed gentry, in September 1929.[103] Fourteen years later, on 20 May 1943, she died in a Glasgow hospital at the age of 48: suicide from an overdose of barbiturates.[104]

Besides composing and editing, Philip continued with his journalistic work and, for a few months, between July and September, some dozen articles (of between 700 and 800 words) signed P. H. appeared in the *Weekly Westminster Gazette* under the general heading 'Music'. Here he seems to have had a pretty free hand and wrote on a number of his favourite composers, such as Liszt, Gesualdo, Sorabji, and van Dieren, as well as subjects which had long fascinated him, 'How is Music Composed' and 'Music in the Mind's Ear'. In August 1923 he also made a brief, five-day visit to Paris with Gerald Cooper to examine some manuscripts at the Conservatoire. It is very likely that the following limerick was written during that particular visit:

> Piss is also the sign of 'The Six'
> (Though five of them only have pricks).
>   But the Penis de Milhaud
>   Piddles more than a kilo—
> God damn these urethrical tricks![105]

Philip continued to send his songs to van Dieren for comment and, as a token of gratitude, dedicated the first of the songs in the *Saudades* ('Along the Stream') to him, writing that he hoped he would forgive him for printing his name over the song, 'but my justification is the command to "Render unto Caesar"'.[106] During the years that followed Philip continued to promote van Dieren's cause as much as he could, enlisting the services of numerous other musicians such as Gerald Cooper, John Goss, and the conductor John Barbirolli (1899–1970).

Despite his busy schedule Philip had not neglected his love life. In September 1923 we find him staying in Essex in a cottage at Rivenhall End near Witham, between Chelmsford and Colchester, for about ten days. To cover his tracks on this occasion he called himself Peter Wood, probably because of the affair he was having at the time with the young, possibly under-age, Judith Wood, who was nicknamed 'Timber'.

In the same month Delius and Jelka came to London for nine days to attend the final rehearsals and premiere of *Hassan*. Delius's health was now beginning to deteriorate visibly and Philip noted in a letter to van Dieren that he had to be carried in and out of the theatre on one of the props, the Caliph's chair of state, until a wheelchair and a attendant could be provided. That September and October Philip went on what he called 'a folk-song hunt with Moeran and a phonograph in the eastern counties'.[107] This was followed almost immediately by a trip to Grez-sur-Loing with Gray, a visit which both Fred and Jelka much enjoyed even though Jelka wrote to Percy Grainger bemoaning the fact that neither of their two guests could play the piano. It was during this visit to Grez that Philip saw some of Grainger's latest compositions which had not yet been printed in England. On 18 November he wrote warmly to Grainger telling him how much he admired his works, arranging at the same time for a copy of his book on Delius to be forwarded to Grainger who was on a concert tour in America at the time. A short time before this Grainger had sent Philip a copy of his two-piano arrangement of Delius's *Dance Rhapsody*, complimenting him on his 'lovely arrangements of Delius works for piano, 4 hands, particularly "North Country Sketches". I admire the fine way you have arranged these exquisite works most warmly & wish to thank you for the pleasure you have given me thru them.'[108] Grainger, of course, would not have been aware that a few years earlier (*c.*1919) Philip had included him in a scurrilous collection of rhymes about contemporary composers entitled 'One dozen Cursory Rhymes dedicated to the Brit. Mus. Soc. & the Soc. of Brit. composers':

> The personal appearance of that ingeniously culinary composer P. GRAINGER
> Was of a kind that frequently causes young virgins to be in grave danger.
> > BUT, ON THE OTHER HAND,
> He had lived with Mama ever since he was a tiny kid,
> > And so
> > He never did.[109]

In a letter written to Grainger later that same November Jelka noted that Philip's book on Delius had 'made a great stir', proudly adding that quotations from it cropped up 'in all sorts of articles everywhere'.[110]

Philip's own original output for 1923 had been considerably smaller than during the previous year. Amongst his compositions are songs such as 'Milkmaids', a strophic setting of great charm, 'Two Short Songs' (poems by Robert Herrick, 1591–1674), the urgent 'I held Love's head', with its dramatic and highly effective piano postlude, and the skittish 'Thou gav'st me leave to kiss'. Another fine song dating from this year, 'Consider', is unique, with its long arching vocal phrases underpinned by a florid, sweeping arpeggio accompaniment. The short cycle *Candlelight* (July 1923), a collection of brief and imaginative settings of twelve nursery rhymes, was probably written for his 6-year-old son, Nigel, at the suggestion of Winifred Baker, a nurse with whom he had a long and close

relationship from about 1919 to the end of his life. She is a rather
shadowy figure of whom we first read in a letter written by Philip
that year. In a reply to one of her letters Philip wrote of her 'mood
to mistrust emotional utterances of all kinds' and her inclination

to see sentimentality everywhere . . . You would probably like me to think of
you as a tragically disillusioned cynic, cautiously limiting your capacity for
sorrow by the most utter scepticism of all possible joys . . . But I, in my simplicity . . . and unfashionable fairy-tale folly, shall persist in regarding you as
an evilly enchanted princess who has yet to be awakened out of sleep.[111]

A decade later she would be a significant yet curious emotional
anchor in his turbulent life.

On 19 December Vaughan Williams duly gave the first performance of Philip's *Three Carols*, with the Bach Choir and orchestra
in Queen's Hall, in a programme which included his own 'Pastoral'
Symphony. Philip had dedicated these carols to Vaughan Williams
who wrote a note to Philip after the concert, to the effect that they
had enjoyed performing the carols very much: 'They went "con
amore" if not with deadly accuracy—the poor old Bach Choir has
never moved so fast before!'[112]

The following year, 1924, was also not a particularly prolific one
for Philip and only a few songs were composed. The hearty 'Twelve
Oxen', a setting of the anonymous sixteenth-century poem for solo
voice, with optional two-part chorus and piano, was written for
John Goss and his Cathedral Male Voice Quartet for performance
in their recitals of 'Sociable Songs'. The delicate setting of 'Sweet
and Twenty' ('O Mistress mine') is one of those compositions which
the hearer instinctively recognizes as a masterpiece, a triumph of art
concealing art. In its 59 bars melody, harmony, and counterpoint
are perfectly fused together with Shakespeare's famous poem. The
skilful use of cross-rhythms and displaced accent give the music just
the right quality of vitality and restlessness, while the shape and
contour of the melodic line has a masterful inevitability. The delicious aptness of the *envoi* with its last five throw-away bars makes it
a perfect gem.

One of Philip's particular gifts as a composer was that of melody
and in this song, as in so many others, he shows his flair for writing
an inspired melody. In *The Sackbut* of March 1921 Philip drew
attention to an attempt by the composer and director of music at
Marlborough College, John Ivimey (1868–1961), to define a tune,
the merits of which Ivimey felt could be tested by singing or playing
it without accompaniment.

A tune that is worthy of the name is one that does not hang fire by harping on one note; does not borrow chromatic notes (notes foreign to the key) to help it; one that shows a good contour when written down, has well-balanced phrases, a medium range, is easily remembered, and gives pleasure by itself alone, sans words, sans accompaniment, sans everything but a good rendering.

In his *Sackbut* article Philip suggested that

> though tune . . . is by no means an essential nor even, at times, a desirable element in modern song, one should never lose sight of the fact that song is in essence unaccompanied tune and on those rare occasions when a modern composer achieves a satisfactory setting of a modern poem by means of a tune which, whatever be the merits and beauties of its accompaniment, satisfies the requirements set forth above, one feels inclined to single out the song for very special commendation.[113]

'A remark', as Gerald Cockshott rightly remarks, 'which is both a statement of Warlock's own procedure and a criticism of the methods of some of his contemporaries.'[114]

Besides the rather ordinary 'I have a garden' (published as a unison choral song in 1925) there is also 'Peter Warlock's Fancy', a typical Warlock drinking-song with a vigorous accompaniment (spiced up with the odd chromatic chord), plenty of thundering left-hand octaves, and a highly effective part for optional chorus. It shows how Philip could write a memorable, first-class melody perfect for a rip-roaring sing-along occasion of the kind for which it was obviously intended. 'Yarmouth Fair', also dating from this period, is another of the Warlock songs which has gained immense popularity. Some years later Moeran told Arnold Dowbiggin about the rather unusual way in which this song came to be composed:

> 'Yarmouth Fair' is not a traditional song in any sense of the word at all. I first of all heard it sung in a pub at Cley-next-the-Sea in 1921 by a villager, John Drinkwater. After he sung it he turned to me and said, 'I picked that old song up by the road-side in an old newspaper'. I said, 'But, how about the tune?' Drinkwater said 'Oh, that sort o' fared to come to me when I was sitting on a pile of stones by the roadside & reading the words over'.
> Now the words were about a 'Magpie': I took them down also. Several years later, Peter got stuck, as all decent composers do sometimes. i.e. ideas wouldn't come to him one day when he was trying to compose. I happened to drop in on him & said, 'If you're hard up for ideas why not arrange a folk-song?' He quite took to the idea, so I showed him my MSS. & gave him some to choose from & he picked 'The Magpie'. The words seemed to have a music-hall tang about them, & the Oxford Press deemed it advisable to enquire about copyright. It turned out that they had appeared in a publication of Francis Day & Hunter's, 'The Mohawk Minstrels' [1896]. Permission to reprint was refused by this firm. A friend of ours, the late Hal Collins, set to work & composed the 'Yarmouth Fair' words to fit Peter's arrangement of

Drinkwater's tune, & the O.U.P. published this. So there is nothing traditional
in the accepted sense of the word.[115]

The tune of this song could not be more straightforward nor
more infectious—once heard, never forgotten, while in the piano
accompaniment Philip shows his considerable skill and ingenuity.
Here he cleverly contrives to incorporate and juxtapose elements as
diverse as lute-like accompaniments, horn fifths, drone-bass pedal-
points, across the barline syncopations, touches of the Tudor
flattened seventh, percussive dissonances, and Delius-like harmonies
rising to the surface as the excitement mounts from verse 3 to the
end. The whole piece, when performed with the almost breathless
exuberance and panache it demands, is a *tour de force* for both
singer and accompanist alike.

There was also good news for Philip that year. In March 1924 he
wrote to tell Fritz Hart that *The Curlew* had been one of five works
selected to represent contemporary British music at the International
Music Festival at Salzburg that year. Philip, however, did not attend
the performance but Hubert Foss, who was present in his capacity
as the recently appointed head of the OUP music department,
received a typical letter from Philip: 'I can't think why you want to
listen to all that filthy music in Salzburg. You'd do much better with
me here in Dorset. I've found a new pub.'[116] Bemoaning the general
state of music in England, Philip cynically concluded his letter to
Hart by adding that Bax continued

to maintain his reputation as the champion musical diarrhoeaist, having a
large new work produced about every three weeks; Ireland churns out laboriously uninspired compositions at much longer intervals; poor old Delius, now
quite a cripple, has apparently dried up for good; and we are left contemplating the melancholy spectacle of Rutland Boughton, [1878–1960] the modern
counterpart of [Michael] Balfe [1808–70] or [Vincent] Wallace [1812–65] (of
'Maritana' fame) achieving 300 performances by the grace of a multi-million-
aire. However, one mustn't grizzle; the standard of dance-music is distinctly
improving![117]

The Deliuses too had not forgotten their younger friend and,
rightly sensing that Philip's finances were in the usual precarious
state, sent him a short letter together with a cheque for £5 which
they hoped would be useful to help balance his budget.[118]

April 1924 found Philip house-bound in Wales as a result of an
accident in which he broke a leg, the result of 'a too too Dionysian
prance down the steep slopes of Montgomery Castle with Mr
Timpany [i.e. Gray]'.[119] During this time of enforced immobility he

read the tarot cards to predict Gray's future, telling him that his present situation was 'rest from strife; pleasure; quick, subtle perceptions; an idea of graceful balancing and unreliability beneath [a] promising exterior'. He added stoically that he had just revised his Serenade for strings (which he intended sending to 'Sir God Damfrey', the conductor, Sir Dan Godfrey, 1868–1939), 'by way of making an excuse for a good debauch at Poole in the autumn. But it is very depressing, all this petty music making; I am no better and no worse than I was seven years ago—just exactly the same—in fact.'[120] The next day, still depressed, he wrote to his old friend Phyl Crocker lamenting the fact that he was 'stretched miserably' on his bed, 'unable to walk and condemned to immobility for another three weeks—a very grisly predicament whose grisliness is intensified by the impossibility of drinking, so that my spirits, like my funds, are at their lowest ebb'.[121]

Philip's feelings about Delius's music had changed dramatically from the early days and in July 1924 he was expressing to Gray the opinion that the less said about the chamber music of Delius the better. He had sent Delius a copy of *The Curlew* but the tone of Delius's reply was a trifle patronizing. Although he found it a very delicate piece of music, he thought that Philip had 'spun it out a little too much . . . but, on no account must you get disheartened about your Music, keep hard at work, & you will eventually do something fine and great'.[122]

By now the claustrophobic atmosphere of Cefn Bryntalch was proving too much for Philip and in June 1924 he made another move, this time returning to live in Chelsea for six months. Oxford University Press had just begun developing their music department under the management of Hubert Foss, and were expanding gradually from educational music to the wider, serious market. Foss had made contact with composers and musical scholars and under his direction the department quickly began to flourish. This seemed an opportune moment for Philip to transfer allegiance and he withdrew the second set of *Peterisms* and the *Serenade* from Chester, selling them to OUP who became his principal publishers until his death. Foss was to become a good friend and admirer of Philip, later writing with great perception about both the man and his music:

Humour in plenty, shyness of an odd kind, a roaring laugh that would give way to a fit of solitude and melancholy—there was Warlock, the man who exquisitely poised the psychologists' requirements of both introvert and extrovert. Add to this an eclectic taste quite out of the common, an almost desperate sense of precision, and a love of male company over pint pots, and you begin to have the man who wrote the music . . .[123]

Philip and Gray had also decided to combine their talents once again, this time to write a book on the fascinating sixteenth-century Italian composer, Gesualdo. Entitled *Carlo Gesualdo: Prince of Venosa: Musician and Murderer*, it was expanded from articles which had previously appeared in October 1920 in *The Sackbut* and the September 1922 volume of *The Chesterian*, and was eventually printed in 1926. One needs to be reminded how original the subject was at that time: much later Stravinsky would take up the cause of Gesualdo and make it his own, if not actually claiming to have put Gesualdo on the map. The collaboration seems not to have been an easy one and Gray later maintained that it was several years before he succeeded in inducing Philip to finish his share of the book, and even then only by threatening to write it himself. In the first two parts of the book Gray wrote on Gesualdo's life and the dramatic murder of his wife, while in the final part Philip gave a brilliant historical survey of chromaticism in music, and an analysis of Gesualdo's genius. He also included several bibliographical appendices with musical examples reproduced in his own handwriting. The subject of Gesualdo inspired a number of witty limericks, two of which actually appeared in the book. He also sent a third one to Gray, jokingly suggesting that it be included in Part II:

> Said the Duke—and his words were not idle—
> To his daughter the day of his bridal:
>   'Now look here, Leonora,
>   Don't *you* play the whore, or
> You'll make poor old Charles homicidal.'[124]

Philip had developed a distinct liking for the seaside town of Poole in Dorset and in the summer of 1924 there were once again mysterious letters to friends which contained intriguing hints and references. Now lodged for a while with Judith Wood at The Lord Nelson, one of the harbour pubs in Poole, he wrote to Gray saying that he was going to start another libel action and might 'be on the track of more good hush-money like Secker's—Gott sei gelobt!'[125] He also wrote in similarly mysterious vein to Colin Taylor who was paying a honeymoon visit to England, telling him that he had had a very strange experience, resulting in an adventure of an incredibly romantic kind which had rejuvenated him both in mind and body. Full of this new life and vigour, Philip was obviously enjoying himself in Dorset, where he drank gin and played skittles all the after-noon, a place which he felt was 'as good as Cornwall, but with pleasant people'.[126] One of the colourful characters whose company he much enjoyed during his time in Dorset was Trelawney Dayrell Reed (b. 1885), a larger-than-life eccentric who, according to their mutual friend Augustus John, was a popular figure in the local pubs, 'often seen wearing a Venetian cape and the beard of an Hidalgo'.[127] Reed had an intimate knowledge of the county and the area in general, later writing a book on Wessex and a treatise on shove-halfpenny, a game often played in English pubs at the time. Reed also provided the English translation for Philip's 'Cornish Christmas Carol' ('Kan Nadelik') when it appeared in print in 1924 and Philip showed his appreciation and admiration by dedicating the drinking-song, 'Peter Warlock's Fancy' to him.

Yet as far as original composition was concerned, he still felt very pessimistic. In a letter to Fritz Hart that October he commented that Hart's 'kind and friendly feelings' led him to exaggerate the value of his compositions:

I myself have no illusions about it, and, much as I appreciate your liking for it, I know that it is but half a pint, so to speak, from a well that is almost dry already. I know that there is practically nothing more to come from that source, and I have no belief in it nor any hopes for the future. I am com-pletely sterile—impotent—in that direction. . . .

I console myself with the reflection that it is better to be sterile than to have musical diarrhoea, as so many English and French composers have at the pre-sent time—though in the end that is poor comfort! If only one had sufficiently little critical sense to believe in one's own works! But then I was always critic first and composer a very long way afterwards—hence these grizzlements.[128]

Instead his energies were now taken up with other projects and at the end of 1924 he was busily engaged on re-scoring his 1916 send-up of César Franck's D minor symphony, 'The Old Codger' for the unlikely combination of piano, banjo, violin, soprano, alto and tenor saxophones, two trumpets, trombone, and tuba. This arrange-ment was for the Savoy Orpheans, formed by Debroy Somers (1890–1952) to play at the Savoy Hotel and one of the most popular of the English dance bands. In early December, Philip compiled an hour-long radio programme for the BBC entitled 'Old English Ayres and Keyboard Music', which he presented on 12 December. Five singers took part in the broadcast, together with Mrs Gordon Woodhouse (1872–1948), a pioneer recorder and broadcaster on the harpsichord. The script was vintage Warlock with its appeal to the ordinary listener and its inevitable dig at the professional:

If people would only listen to music without being obsessed with the notion that they will not understand it unless they are 'educated up to it', they would be surprised at the ease with which they understood it and the increase of pleasure they derived from it. It is a fact that some of the very novel music of the present-day often makes an immediate appeal to the plain music-lover, because he listens to it with unprejudiced ears and lays his mind open to its message, while the professional musician is often unable to free his mind from theoretical preoccupations when listening to something new and unfamiliar—and so the direct appeal of music is lost for him in a tangle of technicalities.[129]

This may have been the occasion of which Jack Lindsay wrote when he related how Philip, 'scheduled to talk about some Elizabethan songs which Victor Carne was to sing on the air . . . went round the BBC staff with a petition for the removal of a musical adviser, unmoved (or rather stimulated) by the fact that the man was in the room'.[130]

By the end of the year Philip had finally decided that it was time to find a new place to stay, preferably near but not in London. After a brief holiday on Majorca, where he spent Christmas in Palma de Mallorca, he moved to Eynsford, a picturesque village in Kent. Here for the next three-and-a-half years he lived in a small cottage formerly rented by Foss and conveniently situated in the main street next to Munns, the grocer, and more important, almost directly opposite the eighteenth-century village pub, The Five Bells, run by the genial Harry Brice, whose family had owned the property since 1855.

As Philip plunged into the next hectic stage of his life he left a trail of damage and ruffled feathers in his wake. His London land-lady wrote a letter of despair to Edith Buckley Jones hoping, if not demanding, to be compensated in some way for the damage wreaked on 6A Bury Street by Philip and his friends during the short time he had stayed there:

it is not re-let yet, it being impossible to do so in the condition it has been left in—the condition of the dining room is very bad, the ceiling & walls being written on. The whole bannister has been very badly damaged in fact has nearly all been broken down—a large divan has been so badly broken that the wooden side is broken to bits . . . with regard to the neighbours complaints they were exceedingly unpleasant . . . it is quite obvious how scandalous the behaviour generally was.[131]

That behaviour would, to a certain degree, now be transferred to rustic Kent.

THE EYNSFORD YEARS
(1925–1928)

Philip was thoroughly delighted with Eynsford, an unspoilt, ancient village in completely rural surroundings on the river Darent. It was a place he found 'peaceful and congenial for work'[1] and had the added advantage of being within commuting distance of London, a mere 20 miles away, as well as having 27 pubs within a 4-mile radius. However, travelling back late at night in the last train after a binge in London sometimes presented problems, should he fall asleep during the journey, as he often did. On such occasions he would wake up in the small hours of the morning in places like Maidstone (some 19 miles from Eynsford) or Whitstable and, finding himself penniless in these towns, was often forced to walk back home. A solution was eventually found: once he was safely on the homeward-bound train, his friends in London would phone the Eynsford station-master to make sure he was taken off the train when it arrived.

Close to the ruins of Eynsford Castle, Philip shared the small main-street cottage with his composer friend, E. J. Moeran, together with a collection of cats and a Maori housekeeper-cum-factotum, Hal Collins (Te Akau) (d. 1929). Collins had previously been a barman at a London drinking club. Gray gave this intriguing description of him:

In contra-distinction to this more or less floating population of cats and women, a permanent member of the establishment was a strange character called Hal Collins . . . whose Maori grandmother had been a cannibal and used, within his memory, to lament the passing of the good old days when she could feast upon her kind. Besides being a graphic artist of considerable talent, particularly in woodcut, he was one of those people who, without ever having learnt a note of music or received a lesson in piano playing, have an inborn technical dexterity and a quite remarkable gift for improvisation. He used to compose systematically, also, but without being able to write it down; I remember him once playing to me a whole act of an opera he had conceived on the subject of Tristram Shandy.[2] A song of his, incidentally, taken down in notation by Peter, called *Forget not yet*,[3] was published by the Oxford University Press,[4] and testifies to his genuine talent. He subsisted chiefly on stout, of which he consumed gargantuan quantities, and when elated would perform Maori war dances with quite terrifying realism. On spirits, however, he would run completely amok, in true native fashion, and on one occasion almost succeeded in massacring the entire household . . . He was devoted to Peter as a dog to its master.[5]

Another permanent member of the household was Philip's mistress, Barbara Peache (b. 1900), whom he had first met at a party in Chelsea in the early 1920s. She lived with him through the Eynsford period until his death, eventually moving to Malta in her later years. Small and trim with bronze hair, sharp, green eyes, and a sharp chin, Eric Fenby described her as 'a very quiet, attractive girl, quite different from Phil's usual types'.[6] For a time she seems also to have been the mistress of Lord Auckland (1895–1941), the sixth Baron, who divorced his American wife in 1925. Philip evidently did not mind her sleeping with Auckland for there was not much jealousy in his nature. He did, however, feel rather sorely about the fact that when the Baron got her pregnant she had to pay for the abortions herself. Philip, on the other hand, conscientiously paid for all the abortions (£5 a time) for which he had been responsible.[7] Judith Wood was another regular visitor and one of Philip's friends at the time, Lionel (later Judge) Jellinek (1898–1979), a keen music enthusiast, recalled that on occasions Philip, Barbara Peache, and Judith Wood slept three to a bed in the Eynsford cottage.

During his years there Philip ran a kind of open house and it is from this period that much of the Warlock 'legend' originates. According to Gray there was a constant stream of visitors including 'poets and painters, airmen and actors, musicians and maniacs of every description, including pyrophils and claustrophobes—everyone who was in any way unusual or abnormal was sure of receiving a ready welcome at Eynsford'.[8] There are many first-hand accounts of the alleged riotous life in the Eynsford commune. Jack Lindsay devoted a whole chapter to Philip in his autobiographical *Fanfrolico and After*, in which he painted a colourful picture of some of the antics at Eynsford. He described Philip as 'rather pallid-faced, but his neat gingery beard, added to his dangerous eyes, gave him the effect of a waspish Elizabethan bravo with a courtly air'. Douglas Goldring confirmed and enlarged on this description when writing about Philip in his book, *The Nineteen Twenties*: 'Tall, pasty-faced, with a wisp of beard, it was his deep-set eyes and demoniac smile—a smile which became more lewdly devilish as the evening proceeded and his blasphemies became more daring—which gave the *clou* to his enigmatic character.'[9] When Lindsay first arrived at the Eynsford cottage, Philip was 'rendering on the piano a Victorian oratorio with an ultra-seriousness carried into parody'. This ill-fated work was *Penitence, Pardon and Peace* by J. A. Maunder (1858–1920), in which a certain passage was sung to the words of the limerick about the Old Man from Newcastle. The daughter of their Eynsford land-lord Mr Munn, the grocer, recalled Philip and Moeran filling big urns at the pub and taking them back to the cottage where the kitchen was 'swimming in beer'.[10] Lindsay's account continues:

We drank up all the beer and hurried across to the Five Bells, where we sat at the back on the garden seats by the rickety table, with the leaves of the trees brushing the sweat from our brows. . . . Then we carried a beer-supply home in a huge earthenware jug . . .

We were now too thoroughly caught up in the steady crescendo of uproari-ous laughters which Philip knew so well how to start off and conduct to a staggering blind-drunk conclusion . . .

Early the second morning I found out how effective a retainer was Hal Collins . . . He was devoted to Philip and watched over him and his interest with a dark and stealthy eye. I had awoken early and felt that I would best restore my stomach and head by a cold shower. The house was dead-quiet and I walked into the unlocked bathroom without knocking. Barbara Peach [sic], the small daintily-made and reserved girl who lived with Philip, was sitting naked in the bath. I muttered an apology and withdrew. Turning, I saw that Hal had come up noiselessly behind me, crouched for a leap if it turned out that I was intentionally intruding on Barbara. Seeing that my action had been innocent, he nodded and went off . . .

On my second visit, Nina [Hamnett] was there, living with Jack Moeran . . . Now at Eynsford she fell flat on her face on the flagged kitchen-floor and damaged her nose, so that she had to be carried to bed in a stunned condi-tion. There Hal the handyman washed her nose in gin and restored her . . .[11]

The painter Nina Hamnett (1890–1956),[12] also recorded her mem-ories of life at Eynsford. She was one of a small number of very good female painters of that period, was a close intimate of the 1920s painters, including Sickert, Pissarro, and Modigliani, and, besides knowing Aleister Crowley, claimed to have introduced James Joyce to Rudolph Valentino. Philip initially invited her to come down and spend an Easter weekend with them:

When I arrived, on the morning of Easter Sunday, the celebration had been going on since Good Friday. On the sitting-room table was the biggest bottle of port that I had ever seen . . .

I tasted some of it and it was very potent—I think that he had bought it for the size of the bottle. The guests had begun the day with doses of Eno's Fruit

Salts and gin, which they assured me gave a most refreshing and invigorating feeling on which to start the day.

We sat in the garden of the pub . . . sang songs of all kinds and drank beer the whole evening. As the Spring was beginning and as I had nothing to do in London and was very bored, I spent a great deal of my time at Eynsford. They were the most sympathetic and intelligent company I had ever been in. Heseltine was a man who really should have lived in about 1400. At any rate, he did his best to put a real English spirit into life in Kent and he was adored by all the farmers and yokels. The landlord of the house, Mr Munn, the grocer, was mentioned by Heseltine in his epitaph . . .

> Here lies Warlock, the composer,
> Who lived next door to Munn, the grocer.
> He died of drink and copulation,
> A great discredit to this nation.

Mr Munn was a most sympathetic character and had a long moustache. When the noise in the evenings was too much and the songs too loud, he would come in and join the party. . . .

On Sundays, a large and important lunch was cooked, everyone in the house helping. Some serious beer-drinking was done in the garden of the pub opposite whilst the food cooked and then a large earthenware jug was filled with ale and brought to the house. . . . Generally, on a Sunday afternoon, as Moeran had a large motor, we would visit a distant pub where drinks could be had. There were several and so our Sundays, instead of being dreadful and boring days, became quite one of the brightest of the week . . .

Next to our house was a [Baptist] chapel. It was surrounded by a small garden and on Sunday mornings we ran a rival show. When the service started, we began with several works by Max Reger, the noisy German composer, some of whose music sounds completely drunk. These were played on the pianola. The 'Fairy Queen' was then played and we ended up by roaring sea songs, ending up with the unexpurgated version of 'Nautical William'.

I heard only recently that the congregation said a prayer every Sunday morning for us. At the evening service they were undisturbed as we were generally drinking in another part of the country and only returned late.

Heseltine had a passion for bonfires and when he felt inclined would start a large one in the garden which smouldered and smelt all night. When Philip had a special job of work to do, he would retire to his room and not speak a word to anyone for days. He worked very hard indeed and when he went out to have a good time he did it equally thoroughly.[13]

Nina Hamnett also related a typical, almost surrealist Warlockian incident in which she was involved during this period:

In a neighbouring village which he visited sometimes, was a pub called the 'Two Brewers'. It was kept by a remarkable character called Robert. Heseltine had arguments with him because he did not like the beer. . . . Opposite the pub was a sort of green with a row of cottages. In one of them lived a girl who was very poor and who came over to see us sometimes. She was good-looking, quite young, and had large, and very beautiful grey eyes. The landlady of the cottage was a very rich and religious woman. We had seen her walking down the village street and she was just the type that Heseltine loathed.

We heard one day from Robert that the landlady was going to have an auction of the poor girl's possessions because she could not pay the rent. Heseltine was delighted to have an opportunity to annoy the old lady. I met him in London, where he was for a few days. He was walking up St Martin's Lane. 'You must come down tomorrow and join us in a protest against injustice. We will buy some masks,' he said. We continued up the street, which leads into the top part of Shaftesbury Avenue, and went into a theatrical costume shop.

In the window were masks, false noses and beards of all shapes and colours. Heseltine thought that a large white death's head mask would be suitable for me. With it I would wear a sheet. It was a terrifying affair and the teeth were painted in black and white stripes. He saw a nose to which was attached a small black beard. He thought it would suit Constant Lambert, who was going to join us. It also resembled a foreign conductor whom Heseltine did not like very much.

I arrived on the following morning. A large motor-car had been hired and a false nose bought for the chauffeur. I wound a sheet around me and the mask was tied on. Constant put on his nose and beard and was quite unrecognisable. Heseltine wore an enormous black hat. It was the largest black hat that I have ever seen and was reputed, at some time, to have belonged to Augustus John. He painted his nose bright red with lipstick and wore a purple Morrocan [sic] robe on which were sewn spangles and small pieces of looking-glass. Moeran stayed behind whilst Heseltine's girl-friend dressed. She did not tell us what she was going to wear.

Heseltine, Lambert and I got into the motor-car. Moeran was to bring the girl along in his car when she was dressed. The auction was arranged for twelve o'clock, so we went to the 'Two Brewers' to see Robert. He hated the old lady as much as Heseltine did and was delighted to have an opportunity to rag her.

The villagers saw us arrive and someone at once telegraphed to the nearest town for an extra large detachment of police. I think they had a suspicion that something unusual was about to happen. Moeran and Philip's friend arrived. She was a very pretty girl; small and well made with blue eyes and did not, as a rule, look more than nineteen or twenty. She was dressed in a child's dress. The skirt was full and very short. She wore flat heeled black shoes and an enormous bow of ribbon on her short hair. She looked about twelve. Her face was made up a very bright pink and her eyes heavily blacked with stage make-up.

A crowd had collected on the green, some with the idea of buying some Sealyhams which the victim of the auction bred, but most of them to see the fun.

At twelve o-clock we crossed the road from the pub. We had to take great care not to drink too much beer in case the police arrived and found us smelling of drink. As soon as the auctioneer started, Heseltine sprang forward in front of him and began to make a speech. We loudly applauded and each time the auctioneer protested, he was greeted by whistles and catcalls, several of the local inhabitants taking our part.

It was a pathetic sale. There were four or five dogs which Robert bought. They were well-bred but not in very good condition. The rest of the poor girl's things consisted of an iron washstand, a bed, a few old chairs, a slop pail, a basin, some pots and pans and a piece of Lifebuoy soap.

When Heseltine thought that the auctioneer had had enough, we made a dash for the motor cars and drove away just as a detachment of mounted police were entering the village.[14]

Not everyone, however, found the Eynsford atmosphere congenial. Shortly after Philip's death Robert Nichols told Gray that what he saw at Eynsford thoroughly alarmed him, with Barbara Peache evidently sharing his alarm:

She was doing her very best—& it appeared to me a brave best but I did not like the look of things & my conversation with Philip created apprehension in me . . . Barbara was for moving out of that house & I seconded her. In addition to other disturbing factors the place had this against it that there seemed to be a sort of taint about it: it was one of the most discouraging houses I have ever been in & one felt in it a spirit that seemed to darken the soul.[15]

Some thirty years later, in a conversation with Robert Beckhard, Barbara Peache confessed that she had tried to break away from Philip many times and wondered why she had actually stayed with him so long. Always feeling that something was wrong, she had realized that the relationship was doomed right from the start and had definitely believed that there was a duality in his personality. She also spoke of 'the bad influence of Delius'.[16]

Among the many weekend visitors at the Eynsford cottage were composers such as Constant Lambert and Lord Berners (1883–1950). Nina Hamnett records how Lambert had found a Victorian duet called 'The Fairy Queen' which contained runs up and down the piano, all kinds of curious trills, and a most ridiculous melody. Moeran and Lambert played it with very serious faces, generally having an argument in the middle when one would push the other off the end of the piano stool. Arnold Bax also stayed at Eynsford for a short time as a guest in 1925 and while there wrote the *Romantic Overture* for small orchestra and piano. Of this period in Bax's life his biographer Lewis Foreman writes:

We may be sure that Bax joined with zest in the Eynsford atmosphere, encountering the young Constant Lambert for the first time, and probably Patrick Hadley[17] also. It is easy to picture the riotous company into which he had strayed where weekends were devoted to the pub, but weekdays to musical hard work, and to imagine his ease at being able to relax after the strain of the previous year. It was doubtless this atmosphere that encouraged him, in an amusing *jeu d'esprit*, to make a two-bar quotation from the César Franck

Symphony in the *Romantic Overture*. The example of *The Old Codger*, one of Warlock's 'Cod Pieces' (where he lampoons the Franck), would have been hard for Bax's sometimes schoolboyish sense of humour to resist.[18]

Bax 'obliged him [Philip] with some special translations from the Irish for the *Merry-Go-Down*[19] anthology'[20] and Philip dedicated the song 'Sorrow's Lullaby' to him. Having been introduced by Philip to Sir Walter Raleigh's poem 'Walsinghame', Bax showed his gratitude for the hospitality by dedicating a setting of the poem (for tenor solo, orchestra, chorus, and obbligato soprano) to him.

For a time the young William Walton was also part of Philip's circle of friends, but after a while he 'found the convivial pressures more than he could manage'.[21] Writing some thirty years later, he acknowledged his debt to Philip, who had introduced him 'to the works of both Schoenberg and Bartók, both of whom were little known in England at that time, and Gesualdo, now so fashionable among the elite'.[22] Lady Walton was, however, later to write that her husband did not care much for Philip. Philip, on the other hand, was greatly impressed with the young Walton and, in one of his last letters to Moeran, written two months before his death, predicted great things for his musical future: 'He is the best musician this country has produced for a long while. Lambert is perhaps more talented, but I do not feel that music is his ultimate mode of expression. His keen observation, sensibility, wit, and critical intellect seem rather to point to literature as his medium, whereas Walton is specifically musical or nothing.'[23]

Philip first met his co-tenant, Moeran, when he (Philip) visited him to tell him how much he had enjoyed one of his songs. He was a composer of Irish descent who had studied at the Royal College of Music under John Ireland and who first attracted public attention in 1924 when Sir Hamilton Harty (1879–1941) commissioned a symphony from him. For a while he had lived in Norfolk, where his father was a vicar, and it was there that he spent some time collecting folk-songs. Moeran has left an interesting account of the way in which Philip worked during their time together at Eynsford:

Warlock's methods as a composer were dictated by the peculiarities of his temperament. For weeks he would be sunk in gloom, unable to think of a note. He would alleviate his melancholy by transcription . . . When the black mood passed he would write a song a day for a week. According to Moeran, 'he went to the piano and began fumbling about with chords, and whistling', quite undisturbed by the conversation from the next room. All his work was written in this way—quickly, at the piano, and often in an atmosphere that was far from quiet.[24]

In his memoir Gray adds some more background, stating that Philip

was genuinely incapable of working steadily at any creative task, over a long period of time. On the other hand, when in the vein, no one had more phenomenal power of concentration and rapidity of execution. He would often work for twenty hours on end, and was able to keep up this rate for comparatively long periods, with the result that in the course of two or three weeks he would produce as much work as the artist of the opposite type would do in six months. The inevitable consequence of such high tension, however, was a violent reaction, and frequently he would be unable to do any work of the slightest value for months on end.[25]

Much mention has been made of Philip's skill at whistling. Robert Nichols noted that 'he whistled more sweetly'[26] than any person he ever knew, while Gray noted how Philip would play through his transcriptions of orchestral scores, whistling instead of singing the vocal parts: 'the sound seemed to come effortlessly from the throat, like the song of a bird, with a sweetness and purity of tone, a perfection of phrasing, a power of dynamic gradation, and a rich, expressive quality such as I have never heard from anyone else'.[27] C. W. Orr also noted its 'flute-like . . . quality and purity'[28] that he never heard equalled.

Given the numerous Warlock legends, it would be easy to imagine that life at Eynsford was one continuous orgy of drinking and carousing. That may have been partly true of weekends but during the week itself there was certainly a great deal of hard work on Philip's part and the Eynsford years were particularly productive. Besides an enormous amount of transcribing, editing, and writing he composed some of his finest songs, as well as the *Capriol Suite* and several choral works. 1925 began auspiciously for Philip. Within a month of his having moved to Eynsford his Serenade for strings was given its first broadcast performance in February, a sign that the Establishment was at last beginning to take his music seriously. In April the venerable Canon Fellowes of Windsor found himself once again the target of Philip's caustic pen. Fellowes had just produced an anthology entitled *English Madrigal Verse: 1588–1632*, which contained all the poems that had appeared, set to music, in the printed books of madrigals published during the Elizabethan and Jacobean periods. Having found over 200 errata in the text, of which few if any, as Philip pointed out, 'could be ascribed to the printer',[29] he wrote a letter to the *London Mercury* in which, quoting page and line in each case, he painstakingly listed all the errata and corrections in a scholarly fashion. Fellowes would hardly have enjoyed the barbed comment: 'In compiling this list I have not concerned myself with the question of conjectural emendations but merely that of textual accuracy. Many of the errors are repeated in Dr Fellowes's edition of the music of the ayres (*The English School of Lutenist Song-Writers*).'[30]

Philip was extraordinarily busy at this time completing his editing of the final volumes of the English ayres, with a volume of French ayres of the same period, and an edition of Ravenscroft's complete rounds and catches soon to follow. He was also completing a book entitled *The English Ayre* (which he dedicated to the memory of Philip Wilson who had died in 1924) as well as the study of Gesualdo. He had long been fascinated by the life and music of this strange composer and had even suggested to Nichols, who was then working as an artistic adviser in Douglas Fairbanks's studio in Hollywood, that Gesualdo's life would make a 'very good spectacular film . . . bizarre and thrilling enough, with a good high-coloured Renaissance setting':[31]

It would certainly be most admirable if you could make a big film out of it, what a setting it could have! . . . we have gleaned a great deal of fresh information from Italy, including a long verbatim report of the inquest held on the murdered wife and her paramour, with all the eyewitness accounts in detail. Also some very interesting medical evidence, to the effect that his Serene Highness was unable to perform the daily function of evacuation without first being flagellated by a valet kept specially for the purpose. In later life there were complaints that he did most shamefully abuse his page-boys; and other interesting little facts.[32]

Besides all this, he had also found time to edit an anthology of twenty-four songs sung at the London Pleasure Gardens (Ranelagh, Vauxhall, Sadlers Wells, etc.) during the latter half of the eighteenth century. Private-press books were having a great surge of popularity in England at the time and *Songs of the Gardens* was printed in 1925 in a limited edition of 875 copies by the Nonesuch Press and produced under the direction of Hubert Foss and the owner of the Press, Sir Francis Meynell (1891–1975). With its attractive layout and adorning woodcuts, this anthology is more of a collector's item than a practical performing edition. Even the songs themselves were not really edited for performance, being mostly printed with figured-bass only, and several in archaic clefs.

Philip's edition of Ravenscroft's complete rounds and catches (numbering 100) entitled *Pammelia and other Rounds and Catches*

was published by the OUP in 1928. Unbeknown to Philip, the publishers also brought out a 'Schools Edition', omitting the rounds the
words of which they considered unsuitable for children. The omission
of round no. 71 led to a typical Warlock piece of mischief-making.
The last line of this round is 'Whip little David's bum, bum, bum,
bum', the voice continuing as a kind of ostinato and the complete
edition included a footnote which instructed the singers 'pronounce
boum, not *bumm*'. The Schools Edition omitted this 'improper'
round, although Philip thought 'it might prove a very salutary lesson
to a classroom of little Davids'. The footnote, however, was accidentally left in and a delighted Philip encouraged friends such as
Dowbiggin to write to Humphrey Milford (1877–1952), the head of
the OUP, to ask 'why this so superogatory *bum* should suddenly
obtrude itself upon an otherwise chaste and blameless page'.[33]

In April Philip wrote to tell Delius that he intended to write a
little book containing detailed descriptions of about fifteen of
Delius's works. The intention was to produce a kind of authoritative
handbook of Delius's works containing music examples and detailed
tempo indications for the use of students and conductors. Although
there is evidence that the OUP were interested in publishing such a
volume (Philip wrote at the end of April that he hoped to produce a
rough draft in a few weeks), the book itself never appeared. It is not
clear as to why the scheme was eventually abandoned although
maybe a clue lies in a letter from Philip to Jelka on 20 July: 'It was
perhaps a mistake to try and get from him [Delius] very detailed
indications as to the tempi of his works . . .'[34]

Round about this time Philip had another of his violent clashes, this
time with a prominent member of the London Musical Establishment,
Percy Scholes (1877–1958), the music critic of the *Observer*, who later
became widely known through his *magnum opus*, the *Oxford Companion
to Music*. This incident is a good example of one of Philip's more
unnerving traits: as Basil Trier described it—'he used to hound
people—he possessed a sort of feminine sustained hostility towards
them'.[35] Sparked off by what Philip considered to be ignorant comments on Liszt (a composer he much admired), he went into battle.
An angry letter from Philip to Nichols gives details of this clash:

And yet things like that stinking bag of putrescent tripe, Percy A. Scholes who
is permitted to gull the readers of 'The Observer' week by week are accus-
tomed to dismiss [Liszt's] entire life's work, together with that of Berlioz, as
unworthy of serious consideration, while columns are devoted to the latest
mess puked up by Gustav Holst and his miserable like. On one occasion when

he had dismissed Liszt *en bloc* in a contemptuous line, I asked Scholes, in the presence of numerous witnesses in the interval at a concert, whether he knew any of the great works of Liszt, mentioning ten or a dozen by name—and he confessed that he did not: whereupon I informed him that he was a most impudent charlatan, obtaining money by false pretences by posing as an authority on a subject of which he was grossly ignorant—and that in no other branch of journalism, even, would such gross incompetence be tolerated.[36]

In June further fuel was added to the fire when Scholes wrote unfavourably about the last of three concerts which Moeran had organized at the Wigmore Hall at his own expense. Besides including his own Piano Trio in this particular concert on 13 June, Moeran had also programmed works by the New Zealand-born composer Hugo Anson (1894–1958), John Ireland, and a *Song-cycle on poems of Thomas Hardy* by Hubert Foss. Philip took great exception to Scholes's review, particularly the comments on Foss's composition, and immediately sent off a scathing attack:

Once again, in your notice of Moeran's concert in to-day's 'Observer', you have given a conspicuous example of your incompetence and dishonesty as a critic. If you had said that Foss 'has still to find a harmonic idiom that means anything' to yourself, you would have been within your rights, but you have no right to saddle Foss with your own utter insensitiveness to any but the most elementary kind of diatonic harmony by suggesting that his own music means nothing to him—in other words that he has deliberately written, rehearsed and performed pages of absolute nonsense; and your statement that he 'introduces long pauses in the singer's part regardless of the sense of the words' is a direct lie.

Foss as a composer is nothing if not strictly self-critical, and as a musical critic he has solid qualifications of musical achievement to qualify him for being one—which is more than can be said for you and most of your journalistic confrères; and the spectacle of you and your pedantic like doing your utmost to thwart the efforts of composers and concert-givers who are doing their best to advance the cause of serious music in this country is becoming more and more disgusting.

Instead of appreciating the initiative of a young and by no means wealthy musician who gives a series of concerts of new and unfamiliar music, you can only complain that they are given on a Saturday afternoon when you would like to be playing tennis instead of earning your ill-gotten living.

Permit me to suggest that, abandoning the pretence that you are in any way qualified to pass judgment on music, you would be much better employed in playing tennis than reporting concerts at any time, and that you would be still better employed in buggering yourself with a pair of exceptionally well-greased bellows.[37]

Scholes was understandably incensed and proceeded to let it be known that he was considering taking legal action. A week later Philip wrote to him again:

I hear you have been talking of having your revenge on me for accusing you of 'incompetence and dishonesty' by having the law on me on account of my last letter. Very well: do so. And let me tell you this:—I have no illusions about the value of my contribution to music as a composer—that will be forgotten, possibly before I am. But there is one thing I *am* out to do and that is to purge musical criticism of reporters who have no qualification whatever for being such.

You are a dirty little place-hunting cur, and if you didn't wear spectacles, I would tell you so in actions rather than words, the next time I set eyes on your exceedingly unprepossessing face.[38]

Brian Lunn related how Scholes had later given him a fuller account of this unpleasant clash:

For months . . . [Philip] had sent him obscene postcards. At all hours of the night he would pour filthy abuse down the telephone. One early morning Scholes had answered the telephone to be greeted with insults from a whole series of drunken men, which ended in an obscene limerick on his name from Heseltine. 'I might have prosecuted him', Scholes added, 'but Philip would not have taken a magistrate's verdict, and if he had appealed he might have got six months. I did not want to send a genius to gaol.'[39]

In fact, Philip was so angry that he proceeded to go round London with an enormous cardboard cylinder containing a petition designed to secure Scholes's dismissal from the newspaper. Angry as he may have been at the time, Philip retained his sharp sense of humour and in June the next year he penned the following letter to Scholes. As one reads it, it seems at first that all has been forgiven until the final brilliant sentence for which Philip reserved his masterstroke:

Dear Mr Scholes,

While sending you an announcement of yet another performance of 'The Curlew', I feel I must write a few words to thank you for the extraordinarily helpful and illuminating commentary which you wrote about this work on the occasion of its recent performance at the Newcastle broadcasting studio. I remember, with profound gratitude, how much trouble you took, when the work was first published, in studying the score and writing the official account of it for the Carnegie trustees' pamphlet, and I must confess that I felt extremely flattered when I saw that you had been kind enough to write yet another article about this little composition of mine—and *such* an article! When I read it, I began to think that I had never yet completely understood the significance of my own work myself,

Yours devotedly, Peter Warlock.[40]

At this time Philip seemed in generally good humour. In June 1925 he wrote to Taylor saying how delighted he had been to find himself portrayed in the novel, *Antic Hay* (1923) by Aldous Huxley

(1894–1963), a contemporary at Eton and also one of Taylor's former piano pupils. He also wrote warmly about another important
figure in his musical life, one of his most loyal friends and supporters, the singer John Goss, who was now one of the advisers for
songs to the Oxford Press. Described as having 'a sympathetic baritone voice and a fine, cultivated musicianship', Goss only seriously
took up singing as a profession in his mid-twenties having previously been 'in a variety of labouring jobs'.[41] Not only did he do
much to promote both the music of Philip and van Dieren, he also
had a male-voice quartet which gave numerous concerts of so-called
'sociable songs'—folk-songs, shanties, hymns, army songs, etc.,
arranged for solo voice, men's voice chorus, and piano—which were
very popular in London at the time. In March 1925 they made some
splendid gramophone records from this repertoire for HMV in
which Hubert Foss provided the piano accompaniment. Perhaps it
was this particular partnership between Goss and Foss which
inspired one of Philip's more outrageous limericks:

> That scandalous pair Goss and Foss
> Once attempted to put it across
>   A girl on a train
>   But their efforts proved vain,
> So Foss tossed off Goss at King's Cross.

Philip proudly plastered the inside of the lavatory door at
Eynsford with similar limericks and 'newspaper cuttings twisted to
read lewdly, [and] with bawdy announcements'.[42] Jack Lindsay later
recalled how Philip had responded with scholarly seriousness, as if
to some important questionnaire on Elizabethan madrigals, when it
was suggested that he might assist in the compiling of a book of
obscene limericks for the American market. Philip evidently 'typed
out a vast number, some by himself, others anonymous, on a toilet-
roll, which he unwound on to a typewriter and then rewound like an
ancient book-roll'.[43] In February 1922 Philip had expounded his
interest in the limerick as a form of poetry to Fritz Hart:

I am interested in the limerick as a literary form—it is conducive to all the
virtues of neat rhyming and terse epigrammatic expression and is the nearest
modern equivalent to the forms used by Catullus and Martial and the Greeks
of the 'anthology'; and I have a large collection of Rabelaisian verses, gleaned
from pubs and other cheery places up and down the country, which I have
thought of printing for private circulation.[44]

Up until now most of them have, alas, had to be circulated
verbally, although a few, such as this oft-quoted one with its clever

double entendre in the last line, have found their way into print in several anthologies:

> The young girls who frequent picture-palaces
> Have no use for this psycho-analysis;
> And although Doctor Freud
> Is distinctly annoyed,
> They cling to their long-standing fallacies.

By June Philip had finished writing *The English Ayre*, as well as his part of the book on Gesualdo, and the following month he and Moeran paid a brief visit to Grez to see Delius, who was now almost totally blind and paralysed. From now on Delius depended more and more on such visits, and an appreciative Jelka wrote to Philip in August telling him that it was a 'great consolation' to her that 'he has all you friends'.[45]

Although in August 1925 Philip had sent a song from his volume *Songs of the Gardens* to Nichols, who was working on a film in Hollywood and had asked for a 'good sentimental tune to associate with our high born heroine',[46] he was gradually becoming more and more disillusioned with original composition. A somewhat cynical letter to Taylor at that time tells how he was busy with literary work, including several books and pamphlets, and editions of old music, as well as a weekly article for *Wireless League Gazette*, a new paper which had started up in August 1925: 'This is much more fun than writing music which one doesn't believe in—and far more paying.'[47]

In the mean time he was still busily pursuing his work as scholar and editor. Although most of his researching and transcribing was done in the British Museum, he occasionally found it necessary to travel to libraries in places such as Oxford and Cambridge for additional material. Some interesting correspondence survives between Philip and George Thewlis (1890–1967), a bass lay-clerk in Christ Church Cathedral Choir, Oxford, for 43 years and conductor of the Oxford Harmonic Society for 21, who also had the distinction of having an honorary MA degree conferred on him in 1948 by the University for his research work in early English music. Thewlis assisted Philip in several ways, notably in the transcription of part-songs by the sixteenth-century composer Thomas Whythorne (1528–96).

One of these letters also shows how meticulous Philip was over his editorial work when he asked Thewlis to check the proofs of some early seventeenth-century songs: 'one cannot be too careful in editing old MSS, and in collating texts, a fresh pair of eyes can often spot errors overlooked by the original transcriber.'[48] Up until his rediscovery by Philip, Whythorne had been rather dismissed out of hand by musicologists. Charles Burney called his music 'truly barbarous' and Ernest Walker in his *History of Music in England* (OUP, 1907) had referred to it as 'miserably feeble rubbish'. Philip wrote a grateful letter to Thewlis at the beginning of December 1925, thanking him for copying the tenor book of Whythorne's songs and telling him that as a result he was able to transcribe all the five-part madrigals from the remaining sources in the British Museum volumes. Philip's correspondence with Thewlis also shows just how charming and helpful he could be. In return for Thewlis's assistance he copied out some music in the British Museum for him, made him a gift of various items of music (his own and also that of other composers), as well as recommending interesting works for Thewlis's choir. Philip also produced a pamphlet of some 2,500 words, *Thomas Whythorne: An Unknown Elizabethan Composer* (OUP, 1925), in an attempt to further the cause of this neglected composer. In May 1927 he sent a copy of this pamphlet to Ernest Walker with the inscription: 'To Dr Walker, hoping he will revise his opinion', surprisingly mild for the usually more waspish Philip. No doubt his admiration for Walker, which dated back to his year at Oxford, had tempered his pen on this occasion. Alas, we shall never know if Walker did, in fact, revise his opinion of Whythorne. A later Oxford musicologist, Jack Westrup (1904–75), would be responsible for removing the disparaging remarks when the book was reprinted in 1952.

Although comparatively few songs were written in 1925, they include the often sung 'Pretty Ring Time', a fine setting of Shakespeare's 'It was a lover and his lass' and yet another example of a truly memorable melody perfectly wedded to the words. In the pert, rhythmical accompaniment there are several appearances of a quotation from the sixteenth-century carol 'Unto us is born a Son', presumably inspired by the line 'This carol they began that hour'. Also written the same year and more serious in nature are the 'Two Short Songs' ('A Prayer to Saint Anthony of Padua' and 'The Sick Heart'), which are meant to be sung consecutively.

By the beginning of 1926 Philip was back again in Oxford, this time to complete some transcriptions of Elizabethan songs with viol accompaniment. In the mean time he had sent his customary Christmas greeting to Taylor:

I had hoped to be able to send you in time for Christmas the two remaining numbers of my choral triptych of dirges from the plays of John Webster;[49] you have the first—'All the flowers of the spring', for mixed voices: the other two are 'Hark, now everything is still'—that grisly poem from 'The Duchess of Malfi', for male voices, and 'Call for the robin-redbreast and the wren', for 4-part female chorus, this last being dedicated to you, the more appropriate because your delightful Madonna songs[50] were the first examples I ever saw of good music for this rather troublesome combination. I have passed the proofs, and copies may arrive any day. With these I shall send you a work for chorus and orchestra by Vaughan Williams, which has lately been published—'Sancta Civitas'—which seems to me to be one of the greatest achievements of our time—certainly with the Pastoral Symphony, the highest point yet reached by a contemporary Englishman . . . Van Dieren is, I am glad to say, at last receiving something like his proper need of recognition. The exquisite 'Serenata' for chamber orchestra was performed by Anthony Bernard's band last week; this is another 'Siegfried Idyll'.[51] The Spenser sonnet for voices and chamber orchestra[52] was given a week or two before—and on the 14th of this month a complete concert of his work takes place.[53]

When Philip sent Balfour Gardiner a copy of 'All the flowers of the Spring' he was delighted, declaring it to be music that he could 'live with for days, in great content. Nowadays I am so starved of musical delights that whenever they come I am endlessly grateful to the author of them.'[54] The other two pieces must surely contain some of Philip's most melancholy and desolate music. Gray thought these pieces 'probably the gloomiest and grisliest music that even Philip Heseltine ever wrote, which is saying a good deal'.[55] Although 'Call for the Robin Redbreast and the Wren' is a difficult, dissonant composition, it is neither as stark nor as bleak as the male-voice dirge, 'The Shrouding of the Duchess of Malfi', having fewer contrapuntal features and tending to be more homophonic in character. In these settings Philip's skilful use of dissonance and other devices (such as bitonality) conveys the atmosphere of the texts with a chilling reality, though the unrelenting and uncompromising chromaticism presents formidable problems of intonation to the finest of choirs. Bax, in an undated letter to Philip, was moved to write the following:

I think *The Shrouding of the Duchess of Malfi* is a masterly piece of tragic writing. You are one of the only modern composers in my opinion whose harmonic invention derives from an emotional and natural source. I would rather hear pure diatonic and nothing else than the damnable brain-spun muddle and mess which is the stuff of most modern music. That is why it is exciting to find someone writing harmony that to my mind is obviously sincere and imaginative and flexible.[56]

The van Dieren concert (mentioned in his letter to Taylor above) had been selflessly promoted by John Goss and included performances of the third String Quartet (Op. 15, 1919), a number of songs, and an excerpt from the opera, *The Tailor*, conducted by a promising young John Barbirolli. In a report of this concert which Philip wrote for the *Musical Times*, he praised this 'noble and generous action' on the part of Goss, although memories of the disastrous van Dieren concert of 1917 still rankled:

Why . . . should one of the best of our younger singers . . . devote a hundred pounds or so of hard-earned fees to giving public testimony to his belief in an almost unknown composer? Why, indeed? To feel passionately about any music is distinctly *démodé*; 'amusing' is the highest adjective of praise permitted in the best circles. The fact that Van Dieren has been acclaimed as a great master by a small group of musicians who have had the privilege of studying each successive work from the manuscript, and so following his development during the last ten years has been said, in the London press, to have prejudiced the public against him. I do not myself believe that the general public accounts it a crime when someone who has found a treasure invites his fellow-citizens to share it with him; but I am, of course, quite willing to admit that it is the height of bad form for mere composers and singers to pronounce emphatically upon the merits of any man's work without waiting for the verdict of the august fraternity of the musical critics. It is now nearly nine years since Mr Cecil Gray gave the first public concert of Van Dieren's work in this country. On that occasion official critical opinion was unanimously hostile; indeed, so great was the derision this music aroused in the corner of Wigmore Hall reserved for official criticism that an attendant had to be deputed to endeavour to mute its all-too-audible expression. Now, after several years of neglect, this 'mystery Dutch musician' has bobbed up again, and has been most effusively greeted as the arch-blackleg of the musical profession. He cannot be classified, he belongs to no recognised school, and as each of his works actually sounds quite different from any of the others, he is said to have no style. It is insinuated that only those who care for no other music can possibly care for his . . .

The general opinion of Van Dieren's work may be aptly summarized by saying . . . that it is divided, those who do not know his works disputing the judgments of those who do. At the risk of being told that I am arousing further prejudice against Van Dieren, I am bound to say that a hearing of several works which I have known intimately on paper for a long time only confirms my opinion that Van Dieren is one of the two or three composers now living who are destined to be ranked among the masters.[57]

In February 1926 at a convivial meeting in The Five Bells in Eynsford, Philip and Moeran combined their talents to compose the rousing drinking-song 'Maltworms' for baritone solo, unison male voice chorus, and piano. Moeran had the poem with him on his midday visit to The Five Bells and had just set the chorus when Philip arrived:

Warlock suggested a tune for the first two lines of the verse, doing, as Moeran put it, 'the steps up'—a series of ascending thirds of which he was very fond.

Moeran then continued with lines three and four. A local dramatic society at Shoreham was putting on some one-act plays and it had been suggested that Philip and Moeran should provide the music. The village boasted a good brass band of from twelve to fifteen players and both composers wanted to make use of it. The band was holding its practice that evening and the two composers therefore went home, harmonized the song and scored the accompaniment. When the accompaniment had been written to the verses, Moeran set to work harmonizing the chorus, while Philip scored the verses in the next room writing out the parts in pencil. There was no full score. Moeran then copied out the parts in ink, the composers caught the seven o'clock bus to Shoreham and the work was rehearsed there and then. Unfortunately the performance never took place. The bandmaster's wife did not hold with play-acting and, on the night, the band was forbidden to appear. The song, however, was given with piano accompaniment; and in place of a Dowland dance which Philip had arranged for brass band the two composers played piano duets. All the band parts have since been lost.[58]

Dating from 1926 is the gentle and sensitive setting of Hilaire Belloc's poem 'The Birds' (written for the boys of Port Regis preparatory school at Broadstairs, not far from where Philip himself went to school). Two other notable songs from this year are the spirited 'Robin Goodfellow' (dedicated to Norman Peterkin, 1886–1981, the song-composer and editor in the OUP music department who had given Philip considerable support) and 'Jillian of Berry' with its almost Bartók-like rhythms. Philip dedicated the latter song to Basil Trier, his friend from the Oxford days and another regular visitor to Eynsford. The rather less-distinguished 'Fair and True' with its somewhat over-harmonized, four-square melody also dates from this period. It is perhaps not without significance that in 1928, when Philip inscribed a copy of this song for the composer John Longmire (1902–86) who was then director of music at Sevenoaks School, he wrote the words: 'To John Longmire, fellow admirer of the Reverend J. B. D[ykes]. from whom this song so obviously derives'.[59] The highly individual setting of 'Sorrow's Lullaby', which dates from May 1926, is one of four vocal chamber pieces by Philip which were conceived with instrumental (not piano) accompaniment and which exist in this form only. This particular song, a setting of a poem by Thomas Lovell Beddoes (1803–49), is a duet for soprano and baritone soloists accompanied by a string quartet. Unfortunately the comparative infrequency of being able to bring together the unusual forces of expert soprano and baritone soloists as well as a string quartet of professional quality for a work of only five pages and lasting for as many minutes mitigates very strongly against its performance. Nor is the whole melodic and harmonic style that of Philip at his most accessible, containing restless chromaticism, evasive tonality, and a seeming lack of harmonic direction. However, given performers of sufficient skill, sensitivity, and commitment, the final result can be a most moving experience. It would be worth performing if only to hear the final string postlude where a wonderful sense of calm repose settles on the work as the dissonance of the last quaver of each bar melts into a resolution of almost numinous quality.

It was during this period that the music publisher Chester commissioned Moeran to write an essay on Philip for a series entitled *Miniature Essays*, inviting Philip at the same time to write a similar one on Moeran for which he was paid two guineas. He had, in fact, already written an article of some 2,000 words on the life and work of Moeran for the June 1924 edition of the *Music Bulletin*, including these amusing words about Moeran's skill as a collector of folksongs:

He collects these songs from no antiquarian, historical or psychological motives, but because he loves them and the people who sing them . . . For him, as for them, the song itself is the thing . . . It is no good appearing suddenly at a cottage door, notebook in hand, as though you might be the bumbailey or the sanitary inspector . . . nor should you spoil the ground for other collectors by forgetting that old throats grow dry after an hour's singing.[60]

In his companion article on Philip, Moeran included an interesting and significant observation regarding 'the influence of van Dieren, from whom Warlock confesses to have learned all that he knows of composition'.[61] Some people, notably Herbert Howells, felt that this influence was not entirely musical and certainly not a good one, either on Philip or, ultimately, on Moeran. In a conversation recorded in 1971, Howells stated that he thought van Dieren the 'evil genius' behind what he called the 'Warlock gang'. Howells then turned the conversation to Philip: 'I don't think I ever met anyone actually more satanic . . . at the same time I had an enormous respect for a lot of his stuff, and for his mind. When you got it away from the bitterness . . . it was quite another personality, he was gentle, appreciative, affectionate, everything that you wish he could have been all the time'.[62] Van Dieren must have been aware of such accusations from the British music fraternity when he wrote the following words after Philip's death:

I have heard him described as Mephistophelian. He certainly had the caustic wit, but he had none of the callousness or of 'the spirit of denial'—on the contrary, he was generous and kind, and possessed the warm-hearted enthusiasm

of the born artist. These were the qualities that in his worldly wisdom he tried
to hide; he knew too well that a man cannot risk the revelation that he
remains a boy, and a rather shy boy. . . . it is this that made him all the more
loveable to those friends who knew him well enough and at the same time
could value his great talents.[63]

Philip equally had little time for Howells, dismissing his church
music as 'effete pseudo catholicism'[64] and producing the obligatory
scatological limerick about him. In the same conversation Howells
also angrily claimed that Philip had been a bad influence on
Moeran, blaming him for Moeran's eventual alcoholism. When
Howells first came across Moeran as a fellow student at the Royal
College of Music he had found him 'one of the gentlest, nicest
people God ever made, and a *very* promising composer. . . . then he
got in with the Heseltine clan, took to drink—you couldn't belong
to that sort of unofficial club without it—and just went to the
dogs'.[65] Commentators are not wholly in agreement as to whether
Moeran's alcoholism was a result of the influence at Eynsford or the
effect of alcohol on a severe head injury sustained in the war.
Maybe it was a combination of both. However, what is clear is that,
whereas Philip produced a constant stream of compositions during
that Eynsford year, in 1925–8 Moeran's creative inspiration seems to
have dried up. Moeran later wrote: 'I lost faith in myself round
about 1926 and composed nothing for several years. I even nearly
became a garage proprietor . . . I had an awfully lazy period in
Eynsford'.[66]

In September 1926 Philip's books on Gesualdo and the English
ayre were finally published, but this was not sufficient to allay his
growing fears about his own creative abilities. Even with this considerable literary success behind him Philip could write a self-doubting
letter to Taylor, adding that as far as original composition was concerned, he had completely dried up. He then related a quite
appalling history of virtual exploitation on the part of his publishers: in the course of seven years his original compositions, his transcriptions of Delius and of early music, as well as his books and
articles on music, had produced a mere £1,100—a little over £150 a
year:

If I had been idiotic enough to accept royalties, I should have had next to
nothing at all. Under the royalty system one is absolutely at the publisher's
mercy. On 'Captain Stratton's Fancy'—my most popular song, an absolute
potboiler which has been published in 3 keys, gramophoned, and continually
broadcasted, I have had less than £3 in four years.[67]

In October that same year Philip wrote what is probably his most often performed and best-known composition, the *Capriol Suite*. Moeran recalled that Philip had written the original piano-duet version in the short time between a Friday and Monday morning when Moeran was away from Eynsford. The suite exists, in fact, in three different versions, all made by the composer himself: for piano duet, for string orchestra, and, finally, one for full orchestra dating from March 1928. Philip dedicated all these versions to his friend the Breton composer Paul Ladmirault, whose music he had long admired and championed. After Philip's death the popularity of the work was such that arrangements were made both for piano solo and for two pianos, while later some of the individual movements were also transcribed for various other instrumental and even vocal combinations.

In 1925 Cyril Beaumont published an English translation of the treatise on dancing by Thoinot Arbeau (1519–95),[68] the 'Orchéso-graphie' of 1588, to which Philip contributed a scholarly preface as well as generally assisting in the project with his considerable editorial expertise. In the preface there is a study of both English and European dance music of the sixteenth century, together with many musical examples reproduced in Philip's own beautiful handwriting. Foss once praised Philip's calligraphy, saying: 'Warlock wrote with exquisite precision . . . the shapes of the note-heads, the uprights, the binds and ties, were of enormous interest to him. He wrote his crotchets and quavers in a handwriting exactly as his ear demanded of the singer and player that they should reproduce his sounds. A Warlock manuscript is a joy to see, and to play from.'[69] The author Spike Hughes (b. 1908) remarked that he was once asked to copy Philip's manuscript piano-reduction score of Bernard van Dieren's 'Chinese' Symphony: 'From all accounts this score had been written by Philip at his drunkest—and Philip could get very, very drunk. But the drunker he had become the more exquisite the handwriting of words and music became.'[70]

Having discovered Arbeau's 'Orchésographie', Philip proceeded to compose his *Capriol Suite*, basing it on some of the dance tunes contained in the original volume. Arbeau had written his treatise in the typical Renaissance dialogue form: in this case between himself, the teacher, and his pupil, Capriol (a lawyer), hence the name of the suite. The string orchestra version was published in 1927 with the two other versions (for piano duet, and full orchestra) appearing the following year. A letter written to his mother in November 1926 suggests that there was at least one performance of the work in its string version before its actual publication. Amazing as it may seem, this was another of those remarkable instances when Philip had difficulty selling a work. After refusing it several times, Curwen eventually offered him 25 guineas on condition that he agreed to accept only 25 per cent of the royalties from the PRS and MCPS, instead of the usual 50 per cent.[71]

Although the six movements are all based on the early melodies, the final result is no mere arrangement or pastiche. Philip's scholarly and intimate knowledge of early music enabled him to take the original and craft it into a living expression of his own art, showing both respect for the original and imprinting his characteristic style on the music with both taste and discretion. Dissonance is not used for its own sake but rather to heighten the effect of the rhythmic drive of movements such as the final one, 'Mattachins'. Harmonic colouring too is used with subtlety, and the one moment of luxuriance at the end of 'Pieds-en-l'air' sounds all the more effective for the general restraint shown in the other movements. It is a moment of sheer unexpected beauty—of 'ambushed emotion which takes one by surprise, by the throat',[72] to use words written to Taylor some nine years earlier. Van Dieren was later to write:

. . . technically he had reached an amazing degree of perfection as for instance in the full score of 'Capriol' which is admirably constructed and most beautifully limned. And the orchestration is crystal clear and powerful in sound. It is all done with so little apparent effort that it makes one feel all the more unhappy that he gained no confidence but retained his exaggerated notion of the ease with which composers may work.[73]

Copley summed up Philip's achievement in the *Capriol Suite*, a work which, in many ways, crystallizes the various influences that produced Warlock, the composer:

Warlock's treatment of the tunes in the *Capriol Suite* shows that in his maturity he had solved the problems that had defeated him nine years previously when he wrote the *Folk Song Preludes* . . . There is nothing of the pseudo-sixteenth century or of the self-consciously archaic about Warlock's treatment of the tunes. The occasional false-relations, 'Elizabethan cadence' formulae, van Dieren chromatics, or melting Delius-like harmonies, are amalgamated in his own individual utterance.[74]

Whilst commenting on attempts to pin down the elusive quality of Philip's music, Moeran wrote the following perceptive paragraph:

Some writers attempt to sum up every composer as though he were a bottle of medicine, compounded of this, that, and the other ingredient; but when we

have admitted that in Warlock's music there is a certain percentage of the harmonic richness of Delius, of the contrapuntal lucidity of the Elizabethans,
welded together by the influence of the textual clarity which is always apparent in the works of Van Dieren, there is yet a residium [*sic*] which cannot be
accounted for by reference to these extraneous influences. This personal element is as apparent in his literary work as in his songs and other compositions. It is a mysterious element . . . one never knows what he has up his
sleeve.[75]

At the end of 1926 Philip collaborated with Jack Lindsay in the production of two books for Lindsay's Fanfrolico Press. The two men
had met some time before in Augustus John's studio, an occasion
which Lindsay remembered vividly. Philip had evidently already
passed out before he arrived and 'was moaning feebly with closed
eyes in the bathroom, where various drunks were trying to revive him
with doses of brandy or douches of cold water. I regarded his tipsily-
pasty face . . . and took my turn at water-sprinkling. "He was talking
of God and then collapsed," said Eugene Goossens.'[76] One of the
Fanfrolico books was *Loving Mad Tom: Bedlamite Verses of the XVI
and XVII Centuries*, illustrated by Lindsay's father, the well-known
Australian black-and-white artist Norman Lindsay (1879–1969), who
had gained a certain notoriety through his erotic illustrations in several editions of Greek and Latin classics. Jack Lindsay edited the
texts, the Elizabethan ballad, *Tom o' Bedlam* together with Francis
Thompson's[77] version, as well as a collection of various seventeenth-
century mad-poems. The distinguished poet Robert Graves
(1895–1985) wrote the foreword, while Philip contributed four musical
transcriptions and three pages of accompanying musical notes. The
title of the other book was *The Metamorphosis of Aiax: A New
Discourse of a Stale Subject by Sir John Harrington and the Anatomie
of the Metamorpho-sed Aiax*. It was a subject which no doubt
appealed to Philip's Rabelaisian sense of humour: a book in which
Elizabeth I's godson extolled the virtues of the water-closet. The final
published version of the book gives no details as to how the editorial
work was shared between the two men but the notes contained in the
appendices characteristically reflect Philip's wide knowledge of
Elizabethan literature. He wrote to his mother in September 1929
that, although it had given him a lot of trouble, the work had been
most enjoyable: 'At least the book will be beautifully produced, and
we hope it will have something of the same success de scandale as it
had when it was first published in 1596, and all the court were laugh-
ing at it.'[78] Moeran later commented that there was a time and place
for everything and that such 'a treatise on shithouses' should best be

read 'over a roaring fire in a London fog in November, preferably in good company & with a bowl of punch'.[79]

On 3 January 1927 Philip's *Serenade* was recorded by the National Gramophonic Society for sale to its subscribing members. This was the Society's first venture into orchestral recording and Philip's violinist friend André Mangeot (1883–1970), the leader of the International String Quartet, formed a chamber orchestra of fourteen string players especially for the occasion. Mangeot invited John Barbirolli to conduct and Philip attended a rehearsal to approve the tempo, about which there had evidently been some doubt.[80] It was released in April on a 12" record to be played at 80 rpm. At this time Mangeot and Philip were busy collaborating in transcribing Purcell's 'Fantasias for Strings' which Curwen published that same year. Some of these had already been recorded in 1927 for the National Gramophonic Society by Mangeot's string quartet, in which Barbirolli had been the cellist.

The year 1927 was also notable for a number of masterly Warlock songs, of which the three settings of poems by Hilaire Belloc ('Ha'nacker Mill', 'My Own Country' and 'The Night') can well lay claim to be some of Philip's finest. In these songs Philip captures perfectly the atmosphere of the poetry: the sadness and desolation of the first, the nostalgia of the second, and the prayerful repose of the last. 'The Lover's Maze', 'Sigh no more, ladies', and 'Mockery' ('When daisies pied') are also particularly fine songs, each variously showing Philip's skill and imagination with melody, harmony, and counterpoint. 'Walking the Woods', on the other hand, is more straightforward: a ballad-type setting of an anonymous sixteenth-century poem which, like so many of Philip's songs, has its obvious roots in the early music in which he was immersed at the time. Of quite different character and mood is the setting of the moving carol-like words of 'The First Mercy' by Bruce Blunt (1899–1967), bon viveur, poet, journalist, and writer on wine, gardening, and the turf, who became one of Philip's closest friends during the last three years of his life. Here, as in so many of his settings of similar religious and quasi-religious poems, Philip captures perfectly the sense of awe and mystery of the scene in the stable at Bethlehem. A medieval atmosphere is here blended together with Philip's own inimitable style to produce a work of timeless beauty. Philip informed Blunt of its completion in typically nonchalant terms, saying that he had set the carol to music, and 'if you like it, we might have a monumental carouse on the proceeds!'[81]

Blunt and Philip had struck up a friendship sometime early in 1927. There are no details as to how or where they met; the first reference to Blunt is a significant press-cutting stuck in Philip's diary for February 1927 which reported that the two of them had been arrested for being drunk and disorderly in Cadogan Street. They were subsequently fined 10s. each for shouting and singing. This was the beginning of a close and fruitful friendship and over the next few years the unique combination of their literary and musical talents resulted in a number of masterpieces. The brief portrait of Philip which Blunt gave in a BBC Home Service programme, 'The World Goes By', on 16 December 1944, is one of the most penetrating that we have:

Peter Warlock was only a pen-name at first, but latterly he used it for every purpose. This started the extraordinary legend that he was really two persons in one, and that the sinister Peter Warlock eventually destroyed the gentle Philip Heseltine. Every time that any reference is made to Peter Warlock or his work, this myth is trotted out. It's time that it was forgotten. At its very mention you instantly think of Dr Jekyll and Mr Hyde, those figures of good and evil splitting a single man. This suggestion of the sinister gives an absolutely false impression of Philip Heseltine, who was fundamentally so simple and sincere. Anyone who has any character at all has many sides to that character, and so it was with Philip. That was all. Of the many times that I was with him, I was quite unaware that a dread figure was my companion. On the contrary.

On expeditions to the country he was the genius of wherever he might be. The country was in his blood. He seemed to be part of the English scene, a timeless being who had always stood and always would stand upon some Kentish hill-top or among the valleys of that land which he loved the best—the stretch of country which lies between Ross-on-Wye and the Black Mountains.

Did I say 'Stand'? As a matter of fact, he had a passion for speed, but speed never blurred his vision. He expected his driver to take in all the details of the passing scene and keep his eyes on the road as well. A rather alarming passenger. Yet, somehow or other, we usually managed to get to the end of our journey, and this, more often than not, was an inn.

Philip's entry into a bar or taproom was apt to be dramatic. That vivid creature, with the handsome face, fair hair and pointed beard, was bound to attract attention. Eyes turned towards him, and talk ceased. But not for long. No-one was quicker at melting barriers than Philip. He was perfectly at ease with all kinds of people, and so were they with him. Many who had known him for only a few hours felt that they had known him all their lives . . . He had that rarest quality in human beings, that when you were with him you were never dull. But what was the secret of that affection which he inspired? He had great charm and a brilliant mind, but these are not enough. Like other people with the quality of true greatness, he was very modest. He never put on airs. And his was a most generous spirit.[82]

In this broadcast it was Blunt's avowed intention to clear away 'the unsavoury legend' which he felt had gathered around Philip. Although he was obviously guarded in this broadcast talk, Blunt was highly critical of Gray's part in building up the sinister Warlock-Heseltine fabrication. Writing to Dowbiggin in 1943, he referred to Gray's memoir as a 'deplorable book', roundly criticizing 'the dual personality nonsense' which 'had done Philip quite enough harm already'.[83] He told Dowbiggin that he thought it would be as well for the whole thing to be allowed to rest for a considerable time, in the hope that 'such vulgar trash' would eventually fade from people's minds.

Philip was still corresponding periodically with his old friend Colin Taylor in Cape Town, reporting on his latest compositions and the current musical life in London. These interesting letters show his likes and dislikes, as well as his enthusiasms—among which was the music of Berlioz. As early as 1919 he had raved to Delius about the *Symphonie fantastique*: 'What a work that is! The Marche au Supplice gave me a feeling of positively physical terror: I have never experienced anything like it in listening to music. Berlioz had the power of the black magicians, and used it, in this work.'[84] Now, eight years later, writing to Taylor, he waxed most excitedly about a Berlioz concert which he had heard on 20 January in the Albert Hall conducted by Hamilton Harty:

. . . a most wonderful and memorable experience—the Hallé chorus with a vast orchestra including 4 of each woodwind, 8 horns, 13 trumpets, 17 trombones, 6 tubas (which ought to be ophicleides) and about a dozen drums. The 'Requiem' is undoubtedly one of the very greatest of all musical creations—worthy to rank with the Matthew-Passion and the 9th Symphony.[85]

Soon after the performance he wrote ecstatically to Harty telling him that he had 'laid us all under a debt of deep gratitude' by his 'splendid work in restoring Berlioz to his rightful place among the greatest masters in music'.[86]

Philip's creative energy seemed to be at a peak early in 1927. On 22 February he spent three days in Cambridge busily working on manuscripts of Dowland's lute music in the University Library. On his return to Eynsford he transcribed the music for piano, working with such remarkable speed that on 2 March he was able to take the completed transcriptions (including a preface) to Curwen as well as the corrected proofs of 'Twenty four French Ayres' to the OUP. Nine days later he was back at work in the British Museum, transcribing more instrumental music, this time three- and four-part viol music by Matthew Locke (1630–77). Yet once again he had difficulty finding a publisher for his transcriptions. Only one suite for string trio was eventually published—by Augener in 1929. Six of Locke's String Quartets, which he had also transcribed that March, had to wait until two years after his death before they were published.

During the five years that had passed since the *Sackbut* débâcle Philip's anger had abated sufficiently for him to contribute an article, entitled 'Purcell's Fantasias for Strings', slightly amended from the preface to the Curwen edition written in March, to the May 1927 issue. In fact an earlier article of his, 'The Editing of Old-English Songs', had appeared in two instalments in the February and March issues of *The Sackbut* the previous year. Here he had pointed out that, despite his constant protests, he still needed to draw attention to the questionable scholarship practised by certain editors. Needless to say, Fellowes had come in for yet more criticism in the second of the two articles, while in the first Philip had already dealt summarily with the organist Sir Frederick Bridge (1844–1924), Arnold Dolmetsch (1858–1940), and Frederick Keel (1871–1954), a baritone and arranger of old Elizabethan songs of whom he was particularly contemptuous. In July 1922 he had already written in scathing terms about Fellowes and Keel in an article for the *Musical Times* entitled 'On Editing Elizabethan Songs':

The average amateur knows little about musical history, and cares less. He is a shy bird when it comes to exploring new fields of music, and anything suggestive of archæology is a sure and certain scarecrow to frighten him away. He merely wants a good song clearly printed in the most readily intelligible form for reading and singing. Let us suppose him an enthusiastic lover of Shakespeare, Ben Jonson, Sidney, and the rest. Someone tells him that the songs of the period are as lovely as the lyrics, and he goes into a music-shop and opens a volume of Dr Fellowes's edition. His eye lights at once on hieroglyphics which have no meaning for him and no connection with any form of musical notation he has ever encountered. Accompanying them he sees three staves of ordinary music-type, but even these present an unfamiliar and forbidding appearance. A bar containing fourteen minims is preceded by one of four minims, and followed by one of two without any warning, and breves— another scarecrow—abound. Small wonder if he turns hurriedly from such pages with the thought that they are not for the likes of him. And if he does not altogether abandon his idea of getting acquainted with the music of Shakespeare's England, he will in all probability turn to some edition of Elizabethan songs as that produced by Mr Frederick Keel. Nothing could be more delightful—to look at . . . Simple tunes in familiar crotchets and quavers, and nice easy accompaniments which anybody could play and many transpose at first sight. So Mr Keel's volumes are purchased and our amateur begins to entertain his friends with Elizabethan love-songs, oblivious of the fact (for Mr Keel's modesty forbade him to mention it in his preface) that the accompaniments bear no relation whatever to the original tablature, having been *entirely composed* by Mr Keel, complete with new basses and all.[87]

Yet despite Philip's continued criticism of Fellowes' editorial practices, by the end of 1926 the two men seemed to have been on amicable terms. On 10 November Edward Dent, who had recently been appointed to the chair of music at Cambridge, wrote to Philip saying that he had seen the 'Abbé' Fellowes and was glad to hear that the two men had 'buried the hatchet. He was quite overcome by your friendliness—though I told him it was nothing unusual.'[88]

Besides all the hard work which marked the Eynsford period—the articles, the editing, the books, and the composing—there was still time for fun. For example, on 6 October 1927 there was a convivial jaunt to The Bull at Wrotham, a village some six miles from Eynsford, for the ceremonial unveiling of a sign painted for the pub by Hal Collins. Praise for Philip's musical achievements was also at last beginning to appear in print. That November a highly complimentary article entitled 'Un grand musicien anglais: Peter Warlock' appeared in the French magazine *Chantecler*. It had been written by Philip's friend, the Breton composer Paul Ladmirault, whose music Philip had been enthusiastically writing about as early as 1916.[89] The two men corresponded regularly from the beginning of 1925 until Philip's death, often sending each other music. Philip also made significant attempts to encourage both the performance and publication of Ladmirault's music in England and a number of letters reveal his generous and untiring efforts in writing to publishers, the BBC, and conductors such as Sir Dan Godfrey, Sir Hamilton Harty, Leslie Heward, and Sir Henry Wood. Ladmirault's article of over 2,000 words comprised a discussion both of Philip's style and some of his compositions. Phrased in most generous terms, it must surely have delighted Philip, who now found himself described as 'un des plus grands compositeurs anglais de notre époque . . . un compositeur rempli à la fois d'érudition et d'imagination . . . de son don superbe d'invention mélodique allié à une opulence harmonique extraordinaire' (one of the greatest English composers of our time . . . of both erudition and imagination . . . [with a] superb gift of melodic invention together with an extraordinary harmonic wealth).[90]

That December saw the composition and publication of one of Philip's most famous carol settings in its original four-part version for choir. Bruce Blunt later related how they were both extremely

hard up that December and, in the hope of being able to get suit-
ably drunk at Christmas, they conceived the idea of collaborating on
another carol to be published in a daily paper. It was whilst walking
on a moonlit night between The Plough at Bishop's Sutton and The
Anchor at Ropley that Blunt thought of the words of 'Bethlehem
Down'. He sent them off next morning to Philip in London, who
completed the carol in a few days and on Christmas Eve it duly
appeared in *The Daily Telegraph*. Blunt was later to write: 'We had
an immortal carouse on the proceeds and decided to call ourselves
"Carols Consolidated".'[91] Few carols written in modern times have
so successfully captured the indefinable essence of this particular
genre and the bitter-sweet imagery of Blunt's poem is perfectly mir-
rored in Philip's finely crafted melody, with its imaginative and sensitive harmony.

In January 1928 yet another angry letter from Philip appeared in
the columns of the *Musical Times*. This was in response to an article, 'A New Light on Purcell' by Arthur Eaglefield Hull
(1876–1928), an organist and writer on music, which had appeared
in the December 1927 edition, where Hull had criticized Philip's new
edition of Purcell's string Fantasias recently published by Curwen.
After some introductory paragraphs in which he wrote about the
music, Hull had suggested that the term 're-discovery' was hardly an
appropriate one, since Purcell scholars had known about these
Fantasias for some time. Of the edition itself Hull wrote:

One would have thought that in the hands of a scholar such as he undoubtedly is, we could have depended on the textual transcription absolutely. Such,
however, proves not to be the case. When I first received the newly-published
score, I came across passage after passage which raised my curiosity and
finally disquieted me so much that I determined to spend a day with the original manuscript. And, alas! my worst fears were realised. The transcription has
been handled in a very loose manner.[92]

After listing a number of supposed errors, Hull questioned some of
the metronome marks, suggesting that the worst feature was the
editing of the accidentals, resulting in what he termed 'a deplorable
amount of wrong notes'. Philip replied immediately in the next issue
selecting his most potent barbs:

Dr Eaglefield-Hull [sic] writes of my transcriptions of Purcell's Fantasias as
though they were as full of gross mistakes as his own notorious translations
from the French; though only one wrong note is adduced as evidence . . .
    Dr Hull goes out of his way to rob me of any credit to which the 're-
discovery' of these Fantasias might entitle me. This is a small and unimportant
matter, but if the 'Purcell research scholars' have known these Fantasias

'long enough', it is hardly to their credit to have kept them so long in the dark . . .

Dr Hull's assurance that he has 'dealt with this important matter in an entirely impersonal manner' is so entirely irrelevant that it actually suggests a guilty conscience for the publication of so many unproven allegations of inaccuracy in an article which is itself so fantastically incoherent and inaccurate.[93]

In February a recording of Philip's 'Captain Stratton's Fancy' was issued on an HMV 10" record which sold for 3s. It was sung by the distinguished Australian bass-baritone, Peter Dawson (1882–1961), accompanied at the piano by a youthful Gerald Moore (1899–1987). This and the Barbirolli recording of the *Serenade* for strings, were the only records of Philip's music to appear in the composer's lifetime.

During the year Philip's friendship with Blunt continued to strengthen, and in April he went to stay in Wake-Robin, Blunt's 'charming old cottage in a wonderful bit of country between Winchester and Petersfield',[94] in Beauworth, Hampshire. With great delight he was later able to enlighten Blunt that he had discovered 'wake-robin' to be 'an ancient specific against inebriety—also, apparently, an aphrodisiac: for an Elizabethan poet writes: "They have eaten so much Wake-Robin that they cannot sleepe for love".'[95]

On a rainy day in May 1928, whilst alighting rather too quickly from the train at Eynsford station, Philip slipped and fell on the wet platform, fracturing his ankle. He later joked that he must have been sober at the time since no drunk ever injures himself! Infuriating and inconvenient as this must have been, the house-bound Philip kept himself busy by making an arrangement of the vocal score of Cecil Gray's opera *Deirdre*, which Gray had commissioned from him. Gray had completed the opera in 1926 and, in a letter to Taylor in September that year, Philip wrote enthusiastically that, 'if it is not entirely a masterpiece, it is certainly one of the most beautiful works that has been made in this country during the present century'. Yet he could not resist adding a cynical remark about opera, saying that he thought there was 'no rottener form in which to cast good music, nor one that militates so against the music's chances of being heard'.[96] The task of transcribing *Deirdre* not only enabled him to spend ten days in bed without being bored, but also provided much-needed cash. He wrote to Gray saying that he thought the work worth about £30, but that he would have no objection if Gray could coax a little bit more out of his mother, who was providing the money. He also badly needed the distraction as he was at the time unable to drink anything alcoholic, since even the smallest amount of alcohol caused painful swelling in his ankle. This transcription of *Deirdre* was Philip's largest single undertaking and one which he found unusually difficult and complicated. The highly intricate score was written on 16-stave paper and the complete vocal parts and duo piano parts were copied in blue ink. The numerous orchestral cues were made either on separate staves or else contained within the duet parts in contrasting green ink, whilst details of the scoring were written in red, the 8-part chorus being skilfully included in the piano parts. The fact that Philip managed to complete all 201 pages of the final score in May 1928, within the short space of a month, is just another example of his amazing capacity for working under pressure. None the less, signs of depression were once again surfacing and Philip attempted to drown his sorrows in the pub. When he was able to resume drinking again he found it difficult to steer himself across the road on one leg and two sticks so Mr Brice thoughtfully produced an antique Bath chair to ferry him ceremoniously to The Five Bells. Sadly declining another invitation to stay at Wake-Robin, he wrote to Blunt, by now one of his chief correspondents, of the excesses of his drinking, saying that he had 'been in soak for several days and even now (10.a.m.) can, as you see, barely hold a pen. . . . I can only just walk as far as the Five Bells (when sober) and am still having massage.'[97]

That summer, in a desperate attempt to augment his income, he rewrote and arranged several of his early Winthrop Rogers songs, including 'The First Mercy' and 'Lullaby', for three-part female voices. He described his acute financial situation to Blunt that September:

As for me, I am at rock bottom—unable either to write anything or to sell the trash and drivel I have managed to knock up during the past few months. There is a frightful slump in the music-publishing business—even the Oxford Press has lost too heavily in the past twelve months to be able to pursue their former spendthrift policy.

As soon as I can pay off the hundred quid I owe in this place (which I hope may be within the next few weeks), I shall clear out and go to London in the hope of finding some menial job that will enable me to drink, occasionally, a few pints of beer.[98]

This proved to be Philip's last prolific year of song-writing, eight out of ten songs composed that year being produced in the short space of a single month, July 1928. The *Seven Songs of Summer*

were originally conceived as a kind of cycle but, as no one firm
would accept the songs as a set, Philip was forced to split them up
and they were eventually published by Augener and Elkin as separate songs, 'The Passionate Shepherd', 'The Contented Lover',
'Youth', 'The Sweet o' the Year', 'Tom Tyler', 'Eloré Lo', and 'The
Droll Lover'. 'Tom Tyler' was, in fact, not entirely Philip's own creation. Writing to Arnold Dowbiggin in July the next year Philip told
him that Hal Collins 'had a great talent but it was quite undeveloped. The tune of my "Tom Tyler" is based almost entirely on an
improvisation of his.'[99] It has been suggested[100] that the melody of
another song from the Eynsford period, 'Passing By', was also composed by Collins, a work which Philip referred to as 'deliberate
spoof'.[101] He added a lush accompaniment in the Victorian ballad
style, producing an unashamed 'potboiler', a word he often used
when describing such songs to Colin Taylor some ten years earlier.
'The Contented Lover' was dedicated to a friend, Gwen Shepherd,
with whom he had corresponded sporadically since 1922, and he
sent the original draft to her on 11 August, the day before her birthday. It was accompanied by a note to the effect that he had been
laid up for three months with 'nothing to do but booze and sweat it
out in sentimental songs—of which I lay one at your feet'. He
added: 'This winter I am really going to learn how to write music,
or perish in the attempt—so I may be able to offer you something
less reminiscent of the glucose in bad beer.'[102] However, despite
these hopes and good intentions, by the autumn of 1928 Philip
found it financially impossible to maintain the Eynsford life-style
and in October he had no option but to move back to Wales again.
He related his problems and feelings of worthlessness in a pathetic
letter to van Dieren: 'This month or next I shall be leaving
Eynsford—owing to financial stress . . . I can no longer sell even the
exiguous amount of trash and drivel that I have hitherto been turning out—sullying the name of music in the process. So I shall
endeavour to find some other, humbler activity.'[103]

RETURN TO LONDON
(1928–1930)

As soon as Philip arrived back in Wales he knew instinctively that there was no way he could survive for any length of time in the stifling atmosphere of Cefn Bryntalch. He wrote to Blunt saying that he had arrived

in a lamentable state of intoxication and magnificent form. Unfortunately, there was a house party, including two Bright Young People who induced in me an all too articulate rage . . . Much as I should like your company, I cannot be so unfriendly as to repeat my suggestion that you should come here. I find I can stand far less than I could then. The atmosphere is all wrong, and I shall leave as soon as possible.[1]

A negative letter sent to Robert Nichols the following week clearly shows his depressed state of mind at this time:

I do very much appreciate your friendly solicitude, but I am afraid you are making the same mistake about me as I have made about myself for some years, in considering me a potential artist. I am not by nature an artist at all. I have no real desire to create anything whatsoever, and my present difficulty is entirely due to my having drifted, more or less by chance, into a milieu where I do not belong and can never really belong—in much the same way that a young man, piously brought up, might drift into the church, only to find some years later that he had no real faith in his religion and certainly no call to expound it to others. The only honest course, a man in this position would feel, would be to resign his living and leave the church—for the weekly sermons and services would entail unbearable hypocrisy for anyone who was sensitive on such a point: but how hard it would be to get out of such a groove after being in it for years, and to turn to other work without experience or qualifications![2]

In his desperate attempts to find some kind of employment he wrote a begging letter to W. C. Smith (1881–1972), Assistant Keeper of Printed Books at the British Museum, asking if there was perhaps an opening 'for one such as myself at the Museum, to assist in cataloguing, or some such job? Times are so bad that it will soon be impossible to eke out even the barest living by composition. If you can suggest anything in this direction for which you think my qualifications would be suitable, I should be most grateful.'³ No offers of employment were, however, forthcoming and, unmotivated to work at anything, Philip spent much of his time either reading Charles Dickens or listening to operas and symphony concerts on the radio and eating 'enormously'. Another letter written to an unidentified correspondent in October 1928 paints a sad and wistful picture:

I have been gathering up the energy to clear out of Eynsford and have got so far as to clear myself out, never to return, though Colly [Hal Collins], cats and Raspberry [Moeran] are remaining until the quite preposterous financial situation is eased a little (though nothing short of a god-from-the-machine can do it). I am still without any plans, hopes, money, or ideas. This solitary place is really beautiful, but I feel like a strayed ghost among such people. From here I seem to see the whole of the immediate past as through the wrong end of a telescope. . . . I feel slightly stupefied by this country-house life, which is really most pleasant when there are no tiresome visitors. One has at least a dozen empty rooms to oneself, and every one with a perfectly amazing view over long vistas of rolling hills and dense woods in all their autumnal brilliance. . . . The prospect of being able to do any work becomes daily more and more remote; but I suppose I could stay here indefinitely, if I wanted do . . . I feel like a vegetable.⁴

Despite the autumnal beauty of his surroundings, in the midst of this isolation Philip's thoughts were turning more and more inwards and he now began to perceive his life as one of misdirection and complete failure. His deep-seated feelings of musical inadequacy began to surface once again and he poured out his frustrations to Nichols, saying that if he had an even moderately comfortable income, or a job that would provide him with one, he would never have anything more to do with music in any shape or form.⁵ To relieve the monotony of life at Cefn Bryntalch he would make occasional excursions into the surrounding countryside where he would sample the local brew. Even this, however, did not satisfy him and he complained critically that the neighbourhood was infested by beer which was either 'as filthy a concoction as one could wish to taste—and most pernicious in its after-effects' or 'weak, and in flavour quite disgusting'.⁶ This interest in alcohol and drinking was to provide a well-timed incentive to complete a drinker's anthology which had first been mooted during the Eynsford days. Nichols had managed to interest the publishers Chatto & Windus in the project and there was now some pressure on Philip to complete the book. By the end of November he had returned to London and, as soon as he had established his base in Pimlico, he busied himself checking sources in the British Museum and searching for original material. He wrote to Blunt telling him that the anthology was making great progress and that he wanted it to be 'a drunkenly haphazard affair—no chapters, or anything of that sort but the items must have an artfully artless juxtaposition, especially in relation to the pictures'.[7]

That same month Philip had written to Francis Toye (1883–1964), the music critic of the *Morning Post*, in a desperate attempt to find some work reviewing concerts. Toye replied that there was unfortunately no regular post going and that he feared that Philip's 'impatience at the great amount of music, bad, badly performed or both' that he would be obliged to hear as a critic would drive him 'into the wildest excesses'.[8] Depressed, and no doubt inspired by his current researchings and writings, Philip attempted to drown his sorrows as long as funds lasted. At the end of November he wrote to Gray telling him that, having consumed his 'entire substance, for a month in advance, in riotous living',[9] he had 'taken perforce a firm seat upon the water waggon'.[10] By now he clearly saw himself as a kind of prodigal son, though with little of the accompanying feelings of repentance. Indeed, a letter written to Blunt at the same time displays an almost boastful air as he relates how he had 'discovered how to drink solidly all day without puking, going to sleep, or feeling bad in the morning . . . I drank a bargee into a state of complete insensibility the other night without any disaster to myself.'[11] As his financial position slowly grew bleaker in those last years his correspondence reveals a despondent and often pathetic figure. In early December 1928, for example, he wrote to Blunt to say that only with great difficulty would he 'be able to buy two very frugal meals a day for the next three weeks; the expenditure of a single shilling on beer is quite out of the question until the anthology or the carol is sold'.[12]

Happily he had found an opportunity to escape from the bleakness of his position by indulging his ailurophile passions. He urged Gray to follow his example and to attend the cat show at the Crystal Palace where he had recently spent an ecstatic couple of hours: 'Such lovely mogs you can't imagine—including *the best cat in the world*, surely—an immense short-haired grey: also the heaviest cat in England, which though physically stoneless, weighs, by a curious chance, *two stones!*'[13] Throughout his life Philip was passionately fond of cats and had even developed 'a special vocabulary for defining the various grades of feline excellence, beginning with "pussum" and culminating in M O G—the supreme cat'.[14] He once told Adrian Allinson that one of his grouses against God was that He had never created a species of woman covered from head to foot in sleek, soft fur! Augustus John related how on a car journey Philip would insist on repeated stops when he would descend from the car 'to caress with loving words some handsome tabby by the roadside'.[15] In his last years his ideal was the rare red self species, a breed with large, round, deep copper-coloured eyes and a deep rich red, long, dense, and silky coat. According to Gray, Philip travelled 'to the other end of London with the sole purpose of seeing one of which he had heard, and to leap off a bus going at full speed, into the middle of the crowded traffic, at the sight of a reddish-hued cat' which they had passed, 'in order to ascertain whether it was of the authentic variety for which he was seeking'.[16] After much searching, he eventually managed to track down one of this rarest of breeds which was destined to play a part in the final dramatic moments of his life. Just as he longed to find the perfect cat, so did he long to find the perfect beer. Gray tells of his quest for 'a beer quite unlike any that he had ever tasted before, a kind of ambrosia or nectar of the gods, but made out of pure hops and nothing else'.[17] By then he had become an authority on pubs throughout England and Wales and would often denounce at length, both in speeches to fellow drinkers and in letters to official bodies, the disgraceful practice of adding chemicals in the manufacture of beer.

The toper's anthology was completed in early December and, as 'it turned out much too improper to offer to Chatto',[18] was eventually published by the Mandrake Press under the colourful title *Merry-Go-Down: A Gallery of Gorgeous Drunkards through the Ages: Collected for the Use, Interest, Illumination, and Delectation of Serious Topers*. In it were included quotations from sources as diverse as the Book of Genesis, Aristotle, Plato, Petronius, Rabelais, Shakespeare, Boswell, Byron, Poe, Dickens, and James Joyce. For this publication Philip used his light-hearted pseudonym, Rab Noolas, the numerous attractive woodcut decorations being provided by Hal Collins. He was delighted with the book when it appeared and even acted as an unofficial salesman. By carrying a set of proofs about with him he managed to collect a number of orders in the various pubs he frequented.

Another project which caught Philip's fancy at this time was the decision by Blunt and J. C. Squire (1884–1958), the editor of the *London Mercury*, to arrange a mid-winter cricket match as a light-hearted protest against the fact that the football season was encroaching more and more into that of cricket. Philip stayed with Blunt that November while the arrangements for the game were being made and, having met several members of the Hambledon Brass Band in the local pubs, The Vine and The George, enthusiastically announced that he would write some music especially for the occasion. This promise resulted in a rousing setting of a new Blunt poem, 'The Cricketers of Hambledon'. Philip thought it 'vulgar', but felt it would sound well, provided the bandmaster could get over 'his astonishment at hearing a brass-band used as a musical instrument and not as an imitation farmyard'.[19] Originally scored for baritone solo and unison male-voice chorus, it was later published as a solo song with piano accompaniment. Philip declared that he was 'rather ashamed of any part in the business: still, a tenner is a tenner'.[20] A companion piece, 'Fill the cup, Philip', a setting of an anonymous sixteenth-century poem, 'a song to be roared, over mugs of beer', was found among Blunt's papers after his death in 1957. Scored for cornet, two saxhorns, two baritones, and euphonium, it had to wait until 1972 before it was eventually published. Both songs typify the 'roystering, swashbuckling, drinking . . . Warlock of popular legend'.[21] The match itself was played between Squire's 'Invalids' and E. Whalley-Tooker's 'Hampshire Eskimos' on a bitterly cold New Year's Day, 1929, on the famous ground at Broadhalfpenny Down, Hambledon, claimed to be the birthplace of cricket. From all accounts it seems to have been a great success, with a large crowd in attendance. The quality of play was evidently not of the highest standard, the match itself being briefly interrupted by the local hunt pursuing a fox across the cricket field. Philip's compositions were duly performed after the game and the only blot on the day was the fact that the historic pub opposite the playing-field, The Bat and Ball, was drunk dry within two hours!

Early in the new year Philip was pressurized by his mother into paying a reluctant visit to his ailing, wealthy uncle Evelyn in Essex. Some two years previously he had dedicated two short unison carols, 'What cheer! Good cheer!' and 'Where riches is everlastingly', to this uncle. He told Taylor his motives for doing so: 'As he is very pious, I dedicated a couple of silly carols to him, in the hope that he might fork out a little dough at Christmas; but alas, the spirit of patronage is not what it was in former ages, and I got nothing beyond a polite letter of thanks.' In the same letter he added some perceptive comments on the contemporary musical scene which included an unexpectedly harsh dismissal of Delius. It would seem as if he were suddenly trying to exorcise his early obsession, at least to Taylor, who had been one of the first to see it manifested in the early Eton days. Or was it simply part of the slow dissolution and disintegration of everything around him, the negativity of the depression that now continually haunted him? Whatever the reason, by the age of 35 he had become a much more advanced critic of Delius's music. Conversely, Philip's previous criticism of the early works of Stravinsky was reassessed; he now saw the music of the first quarter of the twentieth century in perspective and could draw a fine critical line between the Stravinsky of the *Sacre* and the works of Debussy:

Delius, sad to relate, has been completely paralysed and blind for some years. Some people seem to like his piano concerto . . . but it is a most ungrateful work for the soloist, and, I think, both dull and noisy There is a good *Sinfonia concertante* for piano and orchestra, in three movements, by Walton (Oxford Press). His *Portsmouth Point* is exhilarating, but it needs a very large orchestra and is extremely difficult. The only other young Englishman under 25 is Constant Lambert—a more interesting composer and a much finer intelligence than Walton. He has written an admirable *Rio Grande* (nothing to do with sea shantys! [*sic*]) for piano solo and orchestra (strings, brass and percussion only) with a mixed chorus; also an enchanting ballet-suite *Pomona* for small orchestra (O.U.P.). The best new work for chorus and small orchestra that I know is Vaughan Williams's *Flos Campi*; the score and parts are now published (O.U.P.). On the whole, I would bracket V.W.'s *Pastoral Symphony* with Elgar's *Introduction and Allegro* for strings as the best English orchestral music of this century. The only tolerably good orchestral work of Moeran (Rhapsody no. 2) is still in MS . . .

Delius, I think, wears very badly. His utter lack of any sense of construction, coupled with the consistent thickness of texture and unrelieved sweetness of harmony (even at moments where sweetness is the most inappropriate thing in the world) get on one's nerves, and make one long for the clean lines, harmonic purity and formal balance of the Elizabethans and of Mozart—or else for the stimulating harshness and dissonance of Bartók, and the Stravinsky of *Le Sacre du Printemps*, which really sounds very good when it is played, as it was last night at Queen's Hall, by an enormous orchestra, with quintuple wood-wind, 8 horns, 6 trumpets, and a whole regiment of drums. His subsequent works are exceedingly boring . . . Though by no means new, I think the present century has given us few things more lovely than the best works of Debussy . . .[22]

The increasing economic gloom in England was also giving Philip cause for concern. By 1929 the unemployment rate had reached 12 per cent and there were more workers idle than there had been in the General Strike of 1926. In March that year the generous Nichols not only invited Philip to holiday with him on Majorca at his expense but also offered to assist him by paying off some of his debts. Unfortunately, as Philip had just applied for desperately needed work, he had to remain in London in case an opportunity arose. Depressed, he sent a copy of his recently published song, 'And wilt thou leave me thus?', to Arnold Dowbiggin, saying that, owing to the enormous decline in the music publishing trade, he intended devoting himself to other activities than composition and would probably write no more solo songs.

It must have been a great relief when that year, unexpectedly, Beecham invited him to act as editor for a new musical journal which was to run in conjunction with Beecham's Imperial League of Opera (founded in 1927) and also to assist in the organization of a great Delius Festival. In January 1929 Delius had been created a Companion of Honour and the accompanying publicity had resulted in a renewed interest in the man and his music. Beecham now decided that the time was ripe to organize a festival of Delius's music during October and November of that year. Though critical of Philip, the shrewd Beecham knew that he was the best man to assist him in such an undertaking. As Beecham himself said, 'he knew far more about the composer and his music than anyone else in England and possessed a skilled and facile pen, together with a capacity for fiery energy, when his interest was aroused'.[23] Philip's interest was indeed aroused and by July he had established himself in London in the new office of the Imperial League of Opera in Regent Street, where he quickly threw himself into the task. At the festival the major works of Delius were to be performed in six concerts and Philip tackled his work with characteristic enthusiasm and energy. The wheel had come full circle and now his last major musical undertaking was to help in the honouring of the man whose music had meant so much to him in his early days. Within a short time he had drawn up the preliminary prospectus for the festival and was planning the publishing of the new magazine *MILO* (*The Magazine of the Imperial League of Opera*), for which Beecham had given him a free hand. He wrote enthusiastically to Gray in July, telling him that he expected it to expand into a regular monthly journal for the general public and that he hoped they would eventually have yet another *Sackbut*. Three issues appeared between October and December 1929 and included articles on operatic subjects by friends such as Gray, Sorabji, Constant Lambert, and Edwin Evans. Bruce Blunt also contributed a short poem on Delius and Augustus John a sketch of the composer.

In April 1929 Philip had suddenly decided to visit France with a party of friends, Moeran, Anthony Bernard, and the young composer William Wordsworth (1908–88). Eric Fenby who, at the age of 22, had voluntarily gone to Grez to act as amanuensis to the blind and paralysed Delius, later wrote of this visit:

I burned with curiosity to meet that young man who had done so much for Delius since he was little more than a schoolboy—Philip Heseltine. Delius had made scant reference to him when I had enquired about him, and I gathered that there had been some slight estrangement between them, so I dropped the subject.

Imagine my surprise when, one morning, going down to lunch, I discovered that Heseltine and several other people had arrived unexpectedly. They were not at their full strength, they told us, for they had missed 'Old Raspberry' [Moeran] on the way; he would probably be coming along later in the day!

Delius, extremely sensitive at all times to his physical disabilities, and pathetically so in the presence of strangers, was furious, and refused to see Philip . . . Finally, after some gentle persuasion on the part of his wife, Delius agreed to be carried downstairs, and so the whole party stayed to lunch. Conversation was not easy, for the others, excepting Anthony Bernard, appeared to be entirely unmusical, and it was natural that we should want to talk about music. There were, however, occasional flashes of brilliant observation from Heseltine. I envied him his splendid command of words, and liked the way he looked you full in the eye whilst addressing you . . . I shall never forget him for it.

I could see that Delius was still ruffled and not at his ease, and I was relieved when they had taken him away to rest, and I was sauntering down the garden path with Heseltine, leaving Mrs Delius to amuse his friends. We chatted affably enough, but by the time we had reached the pond I found myself wondering whether this could possibly be the same Heseltine who had written that glowing book about Delius and his work, for whenever there was an opening to attack the music he had once championed, he thrust his critical rapier in, hilt and all. I knew nothing at the time of the reactionary phase through which Heseltine was then passing in respect of Delius's music, and it astonished me greatly to hear him say that out of Delius's enormous output, three of the major works only would live—*Sea Drift*, *A Village Romeo and Juliet* and *Appalachia*. . . . I agreed with him that *Sea Drift* and *A Village Romeo and Juliet* were great masterpieces, but I would not have placed *Appalachia* in their company. . . .

(I remember how, after the performance of *Appalachia* at the Delius Festival later that year, we were coming down in the lift together at the Langham Hotel, after having escorted Delius safely across from Queen's Hall, and Heseltine saying, 'Well, Fenby, what do you think of it now? Wasn't it magnificent? It's a superb work!')[24]

It is perhaps significant that from this discussion on Delius their conversation turned to the other important composer in Philip's life, Bernard van Dieren:

Did I know his music, and had I heard the last quartet which van Dieren had dedicated to him? He would send me a score, for it was a 'superlatively fine work'. . . .[25]

After tea Heseltine asked me to take him up to the music-room. He could not believe that 'old Fred' (Delius) was trying to work again, and when he saw what had been done he exclaimed, 'My God, how you both must have slaved at this!'

It was now getting dark, so he proposed that the party should leave, and walk over to Marlotte to see his Uncle Joe (Joe Heseltine). 'No visit to Europe is complete,' said he, 'unless one has seen old Joe's pictures'.[26]

On his return to London, Philip did not forget his promise to the young Fenby. His letter also shows his intimate and encyclopedic knowledge of Delius's music:

I was extremely pleased to find in you one more addition to the increasing number of enthusiastic admirers of the work of van Dieren. I send you a score of his latest string quartet, in the hope that you will enjoy it no less than no. 3. It is a wonderful work.

The 'North Country Sketches' and 'Air and Dance' were brilliantly played in the recording studio yesterday. Bernard's handling of the orchestra was quite masterly. The new piece was most enthusiastically appreciated by all who heard or played it: it will be a big success. It is time that many other works of Delius which are lying in his cupboard should be given a hearing, for there is undoubtedly a great deal of good stuff among his manuscripts.

I am seeing Beecham next Monday, à propos of the programmes of the six-day Delius festival he proposes to give in the autumn, and I shall suggest to him that the interest of the programmes would be greatly increased by the inclusion of some early and unknown works (dated, of course) which, apart from their intrinsic merits, would give people an opportunity of tracing the composer's musical development from one period to another.

If you have the leisure to examine some of these scores, I should be exceedingly grateful for some information about these, as to which, in your opinion, would be worth performing.

I have definite and pleasant recollections of a suite called 'Florida', dating from 1886, but there are many works I know only by name, such as the tone-poem 'Hiawatha' (1888), 'Petite Suite d'Orchestre' (1890), 'Idylle de Printemps' (1889), Suite for small orchestra (1890), Suite for orchestra in three movements: (a) 'La Quadrone' (b) 'skerzo' (c) 'Marche caprice' (1890) Three symphonic poems: (a) 'Summer Evening', (b) 'Winter night', (c) 'Spring morning' (1890). Tone-poem: 'Sur les cimes' (1892) and 'Sommer i Gurre' for voice and orchestra (1902). And, if I remember rightly, there is a beautiful prelude to the opera 'Irmelin' which might be performed separately.

I have written to Mrs Delius on this subject, and it would be as well if you discussed the matter with her before mentioning it to Delius himself.

'The late lark' (Henley) ought certainly to have its first hearing at the festival: and are there completed versions of 'Cynara' (1906–7) and 'Poem of life and love' (1919), or are these only fragments? If you would be so kind as to give me any news of these things, it would be most helpful—provided, of course, that my suggestion is acceptable at all.[27]

Together with Barbara Peache, Philip made a second quick visit to Grez in the first week of May intent on finding some early, unperformed works for the Festival. Fenby gives the impression that he came alone, recalling that after supper one evening Philip suggested that they should walk to nearby Moncourt for a drink. When Fenby hesitated, he looked at him appealingly and said, 'For God's sake, Fenby, do come, I cannot bear to be alone!'[28] But when Jelka Delius had written appreciatively to Philip about his enthusiastic efforts for the forthcoming Festival, she added: 'Please give my love to your friend Barbara; I am afraid she must have bored herself here; had I but known that she was *your great friend*, I should have taken her to my heart at once. Well that is for another time.'[29]

Perhaps one of the most important results of this second visit was the resurrection of the almost completed score of a setting of Ernest Dowson's poem, 'Cynara', dating from 1907. Only the last four lines still remained to be set and these Delius dictated to Fenby in time for the Festival. When the work was eventually published in 1931 Delius added an eight-bar coda based on the opening, but by then Philip was dead and Delius dedicated the work to his memory. Philip's last letter to Taylor tells of these discoveries:

I was over at Delius's home at Grez-sur-Loing lately. The old fellow gets no worse, though he gets no better either, and is naturally very weak. Going through a pile of his old pencil sketches, I came across an almost-completed full score of a song for baritone and orchestra—a setting of Dowson's 'Cynara'—planned on very big lines, and containing some excellent music. I knew he had once attempted this poem, but had no idea he had got so far with it. He had completely forgotten it—it is more than twenty years old—but it was copied out and played to him, and he managed to dictate the last few bars of the music. This, sung by John Goss, will be one of the few novelties of the festival. . . .

I have definitely abandoned musical composition—it is more than a year since I wrote even a potboiler, and the demand for any but purely educational music in this country is absolutely nil: but I am glad to say that I have found plenty of other work in the last few months—indeed, I have never been so busy.

On the 29th [August] I make my first and last appearance as a conductor, when 'Capriol' will be given at the Proms. What a farce this silly 'conducted by the composer' fetish is! One feels that one is merely stuck up at the desk to make the audience laugh, as though one were a dancing bear or something . . .

P.S. I am now officially Peter Warlock for all public communications—it saves trouble and confusion and keeps one's name in people's minds: they cannot remember two at a time.[30]

Elizabeth Poston had amusing memories of Philip's conducting at that particular Prom concert. As he had long since disposed of his

dress clothes, he borrowed Constant Lambert's trousers and John
Ireland's tailcoat for the evening:

Constant had got revoltingly fat, and safety-pinned up with reefs taken in, the
lower half was all right. But John Ireland was rather a mingey little man and
P couldn't move his arms. His conducting was a disaster, his chuckles audible
to the players. The orchestra, going it alone, played like angels and the audience was not aware of anything unusual.[31]

The Times gave the concert a warm review for its British content,
though without specifically commenting on Philip's skill as an
orchestral conductor. Philip himself had no high opinion of his contribution that evening, having nonchalantly written to Blunt the next
month that, as a result of too much drinking, he had experienced
'some very nasty touches of the morning sickness'[32]—the worst
being the day he had to conduct the Queen's Hall Orchestra. He
told Jelka Delius that the orchestra had been 'most sympathetic and
helpful, and played as well as could be expected under such direction. Anyway, the audience seemed pleased enough and I was
recalled four times.'[33] Writing to the conductor of the Barclays
Bank Musical Society after apparently having attended their performance of his *Capriol Suite* in December 1929, Philip was again
scornful about his own efforts: 'I am afraid you were misled, in the
matter of tempi, by my own rendering at Queen's Hall in August
which was atrocious, owing to my complete lack of experience as a
conductor.'[34] Interviewed by the *Evening News* about conducting his
own work, he had caustically remarked: 'It's absurd. I've never conducted at a concert in my life. Why should I conduct because I'm
the composer? Conducting is a highly technical job. Nobody expects
me to sing my own songs in public. Why this curious rage for getting composers to conduct their own compositions?'[35]

During August yet another anxiety had been added to Philip's
growing list of worries. Hal Collins, his loyal companion of the
Eynsford years, who had recently been working as artistic director to
an advertising firm in London, was terminally ill with tuberculosis.
He had been admitted in a very weak state to St George's Hospital
where he was being 'nourished exclusively on brandy, milk and tur-
pentine (the precise function of the latter I know not). Both lungs are
very far gone with tuberculosis, and the doctors have no hope whatever of his recovery.'[36] He died within a few weeks. At this time
Philip was also having a contretemps with Foss and Humphrey
Milford at the Oxford Press and, though the details of this dispute
are not known, his writings on the subject are particularly angry.

The final short reference to Collins's death in this letter to Blunt suggests that he was perhaps venting his personal anger and grief on the OUP management:

Many thanks for the photograph of Mr Fossferine [Foss]. I had occasion to write a lengthy formal complaint about the little beast to Humphrey Bumphrey [Milford] the other day, but, of course, got no satisfaction. However, I have told the Oxford Press that I shall never again have any dealings with them, and that I shall warn every musician I meet of the kind of treatment he may expect if he is fool enough to take his stuff to them.

They are already sick because I have refused to offer them the new Delius works. I am up to my neck in work here, and have to keep very sober of an evening in order to get through the next day's work . . . But I am looking forward to a pint of beer with you after so long a while.

Poor old Colly pegged out last week. He is a great loss, but I am glad the end came quickly and without pain; he had wasted away to a quite horrifying degree.[37]

In the mean time Philip was still corresponding with Jelka Delius about programming details for the Festival. Delius himself was most anxious that none of his family should be involved in providing any of the biographical material and begged Philip not to ask his sisters for any information, adding, 'They will only tell lies.'[38] Now Jelka began to fuss as the actual date drew closer. The ailing Delius had suddenly become pessimistic about being able to travel to London and she was anxious about many of the details: 'I suppose I am to sit with Fred, and then the Bruder nurse must be there and also Fenby. Fred particularly wants Fenby near him to make him note down anything he may wish to tell him about the music. I suppose it will be alright and that there are 2 seats behind us?'[39] Everything was eventually organized and the Deliuses left Grez for London on 7 October, arriving at the Langham Hotel two days later. Philip was pushing himself to his limits in his attempts to ensure the success of the Festival and on the day of the opening concert we find him telling Blunt that it was driving him nearer the asylum than he normally was: 'I am now perforce at the office from 9.30 a.m. till about 8.30 p.m. when I lapse exhausted into "The Antelope". I shall be glad when October is over.' If anyone doubted the success of the whole venture, it was certainly not Beecham. To quote his own rather self-laudatory words: 'The success of the Festival was unquestioned and at none of the six concerts was there a seat unoccupied.'[40]

Once the Festival was over Philip managed to escape from London for a few days' rest in the country, staying with Blunt at

Marriner's Farm, Bramdean, where Blunt had moved in June that year. It was during this time that J. B. Morton (1893–1979), who wrote a regular column in the *Daily Express* under the pseudonym 'Beachcomber', began a light-hearted inquiry into the heseltine/ warlock phenomenon. Eight items on the subject appeared in his column that November and included enquiries as to whether warlocks or heseltines were the same thing and whether they were brown-bearded or hooded. When the following couplet was quoted:

> When heseltines be near
> Good hops do make good beer

there was a response from that well-known figure, Rab Noolas. In an amusing letter he corrected the etymology and enlarged on the heseltine myth:

Beer Deachcomber,
            Your notes about warlocks and heseltines are interesting, but somewhat inaccurate. I have always understood that heseltines are chiefly in evidence, not on May-eve, but in hazel-time, and the philological significance is obvious.
    I know an old man in Hampshire who remembers the Michaelmas-tide custom of 'hunting the heseltine', when the little creatures were lured from their lairs by the repeated beating of pewter upon wood in the copses.
    The Master of the Hampshire Heseltine Hunt was a noted mesmerist named Benn Skinn,[41] who lived at Marriner's Farm, and was capable of reducing the most diabolical heseltine into an uninterruptedly comatose condition between sunset and midnight.
    If you will ask for me at the 'H. H.' inn at Cheriton (again the philological significance is obvious), I shall be pleased to give you any further information which you may, or may not, require.
    Yours faithfully,

                        RAB NOOLAS[42]

The saga continued when Beachcomber quoted a little poem in the following issue:

> Up the airy mountain
> Down the sombre chines,
> We dare not go a-hunting
> For fear of heseltines.

He also produced a quotation from Shakespeare, allegedly from *Henry IV, Part 2*: 'Marry, I had rather be left with a yoke o' bullocks at Stamford Fair than have these same heseltines in mine inn, Hal.'[43] This resulted in two telegrams from Rab Noolas:

10.16 Have captured a heseltine and have it in a bottle can you come down at
    once—Noolas.

10.49 Sorry returned to find heseltine vanished twopence to pay on the empty—Noolas.

After that the correspondence was closed, 'Beachcomber' having decided that heseltines were not malignant unless deprived of their natural sustenance.[44]

Hoping to repeat the Christmas 1927 success of 'Bethlehem Down' with another carol at the end of 1929, Philip and Blunt decided once again to combine their talents. Until then it had been a lean year for Philip as far as original compositions were concerned. Most of his time had been taken up with the Delius Festival, as well as with writing and editing. The result of their Christmas collaboration was 'The Frostbound Wood' which appeared on 20 December 1929 in the Christmas number of the *Radio Times*. Even though Blunt described his poem as a carol, it was hardly cast in the traditional mould, and Philip's setting, a startlingly original creation using only four notes of the pentatonic scale, was certainly not aimed at the popular market. It is, however, a masterpiece of economic writing with a deep-felt intensity that makes it incredibly moving.

The effects of the collapse of the American stock market the previous October were now beginning to have disastrous, world-wide repercussions. The Imperial League of Opera folded at the beginning of 1930 and Philip was out of work once more. On 26 January 1930 Beecham wrote curtly to tell Philip that he did not intend 'to proceed further with "Milo". You need not trouble to make any public announcement about it. I will do that myself.'[45] Philip's life was slowly becoming bleaker and bleaker and in his mounting depression he again felt that his inspiration had finally dried up. Indeed, with the advent of broadcasting and recordings, the market for solo songs had slowly begun to disappear and he was having difficulty selling what songs he had been able to compose. Denis ApIvor suggests a probable explanation of these negative feelings, noting that when Philip

was faced with the 'drying-up' of his early youthful lyrical impulse, he did not have the technique or the sense of direction to move into new fields and exploit new attitudes towards composition, which would have involved some sort of linguistic extension, some enquiry into what his language had been and why it no longer satisfied him or seemed appropriate.[46]

It seems that at some stage Beecham must have offered to programme a new orchestral work by Philip at one of the BBC Symphony Orchestra concerts at Queen's Hall. Advance publicity in the March programme advertised that on 4 April 'A New Work' by Peter Warlock would be included in the Friday evening concert, with Beecham himself conducting. However, no work materialized and the German conductor Oskar Fried (1871–1941) replaced Beecham in a new programme which included Mahler's Fourth Symphony. Given the fact that Beecham had fallen out with the BBC authorities that January and that Philip's prevailing mood was hardly conducive to composing a large-scale work, the non-appearance of a new work is hardly surprising.

It seemed too that he had all but exhausted the supply of early music which he still wished to edit. These factors made him seriously question whether he had achieved anything at all, and the old feelings of self-doubt began to re-emerge in a more menacing form. He asked the tenor Victor Carne to help him find a job at Columbia Gramophones writing notes for recordings and to act as an adviser, offering as a start to conduct his own *Capriol Suite* without a fee: 'The wage he asked was £5 a week; he was turned down. He applied to various official seats of learning; and again was turned down.'[47] Gray later wrote of Philip's other desperate and weird ideas:

Many and various were the projects for earning a livelihood that he considered, some of them touchingly naive, others characteristically fantastic. Among the former should be recorded his approach to various official seats of musical learning in the hope of obtaining some post or other, seemingly quite oblivious of the fact that in such quarters he was probably more bitterly detested than any other living musician; among the latter, a plan he had evolved of buying a certain piece of ground somewhere in Kent or Sussex where there were certain caves which he proposed to furnish and let at high rents to flagellants, who could there pursue their pleasures without disturbing neighbours by screams and groans, and without arousing the undesirable attention of the authorities.[48]

It seems that Philip himself had sadistic tendencies. As early as 1914 he had written to Viva Smith making almost uncomfortably prophetic comments about Frank Wedekind's book on adolescent sexuality, *Frühlings Erwachen* (*Spring's Awakening*, 1891). He described it as being 'very ghastly, but very powerful and a very penetrating study of awakening sex, both in its normal form and inverted: there's a little bit of everything, from Sadism to Suicide!'[49] Jack Lindsay later revealed that Philip's 'exasperation with life developed in a definitely sadistic direction'. A girl had told him how once at a party he had taken her aside and tried to whip her, insisting, 'Come on, you know you want it'. 'Later, sober, he apologized and swore not to repeat the performance; but the next time he got

drunk, he made the same attack. After that she avoided him, decid-
ing that he was mad.'[50] A passing comment at the end of a letter to
Blunt in June 1929 seems to confirm these stories: 'I shall have to
give up Rampayne Mews—so if you want it for a vapulatorium [a
whipping place], let me know at once.'[51] Maybe it was mere light-
hearted banter, but it is worth noting that Rampayne Mews is not
far from Denbigh Street in Westminster where Philip was living at
the time. In a later discussion with Gerald Cockshott, Blunt himself
had actually told Cockshott that Philip used to birch Barbara
Peache.[52]

On 25 February 1930 the *Capriol Suite* was used by the Marie
Rambert Dancers at a matinée of ballet at the Lyric Theatre,
Hammersmith. Constant Lambert had suggested Philip's music to
the dancer and choreographer Frederick Ashton (1906–88), who was
at the time in the process of persuading Marie Rambert to present
an afternoon of ballet using her pupils. It was Ashton who eventually choreographed the ballet and among the dancers were Diana
Gould (later Lady Menuhin) and Ashton himself. The two-piano
version of the suite was used as the accompaniment, presumably for
economic reasons, and the occasion proved popular enough to war-
rant a repeat season from 23 to 25 July in the same theatre. If Philip
attended a performance, he left no written comment.

On 6 March Jelka Delius wrote to Philip from Grez to inform
him that his Uncle Joe had died of blood poisoning, the result of a
bad abscess in a tooth. It was the first time that he was addressed
by either of the Deliuses in a letter as 'Peter Warlock'. Aware of his
dire financial position, Jelka sympathetically hoped that some much-
needed money would perhaps eventually come his way: 'If you could
only get a little something out of the final Sale of Uncle Joe. As far
as I can see his wife is too worn out and ill to do anything and all
will remain as it is till after her death. Then surely you might come
in. He owned those houses you know.'[53]

Despite his personal misfortunes, Philip was, in typical fashion,
continuing his untiring efforts on behalf of colleagues and friends.
Edward Dent, the professor of music at Cambridge, had recently
written an article on Elgar for a German *Handbuch der Musikgeschichte* and in this article Dent had included the following
appallingly dismissive remarks:

Wie Mackenzie, war er Violinspieler von Beruf und studierte Liszts Werke,
welche den konservativen akademischen Musikern ein Greuel waren. Er war
überdies Katholik und mehr oder weniger Autodidakt, der wenig von der liter-

arischen Bildung Parrys und Stanford hatte. . . . Für englische Ohren ist
Elgars Musik allzu gefühlvoll und nicht ganz frei von Vulgarität. Seine
Orchesterwerke, Variationen, 2 Symphonien, Konzerte für Violine und
Violoncell und verschiedene Ouvertüren sind lebhaft in der Farbe, doch pomp-
haft im Stile und mit einer gesuchten Ritterlichkeit des Ausdrucks. . . . Seine
Kammermusik . . . ist trocken und akademisch.[54]

(Like [Sir Alexander] Mackenzie, he [Elgar] was a violin player by profession,
and studied the works of Liszt, which were loathsome to conservative academic musicians. He was, moreover, a Catholic, and more or less self-taught,
possessing little of the literary culture of Parry and Stanford . . . For English
ears Elgar's music is too emotional and not entirely free from vulgarity. His
orchestral works, variations, 2 symphonies, concertos for violin and violon-
cello and various overtures are lively in colour, but pompous in style and with
an attempted nobility of expression. . . . His chamber music . . . is dry and
academic.)

When it was discovered what Dent had written, there was an angry
outcry at the insult to England's greatest living composer. Although
Philip had been on good terms with Dent for a number of years and
had printed two of his songs in *The Sackbut*, he was incensed by the
article and immediately organized a letter of protest which he persuaded a number of distinguished personalities to sign. Among these
were Hamilton Harty, John Ireland, Augustus John, E. J. Moeran,
Landon Ronald, Richard Terry, William Walton, and Bernard
Shaw. The letter, however, only appeared in print after Philip's
death:

We the undersigned, wish to record an emphatic protest against the unjust and
inadequate treatment of Sir Edward Elgar by Professor Dent . . . At the present time the works of Elgar, so far from being distasteful to English ears, are
held in the highest honour by the majority of English musicians and the musical public in general.

Professor Dent's failure to appreciate Elgar's music is no doubt tempera-
mental; but it does not justify him in grossly misrepresenting the position
which Sir Edward and his music enjoy in the esteem of his fellow-
countrymen.[55]

In magnanimous fashion he also attempted to raise funds to
stage van Dieren's unperformed opera, *The Tailor*. Early in January
1930 he wrote giving details to Nichols, who some fourteen years
earlier had been pressurized by Philip and Gray into producing the
original libretto in just a fortnight. He had now managed to find a
sponsor to underwrite a fortnight's run at the Lyric in
Hammersmith and, if it were a success, to take it on to the West
End. Preparations were already in hand and he hoped to be able to
produce the work in the early spring. Alas, like so many projects in

the past, this scheme foundered and in April 1930 a dejected Philip moved temporarily to Blunt's Chelsea apartment in Bramerton Street, telling him that he was still very far from well and now abstaining completely from alcohol. The failure of the opera scheme also had a dreadful effect on van Dieren, who (ill as he was) had completed the full score in eight weeks, but received only £10 of the payment promised.

At the end of April, Philip's wealthy uncle Evelyn died, a week before his eightieth birthday. The funeral, held in what Philip called the 'hideous' church at Great Warley, was attended by most of the family, including Philip, his mother, and stepfather, and also his 14-year-old son, Nigel. The final irony was, however, still to come. Although the old man left an estate of £639,366, to be shared among various members of the Heseltine family (after the servants had been paid six months' wages), Philip was left nothing. Writing to Delius he gave vent to his bitterness, saying that his uncle had given away hundreds of thousands to churches, schools, and the like during his lifetime, 'but never a penny came my way . . . After this I resolved finally to abandon all further use of the family name.'[56] The last words which he had written to Taylor a short while earlier had already hinted at the imminence of such a decision: 'I am now officially Peter Warlock for all public communications'.[57]

Philip's suppressed anger now surfaced in violent disagreements which continued with a vigour reminiscent of the past. A short and intriguing note sent that August to Philip by the composer Frederic Austin (1872–1952) shows how he could still succeed in baiting his victims. It would indeed be interesting to know what incident had sparked off Austin's outburst: 'There are blackguards of so offensive a type that contact with them is so distasteful to the point of nausea. You are one of them.'[58] The animosity between Philip and Austin had been a long-standing one. Years earlier (in about 1919) Philip had been angered by Austin's dismissive remarks about Schoenberg and had included him in his irreverent collection 'One dozen Cursory Rhymes':

Whether it is true or not that Mr. FREDERIC AUSTIN
Has as much creative talent as a Jew has foreskin,
I can testify that one day he exclaimed with considerable animation,
'*Speaking as a composer* I do not think SCHOENBERG's music worthy of my
   consideration.' (A FACT!)[59]

Now Philip retaliated once again, this time producing, for his own amusement, the following little private joke in the style of the James

Joyce stream-of-consciousness technique: 'FredAustingoandbugger-
yourselffishmongerellawheelerwillcocksstandupforgodsavethekingcup-
bearerchequemate.'[60]

From the same period a number of poignant letters allegedly written by Philip to Winifred Baker survive and are extensively quoted
in Gray's memoir. She was the nurse who had loved him since 1919
and was also the dedicatee of two songs, 'Dedication' (1919) and
'The Sick Heart' (1925). The latter song had begun its life as a setting of Yeats's poem 'The Cloths of Heaven' (1919) and was later
wedded to new words, presumably because of copyright difficulties.
On the manuscript copy which he sent to her in 1919, he wrote the
following cryptic message: 'Will you forgive me my somewhat grisly
condition last Saturday week and accept this in lieu of a more articulate apology?'[61] Blunt later claimed that the letters quoted in Gray
were actually written by Philip to himself and not to Winifred Baker
and, as none of the original letters still survive, this may very well
have been the case. She appears to have been to Philip a kind of
idealized woman, though Blunt described her in the most uncomplimentary of terms: 'a lump of a woman, big, with a bad shape . . .
with an ungainly kind of oriental countenance; her eyes were slit-
like, upturned at the outer corners. . . . She was completely dumb,
and never uttered a word; she just used to sit.' Philip's circle of
friends ridiculed her behind her back, calling her 'The British Moth
Work'. Evidently, about once or twice a year, Philip would suddenly
have fits to see her, would go off with her for a day and would then
drop her. Six months later she would come to Eynsford where she
would never drink but simply sit absolutely dumb, though not in
any kind of militant way. Blunt summed her up as 'having no mental or spiritual attraction. Philip never mentioned or discussed her'.[62]
Of her own authenticated letters only a few beautifully worded
examples to van Dieren and Edith Buckley Jones, written shortly
after Philip's death, survive. In some quite inexplicable way, however, she does seem to have been an important figure in Philip's life,
though how she really fitted into the picture is quite impossible to
fathom. Nevertheless, the following extracts from some of Philip's
last letters, allegedly written to her, give a penetrating insight into
his state of mind at the time:

On that miraculous day, now more than two months past, when I was with
you in those lovely places, I was so oppressed by the beauty of it all—and you
were the key to it and all the downs and rivers and birds were you—that I was
quite inarticulate, and even a little afraid of you and all the loveliness around

me. Just so, I think, one who had killed himself might feel if for an hour he might see again from afar the world from which his deed had exiled him. And I resolved to examine myself, to seek out the cause of this spiritual deadness and to try to find a new direction for my being, so that when next I spoke or wrote to you it would be with clear and purposeful words, from my open heart to yours. In the course of the last few bitter and remorseful weeks I have found in myself so many seeds of the soul's death that if I dare still hope for any regeneration, it cannot but be a slow and painful one. I think that I should rightly keep silent until I can come to you as one risen from the dead, yet in these last days I have been filled with apprehensions and forebodings, and something impels me to make certain things clear to you while there is yet time: because, since everything has fallen away from me and I am left empty in mind and spirit, the one light that is left me, burning with ever clearer and intenser flame, is the thought of you who are, who have been and will always be my spirit's companion and my one Reality. I know now—and you have known always, I believe—that in failing you I have deliberately betrayed my own soul and all the faculties of my mind and spirit. I do not pretend to understand the source of the appalling perversity in my nature that has caused me now for years, with deliberate and callous cruelty, to torment and perse-cute that only precious part of myself, which is you, until I know not now whether the semblance of its death is death its very self and no semblance at all. The supreme blasphemy, the sin against the Holy Spirit, is to know the Light and, knowing it, to plunge into the darkness: and I know now by bitter experience that it is not without reason that this sin is called the soul's destruction. You came to me with the most lovely and precious gifts life has to offer—such gifts as *can* be offered only to those who know the light—and stood patiently, offering them again and again, while I betrayed you, reviled, mocked, and ill-used you with a barbarity that must surely have been implanted in me by the fiends of Hell. I do not understand and I cannot explain this devilry. But now that I have seen it face to face, examined it in detail, episode by episode, the memory of it is an incessant torment to me. I have been more vilely cruel to you, the guardian angel of my soul, than I have ever been to a dumb beast; and though you who know my heart have known that I was so encompassing my own destruction, I am writing this because I want to make a full confession to you myself, kneeling at your feet, not for forgiveness but that you may know that all my cruelties have come back to revenge themselves on me, and because my one remaining joy is in an aware-ness of the horrors of my past actions as revealed by the anguish I am suffering at the memory of them—and I like to hope that awareness is itself a sign that I am in some small measure expiating them. I knew love only when I first saw you eleven years ago [1919]—all else that I have called love in my life has been a hideous mockery, a soul-destroying obscenity. All that is good in my work that I have ever done is you and you alone. You have believed in me with a superhuman faith, and I read and re-read in your letters words of love and faith more beautiful than I had ever dared hope would be said to me; and I know now that if any good come of my life now, it will be through the ever-present thought of you and through the integrity of my spiritual kinship with you.[63]

With perceptive insight ApIvor points out that

the constant reference to death of the soul and of the spirit and the expressed desire to say what he had to say 'while there is yet time', indicated the direction in which his thoughts were turning at that moment. But more significant than the references to his bodily or spiritual destruction are the constant suggestions of guilt, his crimes against the spirit. It is the conviction of guilt, of unredeemed crime of a moral kind, of necessity to suffer as a penance for guilt, that is most likely in the circumstances to lead to self-destruction, since the person who experiences these feelings may well come to the conclusion that he is not 'worthy' to live or that death is demanded in expiation of those matters of which he considers himself guilty.[64]

There seemed to be a brief period when depression and self-doubt lifted as Philip wrote to her about composing again:

My mind is slowly awakening from its torpor and I hope to be able to get through a considerable deal of work during the next few weeks. I have actually written some music during the last few days, but rather with the hope of selling it quickly than in the belief that it is any good at all. Still, if I cling to the belief that some day, if ever I can afford a period of intensive study which will enable me to write as I would wish to, the results will be very different from any which I have achieved hitherto.[65]

However, this was only a brief glimmer of light in the ever-darkening gloom and two weeks later he wrote that

Nothing has changed for the better and there is no sign of any improvement on the horizon. I am so steeped in chronic gloom and grisliness that I am no fit correspondent for any normally cheerful person, nor fit company for any but the drunkards who live here. Everything has collapsed like a pricked balloon. I am quite literally dead broke and utterly incapable of any thought or action—my mind simply refuses to function and can produce nothing whatsoever, howsoever bad. It is like being in a cage from which the minutest inspection reveals no way out. London and the company of drunken Hampshire hogs is unbearable, but on the other hand solitude in the country at this time would simply make me suicidal. When I am so insufferably and ignominiously grisly as this, I can't bear to be seen by anyone who matters; my instinct, which I am sure is right, directs me to hide discreetly in a hole. As soon as I become bearably human again (if ever) and there is the faintest glimmer of a possibility of improving the situation in any way, I will write at once and we will meet in Ashdown Forest or where you will—but not in this detestable and increasingly loathly city . . . this abominable impotence in material things is driving me to despair.[66]

Added to all this, his health had been giving him some trouble, as he confided to Arnold Dowbiggin:

Life is very stagnant and dull for me at the moment—my mind is a complete blank and I seem to have become utterly incompetent at any and every sort of work. It is frightfully hot, and I cannot get out for walks in the country owing to the ankle which I broke two summers ago having started to give trouble which I am told is due to uric acid caused by booze—and part of the cure is complete abstention from alcohol! However, it is good to be sober occasionally—one enjoys getting drunk afterwards all the more![67]

In July Blunt invited Philip to spend a fortnight with him at Marriner's Farm in Hampshire and it was here that one of his last original compositions, 'The Fox', was written the same month. It is an inspired, if disturbing, setting of a poem 'of death and dissolution'[68] which Blunt had written. Blunt later related the story of the song's unusual origin:

> . . . as I have hinted before, there are many inns which he only went to once or twice, where people who met him still remember him, and feel more than a vague sorrow that they will never see him there again.
>
> On of the inns which we visited distinctly more than once or twice was 'The Fox' at Bramdean.
>
> On the wall behind the bar hangs a fox's mask—it still hangs there as a matter of fact—and one evening it gave me the idea for the words of 'The Fox' . . .
>
> When we got back home, Philip went almost straight to bed, but I stayed up and opened a bottle of Chablis (what an inadvisable addition to a lot of beer!) and wrote the words.
>
> As I did not go upstairs till about 3.0, I thought that Philip would probably be down before me, so I left the poem on the table with a note to the effect that I thought it was unsuitable for setting to music on account of the shortness of the lines.
>
> When I got down at about noon the next day, I found Philip sitting at the table with the music MS paper in front of him, and he was working at the song. He said 'On the contrary, my dear sir, I think that this is admirably suited for setting to music.'
>
> We were going to Salisbury that afternoon and, when we got there, Philip hired a room with a piano at some music shop, played and whistled the thing over, and finished the song on the spot. So 'The Fox', words and music, was conceived and completed within about eighteen hours, which may, or may not, be a record . . . we duly celebrated the feat at the 'Haunch of Venison' in Salisbury in the evening.[69]

Copley refers to it as 'a gripping and eerie song, words and music together have a chilling intensity of feeling unique among his solo songs'.[70] Foss saw it as 'the Warlock counterpart of Schubert's *Doppelgänger*',[71] while Constant Lambert, perhaps with a certain degree of hindsight, felt it had 'the smell of death about it'.[72] With his cynical thoughts drawn more and more towards death, Philip seems to have identified completely with both the subject and emotion of Blunt's poem. The fox's grin mocks his own dead, wasted years; yet, at the same time, he is the fox, the mask, the warlock who would still have the last laugh. For the supreme irony of this sardonic poem is that, long after huntsmen, horses, and hounds are dead and forgotten, the fox lives on:

> High on the wall
> Above the cask
> Laughs at you all
> The fox's mask.

The fortnight spent with Blunt seemed briefly to refresh Philip and for a while he even entertained brief thoughts of leaving London. By mid-July we find him writing in far more cheerful tones:

The summer winds on this lonely hill-top have blown away much of my town-engendered gloom and I feel transformed, in body and mind. Also I have a hopeful premonition of something extremely fortunate making its way towards me. In any case I shall live no more in London unless I have some definite work to keep me there . . . I shall sell practically everything I have except a few books, and then set out afresh, without impedimenta to tie me long in one place—and hope for the necessary god to descend from his machine.[73]

But alas no *deus ex machina* obliged.

THE END
(1930)

W$_{HEN}$ P$_{HILIP}$ $_{MOVED}$ to Bramerton Street in April he had intended to stay only a short while but, apart from the two weeks spent in Bramdean, he remained there until September, when he finally found a basement flat that suited him. Assisted by a £30 advance from his mother and the loan of a Bechstein piano from Moeran, he and Barbara Peache now moved to 12A Tite Street in Chelsea, which was destined to be the last of his many London addresses.[1] Thanking his mother for the loan, he told her that he found the flat 'quite exceptionally pleasant and sympathetic . . . I am sure I shall be able to do good work there.'[2]

At the end of November he took a short break and went with a friend, Basil Trier, on a motor tour to Wales, his last trip out of London. In recalling this trip to Robert Beckhard years later (and perhaps with a touch of hindsight) Trier had the impression that Philip was on 'a final fling' and had 'a kind of sinister feeling' as Philip began to sort out his papers and prepare fires to burn them. Their route to Cefn Bryntalch took them via Gloucester, Ross, the Black Mountains, Hay, Kington via Knighton (Edith Buckley Jones's birthplace)—a trip which would have evoked many early memories for Philip. In Trier's words, it was 'a kind of wild trek—it looked as if Philip was saying good-bye'. When given the opportunity of taking the wheel, Philip 'drove very fast and nearly wrecked Trier's car'.[3] They returned through Worcester and Chipping Norton, which Philip declared to be 'a very fine drinking centre'.[4] Passing through Oxford they called on Richard Terry, where a 'healthy, tanned, and exuberantly high spirited'[5] Philip was delighted to find him preparing 'a most damning indictment of the much-lauded Oxford Book of Carols'.[6] The only blot on the holiday had been yet another row with his mother because he could not remember whether his son had been baptized or not. It was the last time Edith Buckley Jones would see Philip alive. On his return to

London he wrote about his trip in this humorous letter to Moeran, who was laid up in Ipswich with tuberculosis of the knee:

Ever since last Monday afternoon (starting in Ludlow where they open at 4 every day) I have been almost continuously drunk, with the happily, now usual result that I have drunk myself sober and feel as fit as ever on nothing at all. From the week's haze certain events stand out with the startling quality of objects one just misses while motoring on a foggy night: an elephant in the streets of Chipping Norton who refused a pint of beer because, (so the mahout assured me), he had had so much already that he was tired of it; and a very beautiful woman with one leg who attempted (without success, I may add) to induce me to share a semi- or pseudo-nuptial couch. Also the following passage from 'A plain and easy account of British Fungi' (1871) which I found in the library at Cefn Bryntalch:—

'At first it (the *amanita muscaria*, which Basil tells me can easily be found in Kent) generally produces cheerfulness, afterwards giddiness and drunkenness, ending occasionally in the entire loss of consciousness. The natural inclinations of the individual become stimulated. The dancer executes a *pas d'extravagance*, the musician indulges in a song, the chatterer divulges all his secrets, the orator delivers himself of a philippic, and the mimic indulges in caricature. Erroneous impressions of size and distance are common occurrences: a straw lying in the road becomes a formidable object, to overcome which a leap is taken sufficient to clear a barrel of ale, or the prostrate trunk of a British oak.' But this is not the only extraordinary circumstance connected therewith. 'The property is imparted to the fluid excretion of rendering it intoxicating, which property it retains for a considerable time. A man, having been intoxicated on one day, and slept himself sober on the next, will, by drinking this liquor to the extent of about a cupful, become as much intoxicated as he was before. Confirmed drunkards in Siberia preserve this as a precious liquor in case a scarcity of fungi should occur. This intoxicating property may be communicated to every person who partakes of the disgusting draught, and thus with even the third, fourth, and even fifth distillation. By this means, with a few fungi to commence with, a party may shut themselves in their room and indulge in a week's debauch'.

> He that will a funghouse keep
> Must have three things in store:
> A chamber and a feather-bed,
> Some fungi and a [whore]
>   hey-nonny-nonny, etc.[7]

Moeran's equally exuberant reply gives a good idea of the kind of light-hearted smutty banter they enjoyed:

Thanks for the entertaining letter: I imagine that after a bout of mushrooms the resultant fluid would prove the ideal pick-me-up on which to sober down, and should as such be commended to publicans, who are frequently asked for something with a kick (Two double piss, miss, & a split baby). Seriously though, there might be money to be made by cultivating the amanita muscaria, providing it can be taken without dangerous results. All one would need do would be to collect a company of good fellows, have a glorious blind on fungi, which I suppose could be pleasantly washed down with a barrel of Kenward & Court, afterwards carefully bottling the contents of the jerries & selling them as smuggled Turkish wine of a great and unusual type of potency. Or possibly to import the Lurgi into America: I wonder whether one would be up against the Prohibition act. In this case I think the reputable firm of Hitchcock, Philpot, Chambers & Chambers would give a sound legal opinion . . .

I spend a good deal of time writing music, but lack of privacy prevents me doing anything on a large scale, as I am still too helpless to be free of constant attendance. However, to-day has been a red-letter day in my drab existence. For the first time since May 16th, I have sat down on a civilised seat & enjoyed a good crap. I had no idea that there is such technique in wiping one's ars [sic], that one loses it after a prolonged period of the bedpan. It is really quite difficult for a beginner, but I look forward to making a cleaner job of it to-morrow morning.[8]

Shortly before Philip's death Moeran employed him to make a copy of one of his (Moeran's) recent works. Anne Macnaghten (b. 1908), the violinist and co-founder of the Macnaghten concerts, recounted how she took the fee to his flat in Tite Street. On her way there she saw him in his big camel-hair coat on his way to the pub. He was very pleased to have the 2 guineas, but when she asked him what he would do with it, he only laughed and said 'drink it', brushing aside her protest.[9] Shortly after Philip's death Moeran wrote a bitter letter to Dowbiggin saying that the lamentable neglect of Philip's magnificent output, many of which he considered masterpieces, had embittered him against singers in general:

The majority of his songs he never even heard sung. I cannot help feeling that he might have still been with us, had he been given some of the recognition he deserved. At any rate the musical profession as a whole is to be blamed for allowing a man of his genius to exist very nearly in penury.[10]

Philip's last letter to his mother that November carried little news that was cheerful:

You are right in surmising that my last batch of songs is still unsold. As a matter of fact, after they had been rejected by two publishers, I did not send them out again but kept them by me for revision, since two of them ['The Frostbound Wood' and 'The Fox'] are to form part of a longer series of settings of poems by Bruce Blunt—still unfinished. However, there is absolutely no market for this kind of work at present.[11]

His last original completed work, dated 6 November 1930, was 'The Fairest May', scored for voice and string quartet and written for Arnold Dowbiggin. It is another version of the words 'As Ever I Saw' which he had first set to music as early as 1918. Whereas the earlier setting was in 4/4 time, Philip now employed the by-now-familiar 6/8 rhythm. Of particular note is the skilful use of cross-rhythms and the decorative Elizabethan flourish given to the first violin in the last two bars of the piece.

With the well of creative inspiration apparently run dry, Philip turned once again to the music of a previous era. Up until then his scholarly interests had centred mainly on the works of the Tudor composers. Now his wide-ranging knowledge and interest led him to the symphonies of the neglected English composer, Cipriani Potter (1792–1871), whose compositions had been praised by both Beethoven and Wagner. His last work as a scholar was in the British Museum that November when he began transcribing two of Potter's symphonies for an intended performance the following year. Laying aside this uncompleted task, Philip reworked his beautiful carol 'Bethlehem Down' for a song-recital Dowbiggin was to give in the Priory Church in Lancaster that Christmas. He took the original haunting melody and recast it as a solo song, adding a new organ accompaniment which highlights the inherent sadness of Blunt's poem. What kind of thoughts were going through Philip's troubled mind as he set the words of the final stanza? The last page of the manuscript, dated 1 December 1930, begins with the words 'Here He has peace and a short while for dreaming', accompanied, as Copley points out, by a 'desolate sad motiv that had so often marked his response to profound melancholy'.[12] Indeed, it now seemed that the depression and dejection grew with the approach of Christmas, a season which he had come to dislike more and more. Even a performance at Queen's Hall of his *Three Carols*, written at Vaughan Williams's request some seven years previously, did nothing to cheer him up.

The week before Christmas 1930 was chilly, with heavy winter fogs plaguing London. On Tuesday 16 December, at noon, Philip and two friends spent some time drinking at The Cadogan pub in the King's Road, after which he invited them back to Tite Street where Barbara Peache made lunch for them at about 3.30. After a chat and a short rest they all went out drinking again. That same evening John Goss gave the first performance of some new van Dieren songs for the Chelsea Music Club, which the van Dierens would doubtless have attended, and after the performance Bernard and Frida met Philip in The Duke of Wellington pub in Sloane Square at about 10.45. He was there alone and, after having a drink together, the three went back to his flat. They would be the last people to see Philip alive.

Mrs Mary Venn, the woman who lived above Philip's flat, later recounted how at about 6.40 the next morning she had heard a noise like the shutting of doors and windows (in her statement to the police she had likened the noise to that of taxi-cabs starting off): 'There was a lot of noise. I really wondered what was happening. I got out of bed and looked out of the window. The place downstairs was all lit up, and I heard Mr Heseltine speaking.' Although she could not hear what he was saying, she presumed that a party was in progress and this had annoyed her. An unidentified neighbour interviewed by the *News Chronicle* added to this: 'We heard the piano being played early this morning and the playing continued until about seven o'clock, when it stopped'.[13] The noise, however, did not continue for long and when Mrs Venn got up later that morning, at about 8.20, she was aware of a strong smell of gas. She went over her flat looking for a gas leak and, finding none, phoned the gas company. At about 10.45 Barbara Peache returned home. She had gone to a dance at about eight the previous evening and had spent the night at a hotel: 'Mrs Warlock, as we knew her, came along, and I sent my woman down to see her. She was in the area downstairs, and said she could not get in.[14] She said to my maid, "Send for the police." The police broke the window because it was bolted top and bottom.'

In the yard was a cold and frightened little kitten which Philip had let out earlier that morning. Had the talking that Mary Venn heard just before seven that morning perhaps been Philip speaking his last words to his cat? 'I heard the little thing crying. Apparently Mr Warlock had put some food out. The poor little thing was terrified.' When Constable Alfred Robbins entered the flat he found Philip in the middle room, on a settee in the far corner, unconscious and fully clothed, turned to the wall lying on two cushions with his left hand under his face. 'Mr Warlock was fully dressed except for his shoes, and the appearance of the rooms suggested that he had not slept during the night.'[15] Gas was escaping from the end of a pipe and the plug which had been removed could not be found. Medical evidence showed that on arrival at St Luke's Hospital, Chelsea, Philip had been dead for about three or four hours as a result of coal-gas poisoning. Basil Trier had the grim task of identifying the body at the Chelsea mortuary that same afternoon and, in a brief statement made to the police the following day, Edith Buckley Jones recorded that she had seen the body and identified it as that of her son.

Among the papers found in Philip's flat were some musical manuscripts (including Moeran's Sonata for two violins), a few letters,
and also the pencilled draft of a will. Up till now little attention
seems to have been paid to Philip's attempt to make a new will just
before his death—a mysterious action further compounded by the
fact that in this unsigned draft he bequeathed everything to the enigmatic Winifred Baker. Obviously there can never be a satisfactory
explanation as to why Philip decided to rewrite his will in his last
hours, but the importance of this action should be noted, given
Philip's heartfelt correspondence with Winifred Baker earlier that
year and the fact that in his will dated January 1920 Philip had
made Bernard van Dieren the sole beneficiary. What makes the
whole incident particularly strange is that the rewriting of the will
should have come so soon after Philip's final meeting with van
Dieren that fateful evening. It is possible that Winifred Baker heard
about the contents of this draft will for she wrote to van Dieren on
6 January 1931 declining his invitation to visit his solicitor to see
what she mysteriously described simply as 'those papers'. 'If you
happen to have them in your private possession again at any time
and I could see them unofficially I should like to—simply because
anything which concerned Philip is of great worth to me,' adding, 'I
have written to Trier telling him that I have had all information
from you and I hope that the matter will never be mentioned again.'
Her unceasing devotion to Philip is reflected in her final comment in
the same letter: 'Philip may be dead in the ordinary limited sense of
the word but that he, as an entity, has really ceased to exist in any
sense at all, I find impossible to believe. If one must accept that, the
whole of life becomes a meaningless farce.'[16]

At the inquest[17] on 22 December a number of questions were put
to Edith Buckley Jones by the coroner, Dr Edwin Smith (1870–
1937), who had been trained both as a medical doctor and barrister.
She admitted that Philip was depressed at times, yet strangely
answered in the negative when asked whether he had any financial
difficulties. At this stage Dr Robert Brontë, a Harley Street patholo-
gist and an expert witness in a number of murder trials, was called.
He had conducted the post-mortem examination and in his evidence
added that 'there were no signs whatever of alcohol, and no evidence in the organs to suggest that he was addicted to it, or to any
drug'.

Van Dieren then gave evidence, saying that he had known Philip
for about fifteen years and that he and his wife had been with him

on the night of 16 December from about 10.40 p.m. to 12.15 a.m. In answer to the coroner's questions, van Dieren said that when they left him he had been perfectly all right, normal and sober, and that Philip had apologized for the fact that he did not even have a bottle of beer in the house to offer them. They then had a quiet talk. When asked if he could throw any further light on the matter, van Dieren added:

The only thing I could possibly think of is that he might in the early morning have suddenly awakened, felt miserable for some reason or other, and done something which he could not really have contemplated . . . I can say that when I left him he was in a state of mind in which that should have been the very last thing I could have expected.[18]

Barbara Peache, whose identity was withheld from the jury, then told the court that Philip had on occasion threatened to take his own life, but that she had 'thought it was just talk', significantly adding that Philip had 'said he felt he was a failure, and seemed worried about his work, and that he could not go on. He said he seemed not to be able to do any more.' In her statement to the police on 18 December she had, however, been more specific:

I have an allowance of £200 a year and I helped him materially with the expenses of the home. . . . We were very happy together. . . . On occasions he has been very depressed and he has more than once threatened to commit suicide by gas. The last time was on Sunday 14th Dec. 1930, he was very depressed and he said we had better separate in January and he would commit suicide when everyone was out of the way. I did not take much notice of this as I had heard it before. On Tuesday 16th Dec. deceased came home with two friends at 3.30 p.m. They were all under the influence of drink. I gave them lunch and they went to sleep. Some time later deceased offered me some snuff. I refused it, and we had a few words. I went out of the room and he shut the door. I had a bath and prepared to go out as I had made arrangements to go to a dance with a girl friend.
Deceased knew that I would not be returning that night and when I left him at about 8 p.m. we were on good terms.[19]

Representatives from the gas company then proceeded to point out that no defect had been found with the gas pipe and, although it could not be ascertained whether there had ever been a plug or whether it had recently been removed, the local manager added that 'he could not understand anyone not noticing the escape of gas, since there would be a very strong hissing noise.' In a conversation with Robert Beckhard in 1955 Lionel Jellinek claimed that he had seen Philip in the Tite street flat two or three days before his death. 'The gas tap was so loose it went around with the touch of a finger;

Jellinek warned Philip, who replied that "it may come in very use-ful". In the same conversation Jellinek also told Beckhard that Philip forgot to put a shilling in the gas meter one night when he tried to end his life earlier, adding "it was essential that Philip died, that he had a weak hold on life, that his creative will was stronger than his will to live." '[20]

In his summing up the coroner said:

I have been to the premises and I thought that the tap on the gas turned abnormally easily, so that anyone walking alongside the pipe might turn it on without knowing. It is unlikely, however, they would turn it full on. . . . you would have to remember that if the tap had been turned on he would have smelt the gas before he lay down on the couch, unless he was badly intoxi-cated. The medical evidence does not suggest that he was the worse for alcohol.

Then, of course there was the draft will on the table. That has a significance, and the woman witness has referred to something in the nature of a quarrel. Although that quarrel was of a minor character, it might also be related to the affair.

After deliberating in private for about a quarter of an hour, the jury was unable to say whether Philip's death was due to accident or suicide and the coroner accordingly recorded an open verdict. Offering the family sympathy in Philip's 'tragic death', the coroner added that 'the musical world had lost a figure prominent both in composition and literature'.[21]

In the unpublished typescript of a proposed book on van Dieren, Gray claimed that van Dieren took it to heart more than any of them: 'In fact it is not going too far to say that he was obsessed with the tragedy until the end of his own life . . . It is characteristic that for a long time he would not admit that it had been suicide, but stoutly maintained that it was perfectly explicable as the result of an accident.'[22] However, a moving letter written to Taylor in April 1931 suggests that in his own mind van Dieren had no doubt as to Philip's real intention that fateful night. It is particularly inter-esting to read his account of that last visit and his comments on Philip's personality:

I need hardly tell you how much you have been in my thoughts these last few months. When reading through Philip's papers, I was reminded of you every moment. Your manuscripts had a place of honour and the tone of your corre-spondence showed how you were one of the few for whom he deeply cared. . . .

You can understand what I have suffered—I loved Philip like a brother, a son and a friend all in one. And I admired and loved him for his brilliant gifts. He became ever more dissatisfied with life, and it was impossible to help him at all. Never have I been able to convince him that praise or encourage-ment was more than a somewhat ironic kindness. He was inclined to regard all

I ever said to him as a laborious edifice of charitable deception and I could not make him believe differently. The disharmony between his ideals and life as it revealed itself to him became so unbearable that to endure existence was an ever present pain to him. I was with him till past midnight of his last day and felt terribly unhappy about him. But when I left I am certain he had no thought of anything irrevocable. As for us it is impossible to reconstruct it all, he must early the next morning in an imperative return of his depression have acted automatically.

It was a most terrible shock, and God only knows how I lived through all the subsequent horrors of the inquest and the clashes of friends' and family's interests that converged on me. He had several years ago made me his sole heir and executor and the family solicitor informed me of this a few minutes before I had to go into the witness box![23]

And while I suffered under the irreparable loss of so dear a friend and the terrible tragedy of his whole life, I have had to fight tooth and nail against opposing interests—because only by accepting his will could I deal with his papers and the artistic side of the matter, and it has brought me much misery ever since.

Still I don't like to think how it all might have gone if he had been intestate, so I had no choice. . . .

There were many exquisite things and technically he had reached an amazing degree of perfection . . . I am sure that we might have expected very much more from him still. It is all too heartbreaking.

But at the same time, for those who watched the whole development of his life, the end seemed inevitable. Whatever might have been done for him could only have been done very many years ago, and I fear that just those who had the power to direct his later development could not have been expected to have any notion that they were not perhaps doing the best for him.[24] You, who have known him so young and to whom he was so devoted must have understood that as well as I could and will know how hopeless it is when there occurs such a discord of individual dispositions and formidable conventions.[25]

But perhaps the sensitive and understanding words which van Dieren would have appreciated better than anyone else were written to him on the same day as the inquest by Winifred Baker:

I wanted to speak a word to you this morning but it was all so unreal and inhuman that I did not find it possible.

I am glad that you, with your quietness and your long friendship, were with Philip on that last evening. I had seen him on the Friday before his death & he was more depressed and unhappy than I had ever seen him before and, in some way, remote so that I seemed to be able to do nothing for him—he was, as it were, out of one's reach and I was overwhelmed with pity for his loneliness.

I can feel almost gladness now that it is over—that he has at last found the peace and quietude he so loved and never—or seldom—could find in the world.[26]

On Boxing Day Barbara Peache anxiously wrote to Frida van Dieren, giving her instructions what to do if her diary were found among Philip's effects at Tite Street: 'I am much ashamed of ever writing anything so imbecile and childish. He [Philip] may have destroyed it. If not it will be among my papers & if Mrs B. J. saw it it would upset her. . . . it would be best destroyed at once.'[27] She also destroyed all the letters she had received from Philip, an action she later regretted, describing the letters, apart from anything else, as 'works of art in themselves'.[28]

Delius and his wife were shattered by the news of Philip's death, telling Fenby that they could think of nothing else. In a letter to their novelist friend Sydney Schiff (1869–1944), Jelka wrote poignantly:

We both feel it very deeply. Such an act gives one a sudden insight into depths of disappointment and suffering—that one cannot bear thinking of, as having been endured by a beloved friend. It is true we were rather separated thro' Phil's latter strange way of living and we lost him bit by bit. But all that is swept away by such a catastrophe. I see constantly the beautiful lovable incredibly intelligent and artistic boy of twenty—and that tragic figure lying in a gas-filled room with his face to the wall in the early morning.[29]

Edith Buckley Jones was devastated by her son's death. In his last letter to her, written a month before his death, he had gently declined her invitation to spend Christmas at Cefn Bryntalch:

I would very much rather come and visit you at some time other than Christmas. It is a season of the year that I dislike more and more as time goes on, and the Christmas atmosphere and festivities induce for me an extremity of gloom and melancholy which makes me very poor company at such a time. I find it very much better to remain more or less alone and devote myself to some quiet work. This year, too, some stuff of mine that I have never heard is being sung at Westminster Cathedral and at the Brompton Oratory on Christmas Eve and Boxing Day and I would like to attend the performance.[30]

Preserved in the British Library together with this letter is an undated postcard (illustrated with a reproduction of a drawing of one of his beloved cats) with a Christmas greeting to her which may have been included with the letter. In retrospect this last message must have been particularly heart-breaking for her:

With all my love, dearest Mother, and all that good wishes and affection can do to bring you joy this Christmas tide!
    From your devoted son
        Phil[31]

Edith Buckley Jones's distracted though moving reply to Jelka Delius's letter of sympathy shows that, despite evidence of never really being able to understand her son, her grief was very real:

I have long felt I wished to answer your most kind and sympathetic letter on the death of my own dear Phil, but somehow, I just felt I could not, & even now, I cannot believe the awful tragedy has really happened & that my dear boy has gone, with all his wonderful talents silenced for ever, & it seems all so needless he was all the world to me, & I feel quite heartbroken. I know you and Mr Delius sorrow with me, as he loved Mr Delius and his wonderful music . . . I cannot believe it is of Phil I am writing it seems as if it must be an evil dream. Forgive an incoherant [sic] letter from Phil's most sorrowing Mother.[32]

Jelka replied in January 1931 in a most beautifully worded letter:

I am thinking of you and all you must have lived through since the great sorrow came—constantly—It is a terrible loss to us. It is a sort of consolation to me that he was really happy last year in the activity about the Delius festival, where he really was, next to Beecham, the *soul* of the thing. He wrote to me constantly then about the progress of his activities. I have kept all his letters and cherish them all the more now.

We shall always love dear Phil as the best of friends, ever helpful, ever supremely intelligent and lovable, and we shall sorrow for him and miss him with you.[33]

Philip was buried on Saturday 20 December at 2.30 p.m. in the old Godalming cemetery in Nightingale Road, the service being conducted by the Reverend J. A. Chesterton, of Tenbury Wells. Among those present at the graveside were his mother and stepfather, some of his cousins, and friends such as van Dieren, Gray, Blunt, Trier, Nichols, Lorenz, Arthur Bliss, Constant Lambert, Thomas Earp, and Anthony Bernard.[34] Douglas Goldring wrote of the occasion some years later:

We were an odd lot, and I don't think 'the family' approved of any of us. Our clothes were shabby; we had no crêpe armlets or black ties; we did not lend tone to the proceedings—unless genuine grief, affection and respect on the part of the mourners can lend a funeral 'tone'—and there was a sprinkling, among the musicians and the men of letters, of common beer-drinkers from his favourite pubs. Low fellows, perhaps. But I fancy Warlock was glad to have them there. I know I should have been, in his place.[35]

The question might well be asked why Edith Buckley Jones chose Godalming and not the quiet churchyard in Llandyssil near Cefn Bryntalch where she and Walter Buckley Jones would themselves later be buried. No doubt she wanted to avoid any further unnecessary and unpleasant local publicity and the plot in far-off Godalming provided a ready-made solution. After all, his father and his father's first wife had been buried there many years before.

There always has been, and will continue to be, a great deal of speculation about Philip's death. Fred Tomlinson has some interesting theories on the subject, even though his references to the will do not take into account Philip's final second thoughts:

We may never know the facts, and no doubt the argument will go on. There is no doubt that in 1930 views on suicide were very different from those held now. Relatives were most anxious to avoid the stigma and 'the gentry' were better able to sway a coroner's decision towards 'the sensible thing'. . . .

My opinion . . . is that PH was literally 'sick to death' of a number of things. Bruce Blunt wrote of 'a combination of tendencies, events and atmosphere all meeting at zero hour'[36] and this to me is the key. (Bruce Blunt to Gray, 25 May 1943) Individually each item may not seem sufficient reason for such a drastic step, but consider the cumulative effect, added to his well-known depression at that time of year. (Was this mood brought on by memories of early Christmases with his sanctimonious Uncle Evelyn, who had died a few months earlier leaving over half a million pounds but ignoring PH in his will?)

The market for his songs—his only really successful output—appeared to have dried up. Was this due to PH having exhausted his goodwill, flogging Bernard van Dieren compositions to OUP and Curwen for far more than they could hope to recoup in sales?

He had quarrelled with his girl-friend. However serious that was, she was certainly spending the night elsewhere.

His mentor, Bernard van Dieren, arrived. No one knows what their conversation was about, but judging by existing correspondence it seems safe to bet that money came into it. PH was hopeless about money, and although fed up with van Dieren's importunities his regard for the older composer was never affected.

PH was broke as usual, even without a bottle of beer in the flat. His only source of extra money was his mother, who many years previously had formed a strong antagonism towards van Dieren. Was this final straw the realization by PH that suicide, far from being a negative act, was a positive way of helping van Dieren and annoying his mother?[37]

As has already been noted, John Ireland was one of those who gave evidence at the inquest. Philip had met Ireland in 1928 and shortly before his death was planning to write an article on his recently completed piano concerto (in E flat). In reply to the coroner's question as to whether he could throw any light on the circumstances of his death, Ireland replied that all he could say was that he thought Philip was worried about his work as a composer and possibly felt that he had not yet received the recognition his work deserved. Gray, however, later dismissed these remarks, stating that

quite apart from the fact that there was no lack of appreciation for his work, either in musical circles or with the general public, he was the last man to care, one way or the other. It was not the approbation of others that he desired or sought, and lacked, but of his own self—the only critic, the only audience to whose opinion he attached the slightest weight or consideration.[38]

It was, however, not only Gray who took exception to Ireland's remarks. Sorabji, who had known Philip for 'the best part of twenty years', wrote vehemently about Ireland's evidence in the January 1931 issue of the *New Age*:

It is unpleasant and incongruous to have to introduce a jarring note into this tribute . . . by registering a most emphatic and indignant protest against the entirely gratuitous, offensive and grotesque remarks which a certain composer—a self-alleged 'friend' of Philip Heseltine's—saw fit to make without ever being called upon to give evidence at the inquest. This gentleman . . . had the impertinent fatuity to suggest that a man of Philip Heseltine's mental and moral calibre was depressed by lack of public recognition, a suggestion as fantastic as it was untrue. Philip Heseltine had, and knew he had, the recognition and appreciation of those only whose recognition and appreciation matter to an artist, while his name was a household word with a familiar public, further, whose approval or the reverse it is a damnable insult and slander to his memory to imagine he would have ever condescended to give a moment's thought to . . . it is important for such pestilent nonsense to be contradicted lest Heseltine's memory is wronged by those who did not know him believing it.[39]

Many obituaries and tributes appeared after his death, but it was van Dieren who wrote most movingly of all in the *Musical Times*:

His heaviest burden possibly was his distracting versatility. In his earliest days he found himself burning to write about music, with the conviction that he could say more than others, and say it better. Delius's timely and discerning advice made him see that he was a composer first and foremost. Later, in a brief career as a concert reporter, he speedily discovered that a daily paper is not a suitable medium for the dissemination of ideas or the propagation of convictions.

After he had already established his fame as a composer, he returned again and again to musical journalism with conspicuous success. On a wider basis of literary endeavour he aimed higher, and again justified every ambition. As editor of the *Sackbut* he displayed a brilliance that compelled the admiration of his adversaries, and his own contributions to this and other periodicals always gave proof of an ease beyond his experience, and a knowledge beyond accepted sources. In his independent literary works . . . he eclipsed all these achievements and revealed a mastery of prose style, a lucidity in argument, and a constructive ability that in themselves would suffice to establish an author's reputation.

Neither Philip Heseltine nor 'Peter Warlock' wrote music in the grand manner or planned on a large scale. The very fact compels us to respect his artistic integrity, for he possessed all the technique required. But he distrusted the sweeping gesture as much as he feared the possibility of, like the lesser artist, repeating himself, whether for gain or fame or from habit.

Very much was still to be expected from a man who at thirty-six had acquired a sound scholarship that enabled him to meet with unwavering confidence, and on their own ground, experts schooled in the course of long lives of specialised work.

Such capacities were gained by him while an unabating flow of transcriptions, arrangements, paraphrases and adaptations—all of incontestable merit—came from his pen . . . Here was already a productivity, of high merit, on which a man's fame could securely rest. But yet all this was only part of his activity. He wrote some enchanting works for small orchestra, and enriched music with an impressive number of songs of the most exquisite workmanship, and dictated by real inspiration. I need not draw attention to their liveliness; most of them have already become well-known. In their finely-drawn melodic lines, their beautiful transparency and balanced structure, they show, as in everything Heseltine did, a consummate orderliness, a perspicuity and understanding that makes them worthy counterparts of the words which, with unfailing taste, he selected from the best of English poets. Can one give higher praise? If I knew how to, I would do it.

But if genuine emotion, infinite charm, and grace, can preserve a spirit as a living reality for future generations, the tribute of my admiration is unneeded. Much of 'Warlock's' music will have become a national treasure when all that was ever said or written about it today will be forgotten.[40]

Some eight years after his death Constant Lambert wrote in the *Radio Times* that

It would be an easy matter for me to write down the names of at least thirty of his songs which are flawless in inspiration and workmanship—songs that are the equal in every way of the poems which he always chose with such perfect taste. . . . It is no exaggeration to say that this achievement entitles him to be classed with Dowland, Mussorgsky, and Debussy as one of the greatest song-writers that music has known.[41]

In notes on his correspondence with Philip which Robert Nichols sent to Gray when the latter was writing his memoir, Nichols included the following telling paragraph:

He shared my conviction that music would never be really alive in England till academics were not afraid to hiss or bawl at the conclusion of a piece. It was the passive jelly-fish attitude of the British audiences & the tolerance of execrable performances & their omnivorous indiscriminating acceptance of every item that he particularly abominated. . . . he was not afraid of ticking off incompetence in public & this made him enemies, though, mind you, I think a good many people ultimately admired him for it. They realized that there was no self-advertisement in the process, that what he did was solely dictated by uncompromising love of the art of music and detestation of what he regarded, rightly or wrongly, as want of devotion to it & want of reverence for great composers or pretentious or specious incompetence in speaking or writing on music, performing or composing it. Personally there was nothing in all his character—so subtle & so various—that I admired more than his savage devotion to what he considered the higher interests of his art & the courage & enterprise he displayed in conversations, in writing & in organisation with regard to these interests.[42]

Even Ursula Greville, who had succeeded Philip as editor of *The Sackbut* in 1921, devoted two paragraphs to him (albeit somewhat critically) in the January 1931 number:

In a way, Philip Heseltine was my evil genius. Had he continued to edit this paper when it was taken over by the present proprietors, as they hoped, I should never have adventured, as a stopgap, into the prickly paths of journalism . . .

He had beautiful eyes and a fine forehead, and a mouth that told its own tale, but that might have been moulded to a firm and flexible beauty had his behaviour tallied with the promise his eyes made. But he would sometimes sacrifice a friendship to make a smart saying, so that some who might have been his sincerest friends were not always his most intimate . . . and it was his misfortune to have a commanding influence on those he met, so that the weak ones joined him against the wall, and the strong ones gathered yet more strength from this strange dominating unbridled personality.[43]

Philip was one of the first to recognize the talent of the young South African poet Roy Campbell, and it was in the pages of *The Sackbut* that some of his poems first appeared. It would, therefore, seem fitting to allow Campbell to pay the final tribute to Philip in the poem which appeared in 1936 in a volume entitled *Mithraic Emblems*:[44]

Dedication of a Tree

To 'Peter Warlock'

This laurel-tree to Heseltine I vow
With one cicada silvering its shade—
Who lived, like him, a golden gasconade,
And will die whole when winter burns the bough:
Who in one hour, resounding, clear, and strong,
A century of ant-hood far out-glows,
And burns more sunlight in a single song
Than they can store against the winter snows.

APPENDICES

Philip Heseltine's Dublin Lecture[1]

I should like to dispel at the very outset the impression which some of you may have formed, in anticipation, of the nature of this discourse—an impression that before coming to the real music of the evening, you will have to endure a tedious half-hour of technicalities addressed by a specialist to his fellow-specialists in the art in question. This is not the case. I do not come before you as a specialist nor as a professional musician: I do not come before you to uphold the claims of the specialist or the professional musician, or to extol their virtues. On the contrary, I believe that at present the Art of Music has no greater enemy than the specialist, the professional musician.

If this statement astonishes you, I hope that before the evening is over I shall have done something at least to mitigate your astonishment, if not dispel it entirely.

The specialist, in nine cases out of ten, confines himself to the *letter* of his subject and he takes the *spirit* for granted—which generally means that he ignores it altogether. One may well ask—What do they know of music that only music know?

I do not want to say much about the Letter of Music—about the technique of music; most of you would be profoundly bored if I did and not in the least edified. So I shall confine myself almost entirely to the Spirit of Music—for that, after all, is What Music Is. Spirit, I know, is a vague word—I shall endeavour to define it more explicitly later on—but it stands as a symbol of the very basis of all Art, for no art can be based upon its own technique. One needs no technique to love music and understand it: but the greatest technician may lack both understanding and love. It is absolutely necessary to seek *first* the Kingdom of God within ourselves—and all subsidiary things will be added unto us afterwards.[2]

This simple and fundamental direction will no doubt provoke the same kind of superior sneer in the modern 'intellectuals' as Elisha provoked in that captain of the hosts of Syria whom he bade go and wash seven times in the river Jordan if he would be made whole.[3] Prescribe them a course of the heaviest and abstrusest textbooks and they will pursue it eagerly, even if it lead them nowhere: but bid them listen for the still small voice[4] of the unknown within them and they will jeer at you as an impractical imbecile.

This, however, is only to be expected of the type of mind which rejects the Bible as an old wives' tale, the Bhagavad-Gita[5] as the nebulous rhapsodising of half-civilised maniacs, and acclaims as its prophet an individual of the name of Wells[6] who, having temporarily exhausted the interest of the English suburbs, now deigns to apply his great mind to the 'problem' of God. I, for my part, could wish for no higher compliment than the derision of this kind of 'advanced' and 'intellectual' person.

Now I have often observed amongst people interested in the arts in general that while they take a keen delight in discussing and appraising literature, painting or sculpture—and are quite able to do so with natural insight and intelligence—they adopt quite another tone when they come to deal with music. When the subject is mentioned they at once assume an attitude of extreme humility and almost superstitious deference, as of the uninitiated before a mystery. They 'know what they like' but they are bashful about delivering an opinion of it, pleading lack of sufficient knowledge of music. Now what can this mean? If we were to ask anyone his opinion of a novel or a book of verse it is unlikely that he would say—'I am not a literary man, and therefore have no right to form an opinion on it one way or the other'. If he had read the book, he would doubtless give us his opinion without any further ado or apology. It might be that, having no very comprehensive knowledge of literature, he would lack the *comparative* standard of criticism: but that is by no means a *sine qua non* of literary judgements. Indeed, excessive cultivation of this standard may lead us so far astray that at length we can perceive only the *relative* value of different works, and are made blind to the absolute worth and intrinsic significance of any single one.

Books are not written for literary persons, nor music for musicians. Art is for the world at large—he who hath ears to hear, let him hear.[7]

Professional criticism, in all the arts, is inclined to dwell overmuch upon the means and methods of the creative faculty to the neglect of the created thing itself. Thus the *code* comes to be considered more important than the message, the *sign* than the thing signified.[8] And in this way a great barrier has been interposed between the creative artist and the public to whom he would appeal—a barrier unreal and unsubstantial enough, it is true, but which maintains its existence by sheer virtue of *its being believed in*. The mystery once established, it is natural that those responsible for its perpetuation should turn it to their own pecuniary advantage, arrogating to themselves the sole right of lifting the veil—in return for money, of course. And it is equally natural that, with the passage of time and the continuance of this practise [*sic*], the veil should become heavier and heavier!

One is reminded of the people who enclose within high walls some ancient monument, or some spot of great natural beauty—and charge sixpence for admission where all should be free. It is my object to try and show up the absurdity of this bogey of technical knowledge, to expose some of the machinery of its manipulation, to try and make people understand that they *are free*—to use their own ears and to form their own tastes.[9] I hope also to be able to indicate briefly what education can and can not do with regard to music.

It will be as well to begin at the very beginning, to be quite precise in the definition of every term we employ. I hope thus to render unnecessary the habitual question 'Do you like Music?' which one stranger will ask another without having the least idea what either himself or the other means by Music—as also that equally fatuous question which invariably follows an affirmative answer to the first—'Then what instrument do you play?'

It is necessary to frame a definition of music, to state what is its nature, its function, its scope: and to determine what it is that we require of music—what we turn to music for, that we cannot find elsewhere. And in this enquiry we must be guided not only by the [at this point the text breaks off]

Poems by Philip Heseltine

Wonderment

I watched the moon set in a sea of golden gloom
  Like a soft horn-tone, merging in the twilight chord:
  Yet in the sickle image of the moon a sword
Lurks, and the horn but echoes trumpet shrieks of doom—
And men exult to drink the darkness of the tomb,
To pay the great price for the steely mastery,
And scorn to live and dream, and taste the ecstacy
The moon sheds, sinking in a sea of sable gloom.
14 October 1914[10]

A Delectable Ballad in which is Set Forth ye Futilitie of Remorsefull Retrospection

A signpost at a fork o' the road—
    Two white arms a-poise—
On a bank behind, up in the sunshine,
    A golden noise
        Of gorse rings out aflame. . . .

On a cross set by the roadside
    Hangs a dismal man,
While a lark above him, fluttering and twittering,
    Asks how he can
        Play at such a queer game.

'Alas, in the bridal bed, I
    Slew my purple love,
For which I cannot sufficiently crucify myself,
    Or remove
        The black brand of shame. . . .'

Then up comes a black man
    And 'Ha' and 'Ho' says he,
'I see nothing half as black as the face
    God gave me,
        And that's a fine face, I claim!'
Over the sun-strewn heather
    A wild girl dances
And casts on the man hanging so glib and so glum
    Merry glances,
        And bids him tell his name.
Then on a sudden, what with
    The black man and the girl and the sun,
'Cripes', says he, 'what the Hell am I doing?
    What's done's done,
        Whosoever's to blame.
'Do you suppose I'm Jesus
    Saving humanity,
Or Judas Iscariot, expatiating himself?
    (What vanity!)
        For you know it's all the same.
'No, I'm only an ordinary
    Thief, and old Pilate
Never caught me, yet here I am! Now isn't that
    Something to smile at?
        Down with this bloody frame!
'We're three fine vagabonds.
    The wind and the rain
And empty purses don't matter a damn. Let's go
    Thieving again!
        (Oh, but it's good you came!)
'Now for the rest of time
    We'll wander over
Open country, lie in the fields of
    Sainfoin[11] and clover,
        And sing ourselves to fame.
'And whenever we see a signpost
    With white arms a-poise
Like a blooming crucifix, trying to lead
    Wild girls and boys
        By the hard road to the town

'Of smoke and sacrifices, pretending
   Moors are trespassers' land,
We'll climb up the bank behind it, when it's not looking,
   Into the sunshine, and
       Pull the bloody thing down!'[12]

'You'll never come to Hy-Brasil,'
  —A piskie[13] whispers through your hair—
'By bending to another's will.
  For picks[14] and packs you may not bear
Across the sea to Hy-Brasil
  And you may sweat and you may swear
And swink[15] and think until you're ill
  And die before you're e'er aware;
There's such a place as Hy-Brasil.
  For gold can never pay your fare
(*illegible*)   for Hy-Brasil.
  So have a care, so have a care. . . .
From Trewey Down and Zennor Hill
  You'd ride a puffin through the air
And circle over Hy-Brasil.
  But now from city windows stare—
There's not a sign of Hy-Brasil.
  As if to drive you to despair
The fog sits on your windowsill.
  You take a map and seek the rare,
The golden land of Hy-Brasil.
  You cannot find it anywhere—
The faery isle eludes you still. . . .
  You say it simply isn't there,
And raise a monster you must kill
  (An if you dare, an if you dare)
And lay his bones in Hy-Brasil,
  Or he will hunt you like a hare,
Or grind you in his grisly mill,
  And eat you in his lurid lair.
So never dare to rest until
  You let the piskie in your hair
Whisk you away t'wards Hy-Brasil,
  By your desire, against your will.'
(So piskie sang to piskie Phyl!!)
16 April 1917[16]

An example of Philip's music calligraphy, 'Music, when soft voices die' (1911).

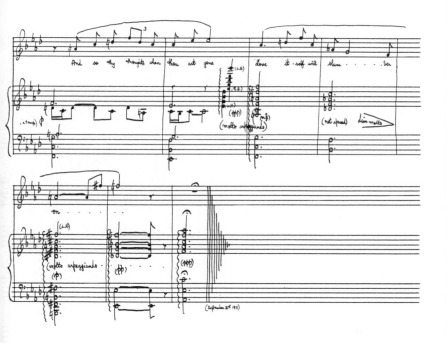

NOTES

Chapter 1

1. R. Bennett, 'Peter Warlock: The Man and his Songs', *Bookman*, 64 (1923), 300–2.
2. Heseltine to Delius, 22 Apr. 1916.
3. Heseltine to his mother, 4 Apr. 1921.
4. C. Gray, *Peter Warlock: A Memoir of Philip Heseltine* (London, 1934), 164–6.
5. Heseltine to Delius, 17 Dec. 1913.
6. J. Lindsay, *Fanfrolico and After* (London, 1962), 87.
7. Heseltine to Viva Smith, 30 Oct. 1913.
8. Joseph Heseltine to his nephew, 23 July 1912, BL, Add. MS 57962.
9. Heseltine to Viva Smith, 20 Sept. 1913.
10. I. Parrott, 'Warlock in Wales', *Musical Times* (1964), 740–1.
11. Heseltine to Gray, 19 Nov. 1921.
12. Ibid.
13. G. Cockshott, 'E. J. Moeran's Recollections of Peter Warlock', *Musical Times* (1955), 128–30.
14. Conversation with the author, 16 Aug. 1992.
15. K. Clark, *Another Part of the Wood: A Self-Portrait* (London, 1974), 52–3.
16. Heseltine to his mother, 29 Apr. 1904.
17. Miss A. L. Cooper to Ian Copley, 4 Feb. 1963, I. Copley, *The Music of Peter Warlock: A Critical Survey* (London, 1979), 1.
18. Florence Peck to Edith Buckley Jones, undated, BL, Add. MS 57964.
19. Copley, *Music of Warlock*, 1.
20. BL, Add. MS 57964.
21. Gray, *Warlock*, 36.
22. Heseltine to Cecil Gray, 14 June 1922.
23. 1905, BL, Add. MS 57967.
24. Herbert Ward to John Bishop, 1 Oct. 1972, PW Society archives.
25. Heseltine to his mother, 1 May 1904.
26. Heseltine to his mother, 3 July 1904.
27. Heseltine to his mother, 21 Sept. 1906.
28. Heseltine to his mother, 23 Sept. 1906.
29. Heseltine to his mother, 19 Mar. 1906.
30. Heseltine to his mother, 12 Dec. 1906.
31. Heseltine to his mother, 29 Apr. 1904.
32. Heseltine to his mother, 16 Dec. 1906.
33. Heseltine to his mother, 2 Apr. 1906.

34. Heseltine to his mother, 1 May 1904.
35. Heseltine to his mother, 20 May 1908.
36. Bennett, 'Peter Warlock', 300–3.
37. Heseltine to Delius, 24 Mar. 1914.
38. Heseltine to Taylor, 25 July 1913.
39. Gray, *Warlock*, 35.
40. Heseltine to his mother, 17 Sept. 1908.
41. Heseltine to his mother, 17 Feb. 1911.
42. Gray, *Warlock*, 37.
43. Heseltine to Delius, 25 Mar. 1912.
44. C. Taylor, 'Peter Warlock at Eton', *Composer*, 4 (1964), 9–10.
45. The Revd G. J. Chitty's Classical Report for Michaelmas School-Time, 1909, BL Add. MS 57964.
46. *Eton College Chronicle* (3 Nov. 1910), 790.
47. A. Rowley, 'The Music of Peter Warlock', *Musical Mirror* (Aug. 1927), 183–4.
48. *Eton College Chronicle* (1 Aug. 1911), 966.
49. Heseltine to his mother, 30 Oct. 1910.
50. Heseltine to his mother, 31 Oct. 1910.
51. Heseltine to his mother, 20 Feb. 1910.
52. Heseltine to his mother, 28 June 1910.
53. Heseltine to his mother, 7 Oct. 1910.
54. Heseltine to his mother, 13 Dec. 1910.
55. Heseltine to his mother, 12 Feb. 1911.
56. G. T. Leigh Spencer lived in the village Clifford, just across the river from Whitney-on-Wye, where the young Heseltine used to visit his aunt at the Rectory. Although Leigh Spencer was some years older than Philip they evidently enjoyed a lively friendship, as can be seen from their correspondence in the BL, Add MS 57964.
57. Heseltine to his mother, 7 May 1911.
58. Heseltine to his mother, 25 May 1911.
59. Heseltine to his mother, 30 May 1911.
60. Heseltine to his mother, 5 June 1911.
61. Heseltine to his mother, 7 June 1911.
62. Taylor, 'Warlock at Eton', 10.
63. Heseltine to his mother, 15 June 1911.
64. Heseltine to his mother, 18 June 1911.
65. Ibid.
66. Heseltine to Delius, 17 June 1911.
67. Heseltine to his mother, 18 June 1911.
68. Delius to Taylor, 18 Dec. 1911, Cape Town, UCT Library, BC76 A4.149.
69. Heseltine to his mother, 21 Mar. 1911.
70. Brinton to Edith Buckley Jones, 5 Apr. 1911, BL, Add. MS 57964.
71. Heseltine to his mother, 7 May 1911.
72. Gray, *Warlock*, 34–5.
73. Heseltine to Taylor, 31 July 1911.

Chapter 2

1. Joseph Heseltine to his nephew, 6 Nov. 1911, BL, Add. MS 57962.
2. Heseltine to Delius, 17 Dec. 1911.
3. Willem Kes (1856–1934), Dutch violinist and conductor.
4. *La Nursery*, piano duets based on French folk-songs by the French composer and conductor Désiré-Émile Inghelbrecht (1880–1965).
5. Heseltine to Delius, 25 Nov. 1911.
6. Heseltine to Delius, 27 Nov. 1911.
7. Ibid.
8. Delius to Heseltine, 26 Nov. 1911.
9. Delius to Heseltine, 4 Dec. 1911.
10. Heseltine to his mother, 5 Dec. 1911.
11. Heseltine to Taylor, 24 Jan. 1912.
12. Heseltine to Taylor, 6 Dec. 1911.
13. Ibid.
14. Heseltine to Delius, 28 Feb. 1912.
15. Ibid.
16. Heseltine to Delius, 15 Dec. 1911.
17. Heseltine to Taylor, 6 Dec. 1911.
18. Heseltine to Delius, 17 Jan. 1912.
19. Heseltine to Viva Smith, 18 Oct. 1913.
20. Heseltine to Taylor, 24 Jan. 1912.
21. P. Heseltine, 'A Note on the Mind's Ear', *Musical Times* (1922), 88–90.
22. C. Gray, *Peter Warlock: A Memoir of Philip Heseltine* (London, 1934), 140.
23. I. Copley, *The Music of Peter Warlock: A Critical Survey* (London, 1979), 55.
24. Heseltine to Delius, 18 Dec. 1912.
25. Heseltine to Taylor, 9 Feb. 1912.
26. This quotation in Gray (*Warlock*, 46) is an amalgam of two letters, one undated and another from Delius to Heseltine, 4 Dec. 1911.
27. Heseltine to Delius, 28 Feb. 1912.
28. Heseltine to Delius, 25 Mar. 1912.
29. Delius to Heseltine, 11 Mar. 1912.
30. Heseltine to Delius, 25 Nov. 1911.
31. Heseltine to Taylor, 27 June 1912.
32. Heseltine to Taylor, 24 May 1912.
33. Delius to Heseltine, 25 Mar. 1912.
34. Delius to Heseltine, 28 Apr. 1912.
35. Delius to Heseltine, 27 July 1912.
36. Rolt to Edith Buckley Jones, 7 June 1912, BL, Add. MS 57964.
37. Heseltine to Delius, 7 July 1912.
38. Heseltine to Delius, 18 Dec. 1912.
39. Heseltine to Delius, 7 July 1912.
40. Rolt to Edith Buckley Jones, 5 Aug. 1912, BL, Add. MS 57964.
41. Heseltine to Taylor, 6 Mar. 1912.
42. Heseltine, 'Mind's Ear', 177.
43. Delius to Heseltine, 24 Sept. 1912.
44. S.O.G., 'What is Cacophony?' *Musical Standard* (Supplement 1912), 40.

45. P. Heseltine, 'Arnold Schönberg and Cacophony', *Musical Standard*, 38 (1912), 233.
46. S.O.G., 'Arnold Schönberg and Cacophony', *Musical Standard* (Supplement 1912), 44.
47. Shakespeare, *Macbeth*, v. vi. 27.
48. Heseltine to Taylor, 2 Oct. 1912.
49. Elgar to Alice Stuart-Wortley, 7 Oct. 1912, Hereford and Worcester County Record Office 705: 445: 7109.
50. Heseltine to Taylor, 9 Oct. 1912.
51. L. Strong, *John McCormack: The Story of a Singer* (London, 1941), 104–5.
52. Heseltine to Taylor, 9 Oct. 1912.
53. Balfour Gardiner to Heseltine, 21 Oct. 1912, photocopy in PW Society archives.
54. Heseltine to Delius, 28 Dec. 1913.
55. Heseltine to Delius, 25 Nov. 1912.
56. Heseltine to his mother, 2 Nov. 1912.
57. Christ Church authorities to Edith Buckley Jones, 14 Dec. 1912, BL, Add. MS 57964.
58. Heseltine to Taylor, 1 Feb. 1913.
59. Eton schoolboy slang for Jesus Christ.
60. Heseltine to Taylor, 17 Feb. 1913.
61. Heseltine to Delius, 8 Jan. 1913.
62. Heseltine to Taylor, 1 Feb. 1913.
63. Delius to Heseltine, 11 Jan. 1913.
64. Heseltine to Taylor, 1 Feb. 1913.
65. Heseltine to Delius, 17 Feb. 1913.
66. Gray, *Warlock*, 56.
67. Ibid. 59.
68. T. Beecham, *Frederick Delius* (London, 1959), 175.
69. Heseltine to Delius, 11 Oct. 1916.
70. Beecham, *Delius*, 176.
71. Ibid. 176–80.
72. Heseltine to Delius, 28 Jan. 1913.
73. Heseltine to his mother, 10 July 1913.
74. Heseltine to Taylor, 7 Apr. 1913.
75. Heseltine to Taylor, 25 July 1913.
76. Heseltine to Taylor, 5 Oct. 1913.
77. Heseltine to Viva Smith, 20 Sept. 1913.
78. Heseltine to Viva Smith, 25 Sept. 1913.
79. Joseph Heseltine to his nephew, 3 Oct. 1913, BL, Add. MS 57962.
80. Heseltine to Viva Smith, 2 July 1914.
81. Heseltine to Taylor, 5 Oct. 1913.
82. *Requiem*, for soprano, baritone, double chorus, and orchestra (1914–16).
83. Heseltine to Viva Smith, undated, Sept., 1913.
84. Heseltine to Taylor, 25 July 1913.
85. Sorabji to Heseltine, 3 Oct. 1913, BL, Add. MS 57963.
86. A. Hinton, 'Kaikhosru Sorabji and Erik Chisholm', *Jagger Journal*, 10 (1989/90), 21.
87. Heseltine to Taylor, 4 Feb. 1914.

Chapter 3

1. Heseltine to Viva Smith, 10 Oct. 1913.
2. M. Deneke, *Ernest Walker* (London, 1951), 66.
3. H. Foss, 'Introductions: XIX. Philip Heseltine', *Music Bulletin*, 6 (1924), 204.
4. Heseltine to his mother, 16 Feb. 1914.
5. Thomas Armstrong to Ian Copley, I. Copley, *The Music of Peter Warlock* (London, 1979), 57.
6. C. Gray, *Peter Warlock* (London, 1934), 63.
7. Viva Smith to van Dieren, 19 Mar. 1934, PW Society archives.
8. Viva Smith to van Dieren, 25 Mar. 1934, PW Society archives.
9. Heseltine to Viva Smith, 25 July 1913.
10. Heseltine to Viva Smith, 1/2 Nov. 1913.
11. Heseltine to Viva Smith, 16 Jan. 1914.
12. Heseltine to Delius, 28 Dec. 1913.
13. Delius to Heseltine, 2 Jan. 1914.
14. Heseltine to Viva Smith, 17 Jan. 1914.
15. Heseltine to Viva Smith, 24/25 Nov. 1913.
16. Heseltine to Viva Smith, 1 Feb. 1914.
17. Heseltine to Viva Smith, 16 Oct. 1913.
18. Heseltine to Delius, 17 Dec. 1913.
19. Heseltine to Viva Smith, 5 Mar. 1914.
20. Heseltine to Viva Smith, 6 Mar. 1914.
21. Heseltine to Viva Smith, 30 Oct. 1913.
22. Heseltine to Viva Smith, 19 June 1914.
23. Diary of Winifred Wood, 15 July 1914, copy in PW Society archives.
24. Gray, *Warlock*, 234.
25. Information from a letter to the author from Robert Beckhard, 5 Mar. 1993.
26. Blunt to Cockshott, July 1943, from notes given to Robert Beckhard by Cockshott in July 1955, and in a letter to the present author, 16 July 1993.
27. Joseph Heseltine to Philip, postcard, c.1911, BL, Add. MS 57962.
28. Joseph Heseltine to Philip, 6 July 1912, BL, Add. MS 57962.
29. Sorabji to Heseltine, 12 Apr. 1922, BL, Add. MS 57963.
30. D. Goldring, *Odd Man Out: The Autobiography of a 'Propaganda' Novelist* (London, 1935), 183.
31. A. Bliss, *As I Remember* (London, 1970), 45.
32. Gray, *Warlock*, 61–92.
33. Ibid. 72.
34. Ibid. 83–5.
35. Heseltine to Delius, 28 Dec. 1913.
36. Heseltine to Nichols, 25 Dec. 1913, BL, Add. MS 57796.
37. Ibid.
38. Heseltine to Viva Smith, 14 Feb. 1914.
39. Sorabji to Heseltine, 8 Dec. 1913, BL, Add. MS 57963.
40. Heseltine to Viva Smith, 24 Aug. 1914.
41. Delius to Heseltine, 2 Jan. 1914.
42. Heseltine to Viva Smith, 12 Feb. 1914.
43. Heseltine to Delius, 11 Feb. 1914.
44. Heseltine to Delius, 24 Mar. 1914.

45. Heseltine to Viva Smith, undated, ?Mar. 1914.
46. Heseltine to Delius, 24 Mar. 1914.
47. Heseltine to his mother, 16 Feb. 1914.
48. Heseltine to Taylor, 3 Apr. 1914.
49. S. G. Owen mark-book, Oxford, Christ Church archives, lxx a.46.
50. Heseltine to his mother, 17 July 1914.
51. Heseltine to Delius, 10 July 1914.
52. B. Lunn, *Switchback: An Autobiography* (London, 1948), 78.
53. Heseltine to Taylor, 7 Sept. 1914.
54. Heseltine to Delius, 18 Oct. 1914.
55. Heseltine to Viva Smith, 24 Sept. 1914.

Chapter 4

1. Heseltine to Delius, 18 Oct. 1914.
2. Ibid.
3. N. Heseltine, *Capriol for Mother* (London, 1992), 119.
4. Heseltine to Delius, 18 Oct. 1914.
5. Heseltine to Fritz Hart, 15 Nov. 1921, photocopy in PW Society archives.
6. Heseltine to Fritz Hart, 7 Feb. 1922, photocopy in PW Society archives.
7. *New Age*, 16 (1914), 134.
8. Ibid. (Dec. 1914).
9. Heseltine to Fritz Hart, 7 Feb. 1922, photocopy in PW Society archives.
10. Heseltine to Viva Smith, 24 Dec. 1914.
11. Heseltine to Viva Smith, 7 Jan. 1915.
12. A. Jenkins, *The Twenties* (London, 1974), 165.
13. Lady Maud Cunard to Heseltine, 3 Feb. 1915, photocopy in PW Society archives.
14. *Daily Mail* (9 Feb. 1915), 3.
15. *Musical Times* (1915), 137.
16. Ibid. 140.
17. Ibid. 141.
18. Heseltine to Delius, 28 Mar. 1915.
19. Lord Alfred Charles William Harmsworth Northcliffe (1865–1922), one of the most successful and powerful newspaper publishers of his day.
20. Delius to Heseltine, ?8 Apr. 1915.
21. Heseltine to Viva Smith, 24 Mar. 1915.
22. Heseltine to his mother, 11 Apr. 1915.
23. Delius to Heseltine, 25 Mar. 1914.
24. Heseltine to Viva Smith, 7 May 1915.
25. J. Rhys, 'Till September Petronella', *London Magazine*, 7 (1960), 19–39.
26. C. Angier, *Jean Rhys: Life and Work* (London, 1992), 90.
27. E. Goossens, *Overture and Beginners* (London, 1951), 111–12.
28. Gardiner to Heseltine, 14 Sept. 1915, photocopy in PW Society archives.
29. E. Goossens, *Overture and Beginners*, 111–12.
30. C. Gray, *Peter Warlock* (London, 1934), 257–8.
31. Lindsay's Fanfrolico Press was begun in Australia in 1922 and re-established in London in 1926.
32. J. Lindsay, *Fanfrolico and After* (London, 1962), 27.

33. Heseltine to Taylor, 12 Nov. 1915.
34. Heseltine to Delius, 22 Aug. 1915.
35. Heseltine to Taylor, 13 Mar. 1916.
36. Heseltine to Delius, 22 Aug. 1915.
37. Heseltine to Taylor, 12 Nov. 1915.
38. Heseltine to Viva Smith, 4 Nov. 1914.
39. B. Lunn, *Switchback* (London, 1948), 92.
40. Heseltine to Taylor, 12 Nov. 1915.

Chapter 5

 1. Heseltine to Viva Smith, 27 Feb. 1914.
 2. Heseltine to Viva Smith, 16 Oct. 1914.
 3. Lawrence to Nichols, 17 Nov. 1915: *The Letters of D. H. Lawrence*, ed.
    G. J. Zytaruk and J. T. Boulton, ii (Cambridge, 1981), 442–3.
 4. Heseltine to Taylor, 25 Nov. 1915.
 5. Lawrence to Henry Savage, 2 Dec. 1913, *Letters*, ii. 113–14.
 6. C. Gray, *Peter Warlock* (London, 1934), 114.
 7. Lawrence to Heseltine, 22 Nov. 1915, *Letters*, ii. 447–8. For Chrustchoff
    see below.
 8. J. Meyers, *D. H. Lawrence: A Biography* (London, 1990), 159.
 9. O. Morrell, *Ottoline at Garsington: Memoirs of Lady Ottoline Morrell
    1915–1918*, ed. R. Gathorne-Hardy (London, 1974), 255.
10. Ch. 8, 'Breadalby'. The 1988 edn. of *Women in Love* quoted throughout
    this chapter uses the text of the 1987 Cambridge edn. in which Lawrence's
    original words are restored. Lawrence was forced to rewrite certain pas-
    sages after Heseltine's threat of a libel action in 1921.
11. Ottoline Morrell to Bertrand Russell, 6 Dec. 1915, P. Delany, *D. H.
    Lawrence's Nightmare: The Writer and His Circle in the Years of the Great
    War* (Hassocks, 1979), 174.
12. Frieda Lawrence to Cynthia Asquith, post 20 May 1916, *Letters*, ii. 606.
13. Lawrence to Ottoline Morrell, 22 Nov. 1915, *Letters*, ii. 449–50.
14. Delius to Heseltine, 24 Nov. 1915.
15. Heseltine to Delius, 15 Dec. 1915.
16. Delius to Heseltine, 21 Dec. 1915.
17. Lawrence to Cynthia Asquith, 5 Dec. 1915: *Letters*, ii. 465–7.
18. Lawrence to Ottoline Morrell, 12 Dec. 1915: ibid. 473–5.
19. Ottoline Morrell's diary, 3 Dec. 1915: *Ottoline at Garsington* (see n. 9), 77.
20. Ibid. 86.
21. J. Huxley, *Leaves of the Tulip Tree* (London, 1986), 48–9.
22. Ibid.
23. C. Gray, *Musical Chairs or Between Two Stools* (London, 1948), 291.
24. Heseltine to Boris de Chrustchoff, 14 Dec. 1915, BL, Add. MS 57794.
25. Lawrence to Heseltine, ?18 Dec. 1915: *Letters*, ii. 480–1.
26. Huxley, *Tulip Tree*, 48–9.
27. Ibid.
28. These details are from Heseltine's marriage certificate. Minnie Channing's
    birth certificate (registration district: Brentford, Chiswick) gives her
    father's name as Robert *Silas* Channing; occupation, hotel waiter.

29. P. Delany 'Halliday's Progress: Letters of Philip Heseltine', *D. H. Lawrence Review*, 13 (1980), 131.
30. Delany, *Lawrence's Nightmare*, 201.
31. Lawrence to Cynthia Asquith, 30 Dec. 1915: *Letters*, ii. 491.
32. Lawrence to Catherine Carswell, 31 Dec. 1915: ibid. 493.
33. Lawrence to Murry, ?9 Jan. 1916, ibid. 500.
34. Heseltine to Delius, 11 Feb. 1916.
35. Lawrence to Ottoline Morrell, 25 Feb. 1916: *Letters*, ii. 556.
36. Heseltine to Delius, 6 Jan. 1916.
37. Delius to Heseltine, 22 Jan. 1916.
38. Heseltine to Delius, 11 Feb. 1916.
39. Lawrence to Ottoline Morrell, 9 Jan. 1916: *Letters*, ii. 501–2.
40. Lawrence to Ottoline Morrell, 13 Jan. 1916: ibid, 503–4.
41. Lawrence to Ottoline Morrell, 17 Jan. 1916: ibid. 506–7.
42. Lawrence to Ottoline Morrell, 9 Jan. 1916: ibid. 501–2.
43. 'As for the Armenian who was here, I had to expel him by violence, he proved so intolerable to all of us and so impervious to all our hints of displeasure at his presence!!' Heseltine to Viva Smith, 16 Feb. 1916.
44. Heseltine to Ottoline Morrell, 28 Jan. 1916, Univ. of Texas at Austin.
45. Heseltine to Viva Smith, 16 Feb. 1916.
46. Ottoline Morrell to Bertrand Russell, 29 Feb. 1916, Delany, *Lawrence's Nightmare*, 194.
47. Lawrence to Ottoline Morrell, 27 Jan. 1916: *Letters*, ii. 517.
48. Lawrence to Ottoline Morrell, 15 Feb. 1916: ibid. 538–40.
49. Lawrence to Ottoline Morrell, 5 Jan. 1916: ibid. 501–2.
50. Lawrence to Bertrand Russell, 13 Jan. 1916: ibid. 505–6.
51. Lawrence to Ottoline Morrell, 25 Feb. 1916: ibid. 556–7.
52. Frieda Lawrence to Mark Gertler, early Mar. 1916: ibid. 548–50.
53. Lawrence to Ottoline Morrell, 15 Feb. 1916: ibid. 538–40.
54. Lawrence to Murry & Mansfield, 24 Feb. 1916: ibid. 548–50.
55. Lawrence to Heseltine, 24 Feb. 1916: ibid. 551.
56. Heseltine to Nichols, 8 Mar. 1916, Gray, *Warlock*, 116.
57. R. Nichols, Notes on the Heseltine correspondence, BL, Add. MS 577965.
58. Lawrence to S. S. Kotelianksy, 25 Feb. 1916: *Letters*, ii. 554.
59. Lawrence to Heseltine, ante 22 Apr. 1916: ibid. 598.
60. Heseltine to Delius, 22 Apr. 1916.
61. Murry to Ottoline Morrell, undated, *D. H. Lawrence Review*, 6 (1973), 42.
62. Murry to Ottoline Morrell, 14 May 1916, Delany, *Lawrence's Nightmare*, 232–3.
63. Heseltine to Delius, 22 Apr. 1916.
64. Gray, *Warlock*, 119.
65. Morrell, *Ottoline at Garsington* (see n. 9), 93.

Chapter 6

1. Heseltine to Delius, 22 Apr. 1916.
2. D. H. Lawrence, *Women in Love* (London, 1988), 63.
3. G. Deghy and K. Waterhouse, *Café Royal: Ninety Years of Bohemia* (London, 1955), 17.

4. A. John, *Chiaroscuro* (London, 1952), 80–1.
5. C. Gray, *Peter Warlock* (London, 1934). 15.
6. Nichols's notes on the Heseltine correspondence, BL, Add. MS 57796.
7. E. Fenby (in conversation with David Cox), 'Warlock as I knew him', *Composer*, 82 (1984), 19–23.
8. J. Epstein, *Let There be Sculpture: An Autobiography* (London, 1940), 138.
9. C. Gray, *Musical Chairs or Between Two Stools* (London, 1948), 98.
10. Ibid. 99.
11. Gray, *Warlock*, 125.
12. 'You remember how Old Mog used to approach when I was playing and seat himself ecstatically upon the lid of the piano?' Heseltine to Gray, 18 June 1920.
13. Gray, *Warlock*, 129.
14. I. Copley, *The Music of Peter Warlock* (London, 1979), 11.
15. E. Poston, script of 'Warlock', BBC broadcast (12 Dec. 1964), 2.
16. Heseltine to Taylor, 5 June 1916.
17. P. Heseltine, *Palatine Review*, 5 (1917), 25–9.
18. B. van Dieren quoted by Arthur Bliss in a BBC broadcast (Apr. 1937).
19. Ibid.
20. *Radio Times* (2 Apr. 1937): F. Tomlinson, *Warlock and van Dieren* (London, 1978), 16.
21. C. Palmer, *Herbert Howells: A Centenary Celebration* (London, 1992), 354.
22. c.1375–1428, Italian theorist and teacher; one of Heseltine's many pseudonyms.
23. Heseltine to van Dieren, 8 June 1916.
24. Heseltine to Taylor, 13 June 1916.
25. Heseltine's manifesto (signed Prosdocimus de Beldamandis), 18 Feb. 1917, sent from 2 Anhalt Studios, Battersea; BL, Add. MS 57961.
26. Gray's programme notes for the concert of van Dieren's works, Wigmore Hall, 20 Feb. 1917, quoted in H. Davies, 'Bernard van Dieren, Philip Heseltine and Cecil Gray: A Significant Affiliation', *Music and Letters*, 69 (1988), 30–48.
27. D. ApIvor, 'Bernard van Dieren: Search and Rescue One Hundred Years on', *Music Review*, 47 (1987), 256.
28. Gray, *Warlock*, 141.
29. *Daily Telegraph* (21 Feb. 1917).
30. *Diaphony* was dedicated to George Macdonald.
31. *The Times* (London, 21 Feb. 1917).
32. *Musical Times* (1917), 166.
33. Davies, 'Van Dieren, Heseltine and Gray', 41.
34. P. Heseltine, *Palatine Review*, 5, (1917), 25–9.
35. P. Warlock, 'Notes on Goossens' Chamber Music', *Music Student* (1916, Chamber Music Supplement, 22*a*), 23–4.
36. Heseltine to Goossens, 12 Sept. 1916, photocopy in PW Society archives.
37. P. Heseltine, 'The Condition of Music in England', *New Age*, 21 (1917), 156.
38. Cyril Beaumont to Ian Copley, 12 July 1962: Copley, *Music of Warlock*, 11.
39. Ibid., 11–12.
40. BL, Add. MS 57968–9.

41. N. Hamnett, *Is She a Lady?* (London, 1955), 30–1.
42. BL, Add. MS 57796.
43. BL, Add. MS 57796. fo. 13.
44. Heseltine to Nichols, 10 Aug. 1916.
45. Delius to Heseltine, 11 June 1916.
46. Heseltine to Delius, 11 Oct. 1916.
47. Heseltine to Goossens, 12 Sept. 1916, photocopy in PW Society archives.
48. Delius to Heseltine, 15 Oct. 1916.
49. Delius to Heseltine, 6 Nov. 1916.
50. Gardiner to Heseltine, 30 Oct. 1916, photocopy in PW Society archives.
51. Delius to Heseltine, 10 Feb. 1917.
52. Heseltine to Viva Smith, 13 May 1917.
53. Heseltine to Gray, undated, ? Aug. 1918.
54. Information supplied by R. Beckhard in a letter to the author, 27 July 1993.
55. Heseltine to Phyl Crocker, 19 Apr. 1917, BL, Add. MS 57794. See Appendix for a poem quoted in the same letter.
56. BL, Add. MS 57796.
57. J. Lindsay, *Fanfrolico and After* (London, 1962), 166.
58. Fenby, 'Warlock as I knew him', *Composer*, 82 (1984) 19–23.
59. Gray, *Warlock*, 231 and 233.
60. Nichols to Gray, 13 Feb. 1933, BL, Add. MS 57795.
61. Heseltine to Viva Smith, 13 May 1917.
62. Heseltine to Nichols, 16 Apr. 1917, Gray, *Warlock*, 145–6.
63. Lawrence to John Middleton Murry, 5 May 1917: *Letters*, iii (Cambridge, 1984), 122.
64. D. H. Lawrence, *Women in Love* (London, 1988), 55.
65. Ibid. 52 and 55.
66. This statement is confirmed in Philip's letter to Delius (11 Feb. 1916) quoted in Ch. 5.
67. *Women in Love*, 57–8.
68. Ibid. 66.
69. Ibid. 70.
70. Heseltine to Nichols, ? May 1917: Gray, *Warlock*, 152–3.
71. Heseltine to Delius, 13 May 1917.
72. Lawrence to Gray, 14 June 1917: *Letters*, iii. 134.
73. Lawrence to Gray, 6 Nov. 1917: ibid. 178–9.
74. Delius to Heseltine, 27 May 1917.
75. Heseltine to Taylor, 17 July 1917.
76. Ibid.
77. P. Heseltine, 'The Condition of Music in England', *New Age*, 21 (1917), 156.
78. Gray, *Warlock*, 78–9.
79. Heseltine to Taylor, 17 July 1917.
80. Copley, *Music of Warlock*, 218.
81. Ibid. 249.
82. Lawrence to Cynthia Asquith, 3 Sept. 1917: *Letters*, iii. 157–8.
83. Lawrence to Gray, 14 June 1917: ibid. 133.
84. Lawrence to David Eder, 24 Aug. 1917: *Letters*, iii. 149–50.
85. Ibid. 150 n.

86. Heseltine to Delius, 10 Dec. 1911.
87. Delius to Heseltine, 28 Apr. 1912.
88. Heseltine to Viva Smith, 25 Sept. 1913.
89. Heseltine to Viva Smith, 27 Apr. 1914.
90. Nichols's notes on the Heseltine correspondence, BL, Add. MS 57796.
91. Heseltine to Gray, 7 Apr. 1918.
92. Heseltine to Gray, 26 June 1917.
93. Heseltine to Taylor, 17 July 1917.
94. Lawrence to Esther Andrews, 23 Aug. 1917, copy in possession of Prof. Mark Kinkead-Weekes.
95. Heseltine to Delius, 22 Apr. 1916.
96. Heseltine to Nichols, 17 June 1917. BL, Add. MS 57796.

Chapter 7

1. J. Lindsay, *Fanfrolico and After* (London, 1962), 91.
2. D. Goldring, *Odd Man Out: The Autobiography of a 'Propaganda' Novelist* (London, 1935), 181–2.
3. L. Shepherd (ed.), *Encyclopedia of Occultism and Parapsychology* (Detroit, 1991), 455.
4. Heseltine to his mother, 1 Oct. 1917.
5. Minnie Lucy Heseltine to Edith Buckley Jones, 1 Oct. 1917, BL, Add. MS 57961.
6. Heseltine to Gray, ? before Mar. 1918.
7. Heseltine to Gray, 9 June 1918.
8. Heseltine to Nichols, 14 May 1918, BL, Add. MS 57795.
9. C. Gray, *Peter Warlock* (London, 1934), 151.
10. i.e. 'alligators', a term used by Philip and Gray for 'cash'.
11. Trans. Professor Kathy Coleman.
12. Jelka Delius to Marie Clews, 20 Dec. 1918, Delius Trust Archive.
13. Goldring, *Odd Man Out* (see n. 2), 183.
14. Heseltine to Taylor, 15 Aug. 1917.
15. Heseltine to Taylor, 24 Sept. 1917.
16. Gray, *Warlock*, 158.
17. Heseltine to Taylor, 12 Sept. 1917.
18. W. Cory, *Ionica* (London, 1891).
19. Heseltine to Taylor, 1 Oct. 1917.
20. L. Cranmer-Byng, quoted by Heseltine on p. 2 of 'Along the Stream', the first of the three *Saudades*.
21. Heseltine to Taylor, 8 Nov. 1917.
22. The work exists in the BL, Add. MS 52904 in piano score only and is signed Huanebango Z. Palimpsest.
23. I. Copley, *The Music of Peter Warlock* (London, 1979), 65 and 261.
24. Heseltine to Gray, 30 May 1918.
25. Heseltine to van Dieren, 18 Feb. 1918, photocopy in PW Society archives.
26. Heseltine to Taylor, 25 Apr. 1918.
27. Heseltine to Gray, ?Jan./Feb. 1918.
28. Van Dieren to Heseltine, undated ?Jan./Feb. 1918, photocopy in PW Society archives.

29. Heseltine to van Dieren, 18 Feb. 1918, photocopy in PW Society archives.
30. A reference to a folk-song, 'Midsummer Fair', which Philip had heard sung at his preparatory school. The chorus was 'My oor, bag boor, bag nigger, bag waller and bantabalor'. Heseltine to his mother, 17 May 1908.
31. Heseltine to van Dieren, 18 Feb. 1918, photocopy in PW Society archives.
32. Goldring, *Odd Man Out* (see n. 2), 182.
33. Shepherd, *Encyclopedia*, 326.
34. Agrippa von Nettesheim, 1486–1535, German writer, soldier, and physician whose writings on the occult gained him a reputation as a magician.
35. Gray, *Warlock*, 163.
36. N. Heseltine, *Capriol for Mother* (London, 1992), 85.
37. Ibid. 167.
38. P. Gray, *Cecil Gray: His Life and Notebooks* (London, 1989), 29.
39. Augustus John to Heseltine, 4 Oct. 1924 and 5 Nov. 1924, National Library of Wales, Aberystwyth, MS 18909D.
40. A Motion, *The Lamberts: George, Constant and Kit* (London, 1986), 166.
41. Éliphas Lévi, pseudonym for Alphonse-Lois Constant, 1810–75, French writer on the occult.
42. Heseltine to Nichols, 14 Dec. 1917, BL, Add. MS 57796.
43. Heseltine to Viva Smith, 12 Nov. 1918.
44. Gray, *Warlock*, 14.
45. Moeran to Cockshott, 13 Sept. 1941, photocopy in PW Society archives.
46. G. Cockshott, 'E. J. Moeran's Recollections of Warlock', *Musical Times*, 96 (1955), 129.
47. Heseltine to Nichols, 14 Dec. 1917, BL, Add. MS 57796.
48. Heseltine to Taylor, ?27 Apr. 1917.
49. Heseltine to Taylor, 31 Oct. 1917.
50. 'Neither shall they say, lo here! or, lo there! for, behold, the kingdom of God is within you': Luke 17: 21.
51. cf. 'for the letter killeth, but the spirit giveth life': 2 Cor. 3: 6.
52. Greek for 'knowledge'.
53. Heseltine is here referring to the later claim by Christian writers to a special *gnosis*, a knowledge of spiritual mysteries, especially a higher knowledge of spiritual things.
54. Heseltine to Taylor, 27 Sept. 1917.
55. Heseltine to his mother, 3 Jan. 1916.
56. D. ApIvor, 'Philip Heseltine (Peter Warlock): A Psychological Study', *Music Review*, 46 (1985), 118–32.
57. Gray, *Warlock*, 236.
58. S. T. Klein, *Science and the Infinite; or, Through a Window in the Blank Wall* (London, 1912).
59. Sydney Turner Klein (b. 1853).
60. J. M. Pryse, *The Magical Message according to Iôannes commonly called the Gospel according to St John: a verbatim translation from the Greek done in modern English with introductory essays and notes* (New York, 1909).
61. Éliphas Lévi, *Histoire de la magie: Avec une exposition de ses procédés, de ses rites et de ses mystères* (Paris, 1860); *Transcendental Magic: Its Doctrine and Ritual* (London, 1896).

62. Inscription at the Delphic Oracle attributed to the Seven Sages (*c*.650–*c*.590 BC).
63. A reference to Plato's Doctrine of Recollection expounded in the *Dialogues* (*Meno, Phaedo*, and *Phaedrus*) which he had studied at Oxford.
64. Heseltine to Taylor, 27 Sept. 1917.
65. Heseltine to Taylor, 31 Oct. 1917.
66. Heseltine to Gray, 7 Apr. 1918.
67. Ibid.
68. Ibid.
69. F. Tomlinson, *Warlock and van Dieren* (London, 1978), 17.
70. BL, Add. MS 57967.
71. 'Formerly a prosperous commercial traveller who had suddenly turned hermit and had lived seven years of monastic solitude and austerity.' Gray, *Warlock*, 160.
72. Heseltine to Taylor, 14 May 1918.
73. Heseltine to Gray, 30 May 1918.
74. Heseltine to Delius, 15 May 1918.
75. Delius to Heseltine, 19 May 1918.
76. Heseltine to Delius, 19 June 1918.
77. Delius to Heseltine, 3 July 1918.
78. Heseltine to Delius, 22 July 1918.
79. Heseltine to Viva Smith, 25 Sept. 1913.
80. Heseltine to Gray, 9 June 1918.
81. Gray, *Warlock*, 188.
82. Heseltine to Gray, 15 June 1918.
83. 'Contingencies', *The Sackbut*, 1 (May 1920), 30.
84. Heseltine to Taylor, 13 June 1918.
85. Ibid.
86. Heseltine to Gray, ? before Mar. 1918.
87. Balfour Gardiner to Heseltine, 6 July 1918, photocopy in PW Society archives.
88. Ibid.
89. Heseltine to Taylor, 19 July 1918.

Chapter 8

1. Heseltine to Taylor, 13 June 1918.
2. Heseltine to Taylor, 2 July 1918.
3. Heseltine to Taylor, 19 July 1918.
4. Rogers to Taylor, 19 July 1918, BL, Add. MS 57794.
5. 'A pretence of Art to destroy Art; a pretence of Liberty to destroy Liberty; a pretence of Religion to destroy Religion'. W. Blake, *Jerusalem* (1804–20), ch. 2, plate 43, pp. 35–6.
6. Heseltine to Taylor, 9 Aug. 1918.
7. Heseltine to Taylor, 22 Aug. 1918.
8. Heseltine to Gray, 15 June 1918.
9. Heseltine to Gray, 21 June 1918.
10. Ibid.
11. Heseltine to Gray, 26 June 1918.

12. Heseltine to Gray, undated, ? Aug. 1918.
13. C. Gray, *Peter Warlock* (London, 1934), 198.
14. Heseltine to Taylor, 19 July 1918.
15. Gray, *Warlock*, 171.
16. A. Dowbiggin, 'Peter Warlock Remembered', *PW Society Newsletter*, 5 (1970), 1.
17. I. Copley, *The Music of Peter Warlock* (London, 1979), 67.
18. E. Poston, Script of 'Warlock', BBC broadcast (12 Dec. 1964), 8–9.
19. Gray, *Warlock*, 204.
20. cf. 'Every good gift and every perfect gift is from above . . .': James 1: 17.
21. cf. 'He that findeth his life shall lose it: and he that loseth his life for my sake shall find it.' Matt. 10: 39.
22. Heseltine to Taylor, 22 Aug. 1918.

Chapter 9

1. C. Gray, *Peter Warlock* (London, 1934), 199.
2. Heseltine to Taylor, 29 Oct. 1918.
3. Heseltine to Taylor, 14 Jan. 1919.
4. Heseltine to Viva Smith, 20 Sept. 1913.
5. Heseltine to Taylor, 14 Jan. 1919.
6. Heseltine to Gray, 14 Jan. 1919.
7. Heseltine to Delius, 13 July 1919.
8. Delius to Heseltine, 17 July 1919.
9. Autolycus [Ernest Newman], 'Unconsidered Trifles', *Musical Opinion* (May 1919), 470–1.
10. Newman to Heseltine, 19 Nov. 1919, I. Copley, *Music of Warlock*, 16.
11. Delius to Heseltine, 29 June 1920.
12. 'Contingencies', *The Sackbut*, 1 (Oct. 1920), 282.
13. *Sunday Times* (1 Mar. 1931), 5.
14. Heseltine to Gray, 18 Apr. 1919.
15. Edward Dent to Heseltine, 5 Sept. 1919, photocopy in PW Society archives.
16. *Musical Times* (1919), 297.
17. Ibid. 367.
18. Ibid. 422.
19. Ibid. 493.
20. Winthrop Rogers to Heseltine, 13 Nov. 1919, BL, Add. MS 57964.
21. 'Six Sketches', Op. 4 (1910–11), pub. by Universal Edition in 1921.
22. A Cornish word meaning a bugbear, a hobgoblin, any frightful object or awkward-looking person.
23. Heseltine to van Dieren, 14 Nov. 1919: F. Tomlinson, *Warlock and van Dieren* (London, 1978), 20.
24. Van Dieren to Heseltine, undated, towards the end of 1919: ibid. 20.
25. Heseltine to van Dieren, 24 Jan. 1920: ibid. 22–3.
26. Van Dieren to Heseltine, undated, early 1920, photocopy in PW Society archives.
27. Van Dieren to Heseltine, ?Nov. 1919. Tomlinson, *Warlock and van Dieren*, 20–1.
28. 'Books', *Sackbut*, 1 (June 1920), 66.

29. 'London', *Music and Letters*, 1 (Jan. 1920), 72.
30. 'London Letter', *Music and Letters*, 2 (Mar. 1920), 164.
31. 'The Scope of Opera', *Music and Letters*, 3 (July 1920), 233.
32. *Musical Times* (1920), 237.
33. Heseltine to van Dieren, 22 Nov. 1919: L. Foreman, *From Parry to Britten: British Music in Letters 1900–1945* (London, 1987), 112.
34. Delius to Heseltine, 24 Mar. 1920.
35. Heseltine to Delius, 16 Apr. 1920.
36. Heseltine to his mother, ?28 Aug. 1920.
37. Heseltine to Delius, 3 May 1920.
38. Heseltine to Gray, undated, ? May, 1920.
39. 'Contingencies', *The Sackbut*, 1 (Dec. 1920), 371–2.
40. Ibid. 372–3.
41. 'Contingencies', *The Sackbut*, 1 (Mar. 1921), 423.
42. H. Foss, 'Introductions: XIX. Philip Heseltine', *Music Bulletin*, 6 (1924), 202.
43. Heseltine to van Dieren, 28 Feb. 1921: Tomlinson, *Warlock and Van Dieren*, 24.
44. Heseltine to Roy Campbell, 28 Feb. 1923, TS copy in the possession of Prof. Peter Alexander.
45. Herbert Hodge to Heseltine, 7 Apr. 1921, BL, Add. MS 57964.
46. Heseltine to his mother, 21 Sept. 1920.
47. M. Gillies, *Bartók in Britain: A Guided Tour* (Oxford, 1989), 122.
48. Heseltine to his mother, 11 Oct. 1920.
49. Heseltine to Delius, 17 June 1922.
50. Delius to Heseltine, 19 Apr. 1920.
51. Delius to Heseltine, 24 Mar. 1920.
52. Delius to Heseltine, 30 Sept. 1920.
53. Heseltine to Gray, 18 June 1920.
54. Heseltine to Gray, 21 June 1920.
55. Heseltine to Gray, 25 June 1920.
56. Heseltine to Gray, 1 July 1920.
57. Heseltine to his mother, 31 Aug. 1920.
58. Heseltine to Gray, 16 July 1920.
59. Heseltine to Gray, 21 Aug. 1920.
60. Rogers to Heseltine, 19 Oct. 1920, BL, Add. MS 57964.
61. Heseltine to Anthony Bernard, 24 Oct. 1920, in the possession of Mary Bernard.
62. Heseltine to van Dieren, 20 Nov. 1920, photocopy in PW Society archives.
63. Heseltine to his mother, 31 Oct. 1920 or 7 Nov. 1920.
64. Heseltine to Gray, 6 Dec. 1920.
65. A pseudonym used by Gray in *The Sackbut*, a play on the word 'Pythagore' (Heseltine to Fritz Hart, 25 Mar. 1924).
66. Heseltine to Gray, 2 Jan. 1921.
67. Heseltine to van Dieren, 28 Feb. 1921: Tomlinson, *Warlock and van Dieren*, 24.
68. Heseltine to his mother, 15 Feb. 1921.
69. For a full account see J. O. Fuller, *The Magical Dilemma of Victor Neuburg* (London, 1965), 154–60.

70. Heseltine to Delius, 28 Mar. 1921. The last sentence refers to Holst's oriental suite for orchestra, *Beni Mora* (1910), a section of which is entitled 'In the Street of the Ouled Naïls'.

71. Heseltine to Fritz Hart, 15 Nov. 1921, photocopy in PW Society archives.

72. Heseltine to his mother, 4 Apr. 1921.

73. D. Dille, 'Vier unbekannte Briefe von Béla Bartók', *Osterreichische Musikzeitschrift*, 20 (1965): Gillies, *Bartók in Britain*, 122.

74. Heseltine to Delius, 21 Apr. 1921.

75. Heseltine to Fritz Hart, 15 Nov. 1921, photocopy in PW Society archives.

76. Heseltine to Taylor, 17 Oct. 1921.

77. Heseltine to his mother, 20 Apr. 1921.

78. Heseltine to his mother, 4 Apr. 1921.

79. Heseltine to Delius, 1 June 1921.

80. Heseltine to Delius, undated (probably 22 May 1921).

81. Heseltine to his mother, 31 May 1921.

82. John Curwen (1881–1935), who had become head of the firm J. Curwen & Sons in 1919.

83. Heseltine to Gray, 21 June 1921.

84. Gray, *Warlock*, 217.

85. Heseltine to his mother, 31 May 1921.

86. Heseltine to his mother, 25 July 1921.

87. Note on back of envelope of letter from Heseltine, 25 July 1921.

88. Heseltine to his mother, 30 July 1921.

89. Heseltine to Fritz Hart, 15 Nov. 1921, photocopy in PW Society archives.

90. Heseltine to Taylor, 17 Oct. 1921.

91. *Musical Times* (1920), 751.

92. *The Times* (London, 6 Mar. 1922), 10.

93. Heseltine to Gray, undated, after Sept. 1921.

94. Tomlinson, *Warlock and van Dieren*, 25.

95. 'Correspondence', *The Sackbut*, 2 (June 1921), 35.

Chapter 10

1. I. Parrott, 'Warlock in Wales', *Musical Times*, 105 (1964), 740–1.

2. Caleb Simper, 1856–1942, composer of simple, popular church music.

3. 'In the right way and backwards'; another name for *canon cancrizans* in which the theme of the canon is performed normally in counterpoint with itself backwards.

4. Heseltine to Gray, 19 Nov. 1921.

5. Harvey Grace in his review of these songs, *Musical Times* (1922), 640.

6. Heseltine to Gray, 6 Jan. 1922.

7. Heseltine to Gray, 8 Feb. 1922.

8. *c*.185–*c*.254, the most important theologian and biblical scholar of the early Greek Church.

9. Heseltine to Gray, 29 Nov. 1921.

10. Heseltine to Delius, 31 Nov. 1921, Gray, *Warlock*, 241.

11. Heseltine to Delius, 27 Jan. 1922.

12. Heseltine to Fritz Hart, 7 Feb. 1922, photocopy in PW Society archives.

13. The unpub. MS (BL, Add. MS 52912) is dated July 1919. It was later adapted as 'The Sick Heart'.

14. Van Dieren to Heseltine, 21 Nov. 1921: Tomlinson, *Warlock and van Dieren*, 25.
15. Lawrence to Catherine Carswell, 21 Nov. 1916: *Letters*, ii. 36.
16. Lawrence to Secker, 10 Nov. 1921: *Letters*, iv. 116.
17. Lawrence to Robert Mountsier, 17 Sept. 1921: *Letters*, iv. 88.
18. Lawrence to Donald Carswell, 15 Nov. 1921: *Letters*, iv. 122–4.
19. Heseltine to his solicitors, Messrs Clifford Webster, Emmet & Coote, ? Nov. 1921: C. Gray, *Peter Warlock* (London, 1934), 221–2.
20. Secker to Heseltine's solicitors, 18 Oct. 1921: *Letters*, iv. 94.
21. Lawrence to Secker, 8 Nov. 1921: *Letters*, iv. 113.
22. Lawrence to Secker, 23 Nov. 1921: *Letters*, iv. 129.
23. Lawrence to Jan Juta, 3 Dec. 1921: *Letters*, iv. 137–9.
24. Gray, *Warlock*, 223.
25. Heseltine to Taylor, 17 Oct. 1921.
26. Heseltine to Taylor, 7 Feb. 1922.
27. I. Copley, *The Music of Peter Warlock* (London, 1979), 228.
28. *Musical Times* (1923), 710.
29. Heseltine to Delius, 17 June, 1922.
30. E. Poston, script of 'Warlock', BBC broadcast (12 Dec. 1964), 8–9.
31. Gray, *Warlock*, 246.
32. Heseltine to Gray, 10 June 1922.
33. Heseltine to Fritz Hart, 15 Nov. 1921, photocopy in PW Society archives.
34. F. Tomlinson, *A Peter Warlock Handbook*, i (London, 1974), 42.
35. Heseltine to Nichols, 15 Jan. 1923, BL, Add. MS 57796.
36. Ibid.
37. Copley, *Music of Warlock*, 12.
38. 'Sir Richard Terry's Tribute': Gray, *Warlock*, 271–3.
39. P. Warlock, 'The Editing of Old English Songs' (1) and (2), *The Sackbut*, 6 and 8 (1926), 183–6 and 215–20.
40. Heseltine to Delius, 5 Mar. 1922.
41. A reference to the song-cycle, *Peterisms*; a word coined from Cephas (the disciple Peter) and masturbate.
42. Heseltine to Gray, 8 Feb. 1922.
43. Copley, *Music of Warlock*, 91.
44. The last page of the MS of this song is reproduced in vol. iv of the Warlock Society Complete Edition of the Songs (London, 1986), 10.
45. *Musical Times* (1922), 88–90.
46. Ibid. 123–5.
47. 'Cambrensis' is the Latin for a Welshman. It is also the name of a Welsh cleric and author, Giraldus Cambrensis (Gerald de Barri), *c.*1146–*c.*1223, mentioned by Heseltine in the article, 'London', *Music and Letters*, I (1920), 71.
48. P. Heseltine, 'A Note on the Mind's Ear', *Musical Times* (1922), 88–90.
49. P. Warlock, 'Mr Yeats and a Musical Censorship', *Musical Times* (1922), 123–4.
50. Ibid. 123.
51. Gray, *Warlock*, 249.
52. Yeats to Ethel Mannin, 6 Jan. 1936: A. Wade, *Letters of W. B. Yeats* (London, 1954), 846–7.

53. *Musical Times* (1922), 124.
54. Heseltine to Gray, 6 Dec. 1921.
55. Heseltine to Gray, 13 Aug. 1922.
56. P. Heseltine, *Delius*, ed. H. Foss (London, 1952), 10.
57. Gray, *Warlock*, 250–1.
58. Heseltine to Taylor, 15 Feb. 1922.
59. Notes by Taylor, Colin Taylor Collection, Univ. of Cape Town.
60. P. Heseltine, 'Music in England: ii. Frederick Delius' (trans. E. Gerhardi), *Musikblätter des Anbruch* (1922), repr. in the *The Delius Society Journal*, 94 (1987).
61. *Musical Times* (1922), 164–7.
62. Heseltine to Gray, 6 Dec. 1921.
63. Parrott, 'Warlock in Wales', *Musical Times*, 105 (1964), 740–1.
64. C. W. Orr to M. J. Wilson: J. Wilson, *C. W. Orr: The Unknown Song-Composer* (London, 1989), 30.
65. Heseltine to Orr, 4 June 1922: ibid. 31–2.
66. Heseltine to Orr, Christmas 1924: ibid. 34–5.
67. C. Lambert, 'Master of English Song', *Radio Times*, 59 (1938), 12–13.
68. Gray, *Warlock*, 204.
69. H. Foss, 'Introductions: XIX. Philip Heseltine', *Music Bulletin*, 6 (1924), 205.
70. Heseltine to Cooper, June 1922: Gray, *Warlock*, 248.
71. Heseltine to Gray, 22 Aug. 1922.
72. E. Goossens, *Overture and Beginners* (London, 1951), 111–12.
73. Heseltine to Taylor, 7 Dec. 1922.
74. Ibid.
75. Heseltine to Fritz Hart, 25 Mar. 1924, photocopy in PW Society archives.
76. H. Foss, 'Peter Warlock (Philip Heseltine)', in A. L. Bacharach (ed.), *British Music of Our Time* (Harmondsworth, 1951), 67–8.
77. Heseltine to Nichols, 15 Jan. 1923, BL, Add. MS 57796.
78. Gray, *Warlock*, 247.
79. E. J. Moeran, 'Peter Warlock (Philip Heseltine)', *Miniature Essays* (London, 1926), 4–5.
80. *Music Bulletin*, 5 (1923), 147.
81. Heseltine to Nichols, 15 Jan. 1923, BL, Add. MS 57796.
82. Ibid.
83. Ibid.
84. Heseltine to George Thewlis, 19 June 1925.
85. Amongst Cecil Gray's papers in the BL, Add. MS 57796, are typewritten notes in the form of an explanatory foreword.
86. BL, Add. MS 57796.
87. Shakespeare, *The Winter's Tale*, IV. iv. 190–4.
88. Heseltine to Taylor, 7 Dec. 1922.
89. Heseltine to Taylor, 19 Dec. 1922.
90. Jelka Delius to Henry and Marie Clewes, 23 Jan. 1923: L. Carley, *Letters*, ii. 263.
91. Heseltine to Delius, 22 Jan. 1923.
92. Delius to Heseltine, 26 Feb. 1923.
93. A. Crowley, *The Confessions of Aleister Crowley: An Autohagiography* (London, 1989), 562.

94. Heseltine to Gray, 22 Jan. 1923.
95. Gray, *Warlock*, 219.
96. Ibid.
97. A reference to *cannabis indica*.
98. Heseltine to Gray, 20 Aug. 1922.
99. Ibid.
100. Herbert Ward to John Bishop, 1 Oct. 1972, photocopy in PW Society archives.
101. Blunt to Cockshott, July 1943, from notes given to R. Beckhard by Cockshott in July 1955, and in a letter to the present author, 16 July 1993.
102. Heseltine to van Dieren, 2 Feb. 1923, photocopy in PW Society archives.
103. Burke's *The Landed Gentry* (London, 1952), 2250. No official record of her divorce from Philip exists.
104. Information from a letter to the author from R. Beckhard, 5 Mar. 1993.
105. Heseltine to Gray, ? Aug. 1923.
106. Heseltine to van Dieren, 20 Sept. 1923, photocopy in PW Society archives.
107. Ibid.
108. Grainger to Heseltine, wrongly dated 17 Nov. 1923, Grainger Museum, Univ. of Melbourne.
109. BL, Add. MS 57969.
110. Jelka Delius to Grainger, 29 Nov. 1923, Grainger Museum, Univ. of Melbourne.
111. Heseltine to Winifred Baker, undated 1919, Gray, *Warlock*, 231–3.
112. Copley, *Music of Warlock*, 195.
113. P. W[arlock], 'The Test of a Tune', *The Sackbut* (Mar. 1921), 421.
114. G. Cockshott, 'Some Notes on the Songs of Peter Warlock', *Music and Letters*, 21 (1940), 249.
115. Moeran to Dowbiggin, 5 Feb. 1931, photocopy in PW Society archives.
116. S. Hughes, *Second Movement: Continuing the Autobiography* (London, 1951), 49.
117. Heseltine to Fritz Hart, 25 Mar. 1924, photocopy in PW Society archives.
118. Delius to Heseltine, 23 Mar. 1924.
119. Heseltine to van Dieren, 22 Apr. 1924: Tomlinson, *Warlock and van Dieren*, 28.
120. Heseltine to Gray, 7 May 1924.
121. Heseltine to Phyl Crocker, 8 May 1924, TS copy in the possession of R. Beckhard.
122. Delius to Heseltine, 18 Sept. 1924.
123. H. Foss, 'Peter Warlock', 68–9.
124. Heseltine to Gray, 31 Aug. 1925.
125. Heseltine to Gray, 16 July 1924.
126. Ibid.
127. A. John, *Chiaroscuro* (London, 1952), 140.
128. Heseltine to Fritz Hart, 10 Oct. 1924, photocopy in PW Society archives.
129. P. Heseltine, script of BBC broadcast, BL, Add. MS 57967.

130. J. Lindsay, *Fanfrolico and After* (London, 1962), 87.
131. Eva Finney to Edith Buckley Jones, 15 Jan. 1925, BL, Add. MS 57064.

Chapter 11

1. Heseltine to Taylor, 25 Feb. 1925.
2. Presumably based on the novel of the same name by the English novelist, Laurence Sterne, 1713–68.
3. Words by Sir Thomas Wyat, 1503–42, English poet and diplomatist.
4. 1928.
5. C. Gray, *Peter Warlock* (London, 1934), 254–5.
6. L. Carley, *Delius: A Life in Letters* (Aldershot, 1988), ii. 351.
7. From conversation between Blunt and Cockshott, July 1943. Information from notes given to R. Beckhard by Cockshott in July 1955 and included in a letter to the author from Beckhard, 16 July 1993.
8. Gray, *Warlock*, 255.
9. D. Goldring, *The Nineteen Twenties* (London, 1945), 101–2.
10. W. G. Duncombe, *The Pubs of Eynsford: Ancient and Modern* (Farningham and Eynsford, 1990).
11. J. Lindsay, *Fanfrolico and After* (London, 1962), 82–4.
12. English illustrator, portraitist, and landscape painter.
13. N. Hamnett, *Is She a Lady?* (London, 1955), 23–33.
14. Ibid. 23–33.
15. Nichols's notes on his correspondence with Heseltine, BL, Add. MS 57796.
16. Information from a letter to the author from R. Beckhard, 5 Mar. 1993.
17. Patrick Hadley (1899–1973), English composer, professor of music at Cambridge (1946–63).
18. L. Foreman, *Bax: A Composer and his Times* (London, 1983), 224.
19. Rab Noolas, decorated by Hal Collins, *Merry-Go-Down: A Gallery of Gorgeous Drunkards through the Ages. Collected for Use, Interest, Illumination and Delectation of Serious Topers* (London, 1929).
20. I. Copley, *The Music of Peter Warlock* (London, 1979), 31–2.
21. Ibid. 18.
22. W. Walton, 'My Life in Music', *Sunday Telegraph* (25 Mar. 1962), 8.
23. Heseltine to Gray, 6 Oct. 1930.
24. G. Cockshott, 'E. J. Moeran's Recollections of Peter Warlock', 128–30.
25. Gray, *Warlock*, 262.
26. Ibid. 64.
27. Ibid. 126.
28. C. W. Orr, 'Recollections of Philip Heseltine ("Peter Warlock")', attachment to *PW Society Newsletter*, 4 (Jan. 1970).
29. P. Heseltine, correspondence, 'English Madrigal Verse', *London Mercury*, 11 (1925), 634–40.
30. Ibid.
31. Heseltine to Nichols, 28 Nov. 1924, BL, Add. MS 57796.
32. Heseltine to Nichols, 24 Feb. 1925, BL, Add. MS 57796.
33. Heseltine to Arnold Dowbiggin, 1 July 1930, photocopy in PW Society archives.

34. Heseltine to Jelka Delius, 20 July 1925.
35. Information from a letter to the author from R. Beckhard, 5 Mar. 1993.
36. Heseltine to Robert Nichols, 24 Feb. 1925, BL, Add. MS 57796.
37. Heseltine to Scholes, 14 June 1925, National Library of Canada, Ottawa.
38. Heseltine to Scholes, 20 June 1925, National Library of Canada, Ottawa.
39. B. Lunn, *Switchback* (London, 1948), 190.
40. Heseltine to Scholes, 12 June 1926, National Library of Canada, Ottawa.
41. Obituary, *Musical Times* (1953), 185.
42. Lindsay, *Fanfrolico*, 86.
43. Ibid. 166.
44. Heseltine to Fritz Hart, 7 Feb. 1922, photocopy in PW Society archives.
45. Jelka Delius to Heseltine, 16 Aug. 1925.
46. Nichols to Heseltine, 22 July 1925, BL, Add. MS 57796.
47. Heseltine to Taylor, 6 Aug. 1925.
48. Heseltine to George Thewlis, 12 June 1925, photocopy in PW Society archives.
49. 1580–1630, English dramatist.
50. 'Three Slumber Songs of the Madonna' for unaccompanied female voices (Novello, 1910).
51. *Siegfried-Idyll* (1870) by Richard Wagner.
52. 'Sonetto VII of Edmund Spenser's "Amoretti"' for tenor and eleven instruments (OUP, 1925).
53. Heseltine to Taylor, 4 Dec. 1925.
54. Gardiner to Heseltine, 13 Aug. 1924, photocopy in PW Society archives.
55. Gray, *Warlock*, 264–5.
56. Bax to Heseltine, undated, Gray, *Warlock*, 265–6.
57. P. H., 'Bernard van Dieren', *Musical Times* (1926), 44.
58. Cockshott, 'Moeran's Recollections', 129.
59. Copley, *Music of Warlock*, 119.
60. P. Heseltine, 'Introductions XVIII: E. J. Moeran', *Music Bulletin*, 6 (1924), 170–4.
61. E. J. Moeran, *Miniature Essays*, 'Peter Warlock', 4.
62. C. Palmer, *Herbert Howells* (London, 1992), 354–5.
63. B. van Dieren, 'Philip Heseltine', *Musical Times* (1931), 117–19.
64. Copley, *Music of Warlock*, 281.
65. Palmer, *Herbert Howells*, 354–5.
66. Moeran to Peers Coetmore, ?1948, quoted in G. Self, *The Music of E. J. Moeran* (London, 1986), 63.
67. Heseltine to Taylor, 5 Sept. 1926.
68. French priest and author. His real name was Jehan Tabournot, of which Thoinot Arbeau is an anagram.
69. H. Foss, 'Peter Warlock', 67.
70. S. Hughes, *Second Movement* (London, 1951), 51–2.
71. F. Tomlinson, 'Chairman's Report 1985 (mostly about *Capriol*)', *PW Society Newsletter*, 35 (1985), 3.
72. Heseltine to Taylor, 24 Sept. 1917.
73. Van Dieren to Colin Taylor, 12 Apr. 1931, in the possession of Hugh Taylor.
74. Copley, *Music of Warlock*, 241.

75. Moeran, *Miniature Essays*, 'Peter Warlock', 6.
76. Lindsay, *Fanfrolico*, 35.
77. 1859–1907, English poet.
78. Heseltine to his mother, 17 Sept. 1927.
79. Moeran to Gerald Cockshott, 22 May 1946, photocopy in PW Society archives.
80. 'National Gramophone Society Notes', *Gramophone*, 4 (1927), 390–1.
81. Heseltine to Blunt, 2 Sept. 1927, photocopy in PW Society archives.
82. B. Blunt, *The World Goes By*, BBC Home Service (16 Dec. 1944).
83. Blunt to Dowbiggin, 20 May 1943, photocopy in PW Society archives.
84. Heseltine to Delius, 15 Oct. 1919.
85. Heseltine to Taylor, 3 Feb. 1927.
86. Heseltine to Hart, 21 Feb. 1927, photocopy in PW Society archives.
87. *Musical Times* (1922), 477–80.
88. Edward Dent to Heseltine, 10 Nov. 1926, photocopy in PW Society archives.
89. 'The other day . . . I scored a charming piece of Paul Ladmirault's.' Heseltine to Taylor, 20 Apr. 1916.
90. *Chantecler* (1927), 3.
91. Blunt to Gerald Cockshott, 20 May 1943: Copley, *Music of Warlock*, 204–5.
92. *Musical Times* (1927), 1075–7.
93. *Musical Times* (1928), 58.
94. Heseltine to his mother, 18 Apr. 1928.
95. Heseltine to Blunt, 3 Dec. 1928, photocopy in PW Society archives.
96. Heseltine to Taylor, 5 Sept. 1926.
97. Heseltine to Blunt, 20 July 1928, photocopy in PW Society archives.
98. Heseltine to Blunt, 12 Sept. 1928, photocopy in PW Society archives.
99. Heseltine to Dowbiggin, 28 July 1930: Copley, *Music of Warlock*, 137.
100. E. Bradbury, 'Lost Magic of Warlock', *Yorkshire Post* (5 Dec. 1979).
101. E. Poston, 'Warlock', BBC broadcast (12 Dec. 1964).
102. Heseltine to Gwen Shepherd, 11 Sept. 1928, photocopy in PW Society archives.
103. Heseltine to van Dieren, 14 Sept. 1928: F. Tomlinson, *Warlock and van Dieren* (London, 1978), 30.

Chapter 12

1. Heseltine to Blunt, 1 Oct. 1928, photocopy in PW Society archives.
2. Heseltine to Nichols, 7 Oct. 1928, BL, Add. MS 57795.
3. Heseltine to W. C. Smith, 2 Oct. 1928, BL, Add. MS 58079.
4. Heseltine to unidentified correspondent, ? Oct. 1928: C. Gray, *Peter Warlock* (London, 1934), 279–80.
5. Heseltine to Nichols, 7 Oct. 1928, BL, Add. MS 57795.
6. Heseltine to Blunt, 23 Oct. 1928, photocopy in PW Society archives.
7. Heseltine to Blunt, 30 Nov. 1928, photocopy in PW Society archives.
8. Francis Toye to Heseltine, 29 Nov. 1928, photocopy in PW Society archives.
9. cf. Luke 15: 13: '. . . and there wasted his substance with riotous living'.

10. Heseltine to Gray, 28 Nov. 1928.
11. Heseltine to Blunt, 28 Nov. 1928, photocopy in PW Society archives.
12. Heseltine to Blunt, 4 Nov. 1928, photocopy in PW Society archives.
13. Heseltine to Gray, 28 Nov. 1928.
14. Gray, *Warlock*, 253.
15. Ibid. 14.
16. Ibid. 253.
17. Ibid. 260.
18. Heseltine to Nichols, 1 Jan. 1929, BL, Add. MS 57796.
19. Heseltine to Blunt, 11 Dec. 1928, photocopy in PW Society archives.
20. Heseltine to Blunt, 17 June 1929, photocopy in PW Society archives.
21. Gray, *Warlock*, 228.
22. Heseltine to Taylor, 19 Jan. 1929.
23. T. Beecham, *Frederick Delius* (London, 1959), 200–1.
24. E. Fenby, *Delius as I knew him* (London, 1936), 59.
25. Ibid. 61.
26. Ibid. 61–3.
27. Heseltine to Fenby, 8 May 1929, in the possession of R. Beckhard.
28. Fenby, *Delius*, 63–4.
29. Jelka Delius to Heseltine, May 1929.
30. Heseltine to Taylor, 6 Sept. 1929.
31. Elizabeth Poston to George Findlay, 8 Dec. 1977, in the possession of Paula Findlay.
32. Heseltine to Blunt, 26 Sept. 1929, photocopy in PW Society archives.
33. Heseltine to Jelka Delius, 1 Sept. 1929.
34. Heseltine to D. Marblacy Jones, 14 Dec. 1929, *Music and Letters*, 66 (1965), 94.
35. *Evening News* (17 Dec. 1930).
36. Heseltine to Blunt, 15 Aug. 1929, photocopy in PW Society archives.
37. Heseltine to Blunt, 26 Sept. 1929, photocopy in PW Society archives.
38. Jelka Delius to Heseltine, 23 Aug. 1929.
39. Jelka Delius to Heseltine, 28 Sept. 1929.
40. Beecham, *Delius*, 205.
41. A play on Benskin's Ale.
42. *PW Society Newsletter*, 32 (1984), 11.
43. The quote from the second part of *Henry IV* (III. ii. 36) is in fact: 'How [much] a good yoke of bullocks at Stamford fair?'
44. *PW Society Newsletter*, 32 (1984), 11–12.
45. Beecham to Heseltine, 26 Jan. 1930, photocopy in PW Society archives.
46. D. ApIvor, 'Philip Heseltine: A Psychological Study', *Music Review*, 46 (1985), 126.
47. J. Lindsay, *Fanfrolico and After* (London, 1962), 185.
48. Gray, *Warlock*, 289.
49. Heseltine to Viva Smith, 8 Mar. 1914.
50. Lindsay, *Fanfrolico*, 88–9.
51. Heseltine to Blunt, 17 June 1929, photocopy in PW Society archives.
52. From a conversation between Blunt and Cockshott, July 1943. Information from notes given to R. Beckhard by Cockshott in July 1955 and included in a letter to the author from Beckhard, 16 July 1993.

53. Jelka Delius to Heseltine, 29 Oct. 1930: L. Foreman, *From Parry to Britten*, 142.
54. G. Adler (ed.), *Handbuch der Musikgeschichte* (Berlin, 1930), 1047.
55. J. Northrop Moore, *Edward Elgar: A Creative Life* (London, 1987), 790.
56. Heseltine to Delius, 29 Sept. 1930: Gray, *Warlock*, 286.
57. Heseltine to Taylor, 6 Aug. 1929.
58. Austin to Heseltine, 28 Aug. 1930, photocopy in PW Society archives.
59. BL, Add. MS 57969.
60. Ibid.
61. I. Copley, *The Music of Peter Warlock* (London, 1979), 81.
62. From conversations with Blunt, quoted in a letter to the author from R. Beckhard, 16 July 1993.
63. Heseltine to Winifred Baker, 7 June 1930: Gray, *Warlock*, 283–4.
64. ApIvor, 'Psychological Study', 131.
65. Heseltine to Winifred Baker?, 15 June 1930: Gray, *Warlock*, 285.
66. Heseltine to Winifred Baker, 30 June 1930: ibid. 285.
67. Heseltine to Dowbiggin, 18 June 1930, photocopy in PW Society archives.
68. Gray, *Warlock*, 301.
69. Taken from Blunt's broadcast script and a letter from Blunt to Cockshott, 20 May 1943: Foreman, *Parry to Britten*, 257.
70. Copley, *Music of Warlock*. 144.
71. H. Foss, 'Peter Warlock' (Philip Heseltine), 72.
72. C. Lambert, 'Master of English Song', *Radio Times*, 59 (1938), 12–13.
73. Heseltine to Winifred Baker, 15 July 1930: Gray, *Warlock*, 286.

Chapter 13

1. The houses were later renumbered and 12A is now no. 30.
2. Heseltine to his mother, 10 Sept. 1930.
3. Information from a letter to the author from Robert Beckhard, 5 Mar. 1993.
4. Heseltine to Moeran, 3 Oct. 1930, BL, Add. MS 57794.
5. C. Gray, *Peter Warlock* (London, 1934), 273.
6. Heseltine to Moeran, 3 Oct. 1930, BL, Add. MS 57794.
7. Ibid.
8. Moeran to Heseltine, 5 Nov. 1930, BL, Add. MS 57794.
9. Macnaghten to Geoffrey Self, 27 June 1983: G. Self, *The Music of E. J. Moeran* (Exeter, 1986), 74.
10. Moeran to Arnold Dowbiggin, 18 Feb. 1931, photocopy in PW Society archives.
11. Heseltine to his mother, 15 Nov. 1930.
12. I. Copley, *The Music of Peter Warlock* (London, 1979), 147.
13. *News Chronicle* (18 Dec. 1930).
14. In her statement to the police at the Chelsea station on 18 Dec. 1930 she had said: 'I tried to open the flat door with my key but I found I could not as the door was bolted.'
15. Unidentified neighbour, *News Chronicle* (18 Dec. 1930).
16. Winifred Baker to van Dieren, 6 Jan. 1931, PW Society archives.
17. For a full account of the inquest see Gray, *Warlock*, 290–5, and *The Times* (London, 23 Dec. 1930).

18. Gray, *Warlock*, 291–2.
19. Statement made by Barbara Peache to the police at the Chelsea station, 18 Dec. 1930.
20. Conversation between R. Beckhard and Jellinek, quoted in a letter to the author from Beckhard, 27 July 1993.
21. *The Times* (London, 23 Dec. 1930).
22. F. Tomlinson, *Warlock and van Dieren* (London, 1978), 35.
23. Philip's will (22 Jan. 1920) stated: 'I devise and bequeath all my real and personal property whatsoever and wheresoever to Bernard van Dieren . . . and appoint him the sole executor thereof.'
24. Taylor has pencilled the name 'Delius?' in the margin of the letter.
25. Van Dieren to Colin Taylor, 12 Apr. 1931, in the possession of Hugh Taylor.
26. Winifred Baker to van Dieren, 22 Dec. 1930, PW Society archives.
27. Barbara Peache to Frida van Dieren, 26 Dec. 1930, PW Society archives.
28. Information from a letter to the author from R. Beckhard, 5 Mar. 1993.
29. Jelka Delius to Sydney Schiff (?Jan. 1931), L. Carley, *Letters*, ii. 378.
30. Heseltine to his mother, 15 Nov. 1930. Part of this letter was read at the inquest.
31. Heseltine to his mother, undated postcard, BL, Add. MS 57961.
32. Edith Buckley Jones to Jelka Delius, 3 Jan. 1931, Melbourne, Grainger Museum, Univ. of Melbourne.
33. Jelka Delius to Edith Buckley Jones: F. Tomlinson, *Warlock and Delius* (London, 1976), 27–8.
34. *The Times* (London, 23 Dec. 1930).
35. D. Goldring, *Odd Man Out* (London, 1935), 184.
36. Bruce Blunt to Gray, 25 May 1943, photocopy in PW Society archives.
37. See correspondence in the *PW Society Newsletter*, 23 (1979), 3.
38. Gray, *Warlock*, 297.
39. K. Sorabji, 'Music', *New Age*, 48 (1931), 128–9.
40. B. van Dieren, 'Philip Heseltine', *Musical Times*, 72 (1931), 117–19.
41. C. Lambert, 'Master of English Song', *Radio Times*, 59 (1938), 12–13.
42. R. Nichols, Notes on his correspondence with Heseltine, BL, Add. MS 57796.
43. U. Greville, 'Excursions of Ursula Greville', *The Sackbut* (Jan. 1931), 148.
44. R. Campbell, *Mithraic Emblems: Poems* (London, 1936).

Appendix

1. BL, Add. MS 57967.
2. cf. 'But seek ye first the kingdom of God, and his righteousness; and all these things shall be added unto you'. Matt. 6: 33.
3. 2 Kings 5: 1–14.
4. cf. 'And after the fire a still small voice.' 1 Kings 19: 12.
5. One of the great religious classics (*c*.AD 400). It is to Hinduism what the Sermon on the Mount is to Christianity.

6. H. G. Wells, 1866–1946, English novelist, journalist, sociologist, and popular historian. Here Heseltine refers to Wells's wartime writings when he turned temporarily to a belief in the transcendental, producing *God, the Invisible King* (1917). In the early 1900s Wells had written a number of novels about lower middle-class life, hence Heseltine's dismissive remarks.

7. cf. 'And he said unto them, He that hath ears to hear, let him hear.' Mark 4: 9.

8. cf. Heseltine's letter to Taylor, 27 Sept. 1917: 'The Christian churches are more remote in spirit from their Founder than the Jewish church was in his own day. The letter has prevailed over the spirit, the sign over the thing signified. . .'.

9. Heseltine pursued this argument further in *The Sackbut*, 1 (May 1920) 8: 'It is to be hoped that something may be done to break down the barrier of unnecessary modesty which so frequently prevents the non-professional music-lover from contributing to discussions on musical subjects, by showing him that music is not the esoteric mystery that many of its professors and pseudo-critical jargon-mongers would have him believe . . .'.

10. C. Gray, *Peter Warlock* (London, 1934), 81.

11. A Eurasian perennial herb.

12. Gray, *Warlock*, 146–8, included in a letter from Heseltine to Nichols, 16 Apr. 1917.

13. Pixie.

14. A scanty meal.

15. Toil.

16. Heseltine to Phyl Crocker, 19 Apr. 1917, BL, Add. MS 57794.

SELECT BIBLIOGRAPHY

(a) Manuscript Sources

British Library, London

Add. MS 52547–52548	Letters from Delius to Heseltine
Add. MS 54197	Letters from Heseltine to Taylor
Add. MS 57794–57803	Cecil Gray papers
Add. MS 57958–57970	Nigel Heseltine papers
Add. MS 58127	Letters from Heseltine to Olivia Smith
Add. MS 71167–71168	Letters from Heseltine to Delius

Peter Warlock Society Archives

National Library of Canada, Ottawa

National Library of Wales, Aberystwyth

University of Cape Town Library

Colin Taylor Collection
SA College of Music Library

University of Melbourne Library

Grainger Museum

University of Texas at Austin

University of Tulsa Library

Allinson, Adrian, *Painter's Pilgrimage*

Private Collections

Various MSS in the possession of Professor Peter Alexander, Robert Beckhard, Mary Bernard, Professor Mark Kinkead-Weekes, and Hugh Taylor.

(b) Books and Articles

Angier, Carole, 'Weekend in Gloucestershire: Jean Rhys, Adrian Allinson and "Till September Petronella"' *London Magazine*, 27 (1987), 30–46.
—— *Jean Rhys: Life and Work* (London, 1992).
ApIvor, Denis, 'Philip Heseltine (Peter Warlock): A Psychological Study', *Music Review* 46 (1985), 118–32.

ApIvor, Denis, 'Bernard van Dieren', *Composer*, 59 (1987), 1–8.

—— 'Bernard van Dieren: Search and Rescue One Hundred Years on', *Music Review*, 47 (1987), 253–66.

Aprahamian, Felix, 'Two Brief Encounters with Peter Warlock', *Peter Warlock Society Newsletter*, 45 (1990), 1–2.

Avery, Kenneth, 'The Chronology of Warlock's Songs', *Music and Letters*, 29 (1948), 398–405.

Beecham, Sir Thomas, *A Mingled Chime: Leaves from an Autobiography* (London, 1944).

—— *Frederick Delius* (London, 1959).

Bennett, Rodney, 'Peter Warlock: The Man and his Songs', *The Bookman*, 64 (1923), 300–2.

—— 'Song-writers of the Day: I. Peter Warlock', *The Music Teacher*, 5 (1926), 300–2.

Bliss, Sir Arthur, *As I Remember* (London, 1970).

Bottomley, Gordon, ' "The Curlew" and Peter Warlock', *The Gramophone* (1931), 259–60.

Bradbury, Ernest, 'Genius Curtailed', *Music and Musicians*, 23 (1974), 16.

—— 'The Lost Magic of Warlock', *Yorkshire Post* (5 Dec. 1979), 8.

Burke's Genealogical and Heraldic History of the Landed Gentry, 17th edn., ed. L. G. Pine (London, 1952).

Carley, Lionel, *Delius: A Life in Letters, 1909–1934* (Aldershot, 1988).

Chisholm, Alastair, *Bernard van Dieren: An Introduction* (London, 1984).

Clark, Kenneth, *Another Part of the Wood: A Self-Portrait* (London, 1974).

Cockshott, Gerald, 'A Note on Warlock's Capriol Suite', *Monthly Musical Record*, 70 (1940), 203–5.

—— 'Some Notes on the Songs of Peter Warlock', *Music and Letters*, 21 (1940), 246–58.

—— 'E. J. Moeran's Recollections of Peter Warlock', *Musical Times*, 96 (1955), 128–30.

—— 'Warlock and Moeran', *Composer*, 33 (1969), 1, 3–4.

Coleman, Stanley M., 'The Dual Personality of Philip Heseltine', *Journal of Mental Science*, 155 (1949), 456–66.

Copley, Ian A., 'Peter Warlock's Vocal Chamber Music', *Music and Letters*, 44 (1963), 358–70.

—— 'Warlock's Cod-Pieces', *Musical Times*, 194 (1963), 410–11.

—— 'Peter Warlock's Choral Music', *Music and Letters*, 45 (1964), 318–36.

—— 'The Published Instrumental Music of Peter Warlock', *Music Review*, 25 (1964), 209–23.

—— 'Warlock in Novels', *Musical Times*, 105 (1964), 739–40.

—— 'The Writings of Peter Warlock (Philip Heseltine) (1894–1930): A Catalogue', *Music Review*, 29 (1968), 288–99.

—— 'Warlock and Delius: A Catalogue', *Music and Letters*, 49 (1968), 213–18.

—— 'Warlock and the Brass Band', *Musical Times*, 109 (1968), 1115–16.

—— *The Music of Peter Warlock: A Critical Survey* (London, 1979).

—— *A Turbulent Friendship: A Study of the Relationship between D. H. Lawrence and Philip Heseltine* ('Peter Warlock') (London, 1983).

Cox, David, 'Unbewitched!', attachment to *Peter Warlock Society Newsletter*, 22 (1978).

—— 'What Music Is', *Peter Warlock Society Newsletter*, 19 (1982), 5–8.

—— 'The Balfour Gardiner Connection', *Peter Warlock Society Newsletter*, 34 (1985), 7–8.

Crowley, Aleister, *The Confessions of Aleister Crowley: An Autohagiography* (London, 1989).

Davies, Hywel, 'Bernard van Dieren, Philip Heseltine and Cecil Gray: A Significant Affiliation', *Music and Letters*, 69 (1988), 30–48.

Delany, Paul, *D. H. Lawrence's Nightmare: The Writer and His Circle in the Years of the Great War* (Hassocks, 1979).

—— 'Halliday's Progress: Letters of Philip Heseltine', *D. H. Lawrence Review*, 13 (1980), 119–33.

Dille, Denijs, 'Vier unbekannte Briefe von Béla Bartók: Vorgelegt und kommentiert von Denijs Dille', *Die Österreichische Musikzeitschrift*, 20 (1965), 449–60.

Fenby, Eric, *Delius as I knew him* (London, 1936).

—— (in conversation with David Cox), 'Warlock as I knew him', *Composer*, 82 (1984), 19–23.

Foreman, Lewis, *From Parry to Britten: British Music in Letters 1900–1945* (London, 1987).

Foss, Hubert, 'Introductions: XIX. Philip Heseltine', *Music Bulletin*, 6 (1924), 202–6.

—— '"Peter Warlock" (Philip Heseltine) 1894–1930', in A. L. Bacharach (ed.), *British Music of Our Time* (London, 1946).

—— *Bax: A Composer and his Times* (London, 1988).

Fuller, Jean Overton, *The Magical Dilemma of Victor Neuburg* (London, 1965).

Gathorne-Hardy, Robert (ed.), *Ottoline at Garsington: Memoirs of Lady Ottoline Morrell 1915–1918* (London, 1974).

Gillies, Malcolm, *Bartók in Britain: A Guided Tour* (Oxford, 1989).

Goldring, Douglas, *Odd Man Out: The Autobiography of a 'Propaganda' Novelist* (London, 1935).

—— *The Nineteen Twenties* (London, 1945).

Goossens, Eugene, *Overture and Beginners: A Musical Autobiography* (London, 1951).

Gray, Cecil, *Peter Warlock: A Memoir of Philip Heseltine* (London, 1934).

—— *Musical Chairs or Between Two Stools: Being the Life and Memoirs of Cecil Gray* (London, 1948).

Gray, Pauline, *Cecil Gray: His Life and Notebooks* (London, 1989).

Hamnett, Nina, *Is She a Lady?* (London, 1955).

Heseltine, Nigel, *Capriol for Mother: A Memoir of Philip Heseltine (Peter Warlock)* (London, 1992).

Hinton, Alistair, 'Kaikhosru Sorabji and Erik Chisholm' *Jagger Journal*, 10 (1989/90), 20–35.

Hold, Trevor, 'Peter Warlock: The Art of the Song-Writer', *Music Review*, 36 (1975), 248–99.

Hughes, Spike, *Second Movement: Continuing the Autobiography of Spike Hughes* (London, 1951).

Hurd, Michael, 'Peter Warlock and his Music', attachment to *Peter Warlock Society Newsletter*, 30 (1983).

Hutchings, Arthur, 'The Heseltine–Warlock Nonsense', *The Listener*, 70 (1963), 34.

—— 'Warlock and a Tite Street Party', *Peter Warlock Society Newsletter*, 33 (1984), 8–10.

Huxley, Juliette, *Leaves of the Tulip Tree* (London, 1986).

Jenkins, Alan, *The Twenties* (London, 1974).

John, Augustus, *Chiaroscuro: Fragments of Autobiography* (London, 1952).

Kaye, Ernest, 'Witches and Warlock', attachment to *Peter Warlock Society Newsletter*, 21 (1978).

Ladmirault, Paul, 'Un grand musicien anglais: Peter Warlock', *Chantecler* (1927), 3.

Lambert, Constant, 'Master of English Song', *Radio Times*, 59 (1938), 12–13.

Lawrence, D. H., *Letters*, ii (June 1913–Oct. 1916), ed. George J. Zytaruk and James T. Boulton (Cambridge, 1981).

—— *Letters*, iii (Oct. 1916–June 1921), ed. James T. Boulton and Andrew Robertson (Cambridge, 1984).

—— *Letters*, iv (June 1921–Mar. 1924), ed. Warren Roberts, James T. Boulton, and Elizabeth Mansfield (Cambridge, 1987).

Lindsay, Jack, *Fanfrolico and After* (London, 1962).

Lloyd, Stephen, *H. Balfour Gardiner* (Cambridge, 1984).

Lowe, Rachel, *A Descriptive Catalogue with Checklists of the Letters and Related Documents in the Delius Collection of the Grainger Museum, University of Melbourne* (London, 1981).

Lunn, Brian, *Switchback: An Autobiography* (London, 1948).

Mellers, Wilfred, 'Bernard van Dieren (1884–1936): Musical Intelligence and "The New Language"', *Scrutiny*, 5 (1936), 263–76.

—— 'Delius and Peter Warlock', *Scrutiny*, 5 (1937), 384–97.

Meyers, Jeffrey, *D. H. Lawrence: A Biography* (London, 1990).

Moore, Harry T., *The Priest of Love: A Life of D. H. Lawrence* (Carbondale and Edwardsville, Ill., 1974).

Moore, Jerrold Northrop, *Edward Elgar: A Creative Life* (Oxford, 1987).

Motion, Andrew, *The Lamberts: George, Constant and Kit* (London, 1986).

Murry, John Middleton, *Between Two Worlds: An Autobiography* (London, 1935).

Orr, Charles W., 'Recollections of Philip Heseltine ("Peter Warlock")', attachment to *Peter Warlock Society Newsletter*, 4 (1970).

Palmer, Christopher, *Herbert Howells: A Centenary Celebration* (London, 1992).

Parrott, Ian, 'Warlock in Wales', *Musical Times*, 105 (1964), 740–1.

Pirie, Peter J., 'The "Georgian" Composers', *Music in Britain: A Quarterly Review*, 69 (1965), 23–7.

—— 'The Lost Generation: (on British Composers between the Two World Wars)', *Music and Musicians*, 20 (1972), 36–40.

Reynolds, Peter J., 'Peter Warlock: His Contemporaries and their Influence', *British Music Society Journal* (1985), 48–58.

Rhys, Jean, 'Till September Petronella', *London Magazine*, 7 (1960), 19–39.

Ross, Charles L., and Zytaruk, George J., 'Goats and Compasses and/or Women in Love: An Exchange', *D. H. Lawrence Review*, 6 (1973), 33–46.

Rowley, Alec, 'The Music of Peter Warlock', *Musical Mirror* (1927), 83 and 88.

Rudland, Malcolm, and Cox, David, 'Elizabeth Poston (1905–1987)', *Peter Warlock Society Newsletter*, 40 (1988), 15.

Self, Geoffrey, *The Music of E. J. Moeran* (Exeter, 1986).

Seymour, Miranda, *Ottoline Morrell: Life on the Grand Scale* (London, 1992).

Shead, Richard, *Constant Lambert* (London, 1973).

Shepherd, L. (ed.), *Encyclopedia of Occultism and Parapsychology* (Detroit, 1991).

Skipwith, Peyton, 'Adrian Allinson: A Restless Talent', *Connoisseur*, 198 (1978), 264–73.

Smith, Barry 'The Colin Taylor Collection', *Jagger Journal*, 10 (1989/90), 1–5.

—— 'Colin Taylor (1881–1973)', *Peter Warlock Society Newsletter*, 45 (1990), 2–3.

Spender, Stephen (ed.), *D. H. Lawrence: Novelist, Poet, Prophet* (London, 1973).

Taylor, Colin, 'Peter Warlock at Eton', *Composer*, 4 (1964), 9–10.

Tomlinson, Fred, 'Cecil Gray Papers in the British Museum', *Peter Warlock Society Newsletter*, 13 (1973), 7–8.

—— 'Colin Taylor, a Tribute', *Peter Warlock Society Newsletter*, 13 (1973), 3–4.

—— *A Peter Warlock Handbook*, i (London, 1974).

—— 'Heseltine MSS in the British Museum', *Peter Warlock Society Newsletter*, 14 (1974), 1–5.

—— 'Peter Warlock (1894–1930)', *Music and Musicians*, 23 (1974), 32–4.

—— *Warlock and Delius* (London, 1976).

—— *A Peter Warlock Handbook*, ii (Rickmansworth, 1977).

—— *Warlock and van Dieren* (London, 1978).

—— 'Capriol Suite', *Peter Warlock Society Newsletter*, 35 (1985), 1–3.

—— 'Philip Heseltine and Kaikhosru Sorabji', *Peter Warlock Society Newsletter*, 42 (1989), 10.

Van Dieren, Bernard, 'Philip Heseltine' (obituary), *Musical Times*, 72 (1931), 117–19.

Walton, William, 'My Life in Music', *Sunday Telegraph* (25 Mar. 1962), 8.

Whittall, Arnold, 'The Isolationists', *Music Review*, 27 (1966), 122.

Wilson, Colin, *The Brandy of the Damned: Discoveries of a Musical Eclectic* (London, 1964).

Wilson, Jane, *C. W. Orr: The Unknown Song-Writer* (London, 1989).

Zytaruk, George J., 'What Happened to D. H. Lawrence's *Goats and Compasses?*', *D. H. Lawrence Review*, 4 (1971), 280–86.

(c) Thesis

Smith, Barry, 'Peter Warlock: A Study of the Composer through the Letters to Colin Taylor between 1911 and 1929', unpublished Ph.D. thesis (Rhodes University, Grahamstown, 1991).

INDEX